Phonology in Perception

Phonology and Phonetics

15

Editor

Aditi Lahiri

Mouton de Gruyter
Berlin · New York

Phonology in Perception

edited by

Paul Boersma
Silke Hamann

Mouton de Gruyter
Berlin · New York

Mouton de Gruyter (formerly Mouton, The Hague)
is a Division of Walter de Gruyter GmbH & Co. KG, Berlin.

♾ Printed on acid-free paper which falls within the guidelines
of the ANSI to ensure permanence and durability.

Library of Congress Cataloging-in-Publication Data

Phonology in perception / edited by Paul Boersma and Silke Hamann.
   p. cm. − (Phonology and phonetics ; 15)
  Includes bibliographical references and index.
  ISBN 978-3-11-021922-7 (hardcover : alk. paper)
  1. Grammar, Comparative and general − Phonology   2. Grammar, Comparative and general − Phonology.   I. Boersma, Paul.
II. Hamann, Silke, 1971−
  P217.52.P46 2009
  414−dc22
                                        2009029565

Bibliographic information published by the Deutsche Nationalbibliothek

The Deutsche Nationalbibliothek lists this publication in the Deutsche Nationalbibliografie;
detailed bibliographic data are available in the Internet at http://dnb.d-nb.de.

ISBN 978-3-11-021922-7
ISSN 1861-4191

Cover design: Christopher Schneider, Laufen.
Printed in Germany.

Table of Contents

Introduction: models of phonology in perception

Paul Boersma and Silke Hamann

The aim of this book is to provide explicit discussions on how perception is connected to phonology. This includes discussions of how many representations a comprehensive view of phonology requires, and how these representations are mapped to each other in the processes of comprehension and production. Of the two directions of processing, this book centres on comprehension, the direction that has received relatively little attention from phonologists.

This introduction makes an attempt at providing a single common formalization for the various models that have been proposed in the literature, including those that are proposed by the authors in this volume.

The first step is to make explicit what representations and processes we are talking about. As for the notations of the representations, we use pipes for lexical or underlying forms (e.g. German |tag + əs| 'day-GENITIVE', with morpheme structure), square brackets for overt or phonetic forms (e.g. ['tʰaːgəs], with articulatory and/or auditory detail), and slashes for any non-underlying non-overt representations (e.g. /(tá.gəs)/, with foot and syllable structure). As for the notations of the processes, we use arrows (e.g. |tag + əs| → ['tʰaːgəs] for phonological-phonetic production, or ['tʰaːgəs] → |tag + əs| for phonological-phonetic comprehension).

The second step is to make explicit how the processes of comprehension and production work. For this introduction we assume that the listener's comprehension process starts from an auditory phonetic representation and aims at arriving at an underlying lexical-phonological representation, and that the speaker's production process starts from an underlying lexical-phonological representation and aims at arriving at an articulatory phonetic representation. All the grammar models we discuss in this introduction agree that these processes are at least partly guided by the grammar. The various models differ, though, in the number and kinds of representations that they consider, and in how they express the relationships between the representations.

1.   The structuralist grammar model

The oldest phonological grammar model in current use is the pre-generative structuralist model depicted in (1).

(1)   *Structuralist grammar model*

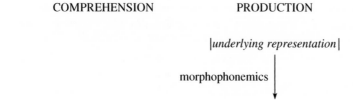

As in all the pictures in this introduction, we draw the comprehension model on the left and the production model on the right. However, the structuralists did not model the comprehension part, so we have a question mark on the left side of (1). On the production side we see three levels of representation, connected with two arrows, each of which represents a module of the grammar.

2.   Chomsky and Halle's grammar model

In *The sound pattern of English*, Chomsky and Halle (1968) deliberately disposed of the intermediate form (the phonemic representation) of the structuralists, as in (2).

(2)   *Early generative phonology*

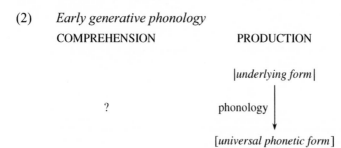

This production model can be looked upon in two ways. One way is to regard it as a single mapping, namely from underlying to surface form, and the other way is to regard it as a sequential series of mappings, starting with the lexical form, going through a multitude of intermediate forms, and ultimately resulting in the surface form. An example from English is shown in (3).

(3)   *Sequentially ordered rules with many unnamed intermediate represen-tations*

COMPREHENSION   PRODUCTION

|ɹait+əɹ, ɹaid+əɹ|
‖ morphological
⇓ bracket erasure
/ɹaitəɹ, ɹaidəɹ/

| syllabification

/.ɹai.təɹ., .ɹai.dəɹ./
| lengthening
↓ before [+voi]

?   /.ɹaitəɹ., .ɹaːi.dəɹ./
| intervocalic
↓ flapping

/.ɹai.ɾəɹ., .ɹaːi.ɾəɹ./
| coda r
↓ vocalization

/.ɹai.ɾəˠ., .ɹaːi.ɾəˠ./
‖ prosodic
⇓ bracket erasure

[ɹaiɾəˠ, ɹaːiɾəˠ]

On the right side of (3) we distinguish two kinds of mappings: universal ones, depicted with double arrows, and language-specific ones, depicted with single arrows. In this picture, the removal of the plusses in the first step can be re-garded as universal if no phonological rules can ever be conditioned by such morphological boundaries. Likewise, the removal of the syllable boundaries in the last step can be regarded as universal if prosodic boundaries have to be universally absent from phonetic forms. The remaining four steps are ordered, language-specific processes and therefore depicted with single arrows. If one's views on what is universal and what is not are different from the ones just ex-pressed, one would draw (3) differently.

The comprehension part in (3) is still a question mark. Comprehension could be implemented as the reverse application of rules until the listener ends up with a form that he/she has stored in the lexicon. In (3) this would indeed work for most of the steps. Starting from the auditory forms [ɹaiɾɚ, ɹaːiɾɚ], the listener could perhaps undo "prosodic bracket erasure" by automatically inserting syllable boundaries (although there may not be any guarantee that syllable boundaries are universally audible). The next step, "coda r vocalization" can be undone by changing every instance of /ɚ/ into /əɹ/; this happens to work in this case because the only source of the retroflex vowel /ɚ/ in English is the sequence /əɹ/ (i.e., /ɚ/ is not the result of a neutralizing rule). The next step, intervocalic flapping, can be undone by changing every /ɾ/ into /d/ after a lengthened vowel and into /t/ after a non-lengthened vowel; this happens to work in this case because the English flapping rule is not completely neutralizing: a cue to the underlying voicing of the plosive is still available in the duration of the preceding vowel. The next step, pre-voice lengthening, can be undone by changing every /aːi/ into /ai/. The next step, "syllabification", can be trivially undone by removing all syllable boundaries. Only the final step, "morphological bracket erasure", is thoroughly problematic, because it is incorrect to assume that a "+" can be inserted before every final /əɹ/ (consider the English monomorphemic words |maitəɹ| 'mitre' and |saidəɹ| 'cider'); to resolve this, an English listener requires lexical information.

Whereas in (3) a listener could reasonably successfully undo each production rule, such a comprehension strategy would not work in general. Especially cases where production rules lead to complete neutralization cannot be undone. Consider the case of the French words |ʒɔli| 'nice', |gʁoz| 'fat', and |pətit| 'small'. That these words must have these underlying forms is known from phrases like [ʒɔliami, gʁozami, pətitami] 'nice friend, fat friend, small friend'; however, in isolation the three words are [ʒɔli, gʁo, pəti]. At some point in the derivation of production, therefore, there must be a rule that deletes final consonants, and this rule is completely neutralizing, i.e., the listener cannot know whether the "final consonant deletion" rule applied in comprehension would have to turn /.pə.ti./ into /.pə.tit./, /.pə.tiz./, or /.pə.ti./. Because of such ambiguities, the listener cannot generally retrace the sequence of the production rules, so in the general case a Chomsky-and-Halle listener would have to consider a large number of underlying forms, compute a surface form from each, and thus decide which underlying form best matches both the incoming phonetic form and information from the lexicon and other modules. This 'considering multiple forms' is something that Optimality Theorists are comfortable with (at least in modelling production), and the next sections will show that indeed the parallel framework of Optimality Theory is better suited to handling comprehension than Chomsky and Halle's sequential rule framework is.

3. McCarthy and Prince's grammar model

Stepping into the field of Optimality-Theoretic proposals, we see that the simplest grammar model, namely that proposed by Prince and Smolensky (1993) and McCarthy and Prince (1995), has only two representations, namely underlying form and surface form.[1] As with the rule-based model of §2, this model is basically production-only, as is shown explicitly in (4).

(4)   *Two-level OT*
       COMPREHENSION   PRODUCTION

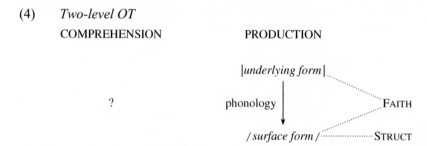

The surface form has been written here between slashes, because it may contain hidden material such as syllable boundaries and foot structure, i.e. it may not be a solely phonetic form. Example (5) applies the format of (4) to the French example discussed in §2.

(5)   *French coda deletion in two-level OT*
       COMPREHENSION   PRODUCTION

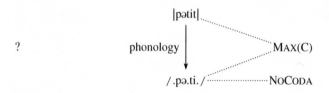

---

1. This formulation simplifies away from the fact that Prince and Smolensky's output candidates were so-called "full structural descriptions" from which both the underlying form and the phonetic form could be derived mechanically, and from the fact that McCarthy and Prince made an additional representational distinction within the surface form, namely that between base and reduplicant. The model in (4) is more representative of the subsequent body of literature that was based on Prince and Smolensky's and McCarthy and Prince's proposals than of the two original proposals themselves.

In (5), comprehension is still depicted by a question mark, because the early OT-ists did not consider it. The most naive way of implementing comprehension would be to copy from the serial-rule framework (§2) the idea of computing surface forms for a large number of underlying forms, then choosing all underlying forms that match the perceived surface form. This 'analysis-by-synthesis' idea was applied to Optimality Theory by Hale and Reiss (1998). However, this way of doing comprehension does not seem to entirely fit the spirit of OT, because the formulation of nearly all constraints proposed in the OT literature seems to allow them to be used in two directions, i.e. for comprehension as well as for production. We will investigate this point in the following sections. First, however, we describe a more elaborate production-only grammar with three representations.

When McCarthy and Prince are asked what the overt phonetic form looks like, they reply that the surface form contains both hidden material and overt phonetic detail. The phonetic form can then be computed in a universal way by removing from the surface form anything that is universally hidden, such as information on foot structure and on syllable boundaries. The grammar model would become:

(6)   *How to include phonetic implementation if one considers it universal*
       COMPREHENSION   PRODUCTION

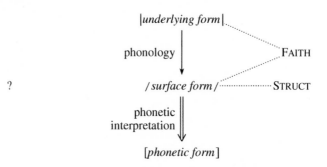

The double arrow here shows the idea that phonetic interpretation is universal. In our French example in (7), for instance, all that happens is that the syllable boundaries are removed.

(7)   *Universal phonetic implementation in French*

COMPREHENSION   PRODUCTION

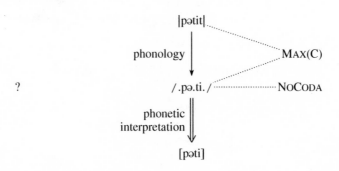

If one thinks that phonetic interpretation is a linguistically relevant language-specific module, one may want to call it 'phonetic implementation' and promote its arrow to a single one. This is what Hayes (1999) did in a footnote (p.250). He proposed that this module was Optimality-Theoretic, but did not supply any constraints or examples. This is shown in (8).

(8)   *Hayes' footnote*

COMPREHENSION   PRODUCTION

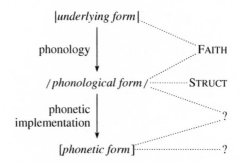

Since the topic of the book is perception, the following sections do away with the question mark on the left side, and consider bidirectional models.

4. Smolensky's bidirectional grammar model (1996)

The simplest *bidirectional* grammar model, i.e. a grammar model that includes both production and comprehension, is that by Smolensky (1996), shown in (9).

(9)   *Smolensky's (1996) grammar model*

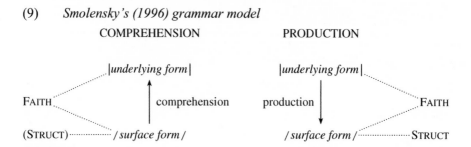

Smolensky proposed that production and comprehension are handled by the same OT constraints with the same rankings, but that the STRUCT constraints do not really work in comprehension, since they evaluate the *input* to comprehension, which is the same for all candidates. Thus, comprehension for Smolensky (1996) is a faithfulness-only mapping, which usually renders it flawless. This allowed Smolensky to explain why young English children may pronounce |kæt| 'cat' as [kæ] themselves but would at the same time object if an adult also pronounces this word as [kæ]. The example is made explicit in (10).

(10)   *Smolensky's (1996) grammar model*

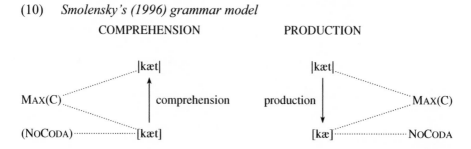

In (10), the surface forms are between square brackets, in (9) between slashes. In a two-level phonology such as this, this choice is not usually so important: one could write slashes because the form may contain hidden material, and brackets because the form contains phonetic detail.

There are several ways to propose constraints in a model like (9). While Smolensky proposed that production and comprehension used the same constraints with the same rankings, one could also use the same constraints with different rankings (Kenstowicz 2001), or one could use partly different sets of constraints (Pater 1999; Broselow 2004; Yip 2006).

5. Bidirectional models with three representations

Four sources of evidence suggest that the bidirectional OT grammar model of (9) might be too simple, in the sense that we might need three representations rather than two. The first source of evidence comes from phonetics and psycholinguistics. Phoneticians could argue that the model in (9) does not really include *perception*. If perception is regarded as the mapping from a universal phonetically detailed form (*overt form*, perhaps) to a language-specific phonological structure (*surface form*, perhaps) without lexical access, an inclusion of perception into the grammar model could require three representations rather than two. Similarly, many psycholinguists, e.g. McQueen and Cutler (1997), argue that comprehension is not a single module but consists of two sequentially ordered modules for prelexical perception and for word recognition, as in the model on the left side in (11). Analogous modularity has been proposed for production, e.g. Levelt (1989), and this is shown on the right side in (11) (also see (8)).

(11)   *Two sequentially modular psycholinguistic models*

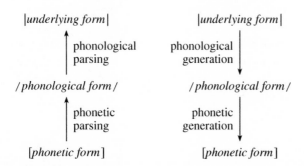

Grammar models with three representations have also been proposed on the basis of linguistic evidence. The listener is confronted with overt phonetic forms from which she has to construct an abstract surface structure in a language-specific way (Tesar 1997 et seq., Boersma 1998 et seq.), and in opposition to Smolensky's (1996) faithfulness-only comprehension model in (9), prelexical perception by young children is not flawless and therefore has to be modelled as a developing constraint system itself (Boersma 1998; Pater 2004).

A simple computational bidirectional grammar model with three representations was devised by Tesar (1997, 1998, 1999, 2000) and Tesar and Smolensky (1998, 2000). It can be abbreviated as in (12).

(12)   *Tesar and Smolensky's grammar model*

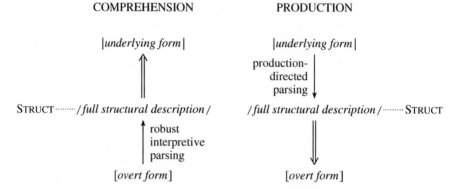

The single arrows here indicate the two processes that are handled by the grammar. The 'robust interpretive parsing' module can be said to perform perception, but since the full structural description *contains* the underlying form (as in Prince and Smolensky's notion of 'containment'), this interpretive parsing may involve lexical access as well. The 'production-directed parsing' module computes the full structural description in production, using the same constraints and rankings as in interpretive parsing. Since the full structural description contains enough information to derive both the underlying form and the overt form without looking at the grammar, the remaining two mappings (which we can equate with recognition and phonetic implementation) are depicted with double arrows. Here is an example:

(13)   *Tesar and Smolensky's metrical phonology learner*

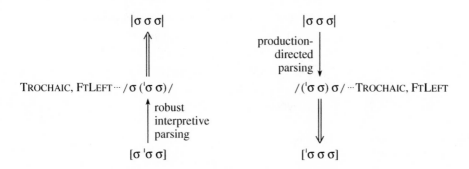

COMPREHENSION   PRODUCTION

This picture shows the reason for the two double arrows: Tesar and Smolensky's mapping from full structural description to underlying form is universal (it removes parentheses and stress marks), as is their mapping from this surface form to the overt form (it removes parentheses).

All the OT bidirectional models with three representations have been informed by considerations of *learning*. Example (13), for instance, shows what happens if the ranking is TROCHAIC >> { IAMBIC, FTLEFT } >> FTRIGHT: when confronted with the second-syllable-stressed overt form [σ 'σ σ], the listener will parse (perceive) it as /σ ('σ σ)/, because that form satisfies the constraints better than its sole competitor /(σ 'σ) σ/ would do; however, when the listener computes what she herself would have said given the underlying form |σ σ σ|, the result is /('σ σ) σ/. This discrepancy between the surface forms in comprehension and production is taken by Tesar and Smolensky as evidence that the listener's grammar is incorrect; as a result, the listener (*learner*) may change the ranking of her constraints.

In an OT model *without* containment, the recognition (lexical access) module will be language-specific, so that the comprehension model will get two single arrows, thus returning to Cutler's psycholinguistic model on the left in (11). Models that implement this were devised by Boersma (1998, 2001), Pater (2004), and Boersma (2007). We will discuss all three in the following.

The model by Boersma (1998, 2000, 2001, 2003) has all the representations in (11), i.e. three representations in comprehension as well as in production,[2] although it lacks a phonetic implementation module in production; instead,

---

2. The actual model also divides up the phonetic form into an articulatory form and an auditory form.

phonetic implementation is implemented as a *perceptual control loop*. An attempt at a visualization is shown in (14).

(14)   *Boersma's (1998) bidirectional grammar model with control loop*

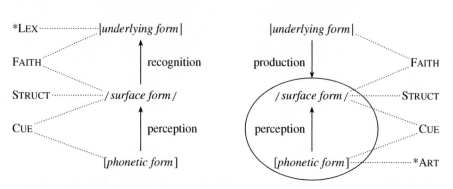

On the comprehension side in (14), we see that in contrast with Tesar and Smolensky's model, the prelexical perception module involves *cue constraints* (Boersma 1998, 2000, 2007; Escudero and Boersma 2003, 2004; Escudero 2005) whose ranking expresses the details of phonological categorization, i.e. the language-specific mapping from auditory cues to phonological elements. In general, then, perception is seen as an interaction between structural restrictions (*STRUCT) and a sort of auditory-to-phonological faithfulness (*CUE); this interaction has been discussed by Boersma (1998, 2000), R.Hayes (2001ab), and Pater (2004). In the present book, the cue constraints are discussed in three chapters: the chapter by **Boersma** discusses how cue constraints interact with structural constraints in perception; the chapter by **Hamann** discusses how various rankings of cue constraints help explain sound change in first-language acquisition; and the chapter by **Escudero** discusses how the ranking of cue constraints changes during second-language acquisition.

Another difference between the model in (14) and Tesar and Smolensky's model is the inclusion of *lexical constraints* (*LEX) in the recognition process. According to Boersma (2001), these constraints use the lexicon to help to resolve ambiguities, a property that improves the bidirectional use of faithfulness constraints.[3] Escudero (2005) used these constraints for modelling the loss of

---

3.   The model by Smolensky (1996), which we discussed in §4, failed to resolve lexical ambiguities. This failure was the reason for Hale and Reiss (1998) to propose the production-only use of faithfulness constraints that we discussed in §3.

phonological categories in second-language acquisition, and Apoussidou (2007) used them for modelling the acquisition of abstract underlying forms.

The third difference is that (14) includes phonetic detail in production. It does so by regarding phonetic implementation as maximally listener-oriented, namely as the speaker's view of how the listener will perceive the speaker's pronunciation. As a result, structural constraints (i.e. constraints against phonological structures and phonotactics) evaluate the output of perception only, both in comprehension and in production. To show that this model handles some perception-precedes-production effects in acquisition, we consider an example from Boersma (1998) in two pictures. In (15) we see a stage in which the learner does not yet perceive the English /s/-/t/ contrast, so that the English word 'see', produced by an adult as [siː], is perceived as /tiː/, hence stored as |tiː|, hence pronounced as [tiː]. The ranking in the perception grammar is *\s/ >> PERCEIVE[fric].

(15)   *Boersma's example of non-adultlike perception and production*

      COMPREHENSION   PRODUCTION

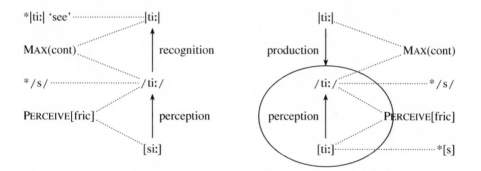

In (16) we see the next stage, in which PERCEIVE[fric] outranks *\s/, so that 'see' is perceived and stored correctly. However, the articulatory-effort constraint against [s] (e.g. against the complicated tongue-grooving gesture) still outranks MAX(cont), so that |siː| is still pronounced [tiː].

(16)   *Boersma's example of adultlike perception and non-adultlike production*

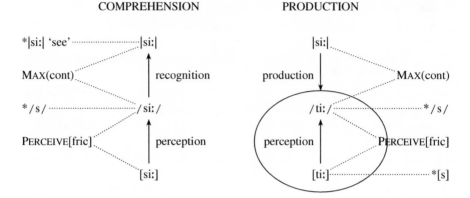

Since the two surface forms, /siː/ in perception and /tiː/ in production, are different, the learner will be able to take action and change the ranking of MAX(cont) and *[s], analogously to what happened in Tesar and Smolensky's case of (13).

Another example of perception-precedes-production is given by Pater (2004), who has the slightly simpler model shown in (17): when compared with (14), this model is identical with respect to comprehension but does not include phonetic detail in production.

(17)   *Pater's partial grammar model*

COMPREHENSION	PRODUCTION

|underlying form| |underlying form|

FAITH_US   phonology   FAITH_US

recognition

STRUCT   / surface form /   / surface form /   STRUCT

FAITH_OS

perception

[overt form]

Pater (2004) uses this model for explaining that children's perception is not always flawless. If the ranking is STRUCT >> { FAITH_US, FAITH_OS }, perception (and therefore production) is non-adultlike, as in the following example of learning to perceive the English word *garage*:

(18)   *Pater's example of non-adultlike perception and production*
                    COMPREHENSION   PRODUCTION

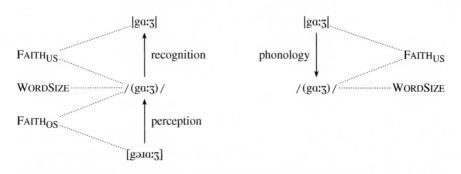

In this example, WORDSIZE is a constraint against polysyllabic words. In the early stage shown here, it limits the output of perception (as in Tesar and Smolensky's model). If in a later stage FAITH$_{OS}$ has risen above WORDSIZE, both perception and lexical storage will be fine, but production is still not adultlike:

(19)   *Pater's example of adultlike perception and non-adultlike production*
                    COMPREHENSION   PRODUCTION

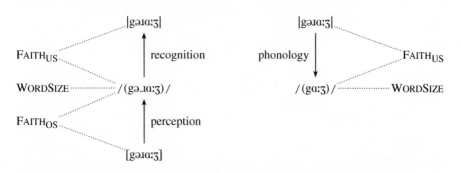

It is straightforward to extend such a model with a phonetic implementation module, bringing it closer to Hayes' footnote and Levelt's modularity. In the most general case, OT constraints would be able to evaluate the results of recognition and phonetic implementation. We would end up with something like (20).

(20)   *The Serial Bidirectional Three-Representation Model*
                      COMPREHENSION   PRODUCTION

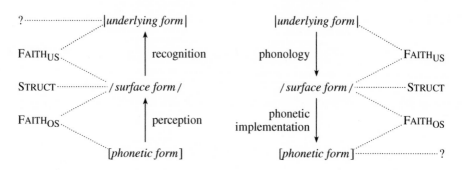

Since as far as we know nobody has ever proposed this model we will simply call it the Serial Bidirectional Three-Representation Model. It can be regarded as Tesar and Smolensky without containment, or as an OT implementation of Cutler and Levelt, or as Hayes' footnote made bidirectional. As an example of the usefulness of this model, consider the Korean example employed by Kabak and Idsardi (2007) (somewhat simplified here) of an underlying |hak+mun| that is produced as /haŋ.mun/, and a phonetic [hakmun] that is perceived by Korean listeners as /ha.kɯ.mun/. This example seems to be handled rather well by the Serial Three-Representation Model, as shown in (21).

(21)   *The Serial Bidirectional Three-Representation Model for two different repairs in Korean*
                      COMPREHENSION   PRODUCTION

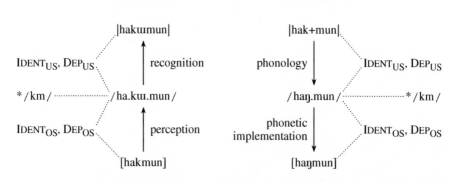

Both in perception and in production, the structural constraint */km/ prevents the occurrence of the phonological surface form */hak.mun/, but in different ways. In production this is possibly caused by the ranking { DEP$_{US}$(V), */km/ }

>> IDENT$_{US}$(nas), in perception possibly by the ranking { IDENT$_{OS}$(nas), */km/ }
>> DEP$_{OS}$(V).

While the model in (20) handles each direction of processing as a sequence of two modules, where the output of one module is the input to the other module, it is also possible, and even more in the spirit of Optimality Theory, to perform the two mappings in parallel. Such a Parallel Bidirectional Three-Representation model is shown in (22).

(22)   *The Parallel Bidirectional Three-Representation Model*

COMPREHENSION   PRODUCTION

*LEX············· |*underlying form*| |*underlying form*|

FAITH   FAITH

STRUCT·············· /*surface form* /   /*surface form* /·············· STRUCT

CUE   CUE

[*phonetic form*]   [*phonetic form*]·············· *ART

In this model the structure of the grammar, namely the representations and the constraints, is identical to that in the bidirectional grammar model with control loop in (14). However, the two models differ in the way the processes of comprehension and production are defined on it. For comprehension, the prelexical perception stage and the word recognition stage are evaluated in parallel, so that structural and cue constraints can interact with lexical and faithfulness constraints; as Boersma (this volume) shows, this can straightforwardly account for several observed phenomena, such as lexical influences on phoneme identification (Ganong 1980) and phonemic restoration (Samuel 1981). For production, the abstract phonology and the concrete phonetics are evaluated in parallel, so that articulatory and cue constraints can interact with structural and faithfulness constraints; this can account for phenomena such as phonetic enhancement (as has been shown by Boersma and Hamann 2008), licensing by cue (as has been shown by Boersma 2008), and incomplete neutralization.

6.   Models with more than three representations

Some models have been proposed that include more than the three representations discussed in §5. Boersma (1998) divided the phonetic representation into an articulatory and an auditory form, where the articulatory constraints evaluate the articulatory form, the cue constraints evaluate the relation between the auditory form and the phonological surface form, and the articulatory and auditory forms are related by sensorimotor constraints (Boersma 2006). Likewise, Apoussidou (2007) divided the underlying representation into a phonological underlying form and the meaning of the morpheme, where lexical constraints evaluate the relation between these two representations; Apoussidou showed that this split enables us to model the acquisition of abstract lexical representations. In this volume, the morphemic meaning representations of 'Focus' and 'Topic' are used by **Féry, Keyser, Hörnig, Weskott and Kliegl** in their OT modelling of intonation contours; these authors also discuss a phonetic form and a surface phonological form, which is directly connected to underlying meaning by association constraints without the intervention of any phonological underlying form.

Once the number of representations can be raised to four or five like this, it becomes imaginable that a realistic OT model of language processing may contain a large number of representations, and that using a single phonetic form, or a single lexical form, or a single phonological form, are all just simplifications. In fact, one can imagine that all the phonological and phonetic forms are connected to a multitude of semantic and syntactic representations, probably via the morphemic meaning mentioned above. An attempt to model this is provided by González (2006), who considers six levels of representation when modelling language mixing in bilinguals.

By providing models for language processing, multi-level OT joins the playing ground of psycholinguistic research. While some observed psycholinguistic phenomena can be replicated by OT models (as mentioned before), some others still pose challenges. An example of this are the *lexical neighbourhood density* phenomena discussed in this volume by **Ussishkin and Wedel**. At first sight, these phenomena seem to require an explanation that involves connections between elements *within* a level of representation, whereas the multi-level OT models discussed above only proposed connections *between* levels. A future solution may be based on realizing that even in these OT models relations within a level automatically exist as a result of bidirectional connections with an adjacent level.

7.   Perception as extralinguistic

If one regards perception and phonetic implementation as universal extralinguistic processes, the grammar model could be the one in (23).

(23)   *Grammar model with extralinguistic perception and phonetic interpretation*

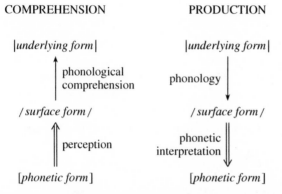

COMPREHENSION   PRODUCTION

This model is compatible with McCarthy and Prince's two-representation model in (6), in which everything to do with overt phonetic forms is outside phonology proper. It seems to be the model *assumed* (not necessarily *defended*) by most phonologists, including people who study the interaction 'between' perception and phonology, such as Steriade (1995, 2001) and Hume and Johnson (2001), and many researchers working on loanword phonology (e.g. La-Charité and Paradis 2005 and Uffmann 2006). Interestingly, the model in (23) seems to be assumed by two opposing schools in loanword research, namely those that think that loanword adaptation is in *phonology* (in the strict sense, i.e. the 'phonology' in the production part of the picture) and those who think that loanword adaptation is in *perception* (for both schools, the 'phonological comprehension' module usually simply stores the perceived surface form in the lexicon unaltered).

Loanword adaptation does not necessarily have to be perception *or* phonology. In fact, the models in (12), (14), (17), (20), and (22) predict that both perception and production are capable of imposing restrictions, and that structural (i.e. phonological) constraints, such as language-specific phonotactics, already determine the perceived surface form. This is in line with the observation by Polivanov (1931) and Dupoux, Kakehi, Hirose, Pallier and Mehler (1999) that Japanese listeners perceive [tak] and [ebzo] as /ta.ku/ and /e.bu.zo/, following Japanese-specific phonotactics (see Boersma this volume for details). In the present book, **Broselow** defends the viewpoint that loanword adaptation is both phonology *and* perception, with a language-specific perception grammar.[4] The contribution by **Balas** also deals with loanword adaptation and puts forward the view that the influence of language-specific perception can be better captured in Natural Phonology than in a two-level representational OT approach.

8.   Conclusion

This book brings together for the first time a number of contributions from different areas of phonology that model the phonological comprehension process by explicit linguistic means. The book contains chapters that provide overviews, case studies, applications to acquisition and change, experimental evidence, and remaining challenges. The book ends with a commentary by **McClelland**, who views the book from the standpoint of cognitive science.

References

Apoussidou, Diana
    2007   *The Learnability of Metrical Phonology*. Ph.D. dissertation, University of Amsterdam.
Boersma, Paul
    1998   *Functional Phonology*. Ph.D. dissertation, University of Amsterdam. The Hague: Holland Academic Graphics.
Boersma, Paul
    2000   The OCP in the perception grammar. *Rutgers Optimality Archive* 435.
Boersma, Paul
    2001   Phonology-semantics interaction in OT, and its acquisition. In: Robert Kirchner, Wolf Wikeley and Joe Pater (eds.), *Papers in Experimental and Theoretical Linguistics*. Volume 6, 24–35. Edmonton: University of Alberta.

---

4. The same point was made by Kenstowicz (2001), Broselow (2004), and Yip (2006). However, they worked within a model with only two levels of representation (§4), so that they had to propose different constraints for comprehension and production. Boersma and Hamann (to appear) work with the three levels of representation discussed in this Introduction, and therefore with the same constraints in both directions of processing.

Boersma, Paul
2003   Overt forms and the control of comprehension. In: Jennifer Spenad-
            er, Anders Eriksson and Östen Dahl (eds.), *Proceedings of the
            Stockholm Workshop on Variation within Optimality Theory*, 47–56.
            Department of Linguistics, Stockholm University.
Boersma, Paul
2006   Prototypicality judgments as inverted perception. In: Gisbert Fanse-
            low, Caroline Féry, Matthias Schlesewsky and Ralf Vogel (eds.),
            Gradience in Grammar, 167–184. Oxford: Oxford University Press.
Boersma, Paul
2007   Some listener-oriented accounts of *h*-aspiré in French. *Lingua* 117:
            1989–2054.
Boersma, Paul
2008   Emergent ranking of faithfulness explains markedness and licensing
            by cue. *Rutgers Optimality Archive* 954.
Boersma, Paul, and Silke Hamann
2008   The evolution of auditory dispersion in bidirectional constraint
            grammars. *Phonology* 25: 217–270.
Boersma, Paul, and Silke Hamann
to appear   Loanword adaptation as first-language phonological perception. To
            appear in: Andrea Calabrese and W. Leo Wetzels (eds.), *Loan phonol-
            ogy*. Amsterdam: John Benjamins. [*Rutgers Optimality Archive* 975]
Broselow, Ellen
2004   Language contact phonology: richness of the stimulus, poverty of the
            base. *North-Eastern Linguistic Society* 34: 1–22.
Chomsky, Noam, and Morris Halle
1968   *The Sound Pattern of English*. New York: Harper and Row.
Dupoux, Emmanuel, Kazuhiko Kakehi, Yuki Hirose, Christophe Pallier and Jacques
Mehler
1999   Epenthetic vowels in Japanese: a perceptual illusion? *Journal of Ex-
            perimental Psychology: Human Perception and Performance* 25:
            1568–1578.
Escudero, Paola
2005   *Linguistic Perception and Second Language Acquistion: Explaining
            the Attainment of Optimal Phonological Categorization*. Ph.D. dis-
            sertation, Utrecht University.
Escudero, Paola, and Paul Boersma
2003   Modelling the perceptual development of phonological contrasts
            with Optimality Theory and the Gradual Learning Algorithm. In:
            Sudha Arunachalam, Elsi Kaiser and Alexander Williams (eds.),
            *Proceedings of the 25th Annual Penn Linguistics Colloquium. Penn
            Working Papers in Linguistics* 8: 71–85.

Escudero, Paola, and Paul Boersma
  2004   Bridging the gap between L2 speech perception research and phono-
                logical theory. *Studies in Second Language Acquisition* 26: 551–585.
Ganong, William F.
  1980   Phonetic categorization in auditory word perception. *Journal of Ex-
                perimental Psychology: Human Perception and Performance* 6:
                110–125.
González, Maria Angélica
  2006   *Inhibition and Activation in Language Mixing by Bilinguals.* M.A.
                thesis, University of Amsterdam.
Hale, Mark, and Charles Reiss
  1998   Formal and empirical arguments concerning phonological acquisi-
                tion. *Linguistic Inquiry* 29: 656–683.
Hayes, Bruce
  1999   Phonetically-driven phonology: the role of Optimality Theory and
                Inductive Grounding. In: Michael Darnell, Edith Moravcsik, Michael
                Noonan, Frederick Newmeyer and Kathleen Wheatley (eds.), *Func-
                tionalism and Formalism in Linguistics*, Volume I: *General papers*,
                243–285. Amsterdam: John Benjamins.
Hayes, Rachel
  2001a   An Optimality-Theoretic account of novel phonetic category forma-
                tion in second language learning. Manuscript, University of Arizona.
Hayes, Rachel
  2001b   The perception of novel phoneme contrasts in a second language: a
                development study of native speakers of English learning Japanese
                singleton and geminate consonant contrasts. In: Rachel Hayes, Wil-
                liam D. Lewis, Erin L. O'Bryan and Tania S. Zamuner (eds.), *Lan-
                guage in Cognitive Science*, (University of Arizona Coyote Working
                Papers 12.) 28–41.
Hume, Elizabeth, and Keith Johnson
  2001   A model of the interplay of speech perception and phonology. In:
                Elizabeth Hume and Keith Johnson (eds.), *The Role of Speech Per-
                ception in Phonology*, 3–26. New York: Academic Press.
Kabak, Barış, and William Idsardi
  2007   Perceptual distortions in the adaptation of English consonant clus-
                ters: syllable structure or consonantal contact constraints? *Language
                and Speech* 50: 23–52.
Kenstowicz, Michael
  2001   The role of perception in loanword phonology: a review of *Les em-
                prunts linguistiques d'origine européenne en Fon* by Flavien Gbéto.
                To appear in *Linguistique Africaine*.
LaCharité, Darlene, and Carole Paradis
  2005   Category preservation and proximity versus phonetic approximation
                in loanword adaptation. *Linguistic Inquiry* 36: 223–258.

Levelt, Willem
1989   *Speaking: From Intention to Articulation.* Cambridge, Mass: MIT Press.

McCarthy, John, and Alan Prince
1995   Faithfulness and reduplicative identity. In: Jill Beckman, Laura Walsh Dickey and Suzanne Urbanczyk (eds.), *Papers in Optimality Theory*, 249–384. (University of Massachusetts Occasional Papers 18.) Amherst, Mass.: Graduate Linguistic Student Association.

McQueen, James M., and Anne Cutler
1997   Cognitive processes in speech perception. In: William J. Hardcastle and John Laver (eds.), *The Handbook of Phonetic Sciences*, 566–585. Oxford: Blackwell.

Pater, Joe
1999   From phonological typology to the development of receptive and productive phonological competence: applications of minimal violation. *Rutgers Optimality Archive* 296.

Pater, Joe
2004   Bridging the gap between perception and production with minimally violable constraints. In: René Kager, Joe Pater and Wim Zonneveld (eds.), *Constraints in Phonological Acquisition*, 219–244. Cambridge: Cambridge University Press.

Prince, Alan, and Paul Smolensky
1993   Optimality Theory: constraint interaction in generative grammar. Technical Report TR-2, Rutgers University Center for Cognitive Science. [published in 2004 by Blackwell, Malden]

Polivanov, Evgenij Dmitrievič
1931   La perception des sons d'une langue étrangère. *Travaux du Cercle Linguistique de Prague* 4: 79–96.

Samuel, Arthur G.
1981   Phonemic restoration: insights from a new methodology. *Journal of Experimental Psychology: General* 110: 474–494.

Smolensky, Paul
1996   On the comprehension/production dilemma in child language. *Linguistic Inquiry* 27: 720–731.

Steriade, Donca
1995   Positional neutralization. Unfinished manuscript, UCLA.

Steriade, Donca
2001   Directional asymmetries in place assimilation: a perceptual account. In: Elizabeth Hume and Keith Johnson (eds.), *The Role of Speech Perception in Phonology*, 219–250. New York: Academic Press.

Tesar, Bruce
    1997   An iterative strategy for learning metrical stress in Optimality
                Theory. In: Elizabeth Hughes, Mary Hughes and Annabel Greenhill
                (eds.), *Proceedings of the 21st Annual Boston University Conference
                on Language Development*, 615–626. Somerville, Mass.: Cascadilla.
Tesar, Bruce
    1998   An iterative strategy for language learning. *Lingua* 104: 131–145.
Tesar, Bruce
    1999   Robust interpretive parsing in metrical stress theory. In: Kimary
                Shahin, Susan Blake and Eun-Sook Kim (eds.), *Proceedings of the
                17th West Coast Conference on Formal Linguistics*, 625–639. Stan-
                ford, Calif.: CSLI.
Tesar, Bruce
    2000   On the roles of optimality and strict domination in language learning.
                In: Joost Dekkers, Frank van der Leeuw and Jeroen van de Weijer
                (eds.), *Optimality Theory: Phonology, Syntax, and Acquisition*, 592–
                620. New York: Oxford University Press.
Tesar, Bruce, and Paul Smolensky
    1998   Learnability in Optimality Theory. *Linguistic Inquiry* 29: 229–268.
Tesar, Bruce, and Paul Smolensky
    2000   *Learnability in Optimality Theory*. Cambridge, Mass.: MIT Press.
Uffmann, Christian
    2006   Epenthetic vowel quality in loanwords: empirical and formal issues.
                Lingua 116: 1079–1111.
Yip, Moira
    2006   The symbiosis between perception and grammar in loanword pho-
                nology. *Lingua* 116: 950–975.

Why can Poles perceive *Sprite* but not *Coca-Cola*? A Natural Phonological account[*]

Anna Balas

1. Introduction

When we ask native speakers of Polish to pronounce the American English word *Sprite* /spraɪt/ they will say [sprajt], but for the word *Coca-Cola* /koʊkəkoʊlə/ they will say [kɔkakɔla], not [kɔwkakɔwla]. Why do Poles, used to pronouncing sound sequences similar to American English diphthongs, substitute Polish vowel plus glide sequences for some English diphthongs, but not for others? The difficulty presumably does not lie in pronunciation, so the explanation must be sought in perception. The aim of this paper is to explain why some American English diphthongs are perceived as Polish vowel plus glide sequences and others as monophthongs, and to test how Natural Phonology and Optimality Theory can deal with the explanation of this difference. The paper is structured in the following way. First, a phonetic description of the phenomenon is presented (§2), and a hypothesis is formulated (§3). Section four is devoted to a comparison of Natural Phonology/Natural Linguistics with Optimality Theory, and of their devices. Then, the Natural Phonological understanding of perception (§5) and underlying representations (§6) is presented. In §7 it is shown how Natural Phonology can account for the perception of American English diphthongs by Polish listeners. In §8 it is shown how classical Optimality-Theoretic constraints fail to account for the phenomenon. It is argued that formalized economical Optimality-Theoretic analysis is not successful in accounting for American English diphthong perception by Polish listeners, because it operates with segmentally categorized input. It is concluded that Natural Phonology can account for the phenomenon, because it explains how uncategorized, auditory-phonetic input is perceived.

---

[*]   I would like to thank Firmin Ahoua, Paul Boersma, Andrzej Dubina, Katarzyna Dziubalska-Kołaczyk, Dafydd Gibbon, Silke Hamann, John Harris, Wiktor Jassem and Geoffrey Schwartz for many insightful comments on this paper or issues addressed in it. All errors are my own. I also gratefully acknowledge the financial assistance of Deutscher Akademischer Austausch Dienst.

2.   Phonetic description of the issue

Before the phonological explanation of English diphthong adaptation into a vowel system of Polish native speakers is offered, a phonetic description of Polish and English vowels is needed. Presented below is a comparative diagram of Polish and American English vowels prepared on the basis of Jassem (2003: 105) and Wells (1982: 486). Polish vowels are presented in brackets.

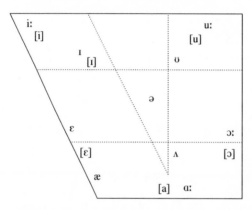

Figure 1.   American English and Polish monophthongs (Polish vowels are in brackets).

Polish sounds possibly substituted for the American English diphthongs /aɪ/ and /oʊ/ are vowels and glides. The four Polish vowels similar to the American English diphthong components are /ɔ/, /a/, /i/, /u/, which do not differ in length or tenseness. Polish has two glide phonemes /j/ and /w/ (Jassem 2003). Strutyński (1999) offers the following description of Polish glides. The sound /j/ is similar to a high front vowel /i/, but the lips are not spread during the articulation of /j/. The sound /j/ is short and it cannot be prolonged or it will become /i/. The glide /j/ can only appear with a syllabic vowel, either before it as in (1), or after it as in (2). Any mid or low vowel next to /j/ is articulated with the tongue raised higher than normal.

(1)   [mjɛtɕ] (have), [pjɛɲ] (song), [vjɛɕ] (village), [zjavitɕ ɕɛ] (turn up)

(2)   [tɕɛmɲɛj] (darker), [krulɔvɛj] (queen-DAT), [daj] (give*e*-IMP)

The glide /w/ is similar to a high back vowel, but, unlike /u/, it does not have to be rounded. It is pronounced in some Greek- or Latin-derived words, like /ɛwfɔrja/ (euphoria), /awtɔ/ (auto), and when the orthographic letter <ł> appears: *kładka* (footbridge) /kwatka/.

Diphthongs do not have a phonemic status in Polish, as the sequences /aj εj ɔj uj iw εw aw ɔw/ are not normally followed by another consonant in the same syllable, which suggests that the glide already occupies the coda position. Moreover, the frequency of occurrence of the vowel plus glide sequences /aj εj ɔj uj iw εw aw ɔw/ is considerably lower than the frequency of occurrence of any simple vowel. For differences related to the formant values and speed of transition based on vector length between British English diphthongs, Polish sequences and English diphthongs produced by Polish learners of English, see Bogacka [Balas] (2007).

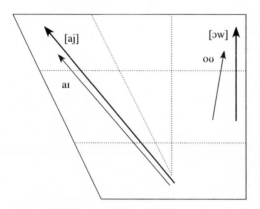

Figure 2. The American English diphthongs /aɪ/ and /oʊ/ and the Polish vowel plus glide sequences /aj/ and /ɔw/ (the Polish vowel plus glide sequences are in brackets).

3. Hypothesis

The comparison of American English (henceforth English) diphthongs and Polish vowels and glides shows that although Polish does not have diphthong phonemes, it has sound sequences very similar to the ones contained in English diphthongs, and that Polish phonotactics allows all the configurations which appear in English diphthongs to appear as sequences of a vowel and glide in the syllable nucleus and coda respectively. Therefore, the null hypothesis is that Polish speakers should both perceive and pronounce the English diphthongs of *Sprite* and *Coca-Cola*, for example, as Polish vowel plus glide sequences, because these Polish sound sequences are very similar to those occurring in English diphthongs. Pronunciation mistakes made by Polish learners of

English and English loanword adaptations into Polish, however, show that Polish native speakers pronounce some English diphthongs as Polish vowel plus glide sequences whereas other English diphthongs are interpreted as Polish monophthongs. Such a difference in the adaptation of foreign sounds into a native language can be claimed to emerge either in speech perception or in speech production. If the twofold adaptation of English diphthongs were to happen in production, we would have to assume that Poles perceive the diphthongs in terms of vowel plus glide sequences and during their production, for some reason, they pronounce some diphthongs as vowel plus glide sequences and others as monophthongs. This hypothesis has to be dismissed as there is no reason why Poles should repair sound sequences which they can otherwise produce in Polish. The twofold adaptation of English diphthongs to Polish categories must happen in perception, then. It is assumed that once Poles *perceive* an English diphthong as a Polish category, they faithfully *produce* it. Speech perception precedes speech production. The paper offers a Natural Phonological explanation of this twofold English diphthong perception pattern by Polish speakers.

A counterargument to the perceptual explanation of the diphthong adaptation could be that mispronunciations and misperceptions or mislexicalizations are based purely on spelling. There are however three arguments against the spelling hypothesis. Firstly, Polish speakers tend to keep as closely as possible to the original pronunciation of any loanwords, including proper names: English *hall* pronounced as [xɔl] and not [xal], English *dealer* is pronounced as [dilɛr], French *fondue* is pronounced as [fɔ̃di] and not as [fɔndi] (usually the second vowel is not rounded, as Polish lacks front rounded vowels). The second argument relates to both spelling-motivated misperception and mislexicalization hypotheses as explanations of the diphthong perception patterns: many adaptations cannot have been influenced by orthography. According to Boersma (1998) and Escudero and Boersma (2004), first spelling causes mislexicalizations and then lexicon-driven perceptual learning explains subsequent misperceptions. A Pole reads an unknown English word spelled with <o>, and creates a lexical entry containing /ɔ/ on the basis of orthography. Upon hearing this word pronounced with the diphthong [oʊ], an early learner may perceive it as /ɔw/, but the lexical representation containing /ɔ/ will suggest that the sound should have been perceived as /ɔ/. The perception grammar will then shift some constraints in such a way that the next incoming English [oʊ] will be more likely to be perceived as /ɔ/. This hypothesis, however, is based on the assumption that first the word has to be read and stored in the lexicon. A counterargument to the mislexicalization or spelling hypotheses as explanations of the English diphthong perception patterns is that these hypotheses do

not explain misperceptions of English words or non-words containing diphthongs by Poles who do not speak English and thus cannot be influenced by
English orthography, or by pre-school children. Thirdly, there is no unified
theory of spelling pronunciation which could predict perception or pronunciation of English words containing diphthongs by Poles on the basis of spelling.
Two kinds of inconsistencies are challenging for a theory of spelling pronunciation: words in which diphthongs are represented by two graphemes are not
necessarily pronounced with diphthongs, and diphthongs represented by one
grapheme can be pronounced as diphthongs. On the one hand, not only English
words spelt with <o> are pronounced with /ɔ/ by Poles, but English words
spelt with <ou> or <oa> are pronounced with /ɔ/ as well. If spelling were the
predominant factor in the adaptation of foreign words, English words containing <ou> or <oa> should be pronounced by Poles as sequences of /ɔ/ plus /w/
or /a/, and they are not. For example, *poultry* is pronounced as [pɔltrɪ], *shoul-
der* as [ʃɔldɛr], *soul* as [sɔl], and *boat* is pronounced as [bɔt], *coast* as [kɔst]
and *loan* as [lɔn]. On the other hand, spelling-based accounts cannot explain
why *Coca-Cola* and other words containing the English diphthong /oʊ/ are
perceived with /ɔ/, but a similar monophthongization process does not apply to
Sprite and other words containing English /aɪ/, which are perceived with a
diphthong. Here it could be hypothesized that the difference between the spelling and pronunciation of the word *Sprite* is big enough for listeners to notice,
especially that the letter corresponding to the vowel is usually read in Polish as
/i/ and the first and more prominent part of the diphthong is /a/. The English
/ɑː/ (as in *father*) and /aɪ/ are faithfully perceived and produced in quantitative
terms, i.e. the former as a monophthong and the latter as a vowel plus glide
sequence. In §7 on the Natural Phonological account of the phenomenon it will
be explained why the auditory difference between the English /ɔː/ and /oʊ/ is
not significant enough for Polish listeners and speakers to distinguish between
the monophthong and diphthong qualities, although they are accustomed to
hearing and producing similar sounds in Polish. The search for the phonological explanation of the twofold perception of Polish diphthongs by Polish
speakers is justified in the light of the three arguments against the alternative
explanation of the phenomenon due to orthography, namely: Polish speakers'
attempts at original pronunciation, misperceptions not motivated by orthography and the lack of unified theory of spelling pronunciation.

4.   Comparison of Natural Phonology, Optimality Theory and their devices

This section is devoted to a comparison of Natural Phonology and Optimality Theory and the devices they use to describe grammars. These two theories offer strategies for interpreting perception, strategies that can be employed in the analysis of the English diphthong perception by Polish speakers. As far as terminology is concerned, two names are used in this section: Natural Phonology and Natural Linguistics. Natural Phonology was founded by Stampe (1969) and developed by Donegan (1978, 1995, 2001), Stampe (1979) and Donegan and Stampe (1979). Natural Linguistics is the name which refers to the model as modified and expanded by Dressler (1984, 1985) and Dziubalska-Kołaczyk (1995, 2002a). The idea of *naturalness* behind linguistic explanations was operationalized in terms of functional and semiotic principles and the framework's explanatory potential was broadened to account for other components of language, i.e. morphonology, morphology, syntax, text, pragmatics and sociolinguistics. The model of Natural Phonology considered in this paper is not only that of Stampe (1969), and the emphasis is on later works: Donegan (1985, 1993, 2001), Dressler (1984, 1985, 1999), Dziubalska-Kołaczyk (1990, 1995, 2001, 2002a, 2007) and Ritt (2001). Natural Phonology, although it does not have an explicit, formal theory of perception, has always used both production- and perception-related phonological reasoning. Natural Phonology distinguishes, for example, between production-driven processes, i.e. lenitions, and perception-driven processes, i.e. fortitions. The Optimality Theory model considered here is the classical one (Prince and Smolensky 2004; McCarthy 2002; Kager 1999), but references are also made to Boersma's (1998, 2000, 2007 and this volume) three-level Optimality Theory, which shares functional interest with Natural Phonology. Classical Optimality Theory does not take into account the potential phonetic or psycholinguistic motivation for constraints, and it is only production-oriented. Boersma's model (1998, 2000, 2007 and this volume), similarly to Natural Phonology, takes into account fortitions in the form of cue constraints in production, and lenitions in the form of articulatory constraints. It is therefore noted how Boersma's (1998, 2000, 2007 and this volume) version of Optimality Theory is more suitable for explaining perception than classical Optimality Theory (Prince and Smolensky 2004; McCarthy 2002; Kager 1999).

Natural Phonology and Natural Linguistics represent a functional approach to language, and rather than aiming at an explicitly formalized model of grammar like Optimality Theory, they are interested in explaining the properties of language in relation to higher-order principles which are applicable to other natural phenomena as well. Natural Phonology and Natural Linguistics, as well as Optimality Theory, are preference theories, but they use different epistemological devices (see Dziubalska-Kołaczyk 2001 and Ritt 2001).

The two theories can be compared in two ways. One is based on the assumption that Natural Phonology could constitute a semantic frame for Optimality-Theoretic constraint rankings. According to such an approach, where Optimality Theory is treated as a metatheory, Natural Phonology would enrich the essential layer of constraints with an additional level of natural, functional explanation. Another way of comparing the theories is based on the assumption that the epistemological devices used by the two theories belong to two different grammar traditions and thus the tertium comparationis is limited. The analysis in the present paper adheres to the second view. The analogies between the two theories are recognized e.g. preferences or considering phonology as a system for both production and perception. Nonetheless, it is assumed that theories with different aims, i.e. functional Natural Phonology and formal Optimality Theory, and different methods, such as Natural Phonological derivations and uncategorized input to perception, and Optimality-Theoretic interaction of constraints and categorized input to perception, cannot be easily reconciled. It is assumed here that enriching Optimality-Theoretic constraints by Natural Phonological preferences would mean that you have to assume the framework of Optimality Theory and the content of another theory which you need to explain a given problem. The unified epistemology of each theory would have to be abandoned. There would be a risk that mingling the two theories could be too costly for explaining phenomena which lie outside the scope of the diphthong adaptation. An endeavor to mix the two theories should therefore be accompanied by testing the consequences for explaining other problems with which either of the theories could deal so far. The comparison below should not defend any of the theories, but serve as the introduction to phonological analysis of second language speech perception in the two theories. There is going to be no ad hoc attempt at unifying Natural Phonology with Optimality Theory in this paper. Nevertheless, reference is going to be made to an alternative, already well-grounded method of analysis (Boersma 1998, 2000, 2007 and this volume), which is cast in the Optimality Theory framework, but includes ideas inherent in Natural Phonology, like for example the handling of sounds in sequences and more than two kinds of representation.

In order to be able to discuss the differences between perception models in Optimality Theory and Natural Phonology/Natural Linguistics, we need a precise description of the devices used by the two theories to model phonological perception and production. In both theories these devices are based on universal but sometimes conflicting principles. Optimality Theory uses the term "constraints," whereas Natural Phonology uses the term "processes" and Natural Linguistics the term "preferences."

Constraints, or rather hierarchies of constraints are employed by Optimality Theory to perform a comparison of candidate forms. Constraints are universal and violable. There are two types of constraint: faithfulness (requiring identity between the input and the output) and markedness (evaluating the form of the output candidate). Every constraint is tested for cross-linguistic consequences and no constraint may be posited on the basis of the analysis of one language only. A grammar of a given language is a specific constraint ranking. It is claimed that classical Optimality Theory is a constraint-based approach, which defines the notion of mapping from underlying to surface representations. However, in a genuine constraint-based approach, the constraints simply filter the underlying representations, therefore a mapping is simply the selection of a subset of input representations. In Optimality Theory however, the constraints are ordered.

Natural Linguistics also uses the term constraint, but to refer to universal, extra-linguistic principles and conditions stemming e.g. from the nature of human bodies (Ritt 2001: 305). A role similar to Optimality-Theoretic constraints may be attributed to processes in Natural Phonology and preferences in Natural Linguistics. It has to be noted here that Natural Phonology distinguishes between phonological processes and rules (Stampe 1969; Donegan 1985). Processes have a synchronic phonetic motivation, they are responses to pronunciation difficulties, they are natural in the sense that they are not acquired cognitively and they apply unconsciously. Some processes always apply in a given language, like for example the word-final devoicing in Polish or German, other processes are optional, i.e. their application depends on the formal or informal style or tempo of speech, etc., like for example the palatalization of alveolar stops and fricatives before /j/ in English. Processes are evident in all kinds of phonological behavior of language users: in normal performance, in child language, in second language acquisition, in aphasia and other types of disorders, in casual speech, in emphatic speech, in slips, errors, language games, whispered and silent speech, and in the changing phonological behavior resulting in sound change. Dziubalska-Kołaczyk (2002b: 114) emphasizes that processes also account for implicational universals by substituting the implying sound by the implied one, and that therefore the task of Natural Phonology is a constant search for processes in the languages of the world. Being strategies of overcoming pronunciation difficulties in a given language, processes are not borrowed in loanword adaptations or transferred in second language speech acquisition. If a process from L1 is adopted in L2 it is first adopted as a rule (Dziubalska-Kołaczyk 1990: 19). Rules, although they might have originated from processes, lack a synchronic phonetic motivation, they are not reactions to pronunciation difficulties. Rules, being morphonological alternations, always operate on phonemes, e.g. /k/ and /s/ in *electric-electricity*, whereas processes operate on features. Rules merely reflect correctness: *dream/dreamt* and, unlike processes, they tolerate exceptions: *dream/dreamed*. Rules are learned, formulated on the basis of observation and their use is habitual. If speakers come across an exception to a rule, they may be surprised or find it difficult to remember, but never to pronounce. Limitations to processes, as attempted when imitating second language sounds or sound sequences, pose pronunciation difficulties, e.g. it is very difficult for Polish learners of English not to devoice word-final obstruents. There is a considerable difference between processes and rules in speech processing. Processes apply to non-lexical results of slips of the tongue and outputs of a secret-language (a system in which messages are enciphered by mixing up, adding or substituting sounds), so they must apply during the processing of speech production. Rules must apply earlier, since slips of the tongue and secret-language rules already operate on the outcome of phonological rules. Morphology can influence the processing of phonological strings only via phonological or prosodic domains. Hence the order: rules > prosodic processes > fortitions > lenitions. In Natural Linguistics the distinction between phonological processes and rules is redefined as the distinction between phonological rules vs. morphonological and morphological rules (Dressler 1984, 1985). Dressler (1985) criticizes a strict process-rule dichotomy, and argues in favor of a gradual relation between them, listing a number of criteria determining the degree of prototypicality of a phonological process and a morphological rule.

Both Optimality-Theoretic constraints and Natural Linguistic preferences are well-formedness conditions describing acceptable structures and violable, universal tendencies (Dziubalska-Kołaczyk 2001: 77). There are two main differences between Optimality-Theoretic constraints and Natural Linguistic preferences. First, Optimality-Theoretic constraints are theory-internal descriptive devices required to model grammars, but they are not designed to reflect the way of functioning of neurally embedded competences of speakers (Ritt 2001: 305). Natural Linguistic preferences are generalizations in the form of statistical implications about the structure of competences, generalizations derived from language external conditions. Dziubalska-Kołaczyk (2001: 77) formulates the difference in the following way: "(…) the constraints are inductive generalizations about grammars of the studied languages while preferences are deductive inferences about grammars based on universal higher-order principles applicable to language as well as to other natural phenomena." So even if an Optimality-Theoretic constraint happens to be similar to a Natural Phonological process or a Natural Linguistic preference, their ontological domains are different, as they refer to different types of entities in their respective frameworks. Classical Optimality-Theoretic constraints do not need to refer to the realm of phonetics or to language-external conditions. Only Functional Phonology (Boersma 1998) and Phonetically Based Phonology (Hayes, Kirchner and Steriade 2004) explicitly claim that constraints are phonetically interpretable, thus phonetically motivated. Natural Phonological processes are by definition phonetically interpretable. One example of a case where an Optimality-Theoretic constraint is identical to a Natural Phonological process concerns voiceless obstruents. An Optimality-Theoretic constraint is the following: *[+voi, −son] meaning: no obstruent must be voiced (Kager, 1999: 40). Stampe (1979: 1) offers a Natural Phonological explanation: "[...] voiced stops are relatively difficult to articulate because their characteristic obstruction of the nose and mouth impedes the air stream on which the glottal vibration of voicing depends. There is a phonological process which avoids this difficulty simply by substituting voiceless stops for voiced; it is observable in the speech of many young children and in the pronunciation of voiced stops by speakers of languages which lack them – Hawaiian, for example." Similar as they are, the constraint and the process differ with respect to the domains they refer to.

The second important difference between Optimality-Theoretic constraints and Natural Linguistic preferences is related to conflict solution strategies. Natural Linguistic preferences are explanatory, because they are based on non-linguistic, external evidence.

> [W]e can arrive at explanations for the regularities within a certain domain by turning to theories that are not theories for that particular domain (e.g., for grammatical theories, these include: theories of phonetic production, perception, learning, memory, communication, action, semiotic theories, etc.). (Vennemann 1983: 9)

Natural Linguistics proposes a "hierarchic, deductive system within which linguistic preferences occupy a general second rank, below higher principles and above the specific linguistic consequences of preferences" (Dressler 1999: 390). Dziubalska-Kołaczyk (2002a: 76) illustrates the levels of the system with the following examples. Higher principles can be cognitive, phonetic, psychological, sociological etc., they are non-linguistic principles, like for example the principle of least effort. Linguistic preferences include for instance a preference for simple phonotactics, for a CV structure. A linguistic consequence of such a preference is then the absence of clusters in a given language. In a conflict situation between preferences "agents strive towards maximal benefit or expected utility" (Dressler 1999: 392). Solutions for conflicts between preferences are to be found in higher-order universal principles and not in language-internal properties, because "preferences in the use and acquisition of language become frozen in preferences of language structure" (Dressler 1999: 394). It is also important to note that resolutions of conflicts can be predicted to a certain extent and therefore testable hypotheses can be postulated, but "total predictability is excluded by interlinguistic and intralinguistic language variation" (Dressler 1985: 294–295).

"The central idea of OT is that surface forms of language reflect resolutions of conflicts between competing demands or constraints" (Kager 1999: xi). In Optimality Theory the only method for explaining how and why languages differ is the constraint ranking, which serves the comparison of candidates and points to the optimal output. Constraints and rankings are defended by their suitability in accounting for a particular grammar. "Thus, there is always a danger of circularity and explanatory emptiness" (Ritt 2001: 308). A constraint may be useful in modeling a grammar and if this constraint is typologically valid, it is introduced without asking the question of why it is employed in languages. A constraint suits other constraints in a model, because they work well in the model, and they work well in the model, because they suit it. In Optimality Theory it does not matter whether the constraints achieve their goals in ways similar to the ones speakers do.

There are attempts by Steriade (2001), Kirchner (2001), Flemming (2001), Hayes (1999) and Hayes, Kirchner and Steriade (2004) at increasing the role of functional explanation in Optimality Theory and introducing phonetic detail into constraints. Kager (1999: 421) concludes about such tendencies that on the one hand they are in line with Optimality-Theoretic reasoning, because Optimality Theory aims at a single-step mapping from the underlying representation directly to the surface representation, without any intermediate representation. On the other hand he criticizes phonetically-oriented Optimality-Theoretic approaches mixing phonological and phonetic features within a single hierarchy with only two levels of representation, because there is evidence for an extra level, the phonological surface representation, which is the output of phonology and the input to phonetic implementation. It is noteworthy, however, that classical Optimality-Theoretic models not necessarily assume an intermediate representation, e.g. Kenstowicz's (2001) model employed in this paper. A model that combines functional explanation with an intermediate abstract surface level is Boersma's (1998, 2000, 2007 and this volume) model. In the comprehension direction, this model has a two-step mapping with an intermediate level. In production, this level is a representation of how the speaker thinks the listener will perceive the utterance.

The derivational approach of Natural Phonology handles abstract phonemic representations and non-distinctive phonetic detail while offering comprehensive functional explanation at the same time. It is assumed that listeners perceive speech in terms of phonemes. Listeners share the knowledge of processes applying in their language with the speakers and therefore listeners can decipher the phonemic makeup of the utterance when lenition processes cause coarticulations or neutralizations. According to Natural Phonology,

> [...] phonology *is* phonetic processing; it is thus the mental (or central-nervous-system) aspect of phonetics. Although certain phonetic *events* may occur in the vocal tract of the speaker, or in the air, or in the ear of the hearer, phonetic processing is a matter of the perception and the production of sounds, and it is thus fundamentally mental. (Donegan 1993: 105)

Donegan (1993) argues that articulatory, acoustic and auditory factors influence categorizations, alternations and substitutions speakers make, but the categorizations, alternations and substitutions are mental. "The relationship between the physical events and the mental processes is what makes phonetics different from physiology or acoustics. Thus, phonology must include matters of 'phonetic detail'." (Donegan 1993: 105). She further argues that unless we believe that differences between sounds in languages and dialects result from differences in speakers' vocal tracts, we must attribute these differences to differences in processing of speech. And characteristics of speech processing consistent across speakers of a particular community are part of phonology. Since phonological processes, having articulatory and perceptual functions, refer to phonetic detail, the phonological features on which phonological processes operate must be mental integrations between articulatory gestures and the perceived effects of those gestures. Phonetic parameters and phonological features should not however be expected to be in simple one-to-one relation. "But until the relationships between articulatory and acoustic parameters can be established, phonological features will be inadequate to account for phonological substitutions and change." (Donegan 1993: 107).

5.   Perception in Natural Phonology

Perception according to Natural Phonology means undoing the derivation until the listener reconstructs a form she has stored in permanent memory (in the case of ambiguity, morphology helps). Undoing the derivation consists in taking into account processes which have applied during the production of the intended form, but perception in Natural Phonology is not merely inverted production. Both production and perception are based on processes, which are shared by the speaker and listener in one person, or which are common to speech production and speech perception capabilities. Being both a speaker and listener, a person controls whether a produced utterance is perceivable, and how the auditory signal reaching the ear might have been produced.

Natural Phonological derivations, which the speaker applies and the listener decodes, do not apply in a linear, serial order as traditional generative grammar rule-based derivations do. Neither are Natural Phonological derivations assumed to be extrinsically ordered, as Optimality-Theoretic constraints are in the rankings. Sequenced substitutions in Natural Phonological derivations result from phonetically motivated process application. All processes which are to apply, apply simultaneously (Donegan and Stampe 1979: 151). Natural Phonological processes are principled within implicational hierarchies, which are revealed by the varying applications of a process depending on the language, time, style, etc (Donegan and Stampe 1979: 140). Working out the details of hierarchies and processes is an ongoing task of Natural Phonology. Natural Phonological derivations obey two general principles: fortitions apply first, lenitions second, and morphological rules apply before phonological processes. Higher order prosodic processes "map words, phrases, and sentences onto prosodic structures, rudimentary patterns of rhythm and intonation" (Donegan and Stampe 1979: 142) before articulatorily- and perceptually-driven processes apply.

Donegan (1985: 37–38) offers the following description of fortitions and lenitions. Fortitions are listener-oriented processes, which increase phonetic properties of phonemes. They strengthen the properties of an individual segment by emphasizing certain phonetic features, sometimes at the cost of other features within the segment. They often function dissimilatively, increasing the contrast between the segment and its context. Most often fortitions are context-free changes, but when they apply in context, they strengthen a phonetic property not shared by adjacent segments and reduce the property shared by adjacent segments, e.g. when /oʊ/ changes into /aʊ/. Fortitions typically apply in 'strong' positions: stressed vowels, syllable-initial consonants and intonations peaks. They apply especially when the increased perceptibility is expected and articulatory effort is high: in slow speech rate, careful articulation and affective style. Summing up, "fortitions (…) limit the inventory of perceptible, intendable, segments in which the forms of lexical items are encoded" (Donegan 2001: 50). An example of a fortition active in English is the denasalization of vowels. Due to this process English native speakers find it very difficult to produce a nasalized vowel when a nasal consonant does not follow. Another example of a fortition is the aspiration of voiceless stops in English. Examples of fortitions in diachronic phonology include the diphthongization of vowels.

Lenitions are speaker-oriented, context-sensitive processes, which optimize the sequences of segments, so that sequences of speech sounds are better adapted to the needs of the vocal tract. They make sound sequences more pronounceable by "assimilating the properties of one segment to those of a neighboring segment, by deleting segments, and by substituting segments that are 'weaker' in some respect for those that are 'stronger'." By decreasing phonetic properties of segments they reduce contrast between the segment and its context. These weakening processes typically apply in 'weak' positions: unstressed vowels, syllable-final consonants, etc. Lenitions apply especially during hypoarticulated speech, in informal situations or situations with predictable content, which allow for lowered articulatory effort: in fast speech, careless articulation and casual styles. Lenitions are applied during speech production, and during speech perception lenitions have to be undone. Listeners have to undo lenitions, so that they can ignore allophonic variation and perceive casually produced speech in terms of phonemes. An example of applying a lenition during speech production by English native speakers is producing a nasalized vowel in assimilation to the following nasal consonant. If listeners are to perceive an oral vowel phoneme, they have to undo the lenition, i.e. attribute the nasalization of the vowel to the influence of the nasal consonant context. Another example of a lenition is the palatalization of consonants preceding high front vowels in Polish.

In one of the latest developments in Natural Phonology, Kul (2007) explicitly defines lenitions as reductions and proposes three types of lenitions: reduction of energy (e.g. a change from a fortis to a lenis sound), reduction of complexity (e.g. vowel centralization, monophthongization, assimilation of place, deletion, etc.), and reduction of aerodynamic unnaturalness (e.g. epenthesis or final devoicing). Such an understanding of lenitions leads to a negative definition of fortition. Fortition is defined as an effortful suppression of lenition (e.g. avoiding /t/-epenthesis in a word like *prince)*. The advantage of these definitions is that they acknowledge the dynamic aspect of speech in terms of gestures and motorics of the vocal tract.

Processes which apply in the mother tongue of foreign language learners determine the way in which they will perceive a second language. As Donegan (1985: 251) notes, fortitions make substitutions for the segments absent from the native language inventory, whereas lenitions are responsible for "'recognizing' certain phonetic segments in particular contexts as substitutions for other more basic segments." An example of a fortition process substituting a sound absent from the first language inventory is a process preventing front vowels from being low, active in Polish, which makes Poles substitute the Polish /ɛ/ for the English /æ/. The substitution takes place when they speak English as well as when they listen to English trying to decode the phonemic makeup of the second language utterance in terms of the first language phonemes. An example of the undoing of a lenition process during second language speech perception is the perception of English velar nasals by Polish listeners. Polish has no velar nasals before sounds other than velars. When Polish listeners hear an English velar nasal they interpret it as a lenited sequence of a nasal and a velar. It means that some phonemes of a second language are interpreted as segments derived by lenitions from other phonemes of the first language. Since second language learners usually want to tailor speech sounds of a second language to the phonemes of their first language, they choose to produce or perceive the basic, non-derived forms. Such attempts result in a foreign accent due to non-native perception and/or the application of processes of the first language to the already ill-perceived second language sounds.

6. Underlying representations in Natural Phonology

If a given utterance is naturally pronounceable as the result of a certain intention, then that intention is a natural perception of the utterance i.e. a possible phonological representation. (Donegan and Stampe 1979: 163)

Underlying representations are defined in Natural Phonology by Stampe and Donegan (1979) as the phonemically fully specified, featurally interpreted (as natural phonological processing refers to features and prosodic domains), forms of the language that speakers store in the long-term memory. They contain all the information that is unpredictable from language-specific processes, but they are also allowed to contain information predictable from the processes and morphology. It is subject to discussion whether recoverability could substitute for the pronounceability of the underlying representation and whether the full specification could be limited and exclude the results of processes which have to apply. The role of phonological processes is crucial in determining underlying representations in a language: the phonological processes determine surface representations and surface representations together with phonological processes determine underlying representations. Such an understanding of underlying representations allows for explaining homophony, phonological change and neutralizations (Donegan 2001: 45).

Underlying representation, a representation of forms in permanent memory, is not understood as a specified level, but as a starting point in speech production and an ending point in speech perception. There can be an unlimited number of representations between the underlying representation and phonetic-auditory form. In Natural Phonology, there are no levels of representations, but kinds of representations. These kinds of representations include, among others: surface phonetic representation, phonemic representation and underlying representation. Perception as understood by Natural Phonology is purely in phonemic terms, but a given phonemic representation of a word does not have to be the only phonemic representation of this word.

> [A] given word may have as many phonemic representations as it has phonemically distinct pronunciations. Unless all the variants and "automatic" alternants of a form have the same phonemic representation, the form in its lexical representation must be represented morphophonemically, or its variants and alternants will not be derivable from that representation. (…) The main significance of the phoneme in lexicon and grammar is that lexical entries and morphological rules are alike "spelled" in terms of phonemes. What one does not perceive, one does not represent in memory, or invent a rule for. (Stampe 1987: 296)

An example illustrating the split of one underlying representation into two phonemic representations is a Polish word *warszawski* (adj. *of Warsaw*), which has one underlying representation having two phonemic representations: /varʃafski/ and /varʃaski/. The question still to be answered by Natural Phonology is whether the two phonemic forms are independent from each other or whether the form /varʃafski/ typical in a formal speaking style is a more basic one, from which we can go either straight to the phonetic implementation or from which we can derive the form /varʃaski/ in casual style. Both interpretations are possible if we take into account that processes apply simultaneously, but not all processes have to apply in a given situation, speaking style, etc.

7.   A Natural Phonological account of the phenomenon

The perception problems second language learners face are the following: second language has different or differently specified phonemes than the first language does (fortitions are responsible), and second language phonology tends to adapt phonemes to the needs of the vocal tract differently than first language phonology does (lenitions are responsible). Second language learners often complain that they do not understand fast speech, and that native speakers of the language they are trying to acquire speak sloppily. Of course native speakers do not speak sloppily, but they allow for the operation of phonostylistic processes which are not employed in the learners' mother tongues. Second language learners try to decode the underlying intention using their native language processes and they are not aware of the fact that the second language has different phonemes and employs different strategies for adapting phonemes to the needs of the vocal tract. If Natural Phonology shows how phonemic representations in the mother tongue arise as a result of the interaction of fortitions and lenitions, it should also be able to account for second language representations referring to processes which operate in the first language and to universal preferences.

The spelling of the English word *Sprite* does not directly resemble any Polish words, but Polish has a word *rajd* (rally) /rajd/ pronounced as [rajt] (due to final obstruent devoicing) and the words *rad* (glad) /rad/ pronounced as [rat] and *rat* (installment- DAT/PLUR) /rat/ pronounced as [rat]. The English *Sprite* is perceived as /sprajt/ by Poles. Polish speakers perceive the English diphthong /aɪ/ as the Polish sequence /aj/, probably because the difference in transition between the Polish /aj/ and the English diphthong /aɪ/ is not substantial. There is a similar situation with other English words containing the diphthong /aɪ/, spelt with <i>, for example: *five, kite, light*, and so on.

The English word Coca /koʊkə/ resembles two Polish words: kołka (peg-gen) /kɔwka/ and koka (bun-gen) /kɔka/. When hearing the English word, Poles report perceiving it as /kɔka/. The English diphthong involves too small a transition for Poles to interpret it as an underlying /kɔwka/ to which a lenition process of smoothing the /ɔw/ sequence has applied. Moreover, the English diphthong followed by a consonant is unlikely to be interpreted as a lenited Polish sequence /ɔw/, because in Polish a lenition process applies to the /ɔw/ sequence only when it is followed by an /ɔ/, like in *koło* (wheel) /kɔwɔ/ which becomes /kɔː/, and this lenition process does not apply before consonants. Also, lenitions are more expected in casual styles, so if Poles hear an English word with an /oʊ/ diphthong in a formal situation, where little casual style is used, e.g. in the classroom, they are even less likely to interpret the English diphthong as a result of the lenition of the vowel plus glide sequence. So if Poles hear the English [koʊkə] they do not interpret the English diphthong as a result of lenition of /kɔwka/, and /kɔka/ is the only possible interpretation left. In derivational terms, a Polish speaker hearing an English word takes into consideration that if an English sound sequence, which is between the two possibilities /ɔ/ and /ɔw/ existing in Polish, cannot be interpreted as a result of a lenition process smoothing the /ɔw/, it has to be /ɔ/. A similar explanation applies to other English words: *telephone, notebook, soap, sofa, smoking, poker*, to list a few. Natural Phonology accounts for this phenomenon, because it takes into consideration the application of lenitions, and because it can also explain where the lenitions cannot apply according to the phonology of a given language.

8.   Optimality-Theoretic formalism

Let us now use the classical OT formalism to illustrate how Polish speakers perceive Polish words that contain vowel plus glide sequences or only vowels, and English words, that contain diphthongs. The ranking used in this paper is compatible with Rubach's (2000, 2004) proposals. In his article dealing with glides, Rubach (2000: 293) suggests the following ranking for Polish:

$$(...) , \text{IDENT(Nuc)} \gg \text{ONSET} \gg *\text{ONSET([u])} \gg \text{DEP(Seg)}$$

The constraint IDENT(Nuc) requires the nucleus to be preserved. The constraint ONSET means "syllables must have onsets." The constraint *ONSET([u]) does not allow [u] in the onset. The constraint DEP(Seg) means "do not insert a segment".

The ranking employed here is also compatible with Burzio's (2001: 674) reply to Rubach (2000). In his article, Burzio (2001: 674) proposes the following constraints and their ranking: ONSET $\gg$ *ONSET([u]) $\gg$ *INDEP([w]). The constraint *INDEP([w]) is meant by Burzio as: "the feature of [w] must be dependent on an adjacent segment" and it was introduced as a means of expressing "an exception to the generalization that [w] in Polish cannot be an onset or part of an onset: namely when [w] is adjacent to [u], as in [pa.pu.was]." The issues that are discussed by Rubach (2000, 2004) and Burzio (2001), namely, the need of introducing derivational levels in a generative sense into Optimality Theory or the problem of dominance of ONSET or *ONSET([u]), are not issues here and they do not influence the rankings in the cases presented in this paper, so differences between the two models will not be addressed. The aim of citing the three articles is to show that the present ranking is compatible with rankings already employed in Optimality-Theoretic analyses.

For the purpose of the analysis of the English diphthong adaptation by Poles in the present paper some constraints were added to the set used by Rubach (2000: 293), in order to accommodate the ranking to account for the perception of simple vowels vs. vowel plus glide sequences. The constraint NO-DIPH, banning diphthongs, is undominated in Polish (Rubach 2000: 278). The constraint *ONSET([u]) is used as meaning that [u] or [w] cannot be a part of the onset. The second faithfulness constraint $\text{MAX}_{\text{IO}}(\text{Seg})$ "a segment in the underlying representation should have a correspondent in the surface form" is also needed, in addition to the constraint $\text{DEP}_{\text{IO}}(\text{Seg})$ "a segment in the surface form should have a correspondent in the underlying form". Last comes a constraint *CODA ([w]) ("[w] cannot be in the coda"), which must be low-ranked in Polish, given the existence of such words as: *piłka* (ball) /piwka/, *orzeł* (eagle) /ɔʒɛw/, *wał* (embankment) /vaw/, *stołka* (stool-ACC) /stɔwka/, *wół* /vuw/ (*ox*), etc. A constraint violation which is fatal for a given candidate is marked by an exclamation mark '!' and the shaded cells reflect the constraints whose violation or satisfaction is no longer relevant for a given candidate, because the candidate has already violated a higher-ranked constraint.

The tables presented below are reversals of production-oriented evaluations usually employed in Optimality-Theoretic accounts. In the following analysis of English diphthong perception by Polish listeners the ranking of constraints evaluates the input to perception and chooses the candidate which maps best onto the underlying form. Input to perception is the phonetic form heard by listeners. Underlying forms are listed as candidates. The underlying forms are postulated on the basis of forms reproduced by Polish listeners. It is assumed that since Poles are able to produce [kɔw.ka] and [kɔ.ka] in Polish, the corresponding underlying forms and their differently syllabified variants are candidates in second language speech perception. The model of perception assumed in the analysis is a two-level Optimality-Theoretic model as postulated by Kenstowicz (2001). It assumes a direct mapping from the phonetic form to the underlying form. This model operates with MAX and DEP constraints, which require the input to be segmented, i.e. a phonetic form is assumed to contain segments. At the same time this model does not allow for the use of constraints referring to sound sequences, which would permit handling the perception of English diphthongs by Polish listeners as one or two segments.

Tableaux 1 and 2 present the perception of Polish words by Polish listeners. If Polish listeners hear a Polish word [kɔwka] (Tableau 1), they do not perceive it as a word containing a diphthong /ɔu/, because there are no diphthongs in Polish, and from this it follows that the constraint NO-DIPH is undominated in Polish. The three-syllable candidate /kɔ.u.ka/ is dismissed, because its middle syllable does not have an onset. The candidate /kɔ.wka/ loses, because it has [w] in the onset. Polish listeners do not perceive [kɔwka] as /kɔ.ka/ either, because they faithfully perceive the segment [w]. The candidate /kɔw.ka/ violates the constraint *CODA([u]) disallowing glides in syllable codas, but this constraint is low-ranked, and the candidate /kɔw.ka/ still wins.

[kɔwka]	No-Diph	Onset	Dep-IO	Max-IO	*Onset([u])	*Coda([w])
/kɔu.ka/	*!					
/kɔ.u.ka/		*!				
/kɔ.wka/					*!	
☞ /kɔw.ka/						*
/kɔ.ka/			*!			

Tableau 1.   Perception: Polish by Polish listeners

When Polish listeners hear the word [kɔka], they perceive it as /kɔ.ka/ (Tableau 2). Other candidates are dismissed: /kɔu.ka/ because it contains a diphthong, /kɔ.u.ka/ because it violates the constraint demanding that syllables have onsets, and /kɔ.wka/ and /kɔw.ka/ because, containing a segment which has not appeared in the input, they violate the MAX constraint (in fact all candidates apart from /kɔ.ka/ violate the MAX constraint, but sometimes higher-ranked constraints are already fatal for them).

[kɔka]	No-Diph	Onset	Dep-IO	Max-IO	*Onset([u])	*Coda([w])
/kɔu.ka/	*!			*		
/kɔ.u.ka/		*!		*		
/kɔ.wka/				*!	*	
/kɔw.ka/				*!		*
☞ /kɔ.ka/						

Tableau 2.   Perception: Polish by Polish listeners

Though accounting for the native perception, the ranking employed in Tableaux 1 and 2 cannot account for the Polish listeners' perception of English words containing diphthongs (see Tableau 3). Candidates remain the same as in the case of perception of Polish words, as it is assumed here that Poles try to perceive the English words in terms of Polish phonemes. Polish has only one high back vowel phoneme /u/, which has a quality between the two English high back vowels /uː/ and /ʊ/. It has been shown on the basis of categorization tests that Poles do not distinguish between the two English high back vowels /uː/ and /ʊ/, neither on the basis of formant differences, nor on the basis of duration differences, and that they categorize the two English high back vowels as exemplars of the Polish /u/ category (Bogacka [Balas] 2004). The phonetic difference between the English [oʊ] and Polish [ɔw] has to be neglected in this two-level Optimality-Theoretic model in which the input to perception already has to be segmented and categorized into phonemes. Acoustically, the English [oʊ] is between Polish [ɔw] and [ɔ]. The ranking favors the candidate /kɔw.ka/, violating only the low-ranked constraint *CODA([u]) banning [u] in the coda. This candidate, however, does not win in the actual perception of English diphthongs by Polish speakers. The faithful candidate /kɔu.ka/ loses, because it contains a diphthong, which does not exist in Polish. Although Polish listeners hear the English word [koʊkə] as /kɔ.ka/, the candidate /kɔ.ka/ cannot win in tableau 3 (because tableau 1 dictates that DEP-IO has to be ranked above *CODA([w])). Quod erat demonstrandum: /kɔ.ka/ violates the constraint DEP banning the deletion of a segment, heard in the input, from the underlying representation. The Optimality Theory formalism cannot account for the perception of English diphthongs, because the constraint ranking favors a candidate that does not win in the actual perception and dismisses the right candidate.

[koʊkə]	NO-DIPH	ONSET	DEP-IO	MAX-IO	*ONSET([u])	*CODA([w])
/kɔu.ka/	*!					
/kɔ.u.ka/		*!				
/kɔ.wka/					*!	
☞ */kɔw.ka/						*
🖙 /kɔ.ka/			*!			

Tableau 3.   Perception: English by Polish listeners

Two factors are responsible for the problem: the lack of recognition of processes applying to specific sound sequences, like the lenition of the glide only before a vowel, and the fact that the perception of English diphthong as a monophthong is based on a feature which is non-distinctive: the rate of transition between the vowel and the glide vowel.

Alternatively, one could argue that since Polish has neither long vowels nor diphthongs, it bans two moras in one nucleus. Therefore, in loanword adaptations or in L2 speech perception, a constraint banning the deletion of a mora (MAXμ) can be violated, and English words with long vowels or diphthongs are interpreted as words containing simple vowels. This would work for the /oʊC/ cases. Such an interpretation, however, is not supported by the treatment of other English words, such as *Sprite* pronounced by Poles as /sprajt/, showing that an English bimoraic nucleus /aɪ/ is reinterpreted by Polish listeners as a single mora nucleus and a glide in the coda.

Neither does it help Optimality Theory to argue that Polish listeners perceive /ɔ/ instead of /oʊ/ before /k/ (though a monophthong is perceived before other consonants, too), because the English velar sounds /ʊ/ and /k/ in a syntagmatic relationship are not distinct enough. As argued by Donegan (2001) attributing the outputs of perception to sequence-optimizing processes is problematic for Optimality Theory. Donegan (2001) claims that the Optimality-Theoretic ranking of constraints cannot explain why Japanese hearers perceive [kɑts] as /kɑtu/, predicting both /kɑtu/ and /kɑtɑ/. The vowel /ɑ/ is by no means more marked than /u/ and therefore it cannot be discarded on the basis of markedness. Donegan emphasizes that the devoicing and deletion of /u/ is *universally* more common than devoicing and deletion of /ɑ/. Therefore the Japanese hearer perceives [kɑts] as /kɑtu/, because he associates [kɑts] with the result of affrication and voiceless vowel deletion. "Perception takes causation into account. Therefore, Sequential Well-Formedness constraints cannot be irrelevant in perception" (Donegan 2001: 63). Donegan's account however, does not take into account that *in Japanese* high vowels are devoiced, whereas /ɑ/ cannot be devoiced. Moreover, the /kɑtu/ case can actually be accounted for in the traditional two-level Optimality Theory, if used bidirectionally (Boersma, personal communication). Since /u/ is often deleted in production, the constraint $MAX_{IO}(u)$ should be ranked low in production. If it is also ranked low in perception, /u/ can be easily inserted in perception. By the same token, $MAX_{IO}(ɑ)$ is ranked higher because /ɑ/ is not prone to devoicing and deletion. So important as Donegan's remark about the sequence-optimizing well-formedness constraints is, it has to be admitted that this very example from Japanese affricate-vowel perception can also be accounted for in two-level Optimality Theory.

The analysis of English diphthong perception by Polish listeners has shown that the issue cannot be accounted for by a two-level Optimality-Theoretic model. The problem is that in two-level Optimality Theory the MAX and DEP constraints can only evaluate (in perception) input that has already been categorized into phonemes. The model requires speech signal segmentation, i.e. a phonological construct, before speech processing has actually begun. Natural Phonological analysis deals well with uncategorized, auditory-phonetic input to speech perception and it can handle sequential issues. One solution to the inadequacy of the two-level Optimality-Theoretic analysis for explaining the issue of English diphthong perception would be the extension of the Optimality-Theoretic model. Such an extension to a three-level model, with functional explanation, constraints of different ontological status – functionally, not only formally, derived, including quantitative constraints, and sequential abstraction devices is provided by Boersma (1998, 2000, 2007 and this volume) and Boersma and Hamann (to appear). According to this model, English [koʊkə] is mapped by Polish listeners onto the surface phonological structure /kɔ.ka/ and this form is then evaluated by faithfulness constraints and mapped onto the underlying |kɔka|. The smoothness of the first-formant transition in English [oʊ] would cause the perception by Poles as /ɔ/ and the abrupt change of the first formant in English [aɪ] would be responsible for the perception as /aj/. Boersma's extended, three-level Optimality-Theoretic model can account for the phenomenon of English diphthong perception by Poles because it shares more features with Natural Phonology than the two-level Optimality Theory does.

There is, however, a factor which makes a Natural Phonological account of perception theoretically better grounded than both two- and three-level Optimality Theory. A Natural Phonological account of perception is based on un-doing of phonological processes and disambiguation heuristics for lenition ambiguities. The logical properties of inference in Optimality Theory can be shown to be less transparent. Optimality Theory claims to be a constraint-based theory. A purely constraint-based theory would be strictly declarative — i.e. the constraints would be unordered "axioms" which apply as they become relevant, using some general procedural principle such as modus ponens, rather than individual principles of application and ordering/ranking for specific "rules". If Optimality Theory were a genuine constraint-based approach, unor-dered constraints would filter the underlying representations in the production direction, and the surface representations in the perception direction. However, Optimality-Theoretic constraints are ranked, i.e. "ordered" (in traditional ter-minology: extrinsically ordered). Different orderings — just like different or-dering of rules in more traditional phonologies – lead to different outputs. Con-sequently, from a logical point of view, Optimality Theory is more appropriately seen as being based on a kind of default logic, with non-monotonic inference. The conclusion to be drawn from this is that the principles of non-monotonic inference must be applied to Optimality Theory. The principles of non-monotonic inference are known to be procedurally intractable except under the closed world condition. Since the Optimality-Theoretic universal candidate generator GEN generates an infinite set of candidates from any input, the closed world condition it not met in the Optimality-Theoretic version of default logic with non-monotonic inference. This means that Optimality Theory in fact does not have a reliable theory of inference. The formal complexity of the model is even more surprising in the light of what Kaplan and Kay (1994) show about phonology and morphology: finite state automata are usually sufficiently expressive as their models. Since a good theory should not involve unnecessary formal mechanisms, and its inferences should be tractable, Optimality Theory should be transformed. Karttunen (1998) proposes a formalization of Optimality Theory which includes no marking or counting of constraint violations, application of constraints within finite-state calculus, merging a system of constraints into a single constraint network. He therefore proves that Optimality Theory is in fact similar to classical rewrite systems and two-level models and that the ranking of constraints corresponds to the ordering of rewrite rules. Jäger (2002) claims that in the case of unidirectional Optimality Theory the premises of Correspondence Theory (McCarthy and Prince 1995) have to be adopted, because then the outputs of GEN are pairs of underlying and surface structures, including correspondence information, thanks to which the input is uniquely recoverable from the output. GEN is one-to-many and the inverse of GEN is a function. All constraints are markedness constraints. In each case it has to be decided whether GEN and the constraints involved can be implemented as rational relations. In bidirectional Optimality Theory the limitation to markedness constraints is too restrictive. Bidirectionally optimal input-output pairs do not form a rational relation and bidirectional optimization with gradient markedness constraints goes beyond the scope of finite-state techniques.

Since Boersma's Functional Phonology model is based on Optimality-Theoretic formalism with elements of bidirectionality, it is still to be examined whether his theory's inference techniques are tractable. Moreover, in his talk McCarthy (2006) argues for an alternative Optimality-Theoretic architecture, where the system of candidate generation has limited access to EVAL, and where candidates include output forms and the information that produced them. Finiteness results from bounded chain construction and evaluation. As a result Optimality Theory now has a minimal inference theory containing the modus ponens rule. The inference rules of OT are more complex: each so-called constraint in the EVAL component is, effectively, the universally quantified premise of a modus ponens inference, and the premises are treated sequentially, i.e. as a multi-stage derivation (Dafydd Gibbon, personal communication). Thus, the question also arises whether Optimality Theory proponents will want and/or be able to adopt their model accordingly.

9. Conclusions

The issue of English diphthong perception by Polish listeners has been explained within Natural Phonology as activity aiming to arrive at an underlying representation, where an underlying representation is understood as consisting of Polish phonemes in configurations allowed by Polish phonotactics. It is assumed that Polish listeners when hearing English phonemes try to derive their underlying forms in accordance with Polish fortition processes, whereby diphthongs have to be reinterpreted as vowel plus glide sequences or vowels. How a given English diphthong gets reinterpreted depends on the possibility of assuming that a diphthong is a result of lenition of a vowel plus glide sequence or the inadequacy of such an assumption in a given phonotactic environment. Inherent in Natural Phonological reasoning is the assumption of the vital role of non-distinctive features and the undoing of sequence-optimizing processes in phonological perception. Natural Phonological reasoning operates with processes which can apply to more than two kinds of representations. These three aspects of perception: non-distinctive features, undoing lenitions and more than two phonological representations are not parts of classical Optimality-Theoretic reasoning. The problem of English diphthong perception is a case, in which classical Optimality Theory, boasting formal predictive power, turns out to be too powerful and selects candidates which, however optimal they could seem, lose in the more rudimentary processing performed by listeners. If a model based on constraint rankings is to account for the issue, it has to be a version extended to include a third level of representation, like e.g. Boersma's model, which bears more resemblance to Natural Phonology than the classical Optimality Theory does.

References

Bogacka [Balas], Anna
    2004   On the perception of English high vowels by Polish learners of English. In: Evangelia Dakalaki, Napoleon Katsos, Marios Mavrogiorgos and Matthew Reeve (eds.), *CamLing 2004: Proceedings of the University of Cambridge Second Postgraduate Conference on Language Research*, 43–50. Cambridge: Cambridge Institute of Language Research.

50 *Anna Balas*

Bogacka [Balas], Anna
2007   *Repopulating Vowel Space: English Diphthong Production by Polish Learners of English.* Ph.D. dissertation, Adam Mickiewicz University, Poznań.
Boersma, Paul
1998   *Functional Phonology.* Ph.D. dissertation, University of Amsterdam. The Hague: Holland Academic Graphics.
Boersma, Paul
2000   The OCP in the perception grammar. *Rutgers Optimality Archive* 435.
Boersma, Paul
2007   Some listener-oriented accounts of *h*-aspiré in French. *Lingua* 117: 1989–2054.
Boersma, Paul
this volume Cue constraints and their interactions in phonological perception and production.
Boersma, Paul, and Silke Hamann
to appear   Loanword adaptation as first language phonological perception. In: Andrea Calabrese and W. Leo Wetzels (eds.), *Loan Phonology.* Amsterdam: Benjamins.
Burzio, Luigi
2001   Zero derivations. *Linguistic Inquiry* 32: 658–677.
Donegan, Patricia
1985   *On the Natural Phonology of Vowels.* New York: Garland Publishing.
Donegan, Patricia
1993   On the phonetic basis of phonological change. In: Charles Jones (ed.), *Historical Linguistics: Problems and Perspectives*, 98–130. London: Longman.
Donegan, Patricia
2001   Constraints and processes in phonological perception. In: Katarzyna Dziubalska-Kołaczyk (ed.), *Constraints and Preferences*, 42–68. Berlin: Mouton de Gruyter.
Donegan, Patricia, and David Stampe
1979   The study of Natural Phonology. In: Daniel A. Dinnsen (ed.), *Current Approaches to Phonological Theory*, 126–173. Bloomington: Indiana University Press.
Dressler, Wolfgang U.
1984   Explaining Natural Phonology. *Phonology Yearbook* 1: 29–50.
Dressler, Wolfgang U.
1985   *Morphonology: The Dynamics of Derivation.* Ann Arbor: Karoma Publishers.

Dressler, Wolfgang U.
1999   On a semiotic theory of preferences in language. In: Michael Jaley
            and Michael Shapiro (eds.), *The Peirce Seminar Papers: Essays in
            Semiotic analysis. Proceedings of the International Colloquium on
            Language and Peircean Sign Theory,* Volume 4, 389–415. New
            York: Berghahn Books.
Dziubalska-Kołaczyk, Katarzyna
1990   *A Theory of Second Language Acquisition within the Framework of
            Natural Phonology.* Poznań: Adam Mickiewicz University Press.
Dziubalska-Kołaczyk, Katarzyna
1995   *Phonology without the Syllable: A Study in the Natural Framework.*
            Poznań: Motivex.
Dziubalska-Kołaczyk, Katarzyna
2001   Phonotactic constraints are preferences. In: Katarzyna Dziubalska-
            Kołaczyk (ed.), *Constraints and Preferences,* 69–100. Berlin: Mou-
            ton de Gruyter.
Dziubalska-Kołaczyk, Katarzyna
2002a   *Beats-and-Binding Phonology.* Frankfurt am Main: Peter Lang.
Dziubalska-Kołaczyk, Katarzyna
2002b   Challenges for Natural Linguistics in the twenty first century: a per-
            sonal view. In: Katarzyna Dziubalska-Kołaczyk and Jarosław
            Weckwerth (eds.), *Future Challenges for Natural Linguistics,* 103–
            128. Munich: Lincom.
Dziubalska-Kołaczyk, Katarzyna
2007   Natural Phonology: universals principles for the study of language
            (insiders meet outsiders). In: Jürgen Trouvain and William J. Barry
            (eds.), *Proceedings of the 16th International Congress of Phonetic
            Sciences,* 1953–1956. Saarbrücken: Saarland University.
Escudero, Paola, and Paul Boersma
2004   Bridging the gap between L2 speech perception research and phono-
            logical theory. *Studies in Second Language Acquisition* 26: 551–585.
Flemming, Edward
2001   Scalar and categorical phenomena in a unified model of phonetics
            and phonology. *Phonology* 18. 7–44.
Hayes, Bruce
1999   Phonetically-driven phonology: the role of Optimality Theory and
            inductive grounding. In Michael Darnell, Edith Moravcsik, Michael
            Noonan, Frederick Newmeyer and Kathleen Wheatley (eds.), *Func-
            tionalism and Formalism in Linguistics,* Volume I, 243–285. Ams-
            terdam: John Benjamins.
Hayes, Bruce, Kirchner, Robert and Donca Steriade (eds.)
2004   *Phonetically Based Phonology.* Cambridge: Cambridge University
            Press.

Jassem, Wiktor
2003   Polish. *Journal of the International Phonetic Association* 33: 103–107.
Jäger, Gerhard
2002   Gradient constraints in finite state OT: the unidirectional and bidirectional case. In: Ingrid Kaufmann and Barbara Stiebels (eds.), *More than Words: A Festschrift for Dieter Wunderlich*, 299–335. Berlin: Akademie Verlag.
Kager, René
1999   *Optimality Theory*. Cambridge: Cambridge University Press.
Kaplan, Roland M., and Martin Kay
1994   Regular models of phonological rule systems. *Computational Linguistics* 20: 331–378.
Karttunen, Lauri
1998   The proper treatment of optimality in computational phonology. In: *The Proceedings of the International Workshop on Finite-State Methods in Natural Language Processing*, 1–12. Bilkent University, Ankara.
Kenstowicz, Michael
2001   The role of perception in loanword phonology: a review of *Les emprunts linguistiques d'origine européenne en Fon* by Flavien Gbéto. To appear in *Linguistique Africaine*.
Kirchner, Robert
2001   Phonological contrast and articulatory effort. In: Linda Lombardi (ed.), *Segmental Phonology in Optimality Theory*, 79–117. Cambridge: Cambridge University Press.
Kul, Małgorzata
2007   *The Principle of Least Effort within the Hierarchy of Linguistic Preferences: External Evidence from English*. Ph.D. dissertation, Adam Mickiewicz University, Poznań.
McCarthy, John J.
2002   *A Thematic Guide to Optimality Theory*. Cambridge: Cambridge University Press.
McCarthy, John J.
2006   Candidates and derivations in Optimality Theory. *Rutgers Optimality Archive* 823-0506.
McCarthy, John J., and Alan Prince
1995   Faithfulness and reduplicative identity. In: Jill Beckman, Suzanne Urbanczyk and Laura Walsh Dickey (eds.), *University of Massachusetts Occasional Papers in Linguistics* 18: 249–384.

Pater, Joe
2004   Bridging the gap between receptive and productive development
                with minimally violable constraints. In: René Kager, Joe Pater and
                Wim Zonneveld (eds.), *Constraints in Phonological Acquisition*,
                219–244. Cambridge: Cambridge University Press.
Prince, Alan, and Paul Smolensky
2004   *Optimality Theory: Constraint Interaction in Generative Grammar*.
                Malden: Blackwell.
Ritt, Nikolaus
2001   Are optimality theoretical "constrains" the same as natural linguistic
                "preferences"? In: Katarzyna Dziubalska-Kołaczyk (ed.), *Con-
                straints and Preferences*, 291–310. Berlin: Mouton de Gruyter.
Rubach, Jerzy
2000   Glide and glottal stop insertion in Slavic languages: a DOT analysis.
                Linguistic Inquiry 31: 271–317.
Rubach, Jerzy
2004   Derivation in Optimality Theory: a reply to Burzio. *Linguistic In-
                quiry* 35: 656–670.
Stampe, David
1969   The acquisition of phonetic representation. *Proceedings of the Chi-
                cago Linguistics Society* 5: 443–453.
Stampe, David
1979   *A Dissertation on Natural Phonology*. New York: Garland Publish-
                ing.
Steriade, Donca
2001   Directional asymmetries in place assimilation: a perceptual account.
                In: Elizabeth Hume and Keith Johnson (eds.), *The Role of Speech
                Perception in Phonology*, 219–250. New York: Academic Press.
Strutyński, Janusz
1999   *Gramatyka Polska*. Kraków: Wydawnictwo Tomasz Strutyński.
Vennemann, Theo
1983   Causality in language change: theories of linguistic preferences as a
                basis for linguistic explanations. *Folia Linguistica Historica* 6: 5–26.
Wells, John
1982   *Accents of English 3: Beyond the British Isles*. Cambridge: Cam-
                bridge University Press.

Cue constraints and their interactions in phonological perception and production[*]

Paul Boersma

This paper shows how one can formalize the phonology-phonetics interface within constraint-based frameworks such as Optimality Theory (OT) or Harmonic Grammar (HG) and why it is necessary and advantageous to do so. I will describe the phonology-phonetics interface in terms of *cue constraints* and illustrate their workings in interaction with each other and in interaction with other classes of constraints. Beside their general usefulness in describing prelexical perception and phonetic implementation, cue constraints help to account for special phenomena such as poverty of the base, the prototype effect, foreign-language perception, and loanword adaptation.

1. Where is the phonology-phonetics interface?

My first task is to make the phonology-phonetics interface explicit. Figure 1 shows where it resides in an explicit multi-level model of phonology and phonetics (Boersma 1998, 2007a; Apoussidou 2007). In the following two sections I briefly clarify why phonological theory requires at least the five representations shown in Figure 1, and why the phonology-phonetics interface must be where it is in Figure 1.

---

* Parts of this paper were presented to audiences at the Meeting on Cochlear Implants and First Language Acquisition in Beekbergen (September 18, 2003), at Edinburgh University (June 3, 2004), at Johns Hopkins University (September 22, 2004), at Utrecht University (April 13, 2006), at the University of Santa Catarina (November 24, 2006), at the III Congresso Internacional de Fonética e Fonologia in Belo Horizonte (November 29, 2006), and at the Workshop on Computing and Phonology in Groningen (December 8, 2006). For comments on earlier versions of the written text I thank Silke Hamann and the phonologists at the University of Tromsø, who include Bruce Morén, Christian Uffmann, Peter Jurgec, Ove Lorentz, Silvia Blaho, and Martin Krämer.

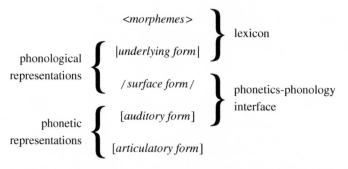

Figure 1.   The BiPhon model (Boersma 2007a, Apoussidou 2007): the five levels of representation minimally required for doing bidirectional phonology and phonetics.

1.1   Phonological theory requires at least five representations

Multiple levels of representation such as those in Figure 1 are common in psycholinguistic models of speech production (e.g. Levelt 1989) and comprehension (e.g. McClelland and Elman 1986, McQueen and Cutler 1997), but are less often seen in phonological theory (I will discuss the exceptions later on). As in my earlier work, I argue in this paper that phonological theory would profit from going beyond its usual two levels, especially by taking the phonetics seriously.

Figure 1, then, contains the minimal number of phonological representations that phonologists can be comfortable working with: the Underlying Form (often called the *input* in the OT literature) and the Surface Form (often called the *output* in the OT literature). The underlying form is the discrete representation of the phonological structure of morphemes in the language user's mental lexicon; the Morpheme (or Lemma) mediates in connecting the phonological underlying form to semantic features in the lexicon (Saussure 1916), which again are probably connected to the meaning of the utterance and from there to the pragmatic context (these are not shown in Figure 1, since they are likely to concern phonological theory to a lesser extent). The surface form is the discrete representation of the phonological surface structure and consists of prosodic elements (feet, syllables, segments) and phonological substance (features, autosegments). For most phonologists, the surface form does not contain any concrete continuous phonetic detail, and this is something I agree with; it means that one can do insightful investigations in many areas of phonology by just considering the two discrete phonological representations.

As for phonetic processing, this is usually regarded as something that comes 'after' the phonology (e.g. Pierrehumbert 1987, Keating 1985, Gussenhoven 2004). Phonologists tend to argue that the phonetics is therefore not really relevant for autonomous phonological processing (e.g. Hale and Reiss 1998), or that it might be relevant but that its modelling is not a priority for phonological theory (e.g. Hayes 1999: fn. 7). On the basis of the abundant existence of seemingly phonetically-inspired processes in segmental phonology, some phonologists have nevertheless tried to include phonetic considerations of articulatory effort and auditory contrast into the usual two-level model of phonology consisting only of underlying and surface form; by doing so, one must either propose that the phonological surface structure somehow includes continuous phonetic detail (Jun 1995, Kirchner 1998; cf. Flemming 1995 for a model without underlying forms but with a phonetically detailed surface form) or that discrete phonological processing is somehow sensitive to extralinguistic information on phonetic detail (Steriade 1995, 2001). Following Boersma (1998), I take the third possible stand, which takes seriously the possible relevance of phonetics for phonological theory without sacrificing the representational modularity of the phonology and the phonetics: in Figure 1, therefore, the phonetic representations are separate from the phonological representations, but are taken just as seriously. The minimum number of phonetic representations that phoneticians can be comfortable working with are two: the Auditory Form and the Articulatory Form. The auditory form is the continuous representation of sound; it consists of noises, pitches, spectra, silences, transitions, and durations. The articulatory form is the continuous representation of the gestures of the human sound-producing mechanism; it consists of the activities of the relevant muscles of the lungs, tongue, throat, larynx, lips and nose and their coordinations.

In the end, whether the phonology and the phonetics are as separated as they appear in Figure 1 is an empirical question. For the moment, however, it seems to suffice to observe that the multi-level model comes with a learning algorithm that has been shown to generate automatically at least three phenomena: (1) the *prototype effect* (Boersma 2006), which leads to the evolutionary emergence of optimal auditory contrast in inventories (Boersma and Hamann 2008); (2) *licensing by cue* (Boersma 2008); and (3) the relation between various properties formerly ascribed to the concept of *markedness* (namely frequency and phonological activity; Boersma 2008). No such explanatory force has been shown to hold for any of the two-level models with which people have tried to explain these phenomena (namely: the MINDIST constraints by Flemming 1995, the P-map by Steriade 2001, and the markedness constraints by Prince and Smolensky 1993 and much following work in OT). The present paper refers to these phenomena and their explanations where they fit naturally in my discussion of the bidirectional use of cue constraints.

To sum up, the present paper assumes (and requires) the five levels of representation mentioned in Figure 1. In real users of language there may well turn out to be more representations than five. For instance, the Underlying Form may turn out to have to be divided up into a Stem Level and a Word Level (Kiparsky 1985, Bermúdez-Otero 1999), and the Auditory Form may turn out to have to be divided into a representation 'before' speaker normalization and a representation 'after' speaker normalization. For the purposes of the present paper, however, the five levels of Figure 1 suffice. The next question is how the two phonological representations connect to the semantic and phonetic ones.

1.2   The phonology-phonetics interface is between Surface and Auditory Form

Given the five levels of representation mentioned in Figure 1, we are left with a couple of possibilities for how and where the phonology interfaces with the morphology (and hence with the semantics) and where it interfaces with the phonetics.

The division of labour between the two phonological representations in this respect seems to be clear: in all published grammar models that make a distinction between underlying and surface form, it is the underlying form that connects to morphemes and meaning (via the lexicon), and it is the phonological surface form that connects to the phonetics (via the phonology-phonetics interface). I see no reason to deviate from this common viewpoint. Figure 1 therefore illustrates my assumption that the connection to the morphology and the semantics is made from the underlying form, and the connection to the phonetics is made from the phonological surface form.

It is a somewhat more controversial matter, however, which of the two phonetic representations (auditory or articulatory) connects to the phonological surface form. The Direct Realist theory of speech perception (Fowler 1986) proposes that auditory speech is directly interpreted in terms of articulatory gestures and that it is these perceived gestures that connect to the phonology. That theory, when confronted with the five representations of Figure 1, would therefore propose that the interface between the phonology and the phonetics resides in a connection between Surface Form and Articulatory Form. While it is thinkable that an explicit model of phonology and phonetics could be based on Direct Realism, such an exercise has yet to be performed. For the present paper I hold the simpler and probably more common assumption that the auditory-phonetic form connects directly to the phonological surface form. This choice is based partly on theoretical simplicity, since it economizes on one level of representation in the speech comprehension process: a listener who follows Figure 1 just starts out with an Auditory Form and can subsequently process the phonology with the ultimate goal of accessing the semantics, all without ever passing through the articulatory form. Moreover, the observation that children can successfully access meaning from sound, while constructing adultlike phonological representations, well before they can produce any speech (Jusczyk 1997), also points to a direct connection between auditory and surface form (Boersma 1998: ch.14).

To sum up, the interface between phonology and phonetics resides in a connection between the phonological surface form and the auditory-phonetic form. It is now time to make explicit what this connection is about.

1.3   The phonology-phonetics interface consists of cues

Now that we assume that the phonology-phonetics interface resides in a connection between auditory forms and phonological surface forms, it becomes relevant to ask how the phonetic literature has been talking about this connection. It turns out that phoneticians talk about this connection in terms of *cues*. In English, for instance, auditory vowel duration (in milliseconds) can be a *cue* to the value (plus or minus) of the phonological voicing feature of the following obstruent, both in comprehension and production: English listeners use vowel duration as a cue for reliably perceiving the value of the phonological voicing of the following obstruent (Denes 1955, Hogan and Rozsypal 1980), and English speakers *implement* (or *enhance*) obstruent voicing by using the vowel duration cue (House and Fairbanks 1953; Peterson and Lehiste 1960). This use of cues is a language-specific issue (Zimmerman and Sapon 1958): while most languages lengthen their vowels slightly before voiced consonants, English does it to an especially large extent (Peterson and Lehiste mention a ratio of 2:3 for an unspecified variety of American English).

1.4   In OT, cues are formalized as cue constraints

Following much earlier work in OT, the present paper assumes that the five levels of representations in Figure 1 are linked by local connections that are implemented as constraints, as in Figure 2.

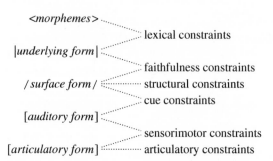

Figure 2.   Formalization of bidirectional phonology and phonetics by means of constraints.

Figure 2 mentions six types of constraints. The *faithfulness constraints* and the *structural constraints* are the same ones that phonologists have been familiar with since Prince and Smolensky (1993), although the explicit division between Underlying Form and Surface Form, and therefore the formulation of the faithfulness constraints, follows more closely the Correspondence account by McCarthy and Prince (1995); the faithfulness constraints therefore evaluate the similarity between underlying and surface form, and the structural constraints evaluate the surface form alone. The *articulatory constraints* are the ones that were proposed by Kirchner (1998) and Boersma (1998), and measure articulatory effort; following Boersma (1998), these constraints evaluate the articulatory-phonetic form, not the phonological surface form. The *lexical constraints* express the relation between underlying form and morphemes (or meaning) in the lexicon; they were discussed by Boersma (2001) and Escudero (2005: 214–236) and formulated in terms of a connection between two separate levels of representation (as in Figure 2) by Apoussidou (2007). The *cue constraints* express the language user's knowledge of cues (§1.3), i.e. the relation between auditory form and phonological surface form; these constraints appeared in Boersma (1998, 2000), Escudero and Boersma (2003, 2004), and Pater (2004), although the term 'cue constraint' was not introduced before Boersma (2007a) and Escudero (2005). Finally, the *sensorimotor constraints* (Boersma 2006) express the language user's knowledge of the relation between articulation and sound; with them, the speaker knows how to articulate a given sound and can predict what a certain articulatory gesture will sound like.

The cue constraints, which are the central subject of this paper, will be seen to be able to interact with all of the remaining five types. This ability crucially relies on two properties of the BiPhon model: *bidirectionality of constraints*, which is the use of the same constraints and rankings by both the listener and the speaker, and *cross-level paralellism*, which is the capability of all the constraints of all the levels to interact with each other. I discuss these two properties in the next two sections.

1.5   Bidirectionality of constraints

Nearly all the constraints in Figure 2 are used both by the speaker and by the listener. The task of the speaker is to turn an intended meaning into an articulation, and the task of the listener is to turn an incoming auditory form into a meaning. Several cases of bidirectional use of constraints have been discussed in the literature, and I review them here.

Bidirectionality of faithfulness constraints. Since Prince and Smolensky (1993) we have known that 'phonological production', i.e. the mapping from underlying to surface form in Figure 2, involves an interaction of structural and faithfulness constraints. Figure 2 makes this interaction explicit by showing that the structural constraints evaluate the output of this mapping, while the faithfulness constraints evaluate the relation between the input and the output of this mapping. Smolensky (1996) has shown that this mapping can be reversed: the mapping from surface to underlying form ('phonological comprehension') is evaluated by the same faithfulness constraints that evaluate phonological production, and with the same rankings. In Figure 2 we see that this mapping is evaluated by faithfulness constraints alone, because there are no constraints that evaluate its output (namely the underlying form). Smolensky makes explicit the point that the structural constraints cannot be involved in this mapping, because these constraints evaluate its input (namely the surface form), which is identical for all candidates; therefore, structural constraints cannot be used bidirectionally in a grammar model with just two levels of representation (underlying and surface form).

Bidirectionality of structural constraints. In a grammar model with three levels of representation, structural constraints can be used bidirectionally, at least if the surface form is the intermediate level. Tesar (1997) proposed a model for metrical phonology with an underlying form, a surface form, and a more 'phonetic' overt form; in that model, structural constraints evaluate both the output of the speaker's phonological production as well as the output of the listener's mapping from overt to surface form ('robust interpretive parsing'). Since the latter mapping may involve additional cue constraints, I discuss this subject in detail in §4.

Bidirectionality of lexical constraints. In comprehension, lexical constraints have been shown to help word recognition, for instance by disambiguating phonologically ambiguous utterances (Boersma 2001, Escudero 2005: 214–236), and in production they have been shown to be able to regulate allomorphy (Apoussidou 2007: ch.6). A discussion of their interactions with cue constraints appears in §8.

Bidirectionality of cue constraints. Cue constraints have been shown to be able to handle the listener's 'prelexical perception', i.e. the mapping from auditory to surface form (Boersma 1998; Escudero and Boersma 2004; Escudero 2005), as well as the speaker's phonetic implementation (Boersma 2006, 2007a, 2008; Boersma and Hamann 2008). The present paper illustrates both of these roles of cue constraints, especially as they interact with structural, faithfulness, articulatory, and lexical constraints.

1.6   Cross-level parallelism

Interactions of cue constraints with all the other types of constraints are not automatically allowed by just any model of processing.

Consider, for instance, the serial processing model in Figure 3. On the left side we see the processing task of the listener, namely mapping an incoming auditory form (sound) all the way to morphemes and meaning. In the serial model of Figure 3, this task consists of three subtasks that process the incoming information sequentially: first, the module of prelexical perception maps the auditory form to a surface form; then, the module of word recognition maps this surface form to an underlying form; finally, the module of lexical access connects the underlying form to the morpheme and meaning.[1] On the right side of Figure 3 we see the processing task of the speaker, namely mapping a morphological (and perhaps semantic) representation all the way to an articulation. In the serial model depicted here, this task consists of four subtasks: a module of lexical retrieval, whose output is the underlying form, which is the input to the phonological production module, whose output is the surface form, which is the input to the phonetic implementation module, whose output is an auditory form (i.e. the speaker's view of what she will sound like), which is the input to the final sensorimotor processing module.

---

1. The dotted curve from auditory to articulatory form in Figure 3 is not part of the comprehension task, but is predicted to occur nevertheless: when a sound comes in, articulatory representations will be automatically activated. The activity of mirror neurons in real human brains may be a sign of this.

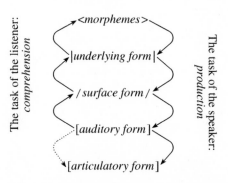

Figure 3. The processing routes of serial comprehension and serial production.

In the serial ('modular') view of comprehension in Figure 3, the extent to which cue constraints can interact with other constraints is quite limited. When comparing the arrows in Figure 3 with the constraints in Figure 2, we see only three modules in which constraints of various types are allowed to interact: on the comprehension side, prelexical perception is handled by an interaction of structural constraints and cue constraints, and on the production side, phonological production is handled by an interaction of structural and faithfulness constraints while sensorimotor processing is handled by an interaction of articulatory and sensorimotor constraints. The remaining four modules are handled by a single type of constraint: word recognition by faithfulness constraints, lexical access and lexical retrieval by lexical constraints, and phonetic implementation by cue constraints. The only interaction that is allowed for cue constraints is an interaction with structural constraints, and this interaction only occurs in comprehension.

The situation is strikingly different for the parallel (or 'interactive') processing model in Figure 4. On the left side we see that comprehension now involves a parallel handling of prelexical perception, word recognition, and lexical access; in Optimality-Theoretic terms, the listener, given an auditory form as input, has to decide on a simultaneously optimal triplet of surface form, underlying form, and morphemes. On the right side of Figure 4 we see that production now involves a parallel handling of lexical retrieval, phonological production, phonetic implementation, and sensorimotor processing; in Optimality-Theoretic terms, the speaker, given a sequence of morphemes as input, has to decide on a simultaneously optimal quadruplet of underlying, surface, auditory and articulatory forms.

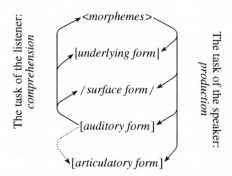

Figure. 4.   The processing routes of parallel comprehension and parallel production.

The parallel view of Figure 4 allows many interactions between many more types of constraints than the serial model of Figure 3 does. In the comprehension direction, cue constraints, structural constraints, faithfulness constraints and lexical constraints can all interact with each other, though not with sensorimotor or articulatory constraints. In the production direction, all the six types of constraints that occur in Figure 2 can interact with each other.

The extent to which linguistic processing is serial or parallel is an open question. Especially in production a good case for extensive parallelism can be made: we have witnessed interactions of faithfulness and articulatory constraints (Boersma 1998), interactions of articulatory and cue constraints (Boersma 2006, Boersma and Hamann 2008), and even quadruple interactions of faithfulness, structural, cue, and articulatory constraints (Boersma 2007a). The present paper discusses most of the possible types of interactions between cue constraints and other constraints, i.e. most of the interactions that involve the phonology-phonetics interface. The focus of the paper (§2–§4) is on interactions of cue constraints and structural constraints in comprehension, because such interactions are predicted both by the serial and by the parallel model; a formalization of these interactions explains several old issues in phonological theory and shows that phonetic considerations have to be formalized in the same way as phonological considerations, because they interact in the same process.

2.   Perception and its formalization

Of the several linguistic processes that involve cue constraints, the first and main one that I formalize is (prelexical) perception. The primacy of this process lies in the fact that it is the process that least controversially involves the phonology-phonetics interface, and at the same time shows that phonological considerations (structural constraints) are in direct competition with more phonetic considerations (cue constraints); their interaction shows that *perception is phonological*.

2.1   What is perception?

In general, perception is the mapping from raw sensory data to more abstract mental representations, or any step therein. In phonology, the perception task for the listener is to map a raw continuous auditory representation (AudF) to a discrete phonological surface structure (SF). This task corresponds to what phoneticians in the lab call an *identification* task.

It is useful to point out to what kind of perception I am *not* referring here. If a listener identifies two different auditory forms as the same phonological structure, I will say that these two forms are 'perceived as the same phonological structure'. But if I say that two auditory forms are perceived as the same phonological structure, I do not mean to say that the listener cannot hear them apart. Listeners can often discriminate sounds that they would classify as the same phoneme. Phoneticians in the lab call this a *discrimination* task. The discriminability of two auditory forms is partly determined by their auditory distance, partly by whether they are classified as the same phonological category in their language: from 9 months of age, human listeners in whose language a certain pair of auditory tokens belongs to two different categories are better at discriminating them than are listeners in whose language this same pair of auditory tokens belongs to a single category (for an overview, see Jusczyk 1997). Thus, the discrimination task measures a partly universal, partly language-specific degree of perceptability of a contrast, whereas the identification task measures what the listener regards as the speaker's most likely intended language-specific phonological surface structure. The two tasks, then, are different, and since the goal of speech comprehension is to reconstruct the speaker's intended message, I will ignore the extralinguistic discrimination task and use the term 'perception' only for the linguistic perception process, which can be equated with the identification tasks that phoneticians conceive in the lab. Other possible terms for the same thing are *prelexical perception* and *phonetic parsing*.

2.2   Modelling robust language-specific perception in OT

To start modelling perception in Optimality Theory, I single out the auditory-to-surface mapping from Figures 2, 3, and 4. This yields Figure 5, which shows both the processing (as a curved arrow) and the grammar (the constraints).

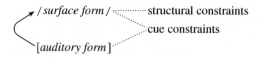

Figure 5.   Prelexical perception.

The structural constraints evaluate the output of the perception process (surface form, SF), and the cue constraints evaluate the mapping between the input (auditory form, AudF) and the output (SF). The structural constraints are the same ones as in production (Prince and Smolensky 1993), where they interact with faithfulness constraints. The cue constraints compare two incommensurable kinds of representations: the auditory form, which consists of universally available continuous formants, pitches, noises and durations, and the phonological surface form, which consists of language-specific abstract discrete structures. Just as the word *faithfulness* the term *cue* implies a relation between two representations ("a surface form can be *faithful* to an underlying form"; "an auditory form can be a *cue* for a surface form"). The cue constraints that have been proposed in the OT literature are OCP (Boersma 1998) and the generalized categorization constraint family "$[x]_{AudF}$ is not perceived as $/y/_{SF}$" (Escudero and Boersma 2003, 2004; Boersma and Escudero 2008; Escudero 2005). Some examples from the pre-OT literature are Polivanov (1931) and Cornulier (1981); I have discussed the latter elsewhere (Boersma 2007a), and discuss the former in the next section.

3.   Polivanov: Japanese learners of Russian[2]

In his discussion of the perception of sounds in a foreign language, Polivanov (1931) proposes an account in terms of inviolable structural constraints and violable cue constraints. This section shows that Polivanov's proposal can be formulated in all details with the decision mechanism of Optimality Theory (Prince and Smolensky 1993) and fits well within the models of Figures 1, 2, 3, 4, and 5.

3.1   Perception

The first example of constraint ranking in perception was provided by Polivanov (1931), who observed that Japanese learners of Russian perceive the Russian pronunciation [tak] (which reflects the underlying form |tak| 'so') as the Japanese phonological surface structure /.ta.ku./. The present section translates this into OT.

In a narrower transcription, the auditory form is [_'a_ᵏ]: as you can see in a spectrogram, this sound consists of (at least) a silence ([_]), followed by a high-frequency brief noise ("burst") ([']), followed by a loud periodic ("sonorant") sound with formants around 1000 Hz ([a]), followed by another silence, followed by a burst with a peak around 2500 Hz ([ᵏ]). A listener of Russian will have to map this sound to the phonological form /.tak./, which is a single syllable (syllables are delimited by periods here) that consists of an ordered sequence of three of the 40 (or so) Russian phonemes ('ordered' because /.kat./ would mean something else). The Russian listener can subsequently easily look this up in her lexicon and finds |tak| 'so', a common interjection expressing agreement. How can we model the Russian perception of [a], or equivalently, [*periodic, sonorant*, F1 = 800 Hz], i.e. an auditorily periodic and sonorant sound with a first formant of, say, 800 Hz? Simply like the following tableau:

---

2.   The observation that Polivanov's account involves the ranking of violable constraints and can therefore be translated directly into an Optimality-Theoretic formalism was made by Escudero and Boersma (2004). The specific formulation of sections 3 and 4 was presented before by the author at Edinburgh University on June 3, 2004, and at Johns Hopkins University on September 22, 2004.

(1)   Russian perception of [a]

[*periodic, sonorant,* F1 = 800 Hz]	*/t/ [*periodic*]	*/b/ [*sonorant*]	*/i/ [F1=800Hz]	*/e/ [F1=800Hz]	*/a/ [F1=800Hz]
☞ /a/					*
/e/				*!	
/i/			*!		
/b/		*!			
/t/	*!				

Russian has vowel phonemes such as /a/, /e/ and /i/, periodic (i.e. voiced) non-sonorant consonant phonemes such as /b/, and non-periodic (i.e. voiceless) phonemes such as /t/. When hearing [a], the listener will have to choose from among at least these 5 sounds. Because the sound is periodic, the speaker cannot have intended to say /t/. This is such an important restriction (constraint) that I put it on top (i.e. in the left column). The *candidate* perception /t/ thus *violates* the constraint "a periodic (voiced) auditory form cannot be /t/" (abbreviated as */t/[*periodic*]). This violation is marked in the first column by an asterisk ("*"). Because this constraint is so high-ranked, its violation immediately rules out the /t/ candidate. In order words, this violation is *crucial*, and we denote that with an exclamation mark ("!").

The second candidate that can be ruled out is /b/, because a sonorant (= loud periodic) auditory form cannot refer to a plosive. This is the second-highest constraint. Regarding only the top two constraints, all vowels are still good candidates, because all vowels are periodic and sonorant. We then look at the formant information. The phoneme /i/ typically comes with an F1 of 300 Hz, /e/ perhaps with 500 Hz, and /a/ perhaps with 750 Hz. If you hear an F1 of 800 Hz, it is very unlikely that the speaker could have intended to put an underlying |i| into your head. That is the third constraint. It must also be slightly unlikely that the speaker's intention was |e|. That is the fourth constraint. There is still a difference between 750 and 800 Hz, but this difference is not so bad, so the fifth constraint is probably really low-ranked. The remaining candidate is /a/; it violates only the fifth constraint, and this violation does not rule out /a/ (since there are no other candidates left), hence no exclamation mark appears in the last column.

This is all the theoretical machinery we need for an Optimality-Theoretic model of perception.

Now consider the auditory form [_'a_^{k}] again. We saw how Russians would perceive it, but how would Japanese perceive it? Japanese words cannot have a plosive at the end of a syllable (i.e. in *coda*). A Japanese listener probably takes that into account when hearing [_'a_^{k}], so the perception /.tak./ is unlikely. So what will a Japanese learner of Russian do when first hearing a Russian say the utterance [_'a_^{k}]?

If the candidate perception /.tak./ is out of the question, perhaps the Japanese listener ignores the [^{k}] release burst and decides to perceive just /.ta./? Or perhaps the Japanese listener hears the [^{k}] release burst and decides that the speaker intended a /k/, which must then have been followed by a vowel, so that some more candidate structures are /.ta.ko./ and /.ta.ku./?

To start to get at an answer, consider what Japanese sounds like. Short high vowels that are not adjacent to a voiced consonant tend to be pronounced voiceless. Thus, the word |káku| is usually pronounced [_^{k}á_^{k}ų]. Such a de-voiced vowel will often lose all of its auditory cues, if there is even a slight background noise. So the auditory form is often not much more than [_^{k}á_^{k}]. Thus, Japanese listeners are used to interpreting a silence, i.e. the auditory form [ ], as the vowel /u/ (at least after a release burst). They will perceive the Russian [_'a_^{k}] as /.ta.ku./. Tableau (2) shows the candidates that I have been discussing, and the reasons why three of them are ruled out.

(2)   Japanese foreign-language perception of Russian

[_'a_^{k}]	NoPlosiveCoda	*/ / [^{k}]	*/o/ [ ]	*/u/ [ ]
/.tak./	*!			
/.ta./		*!		
☞ /.ta.ku./				*
/.ta.ko./			*!	

In Tableau (2) the Japanese ban on plosive codas has been formalized as the constraint NoPlosiveCoda; it assigns a violation mark to any plosive that occurs in a coda position in the surface structure. The listener's resistance to ignoring the [^{k}] release burst is expressed as the cue constraint */ / [^{k}]. The cue constraints against hallucinating the vowels /o/ and /u/ are written as */o/[ ] and */u/[ ]; the Japanese-specific routine of filling in the vowel /u/ is reflected as a low ranking of the latter constraint.

This Japanese behaviour of hallucinating a vowel when confronted with foreign codas generalizes to silences next to voiced consonants, e.g. Japanese have been reported not to hear the distinction between [ebzo] and [ebuzo] at all, interpreting both as /.e.bu.zo./ (Dupoux, Kakehi, Hirose, Pallier and Mehler 1999). It is the cause behind Japanese loanword adaptations, such as /.e.ki.su.to.ra./ for the European word *extra*.

The phenomenon in tableau (2) underlines the language-specificity of perception, because native listeners of Russian will perceive the same auditory form [_'a_^{k}] as the surface structure /.tak./. In tableaus like (2), such an outcome can be achieved by a much lower ranking of NOPLOSIVECODA. The language-specificity of perception, then, corresponds to the freedom that every language possesses to rank the constraints in its own order.

The second 'European' word that Polivanov discusses is *drama*. Its auditory form in Russian is [_^{d}rama], where the funny symbol in the beginning stands for the sound of voicing with your mouth closed, and the superscript ^{d} stands for the "alveolar" (high-frequency) plosive burst.

A Russian listener would perceive this auditory form as the phonological structure /.dra.ma./. A Japanese listener will not perceive it as /.dɾa.ma./, because that form contains a syllable onset that consists of two consonants, and such structures are forbidden in Japanese. The candidate /.dɾa.ma./ therefore violates a structural constraint at Surface Form, say */.CC/ ("no complex onsets"). Tableau (3) makes this explicit.

(3)   Japanese foreign-language perception of Russian

[_{*hi-freq*, *burst*}rama]	*/.CC/	*/ / [*burst*]	*/du/	*/dor/ [*hi-freq*]	*/+cont/ [*burst*]	*/o/ [ ]	*/u/ [ ]
/.dɾa.ma./	*!						
/.ɾa.ma./		*!					
/.du.ɾa.ma./			*!				*
/.gu.ɾa.ma./				*!			*
/.zu.ɾa.ma./					*!		*
☞ /.do.ɾa.ma./						*	

One way to satisfy the Japanese onset constraint is to perceive [_^{d}rama] as /.ɾa.ma./, which does not have a complex onset. This would involve throwing away some positive auditory cues, namely the voicing murmur and the high-frequency (alveolar) burst. As in the case of [_'a_^{k}], Japanese listeners seem not to like throwing away positive cues, i.e. a constraint like */ /[*burst*] is ranked high. This takes care of candidate 2.

The third option is to perceive /.du.ra.ma./, hallucinating an /u/ analogously to the /.ta.ku./ case. But Japanese happens not to allow the structure /du/ on the surface. This is what the third constraint expresses. It is another structural constraint.

The fourth option is to perceive /.gu.ra.ma./. This has the allowed sequence /gu/. But this candidate, with its /dor/ (dorsal) value for the phonological /place/ feature, ignores the high-frequency cues for alveolar place, as expressed by the fourth constraint.

The fifth option is to perceive /.zu.ra.ma./, a phonotactically allowed sequence that would be pronounced as [$_{-}$^{dz}urama]. This does honour the spectral place cues but ignores the auditory cue for plosiveness (namely the burst), positing instead a phonological fricative (denoted in the tableau with the feature value /+cont/). Because this candidate is more or less possible (according to Polivanov), we must conclude that the alveolar place cue is more important than the plosiveness cue. This is an example of *cue weighting*. The tableau shows this as a fixed ranking of the fourth and fifth constraints.

The sixth option is to perceive /.do.ra.ma./. This honours all the place and manner cues for /d/ but has the drawback of hallucinating the full vowel /o/ rather than the half-vowel /u/. It wins because there is no better option.

Please note that the ranking of the constraints in tableau (2) still occurs in tableau (3). This has to be. A single constraint ranking (i.e. a single grammar) has to account for all the forms in the language.

Polivanov suggested that some speakers might choose the fifth candidate. Such speakers would have the ranking in tableau (4).

(4)   Japanese foreign-language perception of Russian

[_ {*hi-freq*, *burst*}rama]	*/.CC/	*/ / [*burst*]	*/du/	*/dor/ [*hi-freq*]	*/o/ [ ]	*/+cont/ [*burst*]	*/u/ [ ]
/.dra.ma./	*!						
/.ra.ma./		*!					
/.du.ra.ma./			*!				*
/.gu.ra.ma./				*!			*
☞ /.zu.ra.ma./						*	*
/.do.ra.ma./					*!		

Polivanov says that for this variation two constraints compete. They are the fifth and sixth constraints in tableau (4). There is a way to express this variation in a single tableau. In tableau (5), the two constraints are ranked at the same height. This is to be interpreted in the following way: when the tableau is evaluated (i.e. when the listener hears [_ᵈrama]), the listener perceives /.zu.ra.ma./ in 50 percent of the cases, and /.do.ra.ma./ in the remaining 50 percent of the cases. Hence the two pointing fingers.

(5)   Two optimal candidates

[_ {hi-freq, burst}rama]	*/.CC/	*/ / [burst]	*/du/	*/dor/ [hi-freq]	*/+cont/ [burst]	*/o/ [ ]	*/d/ [ ]
/.dra.ma./	*!						
/.ra.ma./		*!					
/.du.ra.ma./			*!				*
/.gu.ra.ma./				*!			*
☞ /.zu.ra.ma./					*		*
☞ /.do.ra.ma./						*	

This concludes Polivanov's story. It involves three inviolable structural constraints and two competing cue constraints. In the light of possible abstract analyses of Japanese surface forms, however, the story is not yet complete. I defer this issue to §3.4.

Now that Polivanov's Japanese learner of Russian has perceived the sound [_ᵈrama] as the phonological surface structure /.do.ra.ma./, the next question is what the learner does with this: in what form will he store it in his lexicon, and how will he pronounce it? Although the answer may seem obvious (underlying form |dorama|, pronunciation [_ᵈorama]), we have to check that our OT grammar indeed generates those forms. This is what sections 3.2 and 3.3 do.

3.2   The lexicon: poverty of the base

If Polivanov's Japanese listener wants to learn Russian, he will want to store the *drama* word in his early L2-Russian lexicon. Alternatively, if the European concept of 'drama' is useful and distinctive enough to include into his Japanese vocabulary, he may want to store it as a loanword in his native L1-Japanese lexicon. In either case, the form in which the word is stored is likely to be influenced by his Japanese foreign-language perception of Russian. There are two straightforward strategies for this.

The first straightforward strategy for including the *drama* word into his lexicon relies on *serial comprehension*: the listener takes the output of the prelexical perception, which is /.do.ɾa.ma./, and uses this as the input for the next process, that of word recognition. This is summarized in Figure 6.

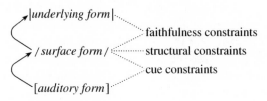

Figure 6. Serial comprehension.

Once the 'serial' listener, given the sound [_ᵈrama], has constructed /.do.ɾa.ma./, he will subsequently map it to the fully faithful underlying form |doɾama|:

(6)   'Recognition' of *drama*

/.do.ɾa.ma./		*/.CC/	DEP	MAX
☞	|doɾama|			
	|drama|		*!	
	|doɾma|		*!	
	|doɾamaɾibo|			*!***

It is worthwhile to look into the details of (6).

First, the structural constraint */.CC/ evaluates surface forms, not underlying forms; therefore, it can only evaluate the input /.do.ɾa.ma./, which is the same for all four candidates and which does not violate this constraint. Specifically, the candidate |drama| does *not* violate */.CC/, because |drama|, as an underlying form, is not affected by structural constraints (see also Figure 6). The same point was made explicit by Smolensky (1996) in a discussion of how young children may be hindered by structural constraints in their productions but not in their comprehension.

Second, the candidate |drama| violates DEP (McCarthy and Prince 1995), a constraint against having surface material (the /o/ in /.do.ɾa.ma./) that is not present underlyingly (in |drama|). Note that although DEP is usually thought of as being an anti-insertion constraint (in a production tableau), in a recognition tableau such as (6) it acts as an anti-deletion constraint: the perceived /o/ is deleted from the recognition output.

Finally, the candidate underlying form |doramaribo| violates fourfold MAX (McCarthy and Prince 1995), a constraint against having underlying material (|ribo|) that does not surface (in /.do.ra.ma./).

In the end, the winner of the recognition process is |dorama|, which is completely faithful to the surface form /.do.ra.ma./. This principle of complete faithfulness is known in phonological theory from the identical process of *lexicon optimization* (Prince and Smolensky 1993), by which actually existing underlying forms come to reflect the language's high-ranked structural constraints indirectly, simply because the surface forms tend to honour these constraints. Here, this idea extends to forms that have been filtered in the first perception step, such as [_ᵈrama]. Thus, the mapping from [_ᵈrama] to |dorama| does not involve a violation of (phonological) faithfulness, because the end result |dorama| is completely faithful to the intermediate form /.do.ra.ma./.[3]

The second straightforward strategy to include the word *drama* in the lexicon relies on *parallel comprehension*: the two processes of perception and recognition are handled at the same time and in interaction. Figure 7 summarizes this.

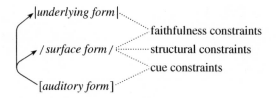

Figure 7.   Parallel (or interactive) comprehension.

The parallel mapping from the auditory form to the surface and underlying forms can be implemented in OT by freely combining pairs of surface and underlying form as candidates in a single *parallel comprehension tableau*, as in (7).

---

3. Cases where faithfulness is instead violated in the recognition process will occur when there are paradigms with alternations. See Apoussidou (2007: ch. 6) and §8.

(7)   Perception and recognition in parallel

[_ {*hi-freq*, *burst*}rama]	*/.CC/	*/du/	DEP	*/+cont/ [*burst*]	MAX	*/o/ [ ]	*/u/ [ ]
/.dɾa.ma./|doɾama|	*!				*		
/.dɾa.ma./|dɾama|	*!						
/.du.ɾa.ma./|duɾama|		*!					*
/.zu.ɾa.ma./|zuɾama|				*!			*
☞ /.do.ɾa.ma./|doɾama|						*	
/.do.ɾa.ma./|dɾama|			*!			*	

In (7) it does not matter how the faithfulness constraints DEP and MAX are interspersed among the structural and cue constraints: since the perceptually optimal candidate pair /.do.ɾa.ma./|doɾama| violates neither DEP nor MAX, this pair will be optimal for the whole comprehension process independently of whether DEP and MAX are ranked high or low (or in the middle, as here).

The lexicon, then, will be genuinely limited by the structural constraints, as long as these outrank the relevant cue constraints. These limitations on lexical structures have been called *poverty of the base* (Boersma 1998: 395; Broselow 2004; see also §4).

3.3   Production

Now that we know that Japanese listeners perceive an overt [_ᵈrama] as /.do.ɾa.ma./ and store it in their lexicon as |doɾama|, what will they pronounce it as? Here again, we distinguish between serial and parallel processing.

In a serial view, phonological-phonetic production consists of three steps, as summarized in Figure 8. First, a process of *phonological production* maps a phonological underlying form to a phonological surface form; subsequently, a process of *phonetic implementation* first maps this surface form to an auditory-phonetic form, and finally maps this auditory form to an articulatory-phonetic form.

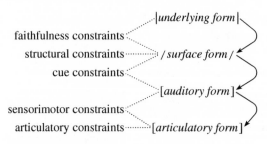

Figure 8.   Serial production.

The first of the three subprocesses, phonological production, maps the underlying |dorama| straightforwardly to /.do.ra.ma./, a form that satisfies both the structural constraints and the faithfulness constraints, as shown in (8).

(8)   Phonological production

|dorama|	*/.CC/	*/du/	DEP	MAX	IDENT
/.dra.ma./	*!			*	
/.du.ra.ma./		*!			*
/.zu.ra.ma./					*!*
☞ /.do.ra.ma./					

The second subprocess maps /.do.ra.ma./ to [_ {hi-freq,burst}orama], a form that satisfies all high-ranked cue constraints, as shown in (9). To rule out weird pronunciations like [zurama], I have added the cue constraint */−cont/[noise], which militates against connecting phonological plosiveness to auditory frication noise, and the cue constraint */o/[u], which militates against having the auditory vocalic material [u] that is inappropriate for the corresponding phonological vowel /o/. Further please note that the notation of phonetic candidates in terms of IPA symbols, such as [_ᵈo], is just a shorthand for an expression in terms of continuous auditory features, such as [*voicing murmur; brief high-frequency noise; loud periodicity with mid F1 and low F2*]; especially, no representational identity with similar-looking surface structures such as /.do./ is intended; indeed, the latter is a shorthand for a discrete phonological structure such as /($_σ$C, −*cont*, −*nas*, *cor*, +*voi*; V, −*high*, −*low*, +*back*)$_σ$/ (or any alternative formulation that suits one's particular theory of phonological features).

(9)   Phonetic implementation

/.do.ra.ma./	*/+cont/ [*burst*]	*/−cont/ [*noise*]	*/o/ [u]	*/o/ [ ]	*/u/ [ ]
[zuɾama]		*!	*		
[zoɾama]		*!			
[ˍᵈuɾama]			*!		
☞ [ˍᵈoɾama]					
[ˍᵈɾama]				*!	

In the mapping from surface form to auditory form, structural constraints play
no role: they would just evaluate the input to this process, which is an invaria-
ble /.do.ra.ma./ shared among all candidates, all of which would therefore
violate the exact same structural constraints. Therefore, the mapping is entirely
determined by cue constraints, and they are in favour of the candidate
[ˍᵈoɾama], which violates none of them.

The third subprocess presumably maps an auditory [ˍᵈoɾama] to an articulatory [ˍᵈoɾama]. I have not formalized the sensorimotor constraints here, and
for simplicity I assume that they favour the articulatory form [ˍᵈoɾama]. If
articulatory constraints are not in the way (see §6), then the speaker will indeed
pronounce [ˍᵈoɾama].

In the parallel view, production consists of a simultaneous mapping from
the underlying form to an optimal triplet of surface form, auditory form, and
articulatory form, as in Figure 9.

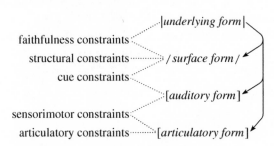

Figure 9.   Parallel (or interactive) production.

Ignoring the articulatory form again, an underlying |dorama| will be mapped
on the surface-auditory pair /.do.ra.ma./[ˍᵈoɾama], just as in the serial view.
This is shown in tableau (10).

(10)   Parallel production

|dorama|	*/.CC/	*/du/	*/+cont/ [burst]	MAX	IDENT	*/o/ [u]	*/o/ [ ]
/.dra.ma./[_^{d}rama]	*!			*			
/.dra.ma./[_^{d}orama]	*!			*			
/.du.ra.ma./[_^{d}urama]		*!			*		
/.zu.ra.ma./[zurama]					*!*		
/.zu.ra.ma./[_^{d}rama]			*!		**		
☞ /.do.ra.ma./[_^{d}orama]							
/.do.ra.ma./[_^{d}rama]							*!
/.do.ra.ma./[_^{d}urama]						*!	

Since the winner in tableau (10) violates none of the constraints, it is optimal regardless of the constraint ranking. The result of parallel production is therefore the same as the result of serial production (in this example; for examples where the two are different see §7.2 and Boersma 2007a, 2008).

The end result is that the modelled Japanese learner of Russian hears an incoming auditory [_^{d}rama] but produces an articulatory [_^{d}orama].

We have to note that in order for this case to have been so interesting that Polivanov used this as an example, the native Russian perception plays a crucial role as well: Polivanov, with his Russian perception, interpreted the original auditory [_^{d}rama] as the Russian-compatible surface structure /.dra.ma./, whereas he interpreted the Japanese pronunciation [_^{d}orama] as the Russian-compatible surface structure /.do.ra.ma./; the discrete difference between the two surface structures is what must have led him to take this as an example for his study on foreign language perception.

3.4   Abstract surface forms

Something is missing in the story of §3.1 through §3.3: the case of [_'r]. The European word *extra*, for instance, is borrowed into Japanese as /.e.ki.su.to.ra./ and not as /.e.ki.su.tu.ra./, with the less audible /u/ vowel. In its choice of the hallucinated vowel the case of [_'r] is therefore similar to the case of [_^{d}r], and a satisfactory account of the perception of Japanese consonant clusters should preferably generalize over the [_^{d}r] and [_'r] cases. We could therefore posit an inviolable constraint */tu/, analogously to */du/, and probably collapse the two into a formulation such as */{C,–cont,–nas,cor}u/.

If one maintains an even more abstract view of Japanese surface forms, however, the analysis with */tu/ (or a generalized formulation) will go wrong. We can see this because the traditional abstract view of the Japanese syllable requires that the surface form /.tu./ exists: on the basis of considerations of distribution and alternations, the Japanese syllable that is pronounced as [_^{ts}u] is regarded as having the surface form /.tu./. For instance, a word that means 'connection' has the surface form /.tu.gi./ although it is pronounced [_^{ts}u _^{ɕ}i]. If the abstract view is correct, there cannot therefore exist a high-ranked constraint */.tu./. Thus, what rules out /.tu.ra./ as the perceptual result of [_'ra] is not the structure /.tu./ in itself, but its associated pronunciation [_^{ts}u]. The solution then lies in the fact that the naked auditory release burst ['], without affrication noise (as in [e_^{k}s_'ra]), cannot be a good representative of the structure /tu/, which must be pronounced with a full affricate [_^{ts}]. The way to handle this is with the cue constraint */tu/[*no noise*], i.e. "the structure /tu/ cannot go without auditory frication noise".

The cue constraint */tu/[*no noise*] handles both perception and production. In (prelexical) perception we get tableau (11).

(11)   Japanese foreign-language perception of Russian -*tra*

[{*hi-freq,burst, no noise*}ra]	*/.CC/	*/ / [*burst*]	*/tu/ [*no noise*]	*/dor/ [*hi-freq*]	*/+cont/ [*burst*]	*/o/ [ ]	*/u/ [ ]
/.tra./	*!						
/.ra./		*!					
/.tu.ra./			*!				*
/.ku.ra./				*!			*
/.su.ra./					*!		*
☞ /.to.ra./						*	

In (11) we see the /tu/-specific cue constraint in the same position as */du/ in previous tableaus; it accomplishes the required elimination of the candidate /.tu.ra./. In production (phonetic implementation), the same cue constraint is again crucial; without it, the surface form /.tu.gi./ would be pronounced [_'u _^{ɕ}i] instead of [_^{ts}u _^{ɕ}i]:

(12)   Phonetic implementation

/.tu.gi./	*/u/ [o]	*/tu/ [no noise]	*/−cont/ [noise]
[_ˡu ̯ ᵍi]		*!	
☞ [_ᵗˢu ̯ ᵍi]			*
[_ˡo ̯ ᵍi]	*!	*	

Perhaps Japanese has a general cue constraint */−cont/[noise] that says that phonological plosives should not be phonetically affricated; such a constraint would account for the affricationless pronunciations of /ta/, /te/, /to/, /pa/, /pe/, /pi/, /po/, /pu/, /ka/, /ke/, /ki/, /ko/, and /ku/, and their voiced coun-terparts. For the affricated exceptions this general constraint has to be overrid-den by more specific constraints such as */tu/[no noise]. Perhaps these excep-tions could be handled by a more general */{C,−cont,−nas,cor}{V, +high}/ [no noise], which would also turn /ti/ into [_ᵗᶜi] and /du/ into [_ᵈᶻu]. Whether such a more general constraint is viable depends on the extent to which [_ˡi] is allowed to contrast with [_ᵗᶜi] in Japanese and on the analysis of the merger of underlying |du| and |zu| into [_ᵈᶻu]. In-depth investigations that could shed light on this matter are outside the scope of the present paper, but I mention the issues here in order to illustrate that one can do 'real' phonology around cue constraints.

The structural constraints discussed in §3 have restricted perception alone; I did not discuss any effect they might have on production. Their truly bidirec-tional effects are illustrated in §4, and for a Japanese-like case in §5.4.

4.   Robust perception: Richness of the Base is in comprehension

The *robust perception* mentioned in §3 is related to two concepts that have been proposed earlier in OT. First there is *richness of the base* (Prince and Smolensky 1993), according to which inputs (to production) can be anything: even hypothetical underlying forms that do not actually occur in the lexicon of the language at hand will be converted by the grammar (constraint ranking) to well-formed surface structures. In the perception case, richness of the base resides in the auditory form, which is the input to perception and can be any-thing: even auditory events that do not normally occur in the listener's lan-guage environment will be converted by the grammar to (more or less) well-formed surface structures. Since we refer to this as *robust perception*, we should perhaps rename Prince and Smolensky's version of richness of the base to robust production, to make its orientation explicit. The second concept related to robust perception is robust *interpretive parsing* (Tesar and Smolensky 1998, 2000), according to which the listener succeeds in making sense of any *overt form* (in Tesar and Smolensky's example this is a sequence of syllables marked for stress) by converting it to a sensible surface structure (in Tesar and Smolensky's example a sequence of feet with head syllables), even if the listener's grammar could never generate such a structure in production. To the extent that Tesar and Smolensky's interpretive parsing can be equated with what others call perception, the concepts of robust perception and robust interpretive parsing are not just related but identical (a difference between them will be discussed later). I will now make plausible that the two concepts can indeed be equated.

As an example of language-dependent interpretive parsing, Tesar (1997) mentions the 'overt form' [σ 'σ σ], which is a sequence of three syllables of which the middle one is stressed. The task of the listener is to map this overt form to a more abstract metrical structure. According to Tesar, the overt form [σ 'σ σ] will be interpreted as the foot structure /(σ 'σ) σ/ in a left-aligning iambic language, and to /σ ('σ σ)/ in a right-aligning trochaic language, depending on the language-specific ranking of the structural (metrical) constraints. This looks straightforwardly like what I have defined as perception. Although Tesar (and Smolensky) never draw a tableau that has the overt form as its input and the interpreted structure as its output (all of their tableaus include the winning candidates in *production*)[4], such a tableau can be drawn easily, as here in tableaus (13) and (14) which use a subset of Tesar's constraints.

(13)   Metrical perception in a left-aligning iambic language

[σ 'σ σ]	FEETLEFT	IAMBIC	TROCHAIC	FEETRIGHT
☞ /(σ 'σ) σ/			*	*
/σ ('σ σ)/	*!	*		

---

4. Tesar's (1997) Table 4, for instance, contains the optimal form in comprehension (called 'winner'), but also contains an even more harmonic form, namely the optimal form in *production* (called 'loser'). This makes it clear that the goal of such tableaus is not to model the comprehension process, but to compare forms on behalf of a learning algorithm. In later work, Tesar (1999: Tableau 8) does provide a tableau like (13) or (14).

(14)   Metrical perception in a right-aligning trochaic language

[σ 'σ σ]	FeetRight	Trochaic	Iambic	FeetLeft
/(σ 'σ) σ/	*!	*		
☞ /σ ('σ σ)/			*	*

While Tesar and Smolensky's surface structures are uncontroversially the same kind of thing as the output of perception in my earlier perception tableaus, the same cannot be immediately claimed about the overt forms in (13) and (14). Are they really auditory forms? After all, the input form [σ 'σ σ] already consists of syllables, which are language-dependent higher-level structures, and my use of the discrete IPA stress symbol already abstracts away from the continuous auditory correlates of stress such as intensity, pitch, and duration. But I want to assert that the foot structures in the *output* candidates of (13) and (14) are even more abstract and high-level than this overt input form. What we see in (13) and (14), then, is a step on the way from the universal auditory form to the language-specific phonological surface structure. Thus, tableaus (13) and (14) represent a step in the perception process. Now, I do not mean to imply that the perception process consists of a sequence of steps. The mapping from auditory cues to segments, from segments to syllables, and from syllables to feet could well be done in parallel. In that case, the mapping from segment to syllable could well depend on the foot structure that the listener has to create at the same time. I assume that, indeed, the various facets of perception work in parallel in much the same way as the various facets of production work in parallel in most published OT analyses. And since in OT analyses of production one can find mappings at various levels of abstraction, I take the liberty of doing the same for perception and declare tableaus (13) and (14) as perception tableaus, thus identifying Tesar and Smolensky's interpretive parsing with the perception process.

The grammatical framework by Tesar and Smolensky is less restrictive than that by Polivanov. Whereas Polivanov assumes that structural constraints are in Gen (inviolable) and cue constraints in Con (violable), Tesar and Smolensky follow the usual Optimality-Theoretical standpoint that structural constraints are violable, i.e. reside in Con. This violability is crucial in tableaus (13) and (14) and I will assume that it is correct. In other words, phonotactic constraints can conflict with each other in perception, in which case their relative ranking becomes crucial.

The robustness of the perception process has already been illustrated with the Japanese perception of a foreign [_'a_^{k}]. Tesar and Smolensky's robustness point applies to first-language acquisition, and specifically to their proposal that a speaker/listener uses the same constraint ranking in production as in perception. A child learning the left-aligning iambic language of tableau (13), for instance, may have at a certain point during her acquisition period the grammar FEETLEFT >> TROCHAIC >> IAMBIC >> FEETRIGHT. This left-aligning trochaic grammar is incorrect, since it causes an underlying |σ σ σ| to be produced as the surface form /('σ σ) σ/. When such a child hears the correct overt form [σ 'σ σ], however, she will interpret it as /(σ 'σ) σ/, which can easily be seen by reversing the two foot-form constraints in (13). Since the child's robust perception can make sense of a form that she would never produce herself, the child is able to notice the discrepancy between the two forms /('σ σ) σ/ and /(σ 'σ) σ/, and can take action, perhaps by reversing the ranking of TROCHAIC >> IAMBIC in her grammar. Thus, Tesar and Smolensky's point is that robustness helps learning. In sum, we conclude that the robustness of the perception process proposed in this section helps in the acquisition of a first and second language and in loanword adaptation.

All of Tesar and Smolensky's examples of robust interpretive parsing are handled with structural constraints alone; in none of their examples do they address the issue of cue constraints. In a full account of stress perception one would have to include constraints for the mapping of stress cues. For instance, language-specific auditory events (intensity, pitch, duration) are cues to phonological stress (i.e. phonological foot headedness for all stressed syllables, and phonological-word headedness for primary-stressed syllables). I will not pursue this any further here. An example of structural constraints that are crucially bidirectional (i.e. that restrict perception as well as production in non-trivial and non-identical ways) and crucially interact with cue constraints is provided in §5.4.

5.   More examples of perception in OT

This section reviews some more examples of how perception has been formalized in Optimality Theory. I investigate none of these examples in full detail; rather, I provide them here in order to familiarize the reader with the directions that full phonological investigations into cue constraints may take.

5.1   Autosegmental constraints on tone

An early example of a structural constraint in phonology is the Obligatory Contour Principle (Leben 1973, Goldsmith 1976). In theories of suprasegmental tone, this constraint militates against the occurrence of two identical tones in a row. Myers (1997) investigated the OCP as a constraint in OT. In Boersma (1998, 2000) the OCP was interpreted as the counterpart of the Line Crossing Condition, in the sense that many structures that violate the OCP do not violate the LCC and vice versa (in this respect, the two constraints are similar to other pairs of opposites such as ALIGNFEETLEFT and ALIGNFEETRIGHT, or IAMBIC and TROCHAIC). The explicit definitions of the two constraints are given in (15).

(15)   Autosegmental constraints

   a.   OCP (*feature value, material*): the surface form cannot contain two instances of *feature value* if not more than a certain amount of material intervenes;

   b.   LCC (*feature value, material*): a single instance of *feature value* in the surface form cannot span across a certain amount of *material*.

These definitions are different from those in Boersma (1998), where these constraints were cue constraints. The current definition is closer to what phonologists are used to (e.g. Myers 1997). Tableaus (16) and (17) show examples from Boersma (2000). In both cases the auditory input consists of two syllables with high level tones (denoted here with acute symbols), but the perceived surface structure depends on the language at hand.

(16)   Shona perception of a suprasyllabic high tone

[ɓáŋgá]	[σ́] → / $\overset{H}{\underset{\sigma}{\mid}}$ /	OCP (H, $\}_\sigma\{_\sigma$)	LCC (H, $\}_\sigma\{_\sigma$)
☞ / $\overset{H}{\underset{\text{ɓ a ŋ g a}}{\diagup\diagdown}}$ /			*
/ $\overset{HH}{\underset{\text{ɓ a ŋ g a}}{\mid\mid}}$ /		*!	
/ $\overset{H}{\underset{\text{ɓ a ŋ g a}}{\mid}}$ /	*!		

(17)   Mandarin perception of a sequence of syllabic high tones

[ʂáfá]	[ʂ]→ / $\overset{\text{H}}{\underset{\sigma}{\mid}}$ /	LCC (H, }σ{σ)	OCP (H, }σ{σ)
/ $\underset{\text{ʂ a f a}}{\overset{\text{H}}{/\backslash}}$ /		*!	
☞ / $\underset{\text{ʂ a f a}}{\overset{\text{H H}}{\mid\ \mid}}$ /			*
/ $\underset{\text{ʂ a f a}}{\overset{\text{H}}{\mid}}$ /	*!		

In Shona, phonological processes of spreading and deletion indicate that disyllabic words with two high-toned syllables, such as [ɓáŋgá] 'knife', have only one underlying H tone (Myers 1997). If prelexical perception is aimed at maximally facilitating lexical access,[5] a sequence of two high-toned syllables should therefore preferably be interpreted on the phonological surface level as having a single high tone (H). Tableau (16) describes in detail how a word with such a sequence is perceived. The auditory form of the word 'knife' is [ɓáŋgá]. The third candidate in (16) is ruled out because there is a cue constraint that says that any high-toned "syllable" in the auditory form[6] has to correspond to a syllable that is linked to an H tone in the (more abstract) phonological structure. The third candidate violates this constraint because the second syllable is auditorily high but not linked to an H in the full structure (the third candidate would be the appropriate structure for the auditory form [ɓáŋgà] instead). The second candidate is ruled out because it has two H tones that are separated by no more than a syllable boundary. This form then violates the tone-specific OCP constraint that says that two H tones cannot be separated by a syllable boundary only. The first form, with a single H tone, then wins, although it violates the generalized line-crossing constraint that says that two H tones cannot be separated by a syllable boundary or more.

---

5. This aim of prelexical perception has been formulated by psycholinguists (e.g. McQueen and Cutler 1997), and has been formulated for OT by Boersma (2000). In multi-level OT, the similarity of surface and underlying forms is generally advocated by faithfulness constraints. Whether faithfulness constraints indeed help the emergence of the OCP and LCC rankings in (16) and (17) during acquisition, or whether they would instead simply override the preferences of OCP and LCC in a parallel comprehension model such as that in Figure 6, could be determined by computer simulations of the concurrent acquisition of structural, cue, and faithfulness constraints, perhaps along the lines of Boersma (2008).

6. Of course the auditory form does not really contain syllables, which are phonological structures. I make the same simplification here as Tesar and Smolensky (see §4).

For the Shona case, the result in (16) reflects the common autosegmental analysis. For Mandarin Chinese, I here try out the slightly more controversial non-autosegmental position, which maintains that in contour-tone systems such as Mandarin the contour tones are "phonologically unitary [...] and not structurally related to a system of level tones" (Pike 1948: 8), a description that extends to any single level tone that a contour-tone language might have (Pike 1948: 12), as is the case in Mandarin. Phonologically speaking, Mandarin Chinese is different from Shona in the sense that every syllable has a separate underlying specification for one of the four possible tones of this language, as a result of which the alternations could perhaps best be described in terms of contour features rather than just H and L (Wang 1967). Even within autosegmental phonology, structural differences between the cases in (16) and (17) have been proposed before (Yip 1989: 166; 2002: 50–56), although they remain controversial (Duanmu 1994). More relevant within the present framework is the observation that if prelexical perception is aimed at maximally facilitating lexical access, a sequence of two high-toned syllables, such as [ṣáfá] 'sofa', should preferably be perceived with two separate H tones, as it is in (17). Indeed the assumption in the phonetic literature is that Mandarin listeners interpret auditory pitch in terms of their four tones rather than in terms of H and L (e.g. Gandour 1978: 45–47).

I have included the difference between the two tone language types here in order to illustrate the possible language-specific perception of phonetic tone stretches, another example of the idea that the phonology-phonetics interface should be handled by linguistic means.

5.2   Autosegmental constraints on nasality

What can be done for tone can be done for any feature that is suprasegmental in one language but segmental in the other. Tableaus (18) and (19), again from Boersma (2000), show examples for nasality.

(18)   Guaraní perception of suprasyllabic nasality

[tũpã]	[Ṽ] → / $\overset{N}{\underset{V}{\mid}}$ /	OCP (*nas*, }σ{σ)	LCC (*nas*, }σ{σ)
☞ / $\overset{N}{\diagup\diagdown}$ t u p a /			*
/ $\overset{N\ \ N}{\underset{t\ u\ p\ a}{\mid\ \ \ \mid}}$ /		*!	
/ $\overset{N}{\underset{t\ u\ p\ a}{\mid}}$ /	*!		

(19)   French perception of segmental nasality

[ʃãsɔ̃]	[Ṽ] → / $\overset{N}{\underset{V}{\mid}}$ /	LCC (*nas*, }σ{σ)	OCP (*nas*, }σ{σ)
/ $\overset{N}{\diagup\diagdown}$ ʃ a s ɔ /		*!	
☞ / $\overset{N\ \ N}{\underset{ʃ\ a\ s\ ɔ}{\mid\ \ \ \mid}}$ /			*
/ $\overset{N}{\underset{ʃ\ a\ s\ ɔ}{\mid}}$ /	*!		

In Guaraní, nasality is assigned at the word level: there are words pronounced as [tũpã] 'God' and [tupa] 'bed', but no words pronounced as *[tũpa] or *[tupã]. The usual view (e.g. Piggott 1992, Walker 1998) is that the form [tũpã] has to be interpreted as having a single nasality (N) value at the surface level. Tableau (18) formalizes this as a high ranking of the OCP for nasality in Guaraní. In French, the nasality of consecutive vowels is uncorrelated, since there are words pronounced as [ʃãsɔ̃] 'song', [lapɛ̃] 'rabbit', [ʃapo] 'hat', and [pɔ̃so] 'poppy'. This means that nasality has to be stored separately with every vowel in the lexicon. If perception is to be aimed at maximally facilitating lexical access, French perception must map the two nasalized vowels in [ʃãsɔ̃] to two different /N/ feature values in the phonological surface structure, as in tableau (19).

Many phonological issues remain that I cannot fully address here. The domain of the single nasal specification in (18), as well as of the single H tone in (16), is the word. But on the prelexical level listeners do not hear word boundaries. The question then is: are phonetic high-tone stretches and phonetic nasality stretches interrupted by word boundaries or not, e.g., would listeners interpret [tũpã] as having two nasals if there were a word boundary between [tũ] and [pã]? They could indeed do this if the lexicon is allowed to pass on information about word boundaries to the lower prelexical level, as in (7). I defer an account of such an interaction to §7.1.

5.3   Loanword adaptation

We are now ready to discuss the subject of loanword adaptation. There has been much controversy as to whether loanword adaptation is due to 'perception' or to 'phonology'. But in an OT account of perception, in which phonological (structural) constraints influence the perception process, there is no dichotomy. Tableaus (20) and (21) give the example (from Boersma 2000: 21–22, 2003) of the adaptation of the Portuguese auditory forms [ʒwẽw̃] 'John' and [sɐbẽw̃] 'soap' by speakers of Desano (Kaye 1971), another nasal harmony language. The structural constraints */{C,−nas}{V,+nas}/ and */{σ,−nas}{σ,+nas}/ militate against nasal disharmony within and across syllables, respectively, and the cue constraints */V,+nas/[nonnasal], */V,−nas/[nasal], */C,+nas/[nonnasal] and */C,−nas/[nasal] express the favoured interpretation of nasality cues for vowels and consonants, respectively.

(20)   Desano adaptation of Portuguese

[ʒwẽw̃]	*/{C,−nas} {V,+nas}/	*/{σ,−nas} {σ,+nas}/	*/V,+nas/ [nonnasal]	*/V,−nas/ [nasal]	*/C,+nas/ [nonnasal]
N / | / ʒ u	*!				
☞ N / /\ / ɲ u					*
/ ʒ u /				*!	

(21)   Desano adaptation of Portuguese

[sɐbẽw̃]	*/{C,–nas} {V,+nas}/	*/{σ,–nas} {σ,+nas}/	*/V,+nas/ [nonnasal]	*/V,–nas/ [nasal]	*/C,+nas/ [nonnasal]
/ $\overset{N}{s\,a\,b\,o}$ /	*!				
/ $\overset{N}{s\,a\,m\,o}$ /		*!			*
/ $\overset{N}{n\,a\,m\,o}$ /			*!		**
☞ /s a b o/				*	

Since Polivanov (1931), then, foreign-language perception and loanword adaptation have been seen by some to involve an interaction between language-specific cue constraints, which partly reflect auditory closeness, and language-specific structural constraints. This is phonology and perception at the same time.

5.4   Korean

Sometimes a phonological process seems to be different in perception than in production. Kabak and Idsardi (2007) mention that Korean avoids [km] (and other) sequences in different ways depending on the direction of processing: speakers turn an underlying |hak + mun| 'learning' into the sound [haŋmun], with assimilation of manner, but often perceive nonnative [km]-containing sounds in the same manner as the Japanese of §3 with epenthesis, e.g. [hak-mun] as /hakumun/. Kabak and Idsardi interpret this as evidence against phonology in perception (p.33): "if Korean listeners hear epenthetic vowels in consonant clusters, they are likely to interpret pairs such as [pʰakma] versus [pʰakɯma] to be the same. If, on the other hand, native phonological processes apply to perception, they should hear pairs such as [pʰakma] versus [pʰaŋma] to be the same."

I will now show that within a three-level account, both the perception and the production are phonological. The idea (also shown in Boersma and Hamann this volume) is that the comprehension process involves a mapping [hakmun] → /.ha.kɯ.mun./ → |hakumun|, whereas the production process involves a mapping |hak + mun| → /.haŋ.mun./ → [haŋmun]. We see here that in both directions the /km/ sequence is avoided, but in different ways. Apparently, a single phonological constraint like */km/ is at work, and it interacts with different types of constraints in perception than in production.

In perception, the structural constraint interacts with cue constraints much in the same way as in the Japanese examples of (2) and (3):

(22)   Korean foreign-language perception of English

[hakmun]	*/km/	*/+*nas*/ [*burst*]	*/ɯ/ [ ]
/.hak.mun./	*!		
/.haŋ.mun./		*!	
☞ /.ha.kɯ.mun./			*

Tableau (22) expresses the idea that */km/ is an inviolable constraint of Korean, and that throwing away the positive nonnasality cue of a plosive burst is worse than hallucinating a vowel for which there are no auditory cues.

In production, the structural constraint interacts instead with faithfulness constraints:

(23)   Korean production

|hak + mun|	*/km/	DEP	IDENT(NAS)
/.hak.mun./	*!		
☞ /.haŋ.mun./			*
/.ha.kɯ.mun./		*!	

Tableau (23) expresses the idea that */km/ is an inviolable constraint of Korean, and that inserting a non-underlying vowel in production (violating DEP; McCarthy and Prince 1995) is worse than changing the value of the nasality feature.

I have thus given an account of an apparent perception-production difference fully in terms of the three levels and the native processing model of Boersma (1998 et seq.), without having to take recourse to any devices specific to foreign-language perception or loanword phonology. This is strikingly different from later accounts of phonological perception in loanword phonology (Kenstowicz 2001, Broselow 2004, Yip 2006), all of which work within a two-level model of phonology and therefore have to posit different faithfulness constraints (or different rankings) in production than in perception. Here as well we *could* say (with Kenstowicz, Broselow and Yip) that in perception the identity constraint outranks the anti-insertion constraint whereas in production the anti-insertion constraint outranks the identity constraint. However, in the three-level model the former anti-insertion constraint is a cue constraint whereas the latter anti-insertion constraint is a faithfulness constraint, and both types of constraints are independently needed to account for native phonological processing. The two types are fundamentally different, and each type comes with its own causes for being ranked high or low. Specifically, the low ranking of */ɯ/[ ] can be explained by the fact that in a noisy environment not all possible auditory cues will always be present, so that listeners have learned to freely hypothesize features and segments for which there is no positive auditory evidence, whereas no such causation mechanism is available for the ranking of DEP (Boersma 2007a: 2021).

We have seen that perception and production do not undergo the same phonological *process* (as Kabak and Idsardi indeed found), but they do undergo the influence of the same phonological *constraint*. By using the decision mechanism of OT, in which a single *constraint* can cause different *processes*, I have thus reconciled one of the phonology-versus-perception debates. For related examples of the interaction of structural and cue constraints in loanword adaptation, see Boersma and Hamann (to appear).

5.5 Arbitrary relations between auditory and surface forms

The cue constraints in (16) to (21) look a bit like faithfulness constraints, e.g. "if there are nasality and vowel cues in the input, the output must have nasality linked to a vowel". Such simplifying formulations disguise what is really going on, namely a partly arbitrary relation between auditory input and phonological output. The arbitrariness becomes especially visible if we consider cases of *cue integration*. Tableaus (24) and (25), from Escudero and Boersma (2004), give examples of the integration of auditory vowel height (first formant, F1) and auditory duration into the single contrast between the English vowels /i/ and /ɪ/.

(24)   Perception of an auditory event in Scottish English

[74 ms, 349 Hz]	*/ɪ/ [349 Hz]	*/i/ [74 ms]	*/ɪ/ [74 ms]	*/i/ [349 Hz]
/ɪ/	*!		*	
☞ /i/		*		*

(25)   Perception of the same auditory event in Southern British English

[74 ms, 349 Hz]	*/i/ [349 Hz]	*/i/ [74 ms]	*/ɪ/ [74 ms]	*/ɪ/ [349 Hz]
☞ /ɪ/			*	*
/i/	*!	*		

The example of tableaus (24) and (25) is a relatively short high vowel. For a Scot, such a token must represent the vowel in *sheep*, because the vowel in *ship* tends to be much more open, and both vowels are short. For a Southern Brit, the same auditory event must represent the vowel in *ship*, because the vowel in *sheep* tends to be much longer, and both vowels are high. These observations are reflected here in the continuous cue constraint families "an auditory F1 of [*x* Hz] should not be perceived as the phonological vowel category /*y*/" and "an auditory duration of [*x* ms] should not be perceived as the phonological vowel category /*y*/". In these tableaus, we again see the language-specificity of perception, as well as the partial arbitrariness of the mapping from auditory to phonological. If the reader does not consider the arbitrariness idea convincing yet (perhaps because auditory F1 could map to a phonological height feature and auditory duration could map to a phonological length feature), the reader might want to ponder the case of the word-final obstruent voicing contrast in English, which involves a single phonological voice feature but multiple auditory cues such as vowel duration, consonant duration and burst strength.

The simplest case of arbitrary categorization constraints is the case of the categorization of a single auditory continuum, say F1, into a finite number of phonological classes, say /a/, /e/, and /i/. Tableau (26) shows how an F1 of [380 Hz] can be perceived as /e/ in language with three vowel heights (from Boersma 2006).

(26)   Classifying F1 into vowel height

[380 Hz]	*/a/ 320 Hz	*/a/ 380 Hz	*/i/ 460 Hz	*/e/ 320 Hz	*/a/ 460 Hz	*/i/ 380 Hz	*/e/ 380 Hz	*/i/ 320 Hz	*/e/ 460 Hz
/a/		*!							
☞ /e/							*		
/i/						*!			

The number of such constraints is very large. Fortunately, the ranking can be learned under the guidance of the lexicon (Boersma 1997; Escudero and Boersma 2003, 2004).

6.   The interaction of cue constraints with articulatory constraints

In sections 3 to 5 we saw interactions of cue constraints with structural constraints. The present section focuses on their interaction with articulatory constraints. I use the example of final voiced obstruents in English.

In English, there are at least two auditory cues to the voicing or voicelessness of a final obstruent: the presence or absence of periodicity (as in most languages), and the lengthening or shortening of the preceding vowel (the size of the effect is specific to English: Zimmerman and Sapon 1958). We can translate this into four cue constraints:

(27)   English cue constraints

*/+voi/[nonperiodic]

*/−voi/[periodic]

*/−son, +voi/[nonlengthened vowel]

*/−son, −voi/[lengthened vowel]

The first use of the cue constraints is in prelexical perception, as before. Most often, the relevant cues agree, so that perception works well. I illustrate this in (28) and (29).

(28)   A perception tableau where the two cues agree

[niːːd]	*/−son, −voi/* [*lengthened vowel*]	*/−voi/* [*periodic*]
/.nit./	*!	*
☞ /.nid./		

(29)   Another perception tableau where the two cues agree

[niːt]	*/−son, +voi/* [*nonlengthened vowel*]	*/+voi/* [*nonperiodic*]
☞ /.nit./		
/.nid./	*!	*

But sometimes the cues disagree. Perception experiments in the lab find that periodicity is the main cue (e.g. Hogan and Rozsypal 1980), but since vowels are much louder than consonant closures, the vowel lengthening constraint must outrank the direct periodicity cue in more natural noisy settings, as in (30).

(30)   A perception tableau with a conflict

[niːːt]	*/−son, −voi/* [*lengthened vowel*]	*/+voi/* [*nonperiodic*]
/.nit./	*!	
☞ /.nid./		*

The same cue constraints that are used in comprehension are also used in the production process, namely in phonetic implementation. It is tempting to regard phonetic implementation as being the inverse of prelexical perception, as in Figure 10.

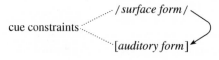

Figure 10.   Phonetic implementation (preliminary version).

Let us see what phonetic implementation would look like if Figure 10 were correct, i.e. if it were handled by cue constraints alone. The most economical assumption to make about the ranking of the cue constraints in phonetic implementation is that this ranking is identical to the ranking of the cue constraints that is optimal for comprehension, i.e. the ranking in (28) to (30). If a speaker of English reuses this ranking in production, she will try to have both cues right, as tableau (31) shows.

(31)　　Phonetic implementation with cue constraints only

/.nid./	*/−son, +voi/ [nonlengthened vowel]	*/+voi/ [nonperiodic]
[niːt]	*!	*
[niːːt]		*!
[niːd]	*!	
☞　　[niːːd]		

But phonetic implementation is not just about rendering cues. It is also about doing so efficiently, i.e. with the minimum expenditure of articulatory effort. Therefore, phonetic implementation is a parallel process that maps from a phonological surface form to a pair of auditory and articulatory form, as in Figure 11.

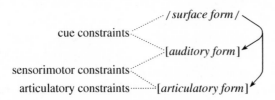

Figure 11.　　Parallel phonetic implementation (full version).

The articulatory form has to be linked to the auditory form in some way. In this paper I simplifyingly assume that this sensorimotor knowledge is perfect, i.e. sensorimotor constraints are either ranked very high or very low. The articulatory-phonetic form itself is evaluated by articulatory constraints (Kirchner 1998, Boersma 1998). In the case at hand, we observe that it is especially difficult to pronounce periodicity in a final plosive. I express this simply with the constraint *[periodic, final plosive]. In a complete phonetic implementation tableau, this constraint must interact with cue constraints. If the articulatory constraint outranks the lower-ranked cue constraint, speakers will implement only the most important cue:

(32)   Interaction of articulatory and cue constraints

/.nid./	*/−son, +voi/ [nonlengthened vowel]	*[periodic, final plosive]	*/+voi/ [nonperiodic]
[niːt]	*!		*
☞ [niːːt]			*
[niːd]	*!		
[niːːd]		*!	

As we saw in the "conflicting perception" tableau, listeners will still perceive this [niːːt] as the intended /.nid./. This means that speakers will easily get away with saying [niːːt].

I have simplified away from a large amount of possible detail. A full modelling of the case probably would require making the sensorimotor constraints explicit, and it would require arbitrary cue constraints like those in §5.5, i.e. the families */±voi/[x percent periodicity] and */±voi/[x milliseconds vowel duration].

The 'superspeaker' of (31), i.e. a speaker who always implements the best cues, probably corresponds to what real humans do when confronted with a prototype task in the lab, where they have to select the best auditory realization of a phonological category by selecting it from among a large number of auditorily presented tokens. That has been modelled within the present framework by Boersma (2006). In real humans, the cue constraints will be counteracted by articulatory constraints, so that an equilibrium emerges (Boersma 2006). This automatic balancing mechanism may lead to the achievement of stable degrees of auditory dispersion in language change, as has been shown in computer simulations of multiple generations of learners (Boersma and Hamann 2008, Van Leussen 2008).

7.   The interaction of cue constraints with faithfulness constraints

While the interaction of cue and articulatory constraints discussed in §6 could be said to take place entirely in the phonetics, there are also cases where cue constraints interact with constraints at the other side of the phonology-phonetics interface. This section discusses their interactions with faithfulness, both in comprehension and in production.

7.1   Interaction of cues and faithfulness in comprehension

If we want to account more fully for the tone and nasality perceptions discussed in §5.1 and §5.2, we have to be able to model explicitly the interactions between cue and faithfulness constraints in parallel comprehension. The present section gives a basic account of a case where it looks as if the lexicon influences prelexical perception.

The example I will discuss is that of a shift of the boundary between two categories on a single auditory continuum. It has been shown that the existence of a form in the lexicon can bias the listener's reported category towards the one that occurs in an existing word, especially if the auditory form is ambiguous between the two categories (Ganong 1980).

I will discuss an example. Suppose the auditory form is a sound that sounds like a typical Spanish *barte* (which is a nonsense word) or *parte* (which means 'part'), or something in between. The following tableaus ignore every auditory aspect of this sound except the voice onset time (VOT) of the initial plosive. I assume that the perceptual boundary between /b/ and /p/ in Spanish lies at −10 milliseconds.

In a serial view of comprehension, prelexical perception is followed by word recognition, as in Figure 6. Step one is prelexical perception, i.e. the mapping from the given Auditory Form to a phonological surface structure (Surface Form). The cue constraints are ranked by distance to the boundary. The worst token of /p/ is one with a very negative VOT such as −100 ms, so the cue constraint that says that */p/[−100] is high-ranked. Likewise, constraints that connect large positive VOT values to /b/ are also high-ranked. An appropriate ranking for perceiving Spanish voicing must be similar to that in tableaus (33) to (35).

(33)   Spanish classification of voicing

[−100 ms]	*/p/ [−100]	*/b/ [+30]	*/p/ [−20]	*/b/ [−20]	*/p/ [+30]	*/b/ [−100]
☞ /.baɾ.te./						*
/.paɾ.te./	*!					

(34)   Spanish classification of voicing

[−20 ms]	*/p/ [−100]	*/b/ [+30]	*/p/ [−20]	*/b/ [−20]	*/p/ [+30]	*/b/ [−100]
☞ /.baɾ.te./				*		
/.paɾ.te./			*!			

(35)   Spanish classification of voicing

[+30 ms]	*/p/ [−100]	*/b/ [+30]	*/p/ [−20]	*/b/ [−20]	*/p/ [+30]	*/b/ [−100]
/.baɾ.te./		*!				
☞ /.paɾ.te./					*	

Step two is word recognition. I will include both the underlying form and the morpheme in the candidates. The lexical entry |paɾte| <part> exists, the underlying form |baɾte| does not (i.e., it is not connected to any morpheme). The perceived form /.paɾ.te./ will easily be recognized with the help of faithfulness constraints:

(36)   Word recognition

/.paɾ.te./	*< > |X|	*|m| /p/	*|m| /b/	*|b| /p/	*|p| /b/
☞ |paɾte| <part>					
|baɾte| < >	*!			*	
|maɾte| <Mars>		*!			

The constraint *< >|X| militates against throwing away phonological material in lexical access (i.e. against linking the material X to no morpheme). Since the winning candidate in (36) violates no constraints at all, a more interesting input form is /.baɾ.te./. What the resulting accessed underlying form is depends on the ranking of the faithfulness constraints. If nasality faithfulness outranks voicing faithfulness, the listener again recognizes |paɾte| <part>:

(37) Word recognition

/.baɾ.te./	*< > |X|	*|m| /p/	*|m| /b/	*|b| /p/	*|p| /b/
☞ |paɾte| <part>					*
|baɾte| < >	*!				
|maɾte| <Mars>			*!		

If, by contrast, voicing faithfulness outranks nasality faithfulness, the listener will recognize |maɾte| <Mars> instead:

(38) Word recognition

/.baɾ.te./	*< > |X|	*|m| /p/	*|p| /b/	*|m| /b/	*|b| /p/
|paɾte| <part>			*!		
|baɾte| < >	*!				
☞ |maɾte| <Mars>				*	

We cannot predict which of the two options, (37) or (38), people will choose. In any case, the choice between these two tableaus does not depend on the degree of ambiguity of the auditory VOT: once prelexical perception has chosen the category, without the help of the lexicon, the probability of subverting the category in the word recognition phase no longer depends on the auditory form.

The situation is different in the parallel model of Figure 7. We first provide a ranking that makes the listener perceive a VOT of −100 ms as /.baɾ.te./, never mind that the faithful lexical item |baɾte| does not exist. If the lexicon is still capable of telling the listener that the word the speaker intended was |paɾte|, the ranking must be similar to that in tableau (39).

(39)   Perception possibly but not really influenced by lexical access

[−100 ms]	*/p/ [−100]	*/b/ [+30]	*<> |X|	*|b| /p/	*|p| /b/	*/p/ [−20]	*/b/ [−20]	*/p/ [+30]	*/b/ [−100]
/.baɾ.te./ |baɾte| <>			*!						*
/.paɾ.te./ |baɾte| <>	*!		*	*					
☞ /.baɾ.te./ |paɾte| <part>					*				*
/.paɾ.te./ |paɾte| <part>	*!								

In the case of a VOT of −20 ms, which was perceived as /b/ in the sequential model, the perception now becomes /p/, as shown in tableau (40):

(40)   Perception possibly and really influenced by lexical access

[−20 ms]	*/p/ [−100]	*/b/ [+30]	*<> |X|	*|b| /p/	*|p| /b/	*/p/ [−20]	*/b/ [−20]	*/p/ [+30]	*/b/ [−100]
/.baɾ.te./ |baɾte| <>			*!			*			
/.paɾ.te./ |baɾte| <>			*!	*		*			
/.baɾ.te./ |paɾte| <part>					*!	*			
☞ /.paɾ.te./ |paɾte| <part>						*			

In this tableau we see that the cue constraints prefer /b/, but the faithfulness constraint, forced by *< >|X|, prefers /p/. What we see in (39) and (40) is that the perceptual shift occurs only in the vicinity of the auditory boundary between the two categories. The parallel comprehension model therefore seems to be more consistent with the Ganong effect than the serial model. This distinction between bottom-up (serial) models and interactive (parallel) models of speech processing has been known for some time. For instance, the TRACE model of speech perception (McClelland and Elman 1986) was designed to be able to produce interactive effects, and one of the simulations performed in the original paper was indeed the Ganong effect. The bottom-up model of speech perception is not dead yet, however: McQueen and Cutler (1997) and Norris, McQueen and Cutler (2000) argue that listeners in the lab base their reported perceptions partly on the phonological surface form and partly on the underlying form, and that this mix can explain the observed boundary shift. This issue seems not to have been settled.

A remaining question is whether the constraint *<>|X| can ever be violated in a winning form. It can, if it is outranked by faithfulness. In such a case, tableau (39) would become tableau (41).

(41)   Recognizing a nonsense word

[−100 ms]	*/p/ [−100]	*/b/ [+30]	*|b| /p/	*|p| /b/	*<> |X|	*/p/ [−20]	*/b/ [−20]	*/p/ [+30]	*/b/ [−100]
☞ /.bar.te./ |barte| <>					*				*
/.par.te./ |barte| <>	*!		*		*				
/.bar.te./ |parte| <part>				*!					*
/.par.te./ |parte| <part>	*!								

If both the cue constraints and the faithfulness constraints are ranked high enough, the auditory form is apparently capable of creating an underlying form not yet connected to a morpheme; perhaps this is the moment for the creation of a new morpheme (Boersma 2001).

A more detailed account of these effects would require computer simulations of the acquisition of all levels of comprehension, building on the simulations in Boersma (2006). Such simulations would also be needed to account for the rankings in §5.1 and §5.2.

7.2   Interaction of cues and faithfulness in production

Computer simulations of the acquisition of cue constraints and faithfulness constraints were performed by Boersma (2008). That paper studied a relatively universal case in which plosive consonants have better place cues than nasal consonants and coronal consonants are more frequent (in word-final position) than labial consonants.

The simulations revealed that both faithfulness constraints and ("identity-preferring") cue constraints ended up being ranked higher for plosives than for nasals and higher for labials than for coronals. The results for the faithfulness constraints explain the automatic mechanism behind Steriade's (1995, 2001) *licensing by cue* as well as the automatic mechanism behind the concept of *markedness*, i.e. the relation between a feature value's frequency and its degree of phonological activity. For the cue constraints, the results show rankings by distance to the boundary, such as those in (41), and the preference of reliable cues over unreliable cues.

8.   The interaction of cue constraints with lexical constraints

Computer simulations of the whole trajectory from the auditory form to the morpheme were performed by Apoussidou (2007). The simulated learners, given pairs of sound and morpheme, had to construct both intermediate forms (surface and underlying), as well as the ranking of all the constraints involved. At the lexical level, the relation between morpheme and underlying form had to be determined by a ranking of lexical constraints, i.e. there were multiple candidate underlying forms for each morpheme. Learners typically came up with rankings that favoured single underlying forms for each morpheme (rather than with allomorph selection), together with a phonology that changed these underlying forms to potentially rather diffferent surface forms.

As for a direct interaction between cue and lexical constraints, Boersma (2007b) considers the case of lexical selection in production: if there is a single morpheme <water>, and it has the two possible underlying forms |#watr#| and |#aː#|,[7] then the choice between the two could partly be based on cue constraints, i.e. on how well the sounds [watr] and [aː] connect to the phonological structures /.watr./ and /.aː./. One can then observe that especially in postconsonantal position the auditory cues for a phonological syllable boundary (and hence the cues for the underlying word boundary) are poorer in [aː] than in [watr]. On this basis, the speaker might select the |#watr#| form even though the lexicon (by means of the ranking of the lexical constraints) may prefer the |#aː#| form (e.g. by means of its slightly better semantic features).

We see here a case of near-maximum interactivity of cue constraints, as they compete directly with constraints that guide connections in the lexicon. This is therefore an interaction that completely bypasses the whole phonology.

---

7.   The "#" sign is the word boundary. This case is loosely based on what must have happened with the 'water' words in Old Germanic. I make here the simplification that the two underlying forms share the same morpheme. It is probably more likely that each is connected to its own morpheme, and that the intended lexical semantic features are instead the same. If so, the cue constraints interact not with the lexical phonological constraints of Figure 1, but with lexical semantic constraints, which can connect the morpheme to a representation above those of Figure 1.

9.   Conclusion

Every OT phonologist agrees that structural constraints, when they appear in the production process, are of a phonological nature. If the same structural constraints dictate the perception process, then the conclusion that I like to draw is that perception is phonological as well. In other words, the perception process is restricted by the same phonological constraints as the production process is. The structural constraints evaluate the output of the mapping from Underlying Form to Surface Form (i.e. phonological production), as well as the mapping from Auditory Form to Surface Form (i.e. prelexical perception). If these constraints are ranked in the OT way, then in order to make the most out of them, they should be integrated in our model of perception to the same extent as they are integrated in our model of production. This argument was valid when Tesar and Smolensky formulated it for overt forms and stress parsing, and it is equally valid for a larger system of representations and constraints, as the one advocated in Figure 1. This means that if the structural constraints that restrict perception are ranked in the OT way (or weighted in the HG way), the cue constraints that compete with them must also be ranked in the OT way (or weighted in the HG way). The present paper has shown how these constraints can interact with other phonetic constraints, with phonological constraints, and with constraints in the lexicon. The resulting grammar model is representationally modular, but entirely interactive when it comes to processing.

References

Apoussidou, Diana
   2007   *The Learnability of Metrical Phonology*. Ph.D. dissertation, University of Amsterdam.
Bermúdez-Otero, Ricardo
   1999   *Constraint Interaction in Language Change: Quantity in English and Germanic*. Ph.D. dissertation, University of Manchester.
Boersma, Paul
   1997   How we learn variation, optionality, and probability. *Proceedings of the Institute of Phonetic Sciences* 21: 43–58. University of Amsterdam.
Boersma, Paul
   1998   *Functional Phonology: Formalizing the Interactions between Articulatory and Perceptual Drives*. Ph.D. dissertation, University of Amsterdam.

Boersma, Paul
2000   The OCP in the perception grammar. *Rutgers Optimality Archive* 435.

Boersma, Paul
2001   Phonology-semantics interaction in OT, and its acquisition. In: Robert Kirchner, Wolf Wikeley and Joe Pater (eds.), *Papers in Experimental and Theoretical Linguistics*. Volume 6, 24–35. Edmonton: University of Alberta.

Boersma, Paul
2003   Nasal harmony in functional phonology. In: Jeroen van de Weijer, Vincent van Heuven and Harry van der Hulst (eds.), *The Phonological Spectrum*, Volume 1: *Segmental Structure*. 3–35. Amsterdam: John Benjamins.

Boersma, Paul
2006   Prototypicality judgments as inverted perception. In: Gisbert Fanselow, Caroline Féry, Matthias Schlesewsky and Ralf Vogel (eds.), *Gradedness in Grammar*. 167–184. Oxford: Oxford University Press.

Boersma, Paul
2007a   Some listener-oriented accounts of *h*-aspiré in French. *Lingua* 117: 1989–2054.

Boersma, Paul
2007b   The evolution of phonotactic distributions in the lexicon. Talk presented at the Workshop on Variation, Gradience and Frequency in Phonology, Stanford, July 8, 2007.

Boersma, Paul
2008   Emergent ranking of faithfulness explains markedness and licensing by cue. *Rutgers Optimality Archive* 954.

Boersma, Paul, and Paola Escudero
2008   Learning to perceive a smaller L2 vowel inventory: an Optimality Theory account. In: Peter Avery, Elan Dresher and Keren Rice (eds.), *Contrast in Phonology: Theory, Perception, Acquisition*. 271–301. Berlin: Mouton de Gruyter.

Boersma, Paul, and Silke Hamann
2008   The evolution of auditory dispersion in bidirectional constraint grammars. *Phonology* 25: 217–270.

Boersma, Paul, and Silke Hamann
this volume Introduction: models of phonology in perception.

Boersma, Paul, and Silke Hamann
to appear   Loanword adaptation as first-language phonological perception. To appear in: Andrea Calabrese and W. Leo Wetzels (eds.), *Loan Phonology*. Amsterdam: John Benjamins. [*Rutgers Optimality Archive* 975]

Broselow, Ellen
2004   Language contact phonology: richness of the stimulus, poverty of the base. *North-Eastern Linguistic Society* 34: 1–22.

Cornulier, Benoit de
1981   H-aspirée et la syllabation: expressions disjonctives. In: Didier L. Goyvaerts (ed.), *Phonology in the 1980's*. 183–230. Ghent: Story-Scientia.

Denes, Peter
1955   Effect of duration on the perception of voicing. *Journal of the Acoustical Society of America* 27: 761–764.

Duanmu, San
1994   Against contour tone units. *Linguistic Inquiry* 25: 555–608.

Dupoux, Emmanuel, Kazuhiko Kakehi, Yuki Hirose, Christophe Pallier and Jacques Mehler
1999   Epenthetic vowels in Japanese: a perceptual illusion. *Journal of Experimental Psychology: Human Perception and Performance* 25: 1568–1578.

Escudero, Paola
2005   *Linguistic Perception and Second-Language Acquisition*. Ph.D. dissertation, Utrecht University.

Escudero, Paola, and Paul Boersma
2003   Modelling the perceptual development of phonological contrasts with Optimality Theory and the Gradual Learning Algorithm. In: Sudha Arunachalam, Elsi Kaiser and Alexander Williams (eds.), *Proceedings of the 25th Annual Penn Linguistics Colloquium. Penn Working Papers in Linguistics* **8.1**: 71–85. [non-misprinted version: *Rutgers Optimality Archive* 439, 2001]

Escudero, Paola, and Paul Boersma
2004   Bridging the gap between L2 speech perception research and phonological theory. *Studies in Second Language Acquisition* 26: 551–585.

Flemming, Edward
1995   *Auditory Representations in Phonology*. Ph.D. dissertation, UCLA. [published in 2002 by Routledge, London]

Fowler, Carol A.
1986   An event approach to the study of speech perception from a direct-realist perspective. *Journal of Phonetics* 14. 3–28.

Gandour, Jackson
1978   The perception of tone. In: Victoria Fromkin (ed.), *Tone*, 41–76. New York: Academic Press.

Ganong, William F. III
1980   Phonetic categorization in auditory word perception. *Journal of Experimental Psychology: Human Perception and Performance* 6: 110–125.

Goldsmith, John
1976   *Autosegmental Phonology.* Ph.D. dissertation, MIT, Cambridge.
            [published in 1979 by Garland Press, New York]
Gussenhoven, Carlos
2004   *The Phonology of Tone and Intonation.* Cambridge: Cambridge University Press.
Hale, Mark, and Charles Reiss
1998   Formal and empirical arguments concerning phonological acquisition. *Linguistic Inquiry* 29: 656–683.
Hayes, Bruce
1999   Phonetically-driven phonology: the role of Optimality Theory and inductive grounding. In: Michael Darnell, Edith Moravcsik, Michael Noonan, Frederick Newmeyer and Kathleen Wheatley (eds.), *Functionalism and Formalism in Linguistics,* Volume I: *General Papers.* 243–285. Amsterdam: John Benjamins.
Hogan, John T., and Anton J. Rozsypal
1980   Evaluation of vowel duration as a cue for the voicing distinction in the following word-final consonant. *Journal of the Acoustical Society of America* 67: 1764–1771.
House, Arthur S., and Grant Fairbanks
1953   The influence of consonant environment upon the secondary acoustical characteristics of vowels. *Journal of the Acoustical Society of America* 25: 105–113.
Jun, Jongho
1995   Place assimilation as the result of conflicting perceptual and articulatory constraints. In: José Camacho, Lina Choueiri and Maki Watanabe (eds.), *Proceedings of the 14th West Coast Conference on Formal Linguistics.* 221–237. Stanford, Calif.: CSLI.
Jusczyk, Peter
1997   *The Discovery of Spoken Language.* Cambridge, Mass.: MIT Press.
Kabak, Barış, and William Idsardi
2007   Perceptual distortions in the adaptation of English consonant clusters: syllable structure or consonantal contact constraints? *Language and Speech* 50: 23–52.
Kaye, Jonathan
1971   Nasal harmony in Desano. *Linguistic Inquiry* 2: 37–56.
Keating, Patricia
1985   Universal phonetics and the organization of grammars. In: Victoria Fromkin (ed.), *Phonetic Linguistics: Essays in Honor of Peter Ladefoged.* 115–132. Orlando: Academic Press.
Kenstowicz, Michael
2001   The role of perception in loanword phonology. Ms. to appear in *Linguistique africaine.*

Kiparsky, Paul
1985   Some consequences of Lexical Phonology. *Phonology Yearbook* 2:
             85–138.
Kirchner, Robert
1998   *Lenition in Phonetically-based Optimality Theory.* Ph.D. disserta-
             tion, UCLA.
Leben, William
1973   *Suprasegmental Phonology.* Ph.D. dissertation, MIT, Cambridge.
             [published in 1980 by Garland Press, New York]
Levelt, Willem
1989   *Speaking: From Intention to Articulation.* Cambridge, Mass.: MIT
             Press.
McCarthy, John J., and Alan Prince
1995   Faithfulness and reduplicative identity. In: Jill Beckman, Laura
             Walsh Dickey and Suzanne Urbanczyk (eds.), *Papers in Optimality
             Theory.* University of Massachusetts Occasional Papers 18. 249–384.
             Amherst, Mass.: Graduate Linguistic Student Association.
McClelland, James L., and Jeffrey L. Elman
1986   The TRACE model of speech perception. *Cognitive Psychology* 18:
             1–86.
McQueen, James M., and Anne Cutler
1997   Cognitive processes in speech perception. In: William J. Hardcastle
             and John Laver (eds.), *The Handbook of Phonetic Sciences.* 566–
             585. Oxford: Blackwell.
Myers, J. Scott
1997   OCP effects in Optimality Theory. *Natural Language and Linguistic
             Theory* 15: 847–892.
Norris, Dennis, James M. McQueen and Anne Cutler
2000   Merging information in speech recognition: feedback is never neces-
             sary. *Behavioral and Brain Sciences* 23: 299–370.
Pater, Joe
2004   Bridging the gap between receptive and productive development
             with minimally violable constraints. In: René Kager, Joe Pater and
             Wim Zonneveld (eds.), *Constraints in Phonological Acquisition.*
             219–244. Cambridge: Cambridge University Press.
Peterson, Gordon, and Ilse Lehiste
1960   Duration of syllable nuclei in English. *Journal of the Acoustical So-
             ciety of America* 32: 693–703.
Pierrehumbert, Janet
1987   *The Phonology and Phonetics of English Intonation.* Bloomington:
             Indiana University Linguistics Club.
Piggott, Glyne
1992   Variability in feature dependency: the case of nasality. *Natural Lan-
             guage and Linguistic Theory* 10: 33–78.

Pike, Kenneth
    1948   *Tone Languages*. Ann Arbor: University of Michigan Press.
Polivanov, Evgenij Dmitrievič
    1931   La perception des sons d'une langue étrangère. *Travaux du Cercle Linguistique de Prague* 4: 79–96. [English translation: The subjective nature of the perceptions of language sounds. In E.D. Polivanov (1974): *Selected works: articles on general linguistics*. The Hague: Mouton. 223–237]
Prince, Alan, and Paul Smolensky
    1993   *Optimality Theory: Constraint Interaction in Generative Grammar*. Technical Report TR-2, Rutgers University Center for Cognitive Science. [published in 2004 by Blackwell, Malden]
Saussure, Ferdinand de
    1916   *Cours de linguistique générale*. Edited by Charles Bally and Albert Sechehaye in collaboration with Albert Riedlinger. Paris: Payot & Cie.
Smolensky, Paul
    1996   On the comprehension/production dilemma in child language. *Linguistic Inquiry* 27: 720–731.
Steriade, Donca
    1995   Positional neutralization. Two chapters of an unfinished manuscript, Department of Linguistics, UCLA.
Steriade, Donca
    2001   The phonology of perceptibility effects: the P-map and its consequences for constraint organization. Unpublished manuscript, Department of Linguistics, UCLA.
Tesar, Bruce
    1997   An iterative strategy for learning metrical stress in Optimality Theory. In: Elizabeth Hughes, Mary Hughes and Annabel Greenhill (eds.), *Proceedings of the 21st Annual Boston University Conference on Language Development*. 615–626. Somerville, Mass.: Cascadilla.
Tesar, Bruce
    1999   Robust interpretive parsing in metrical stress theory. In: Kimary Shahin, Susan Blake and Eun-Sook Kim (eds.), *Proceedings of the 17th West Coast Conference on Formal Linguistics*. 625–639. Stanford, Calif.: CSLI.
Tesar, Bruce, and Paul Smolensky
    1998   Learnability in Optimality Theory. *Linguistic Inquiry* 29: 229–268.
Tesar, Bruce, and Paul Smolensky
    2000   *Learnability in Optimality Theory*. Cambridge, Mass.: MIT Press.
Van Leussen, Jan-Willem
    2008   *Emergent Optimal Vowel Systems*. M.A. thesis, University of Amsterdam. *Rutgers Optimality Archive* 1006.

Walker, Rachel
1998   *Nasalization, Neutral Segments, and Opacity Effects.* Ph.D. disserta-
            tion, University of California, Santa Cruz.
Wang, William
1967   The phonological features of tone. *International Journal of Ameri-
            can Linguistics* 33: 93–105.
Yip, Moira
1989   Contour tones. *Phonology* 6: 149–174.
Yip, Moira
2002   *Tone.* Cambridge: Cambridge University Press.
Yip, Moira
2006   The symbiosis between perception and grammar in loanword pho-
            nology. *Lingua* 116: 950–975.
Zimmerman, Samuel A., and Stanley M. Sapon
1958   Note on vowel duration seen cross-linguistically. *Journal of the
            Acoustical Society of America* 30: 152–153.

The learner of a perception grammar as a source of sound change[*]

Silke Hamann

In this paper, I argue that a regular diachronic sound change is the result of a different interpretation of the same auditory information, as put forward by Ohala (1981 et seq.). Whereas Ohala describes such an account of sound change as purely phonetic, I show that it involves phonological knowledge, namely the language-specific use of auditory cues and their mapping onto language-specific phonological categories.

Two diachronic developments of retroflex segments, namely retroflexion of rhotic plus coronal consonant sequences in Norwegian and retroflexion of labialised coronal obstruents in Minto-Nenana, illustrate these claims. For both, the differences across generations are modelled in Optimality Theory with the help of language-specific cue constraints in a perception grammar (following Boersma 1997 et seq.). This approach is shown to be superior to the descriptive approach of cue re-association proposed by Ohala because it provides a formal account that includes differences in cue weighting (especially the disregard of cues that became unreliable) and differences in emergent phonological categories.

1. Introduction

In recent years, a number of phonological studies have turned their attention to the relation between speech perception and phonology and have highlighted the relevance of this topic, see e.g. the articles in Hume and Johnson (2001a) and in the present volume. The conclusions drawn in these studies, however, diverge. The majority of scientists working on the perceptual basis of phono-

---

*   I want to thank Siri Tuttle for drawing my attention to the Athabaskan data and providing me with literature on this topic. Earlier stages of this research were presented at the *11th Manchester Phonology Meeting*, May 2003; at the *16th International Congress of Historical Linguistics in Copenhagen*, August 2003; and at the ZAS Berlin. I thank the audiences on all three occasions for their comments. I have also received helpful suggestions by Paul Boersma and John Ohala. I gratefully acknowledge a VENI postdoctoral fellowship by the Dutch Science Foundation (NWO; GW 016.064.057).

logical processes, for instance Steriade (1995, 2001), Hume and Johnson (2001b), and Wright (2001), assume or explicitly claim that speech perception informs phonology but lies outside the scope of phonological theory, whereas a few, such as Boersma (1998), Broselow (2004, this volume) and Pater (2004), claim that speech perception is part of our phonological knowledge and therefore has to be included in phonological theory.

One argument against the language-specificity of speech perception put forward by its opponents is the fact that speech perception shares cognitive facilities with general perception, as exemplified with the following citation of Hume and Johnson (2001b: 14):

> [T]o the extent that language sound patterns are caused by external factors such as speech perception, these factors are reflected in the formal phonological theory. Yet, to incorporate them directly into phonological theory erroneously implies that they are exclusive to language.

In the present article I argue that there is no inherent conflict between language-specific perception and our general auditory capacity, but that both are present and apply in the perception of speech sounds.

With respect to sound change, Ohala's (1981) groundbreaking article "The listener as a source of sound change" illustrates that an interaction between sound perception and phonology is one cause of diachronic change. Again, this interaction can be interpreted in two ways. Hume and Johnson (2001b) write that "Ohala's (1981) account of the listener as a source of sound change is one of the most explicit accounts of a *point of contact* between speech perception and language sound structure" (p.7, italics mine), see also Holt (1997) and Mielke (2003) for a similar interpretation. Departing from this interpretation, I show in the present article that Ohala's work on sound change (1974 et seq.) provides no evidence for the independence of speech perception and phonology; on the contrary, it actually supports the phonological nature of speech perception.

In the present study I discuss data of two diachronic developments of retroflexes via re-analysis; both processes and a sample language for each are given in (1) (illustrated by one retroflex segment of each language).

(1)   *Retroflexion*

    a.   *in rhotic context:* *rt > ʈ   Norwegian (North-Germanic)

    b.   *via labialisation:* *ʃʷ > ʂᶫ   Minto-Nenana (Athabaskan)

Bhat (1973), who provides the first comprehensive typological description of retroflexes and includes a short treatise on their diachronic development, mentions that retroflexes are "introduced into a language mainly through the assimilatory influences of neighbouring sounds such as back vowels, velar consonants, r, or at a later stage by other retroflexed consonants" (p.55).[1] Bhat's "assimilatory influence" is thus restricted to *coarticulatory phenomena*.

In the present study the two processes under (1) are shown to involve *perceptual reinterpretation*, which is often based on coarticulatory variation in the input. Due to this variation in the input, the child acquires a perception grammar that differs from the perception grammar(s) of the previous generation. I formalise the acquisition and workings of a perception grammar within the framework of Optimality Theory (McCarthy and Prince 1993, Prince and Smolensky [1993] 2004; henceforth: OT), following Boersma (1997 et seq.), Boersma, Escudero and Hayes (2003), Escudero and Boersma (2003, 2004), and Hamann (2003a). For this, I use the model of *Bidirectional Phonetics and Phonology* (Boersma 2006, 2007, to appear; henceforth: BiPhon) because it is the only linguistic model at present that includes an explicit formalisation of the phonetics-phonology interface with so-called cue constraints, which map the auditory form onto a phonological form and vice versa.[2]

Within OT, sound change is usually assumed to be characterised by a different ranking of the same constraints between two (or more) diachronic stages of a language, see for instance the work by Jacobs (1995), Gess (1996), Green (1997, 2001), Holt (1997), Ham (1998), Bermúdez-Otero (1999), and Hamann (2005). In contrast to these approaches, I propose in the present article that the language learner does not merely construct a different *ranking* of the same constraints from the input, but can employ different *constraints* than the previous generation, see Boersma (1998, 2003) and Gess (2003).[3] My proposal is based on the assumption that constraints and phonological categories are not innate and therefore not universally available to every learner of every language, but have to be constructed language-specifically on the basis of the input that the learner receives. This emergentist or evolutionarist view of phonology is not new, see e.g. Boersma (1997 et seq.) and Mielke (2004) on the

---

1. Retroflexes can also emerge from voiced (implosive) stops, and via areal spread (both are mentioned briefly by Bhat 1973: 41 and 50, respectively, for a detailed account of retroflexion via voiced stops, see Hamann and Fuchs to appear).
2. Alternatively, the mapping between auditory and phonological forms could be modelled for instance with neural networks. Since alternatives that account for the phonetics/phonology interface have not been elaborated yet, and an elaboration would go beyond the focus of the present paper, I employ here the existing and working cue constraints.
3. In contrast to the present study and work by Boersma, Gess (2003) focuses on the role of the speaker in initiating sound change.

non-innateness of phonological features and Haspelmath (1999) and Blevins (2004) on the emergence of typologically similar patterns via diachronic adaptation instead of universal constraints.

The article has the following structure. In §2, I elaborate Ohala's approach to sound change as initiated by the listener. Section 3 contrasts this with the present approach, where the learner of a perception grammar initiates sound change. The workings of the presented model are elaborated in §4. Section 5 provides the data of the two retroflex processes and a formalisation of these changes in terms of OT perception grammars. Conclusions are given in the last section.

2.   Ohala's listener as a source of sound change

The first full-fledged perceptual account of sound change has been proposed by Ohala (1974, 1981, 1986, 1989, 1993b, 1993a, 1995) who attributes a large role in diachronic change to the listener. Ohala's account is reduced to sound changes that have been attested independently in many unrelated languages and that are most likely to arise from physiological factors, excluding changes introduced via spelling pronunciation, paradigm uniformity effects, and other language-specific factors. Ohala illustrates that the listener, when reconstructing what the speaker says, is often confronted with contextual assimilation of sounds, and has to undo these assimilatory changes to derive the correct underlying phonological form (Ohala and Feder 1994; Ohala and Shriberg 1990).

An example recurrently used by Ohala is the contextual influence of a coronal stop /t/ on a back vowel /u/. In this context, the low second formant (henceforth: F2) of the back vowel /u/ is realised with rising F2 transitions for the /t/. These rising F2 transitions can be interpreted as belonging to a more fronted vowel such as /y/, which has higher F2 values than /u/. The contextual influence of a /t/ on a back vowel is stronger in the transitions from vowel to consonant (henceforth: VC) than in the transitions from consonant to vowel (henceforth: CV), because the quick tongue tip gestures are anticipated already during preceding non-coronal sounds but do not carry over onto gestures of following non-coronal sounds. Listeners that hear intended sequences like /ut/ have to subtract the influence of the coronal context from the vowel to derive the intended /u/. Ohala (1981: 181, et seq.) represents this performance of the speaker and the listener as in Figure 1.

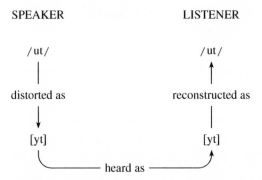

Figure 1.   Ohala's model of a correct speaker – listener interaction.

We have to keep in mind that the use of the symbol [y] for a back rounded vowel in coronal context is a simplification since it implies that this segment is realised identically to a front rounded /y/, which is not the case: listeners of languages that contrast /u/ and /y/ do not generally misperceive [ut] as /yt/. It is, however, the case that in languages with only one high rounded vowel such as English this sound is usually realised less back than in languages that have a backness contrast for high rounded vowels such as French and German (the so-called *dispersion effect*, see e.g. Liljencrants and Lindblom 1972 and Lindblom 1986). As a result, the /u/ in the non-contrasting languages lies perceptually between the /u/ and /y/ in contrasting languages, see for instance Flege's (1987) study where English native speakers perceived both French /u/ and /y/ as English /u/.

In Ohala's model, sound change can occur if the listener performs one of two possible types of "misperceptions", namely uncorrected distortion and dissimilation. In uncorrected distortion, also referred to as *hypocorrection* or *false association*, the listener is unable to correlate the context-induced distortion with the context, which may be almost inaudible due to factors such as loud background noise. The listener thus fails to correct for the context, as in Figure 2a, where the high F2 transition of the coronal plosive is associated with the vowel and thus the intended /ut/ is perceived as /yt/.

In dissimilation, or *hypercorrection*, the listener subtracts what he/she assumes to be due to contextual influence but was actually intended by the speaker, see Figure 2b. Here the high F2 value of the vowel is interpreted as belonging to the coronal plosive, and therefore /yt/ is perceived as /ut/.

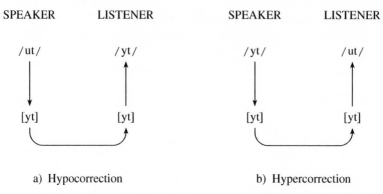

| SPEAKER | LISTENER | SPEAKER | LISTENER |

a) Hypocorrection   b) Hypercorrection

Figure 2.   The two types of Ohala's sound change if the speaker – listener interaction
goes wrong.

According to Ohala, both types of sound changes are some kind of "parsing error[s] by the listener" (1993a: 263), and occur "due to a break-down [...] in the system" (1992: 340). They differ in as far as hypocorrection, which can introduce new phonological categories, is only possible if the listener is linguistically inexperienced and does not know enough about contextual influences yet. Hypercorrection, on the other hand, can occur with adult speakers, since the resulting categories are not new in the language.

In Ohala's model, the listener simply reverses the speaker's task of producing [y] from a phonological form /u/, as can be seen in Figure 1: The listener has to retrieve an /u/ from the phonetic form [y]. He or she does this with the help of what Ohala (1981: 183) terms *"reconstructive rules"*. These rules differ from rules in traditional generative phonology in two ways: They operate on a highly variable input, and they derive more abstract representations from less abstract ones (ibid.). In a later account, Ohala (1992) describes the process of reconstruction as "a cognitive act on the part of the listener" (p.326). He goes on to say "I would be willing to call this a *rule of grammar* although of a type not acknowledged by most phonologists" (ibid., italics mine). Ohala explicitly states that speech reconstruction requires the listener to have an "elaborate knowledge base" (1986: 396) that allows him or her to factor out contextual changes. Nevertheless, he refers to this explanation of sound change as purely phonetic and writes: "this account of sound change also locates the mechanism centrally *in the phonetic domain*" (Ohala 1993a: 263, italics mine).

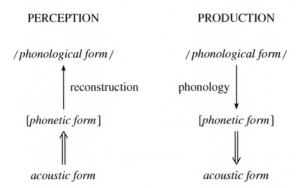

| PERCEPTION | PRODUCTION |

Figure 3.   A depiction of Ohala's grammar modules (double arrows indicating automatic processes).

In line with the notation employed in this book, Ohala's grammar model can be depicted as in Figure 3. Perception is assumed not to involve phonological knowledge in this model. The double arrows from phonetic to acoustic form and vice versa indicate that this is an automatic process, described by Ohala as "is heard as". In this model, phonology maps phonological forms directly onto phonetic forms (without any intermediate phonological representation) and is restricted to the process of speech production, both in line with Chomsky and Halle (1968), as elaborated in Boersma and Hamann (this volume).

3. The present model: phonological speech perception

Based on its rule-like nature and its acquisition on the basis of elaborate knowledge of the language, Ohala's reconstruction module can be interpreted as phonological: It maps auditory information language-specifically to a phonological form. This mapping is only possible when we know what auditory information is of importance in the language under investigation and what phonological categories this language has.

Several studies on cross-language speech perception (e.g. Werker and Logan 1985 and Strange 1995) provide evidence for the language-specificity of the mapping from perceptual information onto phonological form. In psycholinguistics, this mapping is referred to as prelexical speech perception, and complemented by word recognition, where the phonological form is mapped onto a form in the lexicon, see Cutler and Norris (1979), Cutler, Mehler, Norris and Segui (1987), and McQueen and Cutler (1997). Boersma (2006 et seq.) employed such a two-staged speech recognition in the BiPhon model (but see already Boersma 1998), where the mapping between forms is formalised with OT constraints and occurs in parallel. In contrast to Ohala's model in Figure 3 and to earlier phonological models, BiPhon employs two phonological forms, namely a surface and an underlying (or: lexical) form. The surface form contains predictable information like foot structure and stress, whereas the underlying form is stripped from this, and includes only the information that has to be stored in the lexicon. The surface form is connected to the non-discrete phonetic form.

The linguistic modelling of speech recognition in BiPhon is complemented by a model of speech production, which employs the same forms and the same mappings, that is constraints, as the ones used in speech perception. The full BiPhon model is illustrated in Figure 4. Since the present article is concerned with the perception of speech sounds, we will focus on the perception grammar (boldface in Figure 4).

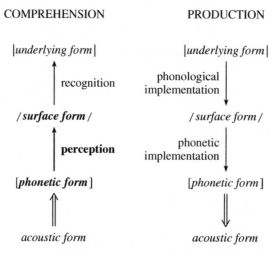

Figure 4. Boersma's BiPhon model, with the additional automatic processing of acoustic forms as auditory forms (double arrows at the bottom).

Before we move on to show how a perception grammar works and can account for sound changes, we have to deal with the claim made by opponents of a phonological view of perception that speech perception cannot be phonological because it is part of our general auditory capacity. Stating that speech perception is phonological does not imply that *all* perception is phonological. Instead, the present article proposes that speech perception *shares* perceptual abilities with general auditory (and visual) perception (see Fowler 1986), namely the ability to turn incoming acoustic data into processable auditory representations. This process is depicted by the double arrow at the bottom left of figure 4. Auditory and speech perception differ in that speech perception has as output phonological categories, i.e. it employs phonology, whereas auditory perception has a non-linguistic output.

Support for this difference between general auditory and language-specific perception comes from neurolinguistics. Best and Avery (1999) tested the perception of Zulu clicks by English and Zulu speakers in a dichotic listening task. Though the two groups had similar overall performance levels, only the Zulu listeners showed a left hemisphere advantage, which is typical for language-specific tasks (Kimura 1961; Studdert-Kennedy and Shankweiler 1970; among others). This result indicates that the Zulu listeners treated the clicks as phonological information, i.e. mapped the incoming data onto phonological categories, whereas the English listeners treated the clicks as general auditory information only. Further evidence comes from Dehaene-Lambertz *et al.* (2005), who found large differences in brain activity between auditory and speech perception. The fact that the perception of speech is processed with general cognitive as well as with language-specific means rebuts the argument by Hume and Johnson (2001b: 14–15) that speech perception cannot be inherent to language because it is part of a general cognitive module.

4.   Sound change as the acquisition of a different perception grammar

The present section is concerned with perceptual cues and how they are mapped onto phonological categories in a perception grammar: §4.1 shows that sound changes do not simply involve a re-association of cues, §4.2 elaborates how the mapping from cues onto categories can be acquired, and §4.3 provides a formalisation of this mapping and its change over two generations of speakers with the example of Ohala's hypocorrection.

4.1   Sound change is more than a change in cue association

In "the perceptual basis of some sound patterns" (1995), Ohala describes the processes of hyper- and hypocorrection by referring to cues, or "phonetic events", as he also calls them (see also Ohala and Busà 1995). Hypocorrection can then be schematically represented as in Figure 5a (leaving aside the dotted lines for the movement): as a process whereby the listener parses a perceptual cue b_1 of the context (segment B) as belonging to segment A. In hypercorrection, a perceptual cue a_2 of a segment A is interpreted as belonging to the context (segment B), see Figure 5b. In this representation of hyper- and hypocorrection we can see that both processes involve perceptual cues that change their *association* from one segment to another.

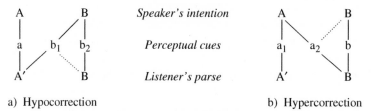

a) Hypocorrection   b) Hypercorrection

Figure 5.   Hypo- and hypercorrection exemplified with cues, based on Ohala (1995: 90). A = original segment, A' = changed segment, B = context.

Re-association of cues is a simplified view of sound change for several reasons. First of all, cues are often associated with more than one segment, that is, they are *shared*. The auditory event of a high F2 transition, for instance, can cue a coronal consonant but also an adjacent front vowel. A hypercorrection of an intended /yt/ as /ut/ is only possible because both /y/ and /t/ share this cue and learners might fail to associate the cue with /y/ since they can already associate it with the coronal. The sharing of a cue is illustrated in Figure 5 with the additional dotted lines: In Figure 5a, the cue b_1 is shared by the younger generation between the segment under investigation and the context, whereas in Figure 5b the cue a_2 was shared by the older generation between segment under investigation and context.

Secondly, sound change can only occur if some perceptual cues are given less importance by the listener, i.e. the younger generation, than by the speaker, i.e. the older generation, or are even totally *ignored*. An intended /yt/ can only be perceived as underlying /ut/ and vice versa if the listeners pay no attention to the F2 values at the beginning or middle of the vowel, where no coarticulatory transitions are observable, and therefore a clear differentiation between /y/ and /u/ is possible. After all, [yt] and [ut] are not confused by listeners of languages that contrast the two high rounded vowels, as mentioned in §2.

Thirdly, sound change is more gradual than a re-association of some cues (and ignorance of others) from one generation to the next suggests. It seems to develop from a change in the *weighting* of cues over generations. Learners acquire a different weighting because one cue is less reliable than it used to be for former generations, whereas others are more or similarly reliable. Such a situation emerges if categories start exhibiting variation along one perceptual dimension, as elaborated in §4.3 below.

Support for a language- and generation-specific difference in cue weighting comes from the fact that listeners do not give equal importance to all cues available to them (as shown e.g. by Dorman, Studdert-Kennedy and Raphael 1977 and by Whalen 1981). As Beddor and Krakow (1998) noted, diachronic change is therefore "not so much a breakdown or failure of normal perceptual processes, but rather a shift in the relative weighting of factors contributing to the linguistic percept" (p. 332).

4.2   The two-staged acquisition of a perception grammar

To acquire the mapping between perceptual information and phonological categories, infants can be assumed to pass through two consecutive stages. In the first stage, at the age of 6–8 months, the infants focus on a few, presumably the most salient, auditory dimensions (such as formant transitions, e.g., Nittrouer 1992). They keep track of the statistical distribution of items along these cue dimensions. Based on the statistical distributions, the infants construct language-specific phonetic categories. Psycholinguistic support for this stage is given for instance by Maye and Gerken (2000), Maye, Werker and Gerken (2002), and Pierrehumbert (2003).

In the second stage, the infants acquire labels for the learnt phonetic categories, and are guided in this by the lexicon. The lexicon informs the learners about the abstract categories necessary to distinguish words in the language and therefore has to be present at that stage. The abstract level created in the second stage also allows the learner to focus on more cues and to map several perceptual dimensions onto the same category (i.e., to integrate cues).

Psycholinguistic studies provide evidence for the two-stage development of perceptual capabilities in infants (e.g. Best 1993; Maye 2000; Stager and Werker 1997; Werker and Pegg 1992). Best, McRoberts and Goddell (2001: 791) describe that infants begin recognizing language-specific phonetic patterns and only later detect phonological classes, "perhaps in relation to increases in size of their early lexicon" (ibid.). The creation of phonetic categories, that is, the end point of the first stage in the acquisition of a perception grammar, explains why infants from nine months of age are no longer able to discriminate all phonetic contrasts but only those that occur in their native language(s) (Werker, Humphrey and Tees 1981; Werker and Tees 1984). Furthermore, it has been observed that infants and children often employ different cues than adults and seem to change their weighting of acoustic cues with more linguistic experience (e.g. Nittrouer Manning and Meyer 1993; Ohde and Haley 1997; Walley and Carrell 1983).[4]

Let us illustrate the two stages with a hypothetical language prone to undergo hypocorrection of /ut/ to /yt/. In this language, the /u/ tokens in coronal context differ from the remaining /u/ tokens with respect to the F2 transitions. We assume that the distribution of both types of tokens along this dimension is bimodal, as shown in figure 6. Infants learning this language hear tokens from this bimodal distribution and keep track of the probabilities of the tokens. On the basis of this input they will construct two separate phonetic categories, which we can term [ut] and [u]. In the second stage of learning, the infants deduct from form alternations with the same meaning that the items with F2 values between 1000 and 1200 Hz (i.e., [ut]) and those with F2 values between 600 and 1000 Hz belong to the same category /u/, and that the former are actually only contextual variants of the latter.

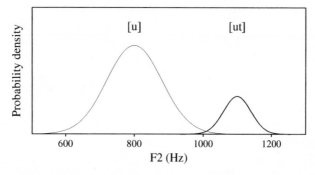

Figure 6.   Assumed distributions for [u] and [ut] allophones along the dimension of F2 transitions.

A bimodal distribution of tokens alone does not trigger a sound change, as we know from the study by Harrington, Kleber and Reubold (2007), where the older generation of English RP speakers showed a similar distribution of /u/ and /ut/ as in Figure 6. This, however, only triggered a gradual shift of the /u/ tokens towards the /ut/ tokens for the younger generation of RP speakers, that is, the category merged again along this perceptual dimension, but no new phoneme /y/ emerged. A sound change in the shape of a split into the two catego-

---

4. Cues are often in a trading relation (e.g., Repp 1979), that is, a cue can receive more weight if certain other cues are not available or less prominent in specific contexts. This fact is not further incorporated in the present account.

ries /u/ and /y/ can only happen if the learners lack phonological or lexical information to associate both phonetic categories with one phonological category.

4.3   The formalisation of a perception grammar

The task of a perception grammar is to map each discrete auditory input onto an abstract phonological category. Within an OT framework, this mapping can be formalised with *cue constraints* (see Boersma 1998 et seq.; and Escudero and Boersma 2003 for the introduction of the term).

Let us take again Ohala's example of hypocorrection to illustrate the workings of cue constraints in a perception grammar. We recall that /ut/ changes to /yt/ because the younger generation uses the high F2 value in the VC transitions as a cue for both /t/ and a front rounded /y/ (the cue is shared), whereas the older generation employed it only to cue a coronal stop. To properly formalize this, we have to distinguish the cue of F2 values at the VC transition, such as [high F2]$_{VC}$, from the cue of F2 values in the middle of the vowel, such as [high F2]$_V$. In the language spoken by our older generation, a [high F2]$_{VC}$ is only a cue for a coronal consonant, expressed as the first cue constraint in (2a). The second cue constraint in (2a) is necessary for the correct perception of a back vowel.[5] It refers to the feature /±back/ but we could have used the features /±front/ or /±round/, instead.[6]

(2)   *Cue constraints for Ohala's example of hypocorrection*

    a. [high F2]$_{VC}$ /cor/: high F2 values in VC transitions cue coronals
        [low F2]$_V$ /+back/: low F2 values in the vowel cue back vowels

    b. [high F2]$_{VC}$ /+front/: high F2 values in VC transitions cue front vowels
        [low F2]$_V$ /−front/: low F2 values in the vowel cue non-front vowels

To correctly formalise the perception of the younger generation, the additional constraints in (2b) are necessary. The younger generation has three high vo-

---

5. The vowel cues in this example are reduced to F2, as we are only interested in the difference in vowel backness and rounding. Further cues necessary for a complete description are F1 and duration. Other consonantal cues than the F2 transition are also not included, since the perception of /t/ as coronal voiceless stop is of no relevance for our example.

6. Backness correlates with rounding for the older generation in the cross-linguistically attested way with front unrounded and back rounded vowels. We have, however, no evidence that speakers of this language employ an additional feature /±round/ to specify their vowels.

wels instead of two. We thus need two features to distinguish these vowels. We will employ /±back/ and /±front/, but in contrast to traditional feature definitions (e.g. Chomsky and Halle 1968) we define /y/ as /–back, –front/, in order to keep the feature system small and to stay close to the acoustic correlate of F2 values. The first cue constraint in (2b) connects the auditory form [high F2]$_{VC}$ with the phonological class of front vowels, and together with the first cue constraint in (2a) it formalises the fact that one cue is shared by two segmental classes. The second cue constraint in (2b) mirrors the fact that the [low F2]$_V$ could also cue the additional high vowel category /y/ that this younger generation created. The four constraints in (2) are sufficient to describe the perception of [ut] by the younger listeners. A full formalisation of the perception grammar of both generations would of course require far more cue constraints than the ones in (2).[7]

As is evident from (2), cue constraints are not universal but depend both on the perceptual cues and the phonological categories that are employed in the respective languages. Thus constraints that refer to /±back/ and /±front/ are only used in a language with more than two distinctions in vowel backness; a language with a two-way distinction only employs one of the two features and the corresponding constraint(s).

In (3) we see perception tableaus for both generations of our assumed language. The input to these tableaus is the auditory form, and output candidates are abstract phonological forms that exist for each generation.

The perception tableaus, just like traditional OT tableaus, allow *Richness of the Base* (Prince and Smolensky [1993] 2004), as there are no language-particular restrictions on the input. In a perception tableau this means that a listener is able to perceive all possible auditory inputs (even though he/she is not always able to assign a linguistic form to them).

---

7. The cue constraints in (2) depart from the ones employed by Boersma (1998 et seq.) in three ways. Firstly, they involve relative cue values instead of concrete ones. This reduces the number of constraints considerably and implies that some kind of speaker normalisation has taken place. Secondly, the cue constraints are positively formulated, based on the assumption that a connection between an auditory form and a phonological form is only ever created if the learner has positive evidence for it. This again reduces the number of cue constraints enormously. Thirdly, the cue constraints refer to (mainly binary) features instead of segments. If the positive cue constraints were formalised in terms of segments, the highest ranked constraint would simply determine the output, even if lower-ranked cue constraints for e.g. less salient cues favour the non-winning candidate (see Boersma and Escudero 2004: 20–21 on the necessity of negatively formalised cue constraints for segmental categories). For instance, [low F2]$_V$ /u/ ≫ [low F2]$_V$ /y/ would never allow the candidate /y/ to win, unless [high F2]$_{VC}$ /y/ was highest ranked (compare to the current formalisation in tableau 3b).

(3)   a. *Perception grammar of an older listener of Ohalaish*[8]

[ut]	[low F2]$_V$ [high F2]$_{VC}$	[low F2]$_V$ /+back/	[high F2]$_{VC}$ /cor/
☞ i. /ut/			
ii. /it/	*!		
iii. /uk/			*!

b. *Perception grammar of a younger listener of Ohalaish*

[ut]	[low F2]$_V$ [high F2]$_{VC}$	[low F2]$_V$ /–front/	[high F2]$_{VC}$ /–back/	[high F2]$_{VC}$ /cor/	[low F2]$_V$ /+back/
i. /ut/			*!		
ii. /it/		*!			*
iii. /uk/			*(!)	* (!)	
☞ iv. /yt/					*

The perception grammars for the two generations differ in several points. They have different sets of output candidates: the younger listener in (3b) has constructed an additional phonological category /y/ (recall the mechanism described in §4.1 that leads to this), which results in the output candidate /yt/. This new category wins because the younger speaker also has a different, high-ranked cue constraint [high F2]$_{VC}$ /–back/, which formalizes that the listener uses the F2 transition as an important cue for a non-back vowel. This constraint rules out candidate (i) with /u/, which did win in the perception tableau of the older listener. The F2 transition is used by both generations to cue the coronal place of the consonant, and the respective constraint [high F2]$_{VC}$ /cor/ is violated by the candidates with non-coronal consonants (iii) in both tableaus.

Though not mentioned by Ohala, the low F2 in the vowel must be considered a very unreliable cue for back or non-front vowels by the young listener

---

8. If the older generation used the feature /±round/ in their phonology (recall footnote 6), we could add a candidate /y/ with the new feature combination /+round/ and /–back/ to tableau (3a), though this vowel itself does not occur in the language. Evidence for the emergence of new combinations of existing features comes for instance from loanword adaptation (Paul Boersma, p.c.). The candidate /y/ would violate a structural constraint */+round, –back/, because this featural combination does not surface in the language of the older generation. The interaction of such structural constraints (militating against non-occurring phonological structures) and cue constraints in the perception tableau illustrates again the phonological nature of speech perception.

(as indicated by the low ranking of [low F2]$_V$ /+back/ in 3b) to allow for the observed change in vowel quality from [ut] to [yt]. As discussed in §4.1 above, such an abrupt change in weighting is not likely to have occurred from one generation to the next. The F2 values of high vowels probably became a more and more unreliable cue over generations. This development might have started with coarticulation of the vowels according to consonantal context, which showed in slightly spread distribution of vowel tokens along the F2 dimension. Learners mirrored this distribution with their cue constraints (recall §4.2) by ranking the constraint [low F2]$_V$ /+back/ lower than the previous generation. The reuse of the same cue constraint ranking in their production grammar (this is one of the essential ideas in BiPhon) caused the learners to produce the same spread token distribution as they had observed in their input. In the production grammar, the cue constraints interact with articulatory constraints. If the language of these learners had high-ranked articulatory constraints that caused more coarticulation, the output tokens of this generation and input to the next would have had even more spread values along the F2 dimension. This gradual coarticulatory change continued until a generation of learners did not profit anymore from using F2 as a main cue to distinguish high vowels, and focussed on other cues instead.[9]

To summarise, an OT perception grammar as employed here expresses the fact that auditory information is not used homogeneously by all speakers across all languages, that no matter what speech sounds we hear we try to assign them abstract categories based on our language-specific knowledge, and that in sound change such language-specific knowledge changes across generations. In contrast to Ohala's account, sound change is not considered a misperception or a break-down in the communicative system. Instead, sound change is the learner's effort to construct the most efficient phonological system and a mapping from auditory form to this phonological system (i.e., a perception grammar) on the basis of the available input.

---

9. The interaction of cue and articulatory constraints in an OT grammar over several generations can account for the aforementioned phenomenon of segmental dispersion, see Boersma and Hamann (2008).

5.   Two diachronic developments of retroflexes

In this section I illustrate that the reinterpretation of auditory information and its formalisation as perception grammars of two generations can account for real instances of hypocorrection. Two diachronic developments illustrating hypocorrection are discussed here, namely those in (4) (repeated from 1).

(4)   *Retroflexion*

    a. *in rhotic context:* *rt   >   ʈ   Norwegian (North-Germanic)

    b. *via labialisation:* *ʃʷ   >   ʂ˖   Minto-Nenana (Athabaskan)

Both processes involve changes from non-retroflex to retroflex coronals. As the accounts for these sound changes are based on the differences in the employment of acoustic information as perceptual cues between adult and language learner, §5.1 gives a short description of the acoustic properties of retroflexes and mentions other segments sharing these properties. Section 5.2 deals with the case of retroflexion in Norwegian (4a), and §5.3 with retroflexion in Minto-Nenana (4b). In these language-specific descriptions, the acoustic properties of the relevant segments are given in relative rather than absolute terms to ease the comparison between the two languages and between the different stages of one language. A further reason for relative descriptions is the lack of acoustic information on the former stages of the two languages.

5.1   Acoustic properties of retroflexes

Retroflex segments are generally distinguished from other coronals by lowered third formant (F3) transitions (both VC and CV; see Stevens and Blumstein 1975 and the summary of language-specific acoustic studies of retroflexes by Hamann 2003b: 59–60). Retroflex sonorants and vowels are furthermore characterised by an inherent low F3. Retroflex fricatives and affricates show a low and narrow frequency spectrum (see e.g. the centre of gravity measurements by Żygis and Hamann 2003 and Hamann and Avelino 2007). The location of F2 formants and formant transitions is the same for retroflexes and non-retroflexes according to Stevens and Blumstein (1975: 219), and seems to depend heavily on the quality of the adjacent vowels.

    Retroflexes share the lowered F3 transitions (and for retroflex sonorants additionally the inherent low F3) with other segmental classes. Rounding in vowels like /u, y/ or labialisation in consonants has the effect of lowering F3 (Stevens 1998). A low F3 can also be found in velarised consonants or back vowels (Brosnahan and Malmberg 1970). Coronal trills show a low F3 (Lindau 1985), too, which might be due to the fact that they are always apical (Recasens 1991) and articulated with a low tongue middle and a retracted tongue back to enable the rapid movement of the tongue tip (see Recasens and Pallarès 1999 and Solé 1999 on the trill in Catalan).[10] This retracted tongue back, i.e. velarisation, causes lowering of the F3.

As we will see below, the similarities in low F3 between coronal rhotics, labialised sounds and retroflexes are responsible for the introduction of retroflex consonants into a number of languages.

5.2   Retroflexion of rhotic plus consonant sequences: Norwegian

In Urban East Norwegian, orthographic forms of <r> plus <t, d, s, n, l> in monomorphemic words are realised by the respective retroflex segments [ʈ, ɖ, ʂ, ɳ, ɭ], see the examples in (5a) (from Kristoffersen 2000). Historically, these forms were pronounced as sequences of rhotic trill plus apical consonant, see Haugen (1982a: 62). In this article, the present-day retroflex segments are assumed to be underlying, for a discussion of alternative views the reader is referred to Jahr and Lorentz (1981) and Hamann (2003b: 84–85).

(5)   *Norwegian*

    a. kart   [kɑʈ]   'map'
       kors   [kɔʂ]   'cross'
       barn   [bɑːɳ]   'child'

    b. bror+s   [bruːʂ]   'brother'possessive cf. [bruːr]   bror
       vår+dag ['ʋoːˌɖɑːg]   'spring day'   cf. [ʋoːr]   vår
       Per ser   [ˌpeːˈʂeːr]   'Per sees'   cf. [peːr]   Per

The examples in (5b) illustrate that Norwegian also has a synchronic process of retroflexion across morpheme and word boundaries. This synchronic process will not be dealt with in the following; for an OT account and a description of exceptions see e.g. Bradley (2007).

---

10. A low F3 does not hold for all coronal rhotics. Ladefoged and Maddieson (1996: 244) describe the retroflex approximants in Hausa and in Arrernte as both having high F3.

The diachronic process of retroflexion in the context of an alveolar rhotic emerged in the transition from Old to Modern Scandinavian (Haugen 1982a); the exact date of this event is difficult to determine (Eliasson 2005: 1124). The following two stages can be assumed:

(6)   *Old Scandinavian*   *Modern Scandinavian/Norwegian*

        *rt, rd, rl, rs, rn   →   ʈ, ɖ, ɭ, ʂ, ɳ

The process in (6) is traditionally referred to as 'postalveolarisation', since the resulting segments are apical postalveolars and do not show a bending-backwards of the tongue tip usually found in the retroflex segments of the In-dian subcontinent (see Hamann 2003b on the definition and occurrence of this type of retroflexion, and Simonsen, Moen and Cowen 2008 on the articulation of present-day retroflexes in Norwegian).

Norwegian also has a retroflex flap /ɽ/, the so-called 'thick l', which is widely agreed to stem from the sequence /rð/ (e.g. Larsen 1907: 70–72; Seip 1955: 177; Haugen 1976: 275). The emergence of this sound is not the topic of the present study, but the interested reader is referred to Molde (2005) for an articulatory explanation and an OT formalisation of this development. Besides postalveolarisation, central Scandinavian also developed a process of 'cacumi-nalisation', whereby heteromorphemic sequences of the so-called 'thick l' /ɽ/ plus following /t, d, s, n/ were realised as apical palatals with a bend-backwards tongue tip (Eliasson 2005: 1124). The older Oppdal dialect of Sør-Trøndelag still has both phonetic series of retroflexion, according to Haugen (1982a: 39–41). In most dialects, however, the results of 'postalveolarisation' and 'cacuminalisation' merged to apical postalveolars.[11]

Let us look at the perceptual cues that were probably involved in the Nor-wegian process. As elaborated in §5.1 above, coronal rhotics have low F3 val-ues during their articulation but also at the transitions to neighbouring seg-ments, fairly similar to the cues of a retroflex consonant. We can therefore assume that whereas Old Scandinavian listeners associated the low F3 values with the rhotic it occurred with, younger generations associated it with the following coronal segment. In Figure 7, the cue re-association is given in Oha-la's notation, with a voiceless stop as representative of the coronal class. Here, the low F3 values of the rhotic are reduced to the transition to the following coronal, transcribed as [low F3]$_{VC}$.

---

11. It has been suggested that the retroflexion of non-rhotic consonants in Middle Scandinavian was first introduced by the retroflex flap, and then this process was transferred to the alveolar trill, see e.g. Torp (1983: 73) and Torp and Vikør (1996: 72). Since there is no evidence for this assumption, the present study treats the process in (6) as an independent development.

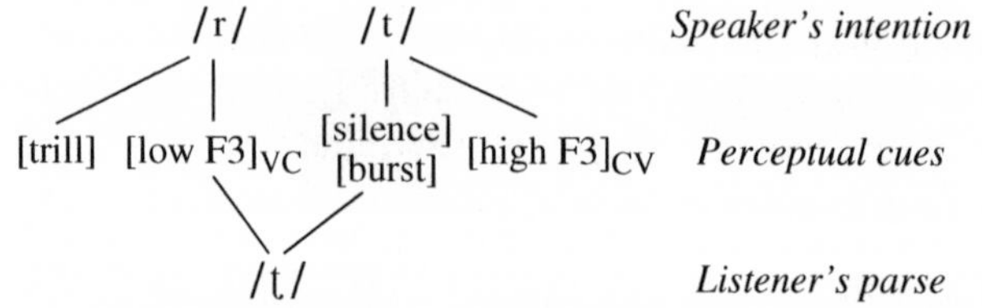

Figure 7.   Development of retroflexion in Norwegian as re-association of low F3.

In Figure 7 we can see that the [low F3]$_{VC}$ which cued the rhotic is used by the younger generation to cue a non-rhotic coronal. Furthermore, the new learner ignores or gives less weight to a number of cues that were of significance to the speakers of the preceding generation, namely the rhotic manner cue (assumedly trill) and the place cue of the anterior coronal (high F3 transition from the consonant to the following vowel, i.e. [high F3]$_{CV}$). In (7) are the cue constraints necessary to formalise the change that took place across the two generations. To reduce the number of cue constraints, we employ only the silence as plosive cue (ignoring the burst), and the low F3 transition as rhotic cue (ignoring the trilling).

(7)   *Cue constraints for Norwegian retroflexion of a plosive*

   a. [low F3]$_{VC}$ /r/: low F3 values in VC transitions cue a rhotic
      [high F3]$_{CV}$ /coronal/: high F3 values in CV transitions cue an (anterior) coronal (probably the only coronal series, and thus not further specified)
      [silence] /plosive/: a silence cues a plosive

   b. [low F3]$_{VC}$ /–anterior/: low F3 values in VC transitions cue a retroflex
      [high F3]$_{CV}$ /+anterior/: high F3 values in CV transitions cue a non-retroflex

The cues in (7a) are the ones necessary to model the older generation, the ones in (7b) replaces the first two in (7a) for the younger generation.

   The development of retroflexion in Norwegian is modelled with the perception grammars in (8) for two generations of Norwegian listeners. I assume that the older generation in (8a) had only one coronal series, and thus no feature such as /±anterior/ available to create a non-anterior, i.e. retroflex, coronal output candidate.

(8)   a. *Perception grammar of an Old Scandinavian listener*

[rt]

[low F3]$_{VC}$ [silence] [high F3]$_{CV}$	[low F3]$_{VC}$ /r/	[silence] /plosive/	[high F3]$_{CV}$ /coronal/
☞ i. /rt/			
ii. /t/	*!		
iii. /r/		*!	
iv. /rk/			*!

b. *Perception grammar of a Modern Norwegian listener*

[rt]

[low F3]$_{VC}$ [silence] [high F3]$_{CV}$	[low F3]$_{VC}$ /–anterior/	[silence] /plosive/	*/r+coronal/	[high F3]$_{CV}$ /+anterior/
i. /rt/	*(!)		*(!)	
ii. /t/	*!			
iii. /r/	*(!)	*(!)		
iv. /rk/	*!			*
☞ v. /ʈ/				*

The learners of the younger generation in (8b) do not interpret any perceived input as a sequence of rhotic plus coronal. This is expressed in the structural constraint */r+coronal/. The same generation gives little weight to the cue of a high F3 in the CV transitions, expressed by the low ranking of the respective constraint. This cue might have been even ignored by this generation, in which case there would be no corresponding constraint at all. A cross-splicing perception experiment conducted by Hamann (2003a) provides psycholinguistic evidence for the low-weighting of [high F3]$_{CV}$. In the experiment, Norwegian listeners did not make use of the VC transitions but categorised coronals almost exclusively by their VC transitions; the latter is reflected in the perception grammar in (8b) by the high-ranked constraint on VC cues.

We can assume, like we did for the example of Ohalaish, that the Norwegian sound change developed more gradual and that there were more than two generations involved. The initial rhotic presumably caused a slightly more postalveolar articulation of the following coronal, leading to a more spread distribution in the coronal input to the following generation. This distribution was replicated with cue constraints by the younger generation, and due to the use of the same constraints and a high-ranked constraint requiring coarticulation in the production grammar, the subsequent generation received even more spread input. Over several generations, this lead to a bimodal distribution of post-rhotic versus post-vocalic rhotics, and since the two are distinguished by meaning in Norwegian, a new generation of learners assigned different abstract categories to them.

The development of retroflexion in rhotic context is cross-linguistically very common. We find it for instance also in Swedish (Eliasson 1986) and Faroese (Sandøy 2005)[12], in the Australian languages Watjarri (Douglas 1981) and Ndjébbana (McKay 2000), in Sanskrit (Whitney 1889), Sardinian (Bhat 1973) and the Iranian languages Yidgha and Munji (Skjærvø 1989). Tibetan languages show that besides apical alveolars also velars and labials can develop into retroflex in rhotic context, cf. the correspondence between orthography and pronunciation in the following words from Ladakhi, spoken in Jammu and Kashmir, India: *drug* 'six' [ʈuk], *phrugu* 'child' [ʈugu], *grodpa* 'belly' [ʈotpa] (Koshal 1982). A similar development can be found in the Tibetan languages Spiti and Lhoke (Grierson 1908).

5.3   Retroflexion of labialised sounds: Minto-Nenana

In Minto-Nenana, a Northern Athabaskan language spoken in Alaska at the Tanana River, retroflex fricatives and affricates were introduced via labialised segments (Krauss 1962; Tuttle 1998). The resulting segmental classes have rhotic releases, see (9a) for examples with fricatives (which show a voiced-voiceless distinction) and (9b) for examples with affricates (which are voiced, voiceless, or voiceless ejective).[13]

---

12. In contrast to Norwegian and Swedish, the retroflexion process in Faroese usually preserves the adjacent rhotic, with the exception of [ʂ], where it is always deleted (Barnes 2005: 1576).

13. Howe and Fullop (2005) discuss the diachronic development of sibilants in Athabaskan, which covers the processes investigated here. They provide an analysis in terms of the features [grave] and [flat], which they claim to be acoustic, not phonological as originally proposed by Jakobson, Fant and Halle (1952). Their proposal suggests that acoustic information is universally mapped onto acoustic features, which in turn are universally mapped onto phonological structures. This goes counter the argumentation and evidence given here that speech perception is language-dependent, i.e. that perceptual cues are weighted language-specifically and that the mapping between these cues and the phonological categories (segments or features) is language-specific.

(9)   a. ṣ̌ᶫa   'sun/moon'
       nəẓ̌ᶫunh   'it is good'

     b. t̪ᶫ'exe   'woman'
        t̪ᶫəx   'he cries'
        d̪ᶫen   'day'

The retroflex fricatives with rhotic releases in (9a) stem from the Proto-Athabaskan fricatives *ʃʷ and *ʒʷ, respectively, as illustrated in (10).

(10)   *Proto-Athabaskan*   *Minto-Nenana*

       *ʃʷ, *ʒʷ   →   ṣᶫ, ẓᶫ

The origin of the retroflex affricate series (9b) is less clear, since the status of the relevant Proto-Athabaskan segments is under dispute. They are assumed to have been either labialised velar stops (Krauss 1973, 1979), labialised alveolar stops (Tharp 1972) (derived from the Proto-Athabaskan-Eyak *kʷ), or labialised postalveolar affricates (Cook and Rice 1989, 1989b; Krauss and Leer 1981), as depicted in the developments in (11a) – (11c), respectively.[14]

(11)   *Proto-Athabaskan*   *Minto-Nenana*

       a. *kʷ, *kʷ', *gʷ   →   t̪ᶫ, t̪ᶫ', d̪ᶫ

       b. *tʷ, *tʷ', *dʷ   →   t̪ᶫ, t̪ᶫ', d̪ᶫ

       c. *t͡ʃʷ, *t͡ʃʷ', *d͡ʒʷ →   t̪ᶫ, t̪ᶫ', d̪ᶫ

The present study follows Tharp (1972) in the assumption that (11b) is correct. This decision is based on the fact that (11b) involves a change from (front) coronal to back coronal and is most similar to the change occurring in the co-ronal fricatives in (10), which allows us to explain the two processes in parallel without any additional assumptions for the affricates.

In the development of retroflexes in Minto-Nenana, the younger generation re-interpreted the perceptual information in a way that departed in a number of points from the representations that the older generation had constructed. The labial release in [ʃʷ, ʒʷ] and [tʷ, tʷ', dʷ] was taken by the younger listeners as a rhotic release because both share long transitions (henceforth: [trans]) and a

---

14. Some scholars (e.g. Leer 1996, 2005: 284 and Rice 2004: 324) assume that the development from labialised to retroflex affricates already took place in the development from Pre-Proto-Athabaskan to Proto-Athabaskan. Leer (1996: 212) includes the stem-final retroflex fricatives in this assumption.

low amplitude, both typical for glides (see Lehiste 1964), and also a lowered F3. The lowered F3 was furthermore interpreted as cue for the retroflexivity of the obstruent segment. For the fricatives, the low frequency friction noise caused by the labialisation was taken by the younger generation as additional cues for the retroflex nature of the fricative. These re-interpretations are graphically represented in Figure 8, with an alveolar labialised voiceless stop as representative of the class of segments that underwent the process (hence fricative-specific cues such as the friction noise are not included).

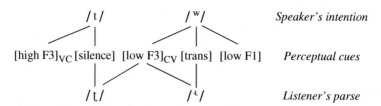

Figure 8.   Development of retroflexion in Minto-Nenana as re-association and interpretation of a low F3.

In the diachronic development of retroflexion in Minto-Nenana, as in Norwegian, the low third formant of a segment (in this case: the approximant release) is associated with the adjacent front coronal, which is interpreted as retroflex. In contrast to Norwegian, the process in Minto-Nenana is not a re-association but a sharing of cues, since the low F3 is also used to cue the retroflex nature of the approximant release. Again, the change can only happen because the learner ignores or gives less weight to other perceptual cues: the high F3 transition into the alveolar stop and the low F1 typical for labialised approximants.

The following cue constraints are minimally necessary to model the change in Minto-Nenana, again restricted to the voiceless stop. The list in (12) does not include the low F1 values as cue for the labialised approximant release and the long transitions for any kind of approximant release. In (12a) are the constraints necessary for the older generation of Minto-Nenana, in (12b) those necessary for the younger generation.

(12)   *Cue constraints for Minto-Nenana retroflexion*

    a. [high F3]$_{VC}$ /coronal/: high F3 values in the VC transitions cue an (anterior) coronal
    [silence] /plosive/: a silence cues a plosive
    [low F3]$_{CV}$ / ʷ/: low F3 values in the CV transitions cue a labialised approximant release

b. [high F3]$_{VC}$ /+anterior/: high F3 values in the VC transitions cue an
anterior coronal
[silence] /plosive/: a silence cues a plosive
[low F3]$_{CV}$ /–anterior/: low F3 values in the CV transitions cue a retroflex
[low F3]$_{CV}$ /ɭ/: low F3 values in the CV transitions cue a (retroflex)
approximant release

The perception tableaus in (13) show the application of these cue constraints in
the modelling of the two generations of listeners.

(13)   a. *Perception grammar of a Proto-Athabaskan listener*

[tʷ]	[low F3]$_{VC}$ [silence] [high F3]$_{CV}$	[low F3]$_{VC}$ /coronal/	[silence] /plosive/	[low F3]$_{CV}$ /ʷ/
☞ i. /tʷ/				
ii. /t/				*!
iii. /kʷ/	*!			
iv. /ʷ/	*(!)		*(!)	

b. *Perception grammar of a Minto-Nenana listener*

[tʷ]	[low F3]$_{VC}$ [silence] [high F3]$_{CV}$	[low F3]$_{VC}$ /–anterior/	[silence] /plosive/	[low F3]$_{CV}$ /ɭ/	[high F3]$_{VC}$ /+anterior/
i. /t/	*(!)			*(!)	
☞ ii. /tɭ/					*
iii. /kɭ/	*!				*
iv. /ɭ/			*!		*

The candidate lists in both grammars only include segments or feature combinations that actually occur in the respective language, thus Proto-Athabaskan in
(13a) does not have any retroflex sounds, and Minto-Nenana no labialised
approximant releases. As a result, the cue constraints for Proto-Athabaskan
involve unspecified but assumedly anterior coronals and labialised approximants, whereas that for Minto-Nenana employ retroflex and non-retroflex
coronals and retroflex approximants.

The cue [high F3]$_{VC}$ is weighted very low or not considered at all by the listeners of Minto-Nenana, and therefore the respective constraint is ranked below the three decisive constraints in tableau (13b). We can assume again that the different weighting did not happen within two generations. It seems very likely that first a re-interpretation of the labialised release as retroflex took place (due to the weak cues involved), and at a later stage an assimilation of the obstruent to its retroflex release happened.

The retroflexion process of Minto-Nenana occurred cross-linguistically very seldom, a number of other Northern Athabaskan languages underwent it, namely Ingalik (or Deg Hit'an), Kolchan, Han, and Eastern and Western Kutchin (or Gwich'in) (Krauss and Golla 1981: 72). Smith River Athabaskan, an Athabaskan language belonging to the Pacific Coast subdivision, has only two retroflexes, a voiceless ejective affricate [ʈʂ'] and a voiceless fricative [ʂ], both seem to derive from the same Proto-Athabaskan sounds as the Northern Athabaskan retroflexes (with a collapse of the voicing distinction), see Bright (1964). A reason for the rarity of such a retroflexion process may be the typological unusualness of labialised coronals.

6.   Conclusion

In the present paper I provided data from two diachronic changes that introduced retroflexes and argued that they happened because learners of both languages interpret the auditory information in a different way than previous generations. I illustrated that both changes belong to what Ohala (1981 et seq.) defines as "hypocorrection". Departing from Ohala's definition, I showed that these diachronic developments do not only involve some kind of re-association of perceptual cues but also a difference in cue weighting, where some cues are given much less (or no) weight by the younger generation than they received by the parent generation. I proposed that such a change in weighting occurs because some cues become less reliable due to variation in their distribution.

It was furthermore shown that the association of cues with phonological categories is an integral part of explaining speech perception and sound change. This association is not trivial, and involves both our phonetic and phonological knowledge. For this reason, I argued that speech perception is phonological and can be modelled by linguistic means, namely with a perception grammar in the linguistic framework of BiPhon (Boersma 2006 et seq.). The perception grammars for two generations of Norwegian and Minto-Nenana listeners yielded a straightforward formalisation of a difference in cue weighting and of its results for the categorisation of an incoming auditory signal.

Not only the mapping between cues and phonological categories were shown to differ from generation to generation. The phonological categories and features themselves were assumed to be emerging and not universal, and therefore also variable across generations. An assumption of universal categories and features, by contrast, raises the question whether the mapping between cues and such categories is also universal (this would not allow changes in mapping like the ones we provided evidence for) or, if it is not, how the learning infant can activate the correct universal category when confronted with varying cues in the input.

The reader might wonder whether the present model disposes of everything that might be universal in sound change. This is not the case. It is well-known that a large number of frequently occurring diachronic changes are due to universal phonetic characteristics such as the acoustic similarity between segments (e.g., Winitz, Scheib and Reeds 1972) or aerodynamic preferences (e.g., Ohala 1983). Such universals grounded in the vocal tract or the hearing apparatus can be included in a formal model of phonetics as general restrictions or preferences, and are not influenced in any way by the language-specificity of the phonological categories. This independence of phonetics and phonology is expressed in BiPhon by separate representations, and their interaction can be modelled by a parallel evaluation of the representations. The independence but cooperation of phonetics and phonology makes BiPhon resistant to criticism voiced repeatedly that phonological accounts of perceptually-motivated diachronic processes reduplicate phonetic information or incorporate phonetic markedness into phonology (see, e.g., Blevins 2004, Ohala 2005 and Howe and Fulop 2005[15]).

A remaining question is whether the present proposal of the listener as the initiator of sound change generalises from the discussed cases of hypocorrection to other types of diachronic developments. Not all sound changes seem to be initiated by the learning child. Let us look at two cases where adults seem to be actively involved. The first one is the well-known example of the British queen, who altered her pronunciation over the last 50 years (Harrington, Palethorpe and Watson 2000). We know that the queen did not initiate a sound change but instead slightly adjusted her own pronunciation to the Received Pronunciation of English spoken nowadays (see the illustration of the change in the articulation and perception of /u/ across three generations by Harrington, Kleber and Reubold 2007). This example only illustrates that even adult

---

15. Howe and Fulop (2005) argue "that sound change has its source in phonetics, not phonology [...] and that phonetics and phonology are distinct modules, each with its privileged principles and elements, including features" (p.1). Their acoustic features [grave] and [flat], however, seem to duplicate the task of phonological abstraction within phonetics.

speakers continuously adjust the rankings of their cue constraints on the basis of the perceived input.[16] The actual sound change is the change in the input, which is to a large part produced by adults. A better example for sound change initiated by adults might be adult misperceptions, such as Ohala's hypercorrection elaborated in section 2. Adult misperceptions, however, do not usually lead to change. Listeners are used to misperceive all the time (due to background noise and other factors), but mostly correct their percept with the help of semantic context and the mental lexicon. Only highly infrequent words stand a chance of being permanently stored with a representation that departs from that of other speakers. Still, an idiosyncratic pronunciation of a highly infrequent word by a single speaker does not constitute a sound change. In order to be considered a sound change, such a pronunciation of a word has to spread in the population of speakers and to the pronunciation of other words, and this seems to involve again infant learners. It remains a topic for future studies to test whether adults alone can initiate and propagate a sound change.

References

Barnes, Michael
  2005   The standard languages and their systems in the 20th century II: Fa-
              roese. In: Oskar Bandle, Kurt Braunmüller, Ernst Håkon Jahr, Allan
              Karker, Hans-Peter Naumann and Ulf Teleman (eds.), *The Nordic
              Languages: An International Handbook of the History of the North
              Germanic Languages*, 1574–1584. Berlin: Walter de Gruyter.
Beddor, Patrice Speeter, and Rena Arens Krakow
  1998   Perceptual confusion and phonological change: how confused is the
              listener? In: Benjamin K. Bergen, Madelaine C. Plauché and Ashlee
              C. Bailey (eds.), *Proceedings of the Twenty-Fourth Annual Meeting
              of the Berkeley Linguistics Society*, 320–334. Berkeley: Berkeley
              Linguistics Society.
Bermúdez-Otero, Ricardo
  1999   *Constraint Interaction in Language Change: Opacity and Globality
              in Phonological Change*. Ph.D. dissertation, University of Manchester.

---

16. Updating the cue ranking on the basis of the input has less drastical effects the more experienced (i.e., older) the listener gets.

Best, Catherine T.
1993   Emergence of language-specific constraints in perception of non-native speech: a window on early phonological development. In: Bénédicte de Boysson-Bardies, Scania de Schonen, Peter W. Jusczyk, Peter F. MacNeilage and John Morton (eds.), *Developmental Neurocognition: Speech and Face Processing in the First Year*, 289–304. Dordrecht: Kluwer Academic Press.

Best, Catherine T., and Robert A. Avery
1999   Left-hemisphere advantage for click consonants is determined by linguistic significance and experience. *Psychological Science* 10: 65–69.

Best, Catherine T., Gerald W. McRoberts and Elizabeth Goodell
2001   Discrimination of non-native consonant contrasts varying in perceptual assimilation to the listener's native phonological system. *Journal of the Acoustical Society of America* 109: 775–794.

Bhat, D. N. S.
1973   Retroflexion: an areal feature. *Working Papers on Language Universals* 13: 27–67.

Blevins, Juliette
2004   *Evolutionary Phonology.* Cambridge: Cambridge University Press.

Boersma, Paul
1997   How we learn variation, optionality, and probability. *Proceedings of the Institute of Phonetic Sciences of the University of Amsterdam* 21: 43–58.

Boersma, Paul
1998   *Functional Phonology: Formalizing the Interaction between Articulatory and Perceptual Drives*, Ph.D. dissertation, University of Amsterdam, The Hague: Holland Academic Graphics.

Boersma, Paul
2003   The odds of eternal optimization in Optimality Theory. In: D. Eric Holt (ed.), *Optimality Theory and Language Change*, 31–65. Dordrecht: Kluwer.

Boersma, Paul
2006   Prototypicality judgments as inverted perception. In: Gisbert Fanselow, Caroline Féry, Matthias Schlesewsky and Ralf Vogel (eds.), *Gradience in Grammar*, 167–184. Oxford: Oxford University Press.

Boersma, Paul
2007   Some listener-oriented accounts of *h*-aspiré in French. *Lingua* 117: 1989–2054.

Boersma, Paul
to appear   A programme for bidirectional phonology and phonetics and their acquisition and evolution. In: Anton Benz and Jason Mattausch (eds.), *Bidirectional Optimality Theory*. Amsterdam: John Benjamins.

Boersma, Paul, and Paola Escudero
    2004   Learning to perceive a smaller L2 vowel inventory: an Optimality
                    Theory account. *Rutgers Optimality Archive* 684.
Boersma, Paul, Paola Escudero and Rachel Hayes
    2003   Learning abstract phonological from auditory phonetic categories: an
                    integrated model for the acquisition of language-specific sound cate-
                    gories. In: Marie-Josep Solé, Daniel Recasens and Joaquín Romero
                    (eds.), *Proceedings of the 15th International Congress of Phonetic
                    Sciences*, 1013–1016. Barcelona.
Boersma, Paul, and Silke Hamann
    2008   The evolution of auditory dispersion in bidirectional constraint
                    grammars. *Phonology* 25: 217–270.
Boersma, Paul, and Silke Hamann
    this volume   Introduction: models of phonology in perception.
Bradley, Travis G.
    2007   Morphological derived-environment effects in gestural coordination:
                    a case study of Norwegian clusters. *Lingua* 117: 950–985.
Bright, Jane O.
    1964   The phonology of Smith River Athapaskan (Tolowa). *International
                    Journal of American Linguistics* 30: 101–107.
Broselow, Ellen
    2004   Language contact phonology: richness of the stimulus, poverty of the
                    base. *Proceedings of the North-Eastern Linguistic Society* 34: 1–22.
Broselow, Ellen
    this volume   Stress adaptation to loanword phonology: perception and learnability.
Brosnahan, Leonard Francis, and Bertil Malmberg
    1970   *Introduction to Phonetics*. Cambridge: Heffer & Sons.
Chomsky, Noam, and Morris Halle
    1968   *The Sound Pattern of English*. New York: Harper and Row.
Cook, Eung-Do, and Keren D. Rice
    1989   Introduction. In: Eung-Do Cook and Keren Rice (eds.), *Athapaskan
                    Linguistics: Current Perspectives on a Language Family*, 1–62. Ber-
                    lin: Mouton de Gruyter.
Cutler, Anne, and Dennis Norris
    1979   Monitoring sentence comprehension. In: William E. Cooper and
                    Edward C.T. Walker (eds.), *Sentence Processing: Psycholinguistic
                    Studies Presented to Merrill Garrett*, 113–134. Hillsdale: Erlbaum
                    Associates.
Cutler, Anne, Jacques Mehler, Dennis Norris and Juan Segui
    1987   Phoneme identification and the lexicon. *Cognitive Psychology* 19:
                    141–177.

Dehaene-Lambertz, Ghislaine, Christophe Pallier, Willy Serniclaes, Liliane Sprenger-Charolles, Antoinette Jobert and Stanislas Dehaene
  2005   Neural correlates of switching from auditory to speech perception. *NeuroImage* 24: 21–33.
Dorman, Michael F., Michael Studdert-Kennedy and Lawrence J. Raphael
  1977   Stop-consonant recognition: release bursts and formant transitions as functionally equivalent, context-dependent cues. *Perception & Psychophysics* 22: 109–122.
Douglas, Wilfrid H.
  1981   Watjarri. In: Robert M. W. Dixon and Barry J. Blake (eds.), *Handbook of Australian Languages*, Volume 2, 197–273. Amsterdam: Benjamins.
Eliasson, Stig
  1986   Sandhi in Peninsular Scandinavian. In: Henning Andersen (ed.), *Sandhi Phenomena in the Languages of Europe*. Berlin: de Gruyter.
Eliasson, Stig
  2005   Phonological developments from Old Nordic to Early Modern Nordic IV: a typological and contrastive survey. In: Oskar Bandle, Kurt Braunmüller, Ernst Håkon Jahr, Allan Karker, Hans-Peter Naumann and Ulf Teleman (eds.), *The Nordic Languages: An International Handbook of the History of the North Germanic Languages*, 1116–1128. Berlin: Walter de Gruyter.
Escudero, Paola, and Paul Boersma
  2003   Modelling the perceptual development of phonological contrasts with Optimality Theory and the Gradual Learning Algorithm. In: Sundha Arunachalam, Elsi Kaiser and Alexander Williams (eds.), *Proceedings of the 25th Annual Penn Linguistics Colloquium* (Penn Working Papers in Linguistics 8.1), 71–85.
Escudero, Paola, and Paul Boersma
  2004   Bridging the gap between L2 speech perception research and phonological theory. *Studies in Second Language Acquisition* 26: 551–585.
Flege, James E.
  1987   The production of "new" and "similar" phones in a foreign language: evidence for the effect of equivalence classification. *Journal of Phonetics* 15: 47–65.
Fowler, Carol A.
  1986   An event approach to the study of speech perception. *Journal of Phonetics* 14: 3–24.
Gess, Randall
  1996   *Optimality Theory in the Historical Phonology of French*, Ph.D. dissertation, University of Washington.

Gess, Randall
2003   On re-ranking and explanatory inadequacy in a constraint-based theory of phonological change. In: D. Eric Holt (ed.), *Optimality Theory and Language Change*, 67–90. Dordrecht: Kluwer.

Green, Antony Dubach
1997   *The Prosodic Structure of Irish, Scots Gaelic, and Manx*, Ph.D. Dissertation, Cornell University.

Green, Antony Dubach
2001   The promotion of the unmarked: representing sound change in Optimality Theory. Manuscript, University of Potsdam.

Grierson, George
1908   *Linguistic Survey of India*. Volume III: *Tibeto-Burman Family*. Delhi: Motilal Banarsidass.

Ham, William H.
1998   A new approach to an old problem: gemination and constraint reranking in West Germanic. *Journal of Comparative Germanic Linguistics* 1: 225–262.

Hamann, Silke
2003a   Is retroflexion licensed by VC cues only? Observations from Norwegian. *Nordlyd* 31: 63–77.

Hamann, Silke
2003b   *The Phonetics and Phonology of Retroflexes*, Ph.D. dissertation, Utrecht University.

Hamann, Silke
2005   The diachronic emergence of retroflex consonants in three languages. *LINK: Tijdschrift voor Linguistiek te Utrecht* 15: 29–48.

Hamann, Silke, and Heriberto Avelino
2007   An acoustic study of plain and palatalized sibilants in Ocotepec Mixe. In: Jürgen Trouvain and William J. Barry (eds.), *Proceedings of the 16th International Congress of Phonetic Sciences*, 946–952. Saarbrücken.

Hamann, Silke, and Susanne Fuchs
to appear   Retroflexion of voiced stops: data from Dhao, Thulung, Afar and German. *Language and Speech* 53.

Harrington, Jonathan, Sallyanne Palethorpe and Catherine I. Watson
2000   Monophthongal vowel changes in Received Pronunciation: an acoustic analysis of the Queen's Christmas broadcasts. *Journal of the International Phonetic Association* 30: 63–78.

Harrington, Jonathan, Felicitas Kleber and Ulrich Reubold
2007   /u/-fronting in RP: A link between sound change and diminished perceptual compensation for coarticulation? In: Jürgen Trouvain and William J. Barry (eds.), *Proceedings of the 16th International Congress of Phonetic Sciences*, 1473–1477. Saarbrücken.

Haspelmath, Martin
1999   Optimality and diachronic adaptation. *Zeitschrift für Sprachwissenschaft* 18: 180–205.
Haugen, Einar
1976   *The Scandinavian Languages: An Introduction to their History.* London: Faber and Faber.
Haugen, Einar
1982a   *Scandinavian Language Structures: A Comparative Historical Survey.* Tübingen: Niemeyer.
Haugen, Einar
1982b   *Oppdalsmålet: Innføring i et Sørtrøndsk Fjellbygdmål.* Oslo: Gyldendal.
Holt, D. Eric
1997   *The Role of the Listener in the Historical Phonology of Spanish and Portuguese: An Optimality-Theoretic Account*, Ph.D. dissertation, Georgetown University.
Howe, Darin, and Sean A. Fulop
2005   Acoustic features in Athabaskan. Paper presented at the *Annual Meeting of the Linguistic Society of America*, Oakland.
Hume, Elizabeth, and Keith Johnson (eds.)
2001a   *The Role of Speech Perception in Phonology.* San Diego: Academic Press.
Hume, Elizabeth, and Keith Johnson
2001b   A model of the interplay of speech perception and phonology. In: Elizabeth Hume and Keith Johnson (eds.), 3–26.
Jacobs, Haike
1995   Optimality Theory and sound change. *Proceedings of the Annual Meeting of the North-Eastern Linguistic Society* 2: 219–232.
Jahr, Ernst H., and Ove Lorentz
1981   *Fonologi/Phonology.* Oslo: Novus.
Jakobson, Roman, Gunnar Fant and Morris Halle
1952   *Preliminaries to Speech Analysis: The Distinctive Features and their Correlates.* Cambridge (Massachusetts): MIT Press.
Kimura, Doreen
1961   Cerebral dominance and the perception of verbal stimuli. *Canadian Journal of Psychology* 15: 166–171.
Koshal, Sanyukta
1982   *Conversational Ladakhi.* Delhi: Motilal Banarsidass.
Krauss, Michael E.
1962   Minto phonology. Manuscript, Alaska Native Language Center.
Krauss, Michael E.
1973   Na-Dene. In: Thomas A. Sebeok (ed.), *Linguistics in North America* (Current Trends in Linguistics, Volume 10), 903–978. The Hague: Mouton.

1979   Na-Dene and Eskimo-Aleut. In: Lyle Campbell and Marianne Mithun (eds.), *The Languages of Native North America: An Historical and Comparative Assessment*, 803–901. Austin: University of Texas Press.

Krauss, Michael E., and Victor K. Golla
1981   Northern Athapaskan languages. In: June Helm (ed.), *Handbook of North American Indians*, 67–85. Washington: Smithsonian Institution.

Krauss, Michael E., and Jeff Leer
1981   Athabaskan, Eyak and Tlingit sonorants. *Alaska Native Language Center Research Papers* 5.

Kristoffersen, Gjert
2000   *The Phonology of Norwegian.* Oxford: Oxford University Press.

Ladefoged, Peter, and Ian Maddieson
1996   *The Sounds of the World's Languages.* Oxford: Blackwell.

Larsen, Amund B.
1907   *Kristiania Bymål.* Kristiania: Cammermeyer.

Leer, Jeff
1996   The historical evolution of the stem syllable in Gwich'in (Kutchin/Loucheux) Athabaskan. In: Eloise Jelinek, Sally Midgette, Keren Rice and Leslie Saxon (eds.), *Athabaskan Language Studies: Essays in Honor of Robert W. Young*, 193–234. Albuquerque: University of New Mexico Press.

Leer, Jeff
2005   How stress shapes the stem-suffix complex in Athabaskan. In: Sharon Hargus and Keren Rice (eds.), *Athabaskan Prosody*, 277–318. Amsterdam: John Benjamins.

Lehiste, Ilse
1964   Acoustical characteristics of selected English consonants. *International Journal of American Linguistics* 30.

Liljencrants, Johan, and Björn Lindblom
1972   Numerical simulation of vowel quality systems: the role of perceptual contrast. *Language* 48: 839–862.

Lindau, Mona
1985   The story of /r/. In: Victoria Fromkin (ed.), *Phonetic Linguistics: Essays in Honour of Peter Ladefoged*, 157–168. Orlando (Florida): Academic Press.

Lindblom, Björn
1986   Phonetic universals in vowel systems. In: John J. Ohala and Jeri J. Jaeger (eds.), *Experimental Phonology*, 13–44. Orlando: Academic Press.

Maye, Jessica
2000   *Learning Speech Sound Categories from Statistical Information*, Ph.D. dissertation, University of Arizona.

Maye, Jessica, and LouAnn Gerken
2000   Learning phonemes without minimal pairs. *Proceedings of the 24th Annual Boston University Conference on Language Development*: 522–533.

Maye, Jessica, Janet F. Werker and LouAnn Gerken
2002   Infant sensitivity to distributional information can affect phonetic discrimination. *Cognition* 82: B101–B111.

McCarthy, John J., and Alan Prince
1993   Prosodic morphology I: constraint interaction and satisfaction. Manuscript, University of Massachusetts and Rutgers University.

McKay, Graham
2000   Ndjébbana. In: Robert M. W. Dixon and Barry Blake (eds.), *Handbook of Australian Languages*, Volume V, 155–354. Oxford: Oxford University Press.

McQueen, James, and Anne Cutler
1997   Cognitive processes in speech perception. In: William J. Hardcastle and John Laver (eds.), *The Handbook of Phonetic Sciences*, 566–586. Oxford: Blackwell.

Mielke, Jeff
2003   The interplay of speech perception and phonology: experimental evidence from Turkish. *Phonetica* 60: 208–229.

Mielke, Jeff
2004   *The Emergence of Distinctive Features*, Ph.D. dissertation, Ohio State University.

Molde, Ann-Kristin
2005   *Innføringen av Tjukk l og Retroflekser i Østlandsk: En Empirisk Avklaring og Optimalitetsteoretisk Analyse*, M.A. thesis, Universitetet i Bergen.

Nittrouer, Susan
1992   Age–related differences in perceptual effects of formant transitions within syllables and across syllable boundaries. *Journal of Phonetics* 20: 351–382.

Nittrouer, Susan, Carol Manning and Carol Meyer
1993   The perceptual weighting of acoustic cues changes with linguistic experience. *Journal of the Acoustical Society of America* 94: 1865.

Ohala, John J.
1974   Experimental historical phonology. In: John M. Anderson and Charles Jones (eds.), *Historical Linguistics II: Theory and Description in Phonology*, 353–389. Amsterdam: North-Holland Publishing.

Ohala, John J.
1981   The listener as a source of sound change. In: Carrie Masek, Roberta A. Hendrik and Mary Frances Miller (eds.), *Proceedings of the Chicago Linguistics Society* 17, 178–203. Chicago.

Ohala, John J.
1983   The origin of sound patterns in vocal tract constraints. In: P.F. Mac-
            Neilage (ed.), *The Production of Speech*, 189–216. New York:
            Springer.

Ohala, John J.
1986   Phonological evidence for top-down processing in speech percep-
            tion. In: Joseph S. Perkell and Dennis H. Klatt (eds.), *Invariance and
            Variability of Speech Processes*, 386–401. Hillsdale: Erlbaum Asso-
            ciates.

Ohala, John J.
1989   Sound change is drawn from a pool of synchronic variation. In: Leiv
            Earl Breivik and Ernst Håkon Jahr (eds.), *Language Change: Con-
            tributions to the Study of its Causes*, 173–198. Berlin: Mouton.

Ohala, John J.
1993a   Sound change as nature's speech perception experiment. *Speech
            Communication* 13: 155–161.

Ohala, John J.
1993b   The phonetics of sound change. In: Charles Jones (ed.), *Historical
            Linguistics:Problems and Perspectives*, 237–278. London: Longman.

Ohala, John J.
1995   The perceptual basis of some sound patterns. In: Bruce A. Connell
            and Amalia Arvaniti (eds.), *Phonology and Phonetic Evidence: Pa-
            pers in Laboratory Phonology IV*, 87–92. Cambridge: Cambridge
            University Press.

Ohala, John J.
2005   Phonetic explanations for sound patterns: implications for grammars
            of competence. In: William J. Hardcastle and M. Beck (eds.), *A Fig-
            ure of Speech: A Festschrift for John Laver*, 23–38. London: Erl-
            baum.

Ohala, John J., and Elizabeth E. Shriberg
1990   Hypercorrection in speech perception. *Proceedings of the Interna-
            tional Conference on Spoken Language Processing*, 405–408. Kobe.

Ohala, John J., and Deborah Feder
1994   Listeners' identification of speech sounds is influenced by adjacent
            "restored" phonemes. *Phonetica* 51: 111–118.

Ohala, John J., and Grazia Busà
1995   Nasal loss before voiceless fricatives: a perceptually-based sound
            change. *Rivista di Linguistica* 7: 125–144.

Ohde, Ralph N., and Katarina L. Haley
1997   Stop-consonant and vowel perception in 3- and 4-year-old children.
            Journal of the Acoustical Society of America 102: 3711–3722.

Pater, Joe
2004   Bridging the gap between perception and production with minimally violable constraints. In: René Kager, Joe Pater and Wim Zonneveld (eds.), *Constraints in Phonological Acquisition*, 219–244. Cambridge: Cambridge University Press.

Pierrehumbert, Janet B.
2003   Phonetic diversity, statistical learning, and acquisition of phonology. *Language and Speech* 46: 115–154.

Prince, Alan, and Paul Smolensky
2004   *Optimality Theory: Constraint Interaction in Generative Grammar*. London: Blackwell. First appeared as Technical Report of the University of Colorado Computer Sience Department [1993].

Recasens, Daniel
1991   On the production characteristics of apicoalveolar taps and trills. *Journal of Phonetics* 19: 267–280.

Recasens, Daniel, and Maria Dolors Pallarès
1999   A study of /flap/ and /r/ in the light of the "DAC" coarticulation model. *Journal of Phonetics* 27: 143–169.

Repp, Bruno
1979   Perceptual trading relation between aspiration amplitude and VOT. In: Jared J. Wolf and Dennis H. Klatt (eds.), *Speech Comunication Papers*, 53–56. New York: Acoustical Society of America.

Repp, Bruno
2004   Language contact, phonemic inventories, and the Athabaskan language family. *Linguistic Typology* 8: 321–383.

Sandøy, Helge
2005   The typological development of the Nordic languages I: phonology. In: Oskar Bandle, Kurt Braunmüller, Ernst Håkon Jahr, Allan Karker, Hans-Peter Naumann and Ulf Teleman (eds.), *The Nordic Languages: An International Handbook of the History of the North Germanic Languages*, 1852–1871. Berlin: Walter de Gruyter.

Seip, Didrik Arup
1955   *Norsk Språkhistorie til Omkring 1370*. Oslo: Aschehoug, 2nd edition.

Simonsen, Hanne G., Inger Moen, and Steve Cowen
2008   Norwegian retroflex stops in a cross linguistic perspective. *Journal of Phonetics* 36: 385–405.

Skjærvø, Prods
1989   Modern East Iranian languages. In: Rüdiger Schmitt (ed.), *Compendium Linguarum Iranicum*, 370–383. Wiesbaden: Reichert.

Solé, Maria-Josep
1999   Production requirements of apical trills and assimilatory behavior.
                In: John J. Ohala, Yoko Hasegawa, Manjari Ohala, D. Granville and
                Ashlee C. Bailey (eds.), *Proceedings of the XIVth International
                Congress of Phonetic Sciences*, 77–94. San Francisco.
Stager, Christine L., and Janet F. Werker
1997   Infants listen for more phonetic detail in speech perception than in
                word-learning tasks. *Nature* 388: 381–382.
Steriade, Donca
1995   Positional neutralization. Unpublished manuscript, University of Cali-
                fornia, Los Angeles.
Steriade, Donca
2001   Directional asymmetries in place assimilation: a perceptual account.
                In: Elizabeth Hume and Keith Johnson (eds.), 219–250.
Stevens, Kenneth N.
1998   *Acoustic Phonetics*. Cambridge (Massachusetts): MIT Press.
Stevens, Kenneth, and Sheila Blumstein
1975   Quantal aspects of consonant production and perception: a study of
                retroflex stop consonants. *Journal of Phonetics* 3: 215–233.
Strange, Winifred
1995   Cross-language studies of speech perception: a historical review. In:
                Winifred Strange (ed.), *Speech Perception and Linguistic Expe-
                rience: Issues in Cross-language Research*, 3–45. Timonium: York
                Press.
Studdert-Kennedy, Michael, and Donald Shankweiler
1970   Hemispheric specialization for speech perception. *Journal of the
                Acoustical Society of America* 48: 579–594.
Tharp, George
1972   The position of Tsetsaut among the Northern Athapaskans. *Interna-
                tional Journal of American Linguistics* 38: 14–25.
Torp, Arne
1983   Nokre tankar om inndeling av folkemålet i Skandinavia.
                Folkmålsstudier 28: 45–92.
Torp, Arne, and Lars S. Vikør
1996   *Hovuddrag i Norsk Språkhistorie*. Oslo: Gyldendal.
Tuttle, Siri
1998   *Metrical and Tonal Structures in Tanana Athabaskan*, Ph.D. disser-
                tation, University of Washington.
Walley, Amanda C., and Thomas D. Carrell
1983   Onset spectra and formant transitions in the adult's and child's per-
                ception of place. *Journal of the Acoustical Society of America* 73:
                1011–1022.

Werker, Janet F., and Richard C. Tees
1984   Cross-language speech perception: evidence for perceptual reorgani-
            zation during the first year of life. *Infant Behavior & Development* 7:
            49–63.
Werker, Janet F., and John S. Logan
1985   Cross-language evidence for three factors in speech perception. *Per-
            ception and Psychophysics* 37: 35–44.
Werker, Janet F., and Judith E. Pegg
1992   Infant speech perception and phonological acquisition. In: Charles
            A. Ferguson, Lise Menn and Carol Stoel-Gammon (eds.), *Phonolog-
            ical Development: Models, Research, Implications*, 285–311. Timo-
            nium: York Press.
Werker, Janet F., John H. V. Gilbert, Keith Humphrey and Richard C. Tees
1981   Developmental aspects of cross-language speech perception. *Child
            Development* 52: 349–355.
Whalen, Doug H.
1981   Effects of vocalic transitions and vowel quality on the English /s/ - /ʃ/
            boundary. *Journal of the Acoustical Society of America* 69: 275–282.
Whitney, William Dwight
1889   *Sanskrit Grammar*. Cambridge: Harvard University Press.
Winitz, Harris, M. E. Scheib, and James A. Reeds
1972   Identification of stops and vowels for the burst portion of /p, t, k/
            isolated from conversational speech. *Journal of the Acoustical Socie-
            ty of America* 51: 1309–1317.
Wright, Richard
2001   Perceptual cues in contrast maintenance. In: Elizabeth Hume and
            Keith Johnson (eds.), 251–277.
Żygis, Marzena, and Silke Hamann
2003   Perceptual and acoustic cues of Polish coronal fricatives. In: Marie-
            Josep Solé, Daniel Recasens and Joaquín Romero (eds.), *Proceed-
            ings of the 15th International Congress of Phonetic Sciences*, 395–
            398. Barcelona.

The linguistic perception of SIMILAR L2 sounds

Paola Escudero

1. Introduction

In this paper, I discuss a linguistic model for explaining native and second-language (L2) sound perception. In §2, I discuss the Linguistic Perception (LP) model for general sound perception and L1 acquisition. In §3, I illustrate the L2 Linguistic Perception (L2LP) model with the learning of L2 SIMILAR sounds, which are L2 sounds that are phonologically equivalent but yet phonetically different from the sounds in the learner's first language (L1) that are acoustically most similar. In this introductory section, I argue why we need a linguistic model for sound perception (§1.1) and discuss the characteristics that such a model should have to adequately describe and explain the phenomenon at hand (§1.2).

1.1 Why a phonological model for sound perception?

It is widely accepted that the human perceptual system organizes raw sensory input into abstract mental representations. For speech perception, this means that the listener converts raw auditory input into linguistic units such as vowels and consonants, as illustrated in Figure 1. For instance, English listeners will categorize a vowel with a short duration, a high first formant (F1), and a high second formant (F2) as the vowel /æ/ in the word *cat*, probably because English speakers tend to pronounce the vowel in *cat* with those same properties.

Typically, linguistic proposals that model the role of speech perception in phonology refer to the perceptual mapping of the speech signal as an extra-linguistic, general auditory and universal phenomenon.[1] Within this view, speech perception plays a role in shaping phonological systems but it is not modelled within the linguistic knowledge of language-specific sound structure. For instance, Hyman (2001: 145) argues that speakers do not need to 'know'

---

1. Here the idea that speech perception is a 'universal phenomenon' is taken to mean that human listeners perceive speech sounds in exactly the same manner because humans share the same physiology.

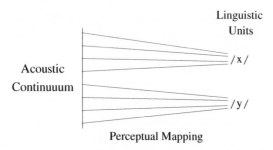

Figure 1.   Speech perception as the mapping of the speech signal onto linguistic units.

the universal phonetics involved in speech perception because no evidence is available for phonology being stored in phonetic terms.[2] Likewise, Hume and Johnson (2001)'s model refers to speech perception as an 'external force' whose elements are tied up with the transduction of speech sounds in the auditory periphery. These authors claim that it would be erroneous to directly incorporate speech perception into phonological theory because it would imply that perception is exclusive to language (p. 14). Similarly, Steriade (2001: 236) proposes an external or extra-linguistic *perceptibility map* (P-map) to formalize the universal perceptual similarity constraints that have an effect on phonological phenomena, such as place assimilation. Finally, Brown (1998) refers to the phonetic mapping of the speech signal as a universal and general auditory phenomenon and, consequently, assumes that it occurs automatically and needs no phonological explanation.

Contrary to the above views, I argue that speech perception is a language-specific phenomenon that involves linguistic knowledge. This claim is not at all new to most phoneticians and psycholinguists and it is supported by a large body of empirical evidence. Cross-linguistic studies (cf. Strange 1995) have shown, for instance, that experience with the fine-grained acoustics of a specific language environment shapes listeners' perception of the speech signal in a linguistic way. This environmental dependence is observed in two of the basic properties of speech perception, namely the categorization of acoustic continua and the perceptual integration of multiple acoustic dimensions. These properties of speech perception have been shown to differ cross-linguistically (cf.

---

2.   As will be mentioned in the following paragraphs, empirical evidence suggests that phonetic properties are produced and heard differently depending on the speaker/listener's linguistic background. In the next section, it will be proposed that a phonological grammar which contains phonetic terms or phonetic values is needed to account for the knowledge underlying the categorization of sounds, which is a phonological phenomenon because it is specific to each language or language variety.

Gottfried and Beddor 1988; Escudero and Polka 2003; Escudero, Benders and Lipski in press; and, even, cross-dialectally, cf. Miller and Grosjean 1997; Escudero 2001; Escudero and Boersma 2003, 2004b).

Furthermore, infant speech perception studies have shown that, within their first year of life, babies develop speech perception capabilities that are appropriate for their specific language environment exclusively (cf. Werker and Tees 1984; Jusczyk, Cutler and Redanz 1993; Polka and Werker 1994). This finding leads Kuhl (2000) to argue that infants develop from universal acoustic discrimination to *filtered* or *warped* language-specific perception. This means that the language-specific filtering or mapping of speech input alters the universal acoustic dimensions of the speech signal in order to highlight differences between the categories of our native language. Moreover, Kuhl claims that "no speaker of any language perceives acoustic reality; in each case, (speech) perception is altered in the service of language" (2000: 11852). However, this altering of the perceptual space seems to apply to speech only because, as shown by phonetic and psycholinguistic studies, speech perception involves different means and processes than those required by the perception of other auditory stimuli (cf. Miyawaki *et al.* 1975; Werker and Logan 1985; Jacquemot *et al.* 2003).

I interpret the evidence as supporting the claim that speech perception is not *solely* performed by our general auditory system but also by perceptual mappings that are language specific and exclusively appropriate for the language (or languages) that we have learned. Consequently, the perceptual mapping of the speech signal should be modelled within phonological theory. This line of thinking has recently been followed by a number of phonologists to model different aspects of speech perception, e.g. Boersma (1998), Tesar and Smolensky (2000), Broselow (2004), Pater (2004). Importantly, the L2 proposal that I will discuss in this paper belongs to the tradition of modelling sound perception with Stochastic Optimality Theory started by Boersma (1998), which was extended to L1 and L2 acquisition by Escudero and Boersma (2003, 2004b) and Boersma, Escudero and Hayes (2003). Before moving onto the proposed model, the next section discusses a number of criteria that a comprehensive model of sound perception should incorporate, in light of the available phonetic and psycholinguistic empirical evidence.

1.2   Criteria for a comprehensive model of sound perception

A comprehensive model of sound perception needs to consider (a) the *definition* of this phenomenon, i.e. what we mean by the mapping of the speech signal, (b) the *type of process* involved, i.e. is it universal or language-specific, (c) the *elements* involved in this processing, i.e. representations, processing mechanisms or a combination of these, and (d) the *relationship between the elements* assumed to be involved in speech perception. Thus, with respect to (a), the definition of speech perception, we assume that it refers to the decoding of the variable and continuous acoustic dimensions of the speech signal. Concerning (b), the type of process involved, it is proposed here that speech perception is a linguistic and language-dependent procedure, i.e. during language development the specific language environment shapes the decoding of the speech signal. Concerning (c), the elements involved in the processing of the signal, it is proposed here that speech perception involves both abstract representations and perceptual mappings. Finally, concerning (d), it is proposed that the degree of abstraction of sound representations depends on the acoustic properties of the signal and the way in which these properties are encoded in the perceptual mappings. I argue that all of these aspects contribute to an adequate modelling of speech perception. Thus, Table 1 shows possible ways of modelling the four essential aspects of sound perception proposed here.

Table 1.   Notions associated with speech perception, and criteria for their modelling.

Sound perception	Proposed modelling of sound perception
Definition: Decoding of acoustics	Phonetic-to-phonological mappings
Type of process: Language-specific and language-dependent	Linguistic knowledge underlies speech perception: Grammatical rules or grammatical constraints
Elements: Speech signal + mappings + abstract categories	Perceptual mappings connect the signal with the listener's abstract representations
Relationship between elements: The nature of categories depends on the signal and the mappings	The input generates the mappings and they, in turn, generate sound representations.

The modelling possibilities shown in Table 1 would integrate phonetic and phonological approaches to sound perception. However, a comprehensive model of sound perception would also need to incorporate two psycholinguistic constructs, viz., the pre-lexical and bottom-up nature of speech perception. That is, psycholinguistic research has shown that the decoding of the acoustic properties of the speech signal precedes the access of meaning (cf. McQueen 2005). In addition, it has been shown that speech perception takes place without the aid of word knowledge (cf. Miller and Dexter 1988; Schachter and Church 1992; Pitt and McQueen 1998; Bürki-Cohen, Miller and Eimas 2001;

Dupoux, Pallier, Kakehi and Mehler 2001). The phonological framework that will be discussed in the next section incorporates all of the criteria suggested here.

2. Linguistic Perception

The explicit modelling of speech perception as linguistic knowledge started with Boersma (1998)'s Optimality-Theoretic (OT, Prince and Smolensky 1993) *perception grammar*, which was proposed to underlie the perception of the sounds of a language. This perception grammar implements the *optimal perception hypothesis*, which states that an *optimal* listener will construct those vowels and consonants that are most likely to have been intended by the speaker. Escudero and Boersma (2003)'s proposal extends Boersma's perception grammar by introducing *auditory-to-segment cue constraints* which explain how multiple auditory cues are perceptually integrated in order to map the speech signal onto phonological categories like place of articulation or voicing.

In this paper, I refer to the combination of Boersma's pioneering work on perception (and recognition) grammars and Escudero and Boersma's extension with cue constraints as the *Linguistic Perception* (LP) model, a term that was first used in Escudero (2005). This model is illustrated in Figure 2.

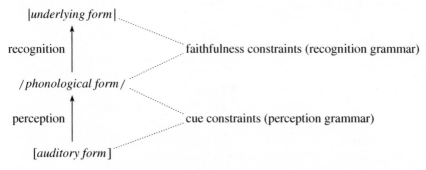

Figure 2.   A model for speech comprehension composed of two sequential mappings (perception and recognition), and three representations (auditory, phonological and underlying form).

Thus, the LP model makes two main assumptions. First, it assumes that speech comprehension is a two-step process that involves two mappings, namely speech perception and speech recognition. Second, it assumes that speech perception is a pre-lexical and bottom-up process. These two assumptions are also found in the psycholinguistic models mentioned in §1.2. In addition, the model incorporates the idea that both speech perception and recognition are handled by linguistic grammars, depicted as single arrows in the figure.

2.1   Optimal Linguistic Perception

Within the LP model, it is proposed that the auditory-to-abstract mapping of the speech signal depends on the specific properties of the language environment involved. Specifically, Escudero and Boersma (2003) argue that, for speech perception, listeners integrate the different auditory dimensions that they hear in ways that resemble the manner in which such dimensions are combined in speech production. This claim was formalized as the *optimal perception hypothesis*, which states that an optimal listener will prefer auditory dimensions that reliably differentiate sounds in the production of her language. In addition, such an optimal listener will identify auditory inputs as the vowels or consonants that are most likely to have been intended by the speaker. Therefore, an important prediction of this hypothesis is that differences in the productions of two languages or language varieties will lead to differences in their respective optimal perception of these two languages or language varieties. Specifically, if two languages differ in the way acoustic dimensions are used and integrated in production, the optimal listeners of these languages will have different ways of perceiving these languages. For instance, Escudero and Boersma (2003) found that Southern British English and Scottish English speakers used F1 and duration differently when producing the vowels /i/ and /ɪ/, and they hypothesized that the optimal perception of these two languages would exhibit differences in line with the attested production differences. The data reported in Escudero (2001) showed that their hypothesis was borne out. It was shown that Scottish English listeners relied almost exclusively on F1 differences to categorize tokens of /i/ and /ɪ/, while Southern British English listeners used both F1 and duration differences to categorize the same stimuli. Thus, this perceptual difference between language varieties closely resembles the different ways in which acoustic dimensions are used in production.

Escudero and Polka (2003)'s findings demonstrate that optimal perception also applies to other cases. These authors found large differences between the productions of the vowels /æ/ and /ɛ/ in Canadian English (CE) and Canadian French (CF), which led to the same large differences in the perception of these vowels by native listeners of the two languages. In their production experiment, Escudero and Polka recorded the /æ/ and /ɛ/ productions of 6 (3 male, 3 female) monolingual CF speakers and 6 (3 male, 3 female) monolingual CE speakers. The vowels were produced in five different Consonant-Vowel-Consonant (CVC) environments and embedded in a carrier French or English sentence. Figure 3 shows the F1 and duration values of the 60 tokens produced in each language.

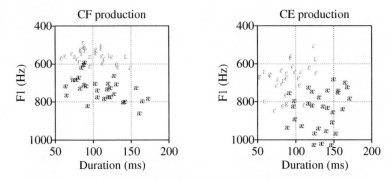

Figure 3.   F1 and duration values of the 60 CE and 60 CF tokens.

We can see that although the productions of the vowels occupy similar acoustic regions, it is clear that the use of F1 and duration is rather different. Thus, we can easily observe that while the CE vowels (on the right) are produced with dissimilar F1 and duration values, the CF vowels (on the left) are produced with different F1 values only. That is, intended CE /æ/ tokens usually have a high F1 value together with a long duration, while intended CE /ɛ/ tokens have a lower F1 value together with a short duration. For instance, the great majority of vowel tokens produced with an F1 value of 700 Hz are intended as CE /æ/ if they are longer than 110 ms but as CE /ɛ/ if shorter than 110 ms. By contrast, although intended CF /æ/ tokens also have higher F1 values than intended CF /ɛ/ tokens, the two CF vowels freely vary between long and short values. For instance, CF tokens produced with values around 700 Hz are almost always intended as /æ/ and almost never as /ɛ/, regardless of their duration values. In addition, Figure 4 shows that the average productions, represented by the symbols, and the variation between speakers, represented by the ellipses, differ across languages. Note that the dotted curve represents the *equal-likelihood* line as computed in Escudero and Boersma (2004a), which is the line along which tokens are likely to be intended as either of the two vowels.

    In these average production distributions, we can again observe that the acoustic dimensions are combined in a language-specific way because the directions of the ellipses in the two plots are different. That is, the ellipses for the

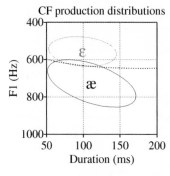
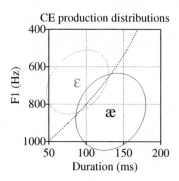

Figure 4.   CE and CF average and distributions for /æ/ and /ɛ/. Dotted curve: equal-likelihood.

CF vowels are almost horizontal, which means that CF speakers almost exclusively use the F1 dimension to distinguish between the two vowels. In contrast, the CE vowels have a completely diagonal shape, which means that CE speakers use a combination of F1 and duration when distinguishing the two vowels. Along with these dissimilarities in the integration of acoustic dimensions, the two languages exhibit differences in F1 distributions for the production of the two vowels. That is, the mean F1 productions of CE /æ/ and /ɛ/, viz. 840 and 681 Hz respectively, are higher than their CF counterparts, which have F1 values of 728 and 557 Hz respectively.

According to the optimal perception hypothesis, these differences in vowel production should lead to differences in perception. This is because the optimal perception of a language should resemble its production distributions and therefore the equal-likelihood line in production should resemble the perceptual category boundary. Thus, it was predicted that an optimal CF listener would rely almost exclusively on F1 and hardly on duration when distinguishing between /æ/ and /ɛ/, whereas an optimal CE listener would rely on both duration and F1 for categorizing the same vowels. Likewise, the differences in F1 distributions should lead to differential categorization of the same vowel tokens. Figure 5 shows that the optimal *perceptual category boundary* of CE and CF listeners, which is represented as a solid line, coincides with the respective *production equal-likelihood* line in Figure 4. As an example of language-specific optimal perception, we observe that the same token [785 Hz, 85 ms], which is depicted by a diamond, is perceived as /æ/ in CF but as /ɛ/ in CE.

This optimal perception hypothesis needed to be validated with the perception of *real* CE and CF listeners. Thus, Escudero and Polka (2003) tested the perception of the 60 CE and the 60 CF vowel tokens by eight monolingual CE

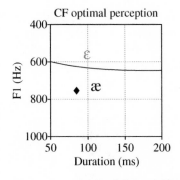
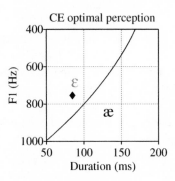

Figure 5.   Optimal CE and CF categorization of [785 Hz, 85 ms].

listeners and eight monolingual CF listeners. These listeners performed a native vowel categorization test. They were told that all of the stimuli were from their native language and were asked to choose between five of their native vowels. Thus, the CE listeners' options were *see* [siː], *it* [ɪt], *say* [seɪ], *pet* [pɛt], and *at* [æt], while the CF listeners' options were *bise* [biz], *biss* [bɪs], *bess* [bɛs], *be* [be], and *bace* [bæs].[3] Figure 6 shows the perceptual category boundary for the two groups as computed in Escudero and Boersma (2004a).

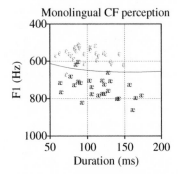
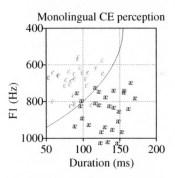

Figure 6.   Monolingual perception of the 60 CE and the 60 CF tokens.

We can see that the CE and CF listeners perceived the productions of their respective native language in a way that matches their predicted optimal perception. Thus, when comparing Figures 4, 5 and 6, the perceptual category boundaries of real listeners resemble their language-specific equal-likelihood line in production in Figure 4 and their optimal category boundaries in Fig-

---

3. The majority of the French category responses were non-sense words whose pronunciations undoubtedly led to the expected vowels.

ure 5. As for the mechanism that leads to this perceptual behaviour, the LP model presupposes that linguistic knowledge in the form of a perception grammar underlies the attested language-specific optimal perception. Such an adult perception grammar can be formalized in OT by means of the cue constraints in (1), formulated by Escudero and Boersma (2003: 77–78).

(1)   **Cue constraints** for adult sound perception
"A value x on the continuum f should not be mapped to the phonological category y"[4]
e.g.   [F1=260 Hz] *→ /i/
[F1=500 Hz] *→ /e/
[duration=120 ms] *→ /i/
[duration=60 ms] *→ /e/
[F2=2800 Hz] *→ /i/
[F2=1400 Hz] *→ /e/, ...
and so on for every duration, F1, F2 value and for every vowel.

According to the model, the constraints are ranked with respect to their distance from the centres of the production distributions of the vowels. In the case of the CF grammar, the mean F1 and standard deviation (s.d.) for /æ/ and /ɛ/ are 748 Hz (60) and 557 Hz (40) respectively. Thus, for a token with values [785 Hz, 85 ms], like the diamond in Figure 5, the constraint that says "do not perceive 785 Hz as /ɛ/" will be higher ranked than the one that says "do not perceive 785 Hz as /æ/" because 785 Hz is 5.7 s.d. away from the mean F1 value for /ɛ/ but only 0.61 s.d. from the mean F1 for /æ/. Regarding vowel duration, 85 ms is 0.87 s.d. away from the mean duration value for /æ/ and 0.61 from that of /ɛ/. The tableau in (2) shows the *distance-based ranking* of the constraints in the CF perception grammar. Given this ranking, an optimal CF listener will perceive [785 Hz, 85 ms] as CF /æ/ because a token with such a F1 value is highly unlikely to have been intended as /ɛ/ in the CF production environment.[5]

---

4.   These constraints are different from those proposed by Boersma (1998: 163–172) because the latter evaluate a mapping from values of a certain auditory continuum to other values on the same continuum. Boersma's constraints can be called *auditory mapping* constraints and can be said to be relevant for infant perception, as will be described in § 2.2. Importantly, Escudero and Boersma (2004b) show that these auditory constraints would have trouble handling the integration of multiple cues in L1 and L2 sound perception.

5.   The dotted line in the tableau shows that the constraints "do not perceive 785 Hz as /æ/" and "do not perceive 85 ms as /ɛ/" are ranked at the same height because such F1 and duration values are equally distant from the mean values of the respective vowel. However, because the highest ranked constraint rules out /ɛ/ as a candidate, this duration constraint can no longer

(2)   The constraints and constraint rankings relevant for the categorization of [785 Hz, 85 ms] in the optimal CF perception grammar

[785 Hz, 85 ms]	785 Hz not /ɛ/	85 ms not /æ/	85 ms not /ɛ/	785 Hz not /æ/
/bɛk/	*!		*	
☞ /bæk/		*		*

Tableau (3) shows that the same four constraints have a different ranking in the CE optimal perception grammar. This is because the mean F1 and duration distributions of the CE vowels (F1 /æ/ = 840 (103) Hz, F1 /ɛ/ = 681 (86) Hz, duration /æ/ = 133 (23) ms, and duration /ɛ/ = 88 (21) ms, are very different from those of the CF vowels. Thus, 85 ms is 2.1 s.d. away from the mean duration value for /ɛ/ but only 0.14 away from that of /æ/, while 785 Hz is 1.2 s.d. away from the mean F1 value for /ɛ/ and 0.53 s.d. away from that of /æ/. Consequently, the resulting distance-based ranking shown in Tableau (3) has the constraint "do not perceive 85 ms as /æ/" as the highest ranked, because a token with such duration value is very unlikely to have been intended as the vowel /æ/ in the CE production environment. Note that this ranking is the only possible one if we follow the model's ranking proposal, which is based on the distances between auditory values. Thus, in the optimal CE grammar, duration constraints play an important role in determining the perceived vowel category, a situation which contrasts with that of the optimal CF perception grammar shown in Tableau (3). As a consequence, a token with short vowel duration such as 85 ms is categorized as /ɛ/, irrespective of its F1 value. This vowel categorization is different from the one resulting from the CF perception grammar. It is proposed here that the difference in the constraint rankings of the two perception grammars underlies the cross-linguistic perceptual difference shown in Figure 6.

(3)   The constraints and constraint rankings relevant for the categorization of [785 Hz, 85 ms] in the optimal CE perception grammar

[785 Hz, 85 ms]	85 ms not /æ/	785 Hz not /ɛ/	785 Hz not /æ/	85 ms not /ɛ/
☞ /bɛk/		*		*
/bæk/	*!		*	

---

play a role in the categorization of this token, as depicted by the gray shading of the column. Thus, a vowel token with a high F1 value such as 785 Hz will always be categorized as CE /æ/, irrespective of its duration value.

In sum, the LP model is able to account successfully for the way in which real adult listeners perceptually map the auditory dimensions of the speech signal onto sound categories. Perhaps more importantly, the model is able to formalize the linguistic knowledge that underlies the attested perceptual behaviour by means of a phonological implementation of the optimal perception hypothesis.

2.2   L1 acquisition of Linguistic Perception

The next question in the modelling of sound perception is how adult listeners attain optimal perception. In answering this question, Boersma, Escudero and Hayes (2003) put forward an account of the path that an infant follows when learning to perceive sound categories. They proposed that the three auditory-mapping constraint families described in (4) are first introduced in the infant perception grammar. These three types of constraints are similar to Boersma's perception grammar constraints (Boersma 1998).

(4)   Auditory mapping constraints in the infant perception grammar

PERCEIVE $(f: x)$
"Map the value x along the continuum f to some value along that same continuum"

*CATEGORIZE $(f: y)$
"Do not perceive anything as the value y along the continuum f"

*WARP $(f: d)$
"Do not perceive a value along a continuum f as a value that is a distance d (or more) away along that same continuum"

As we can see, PERCEIVE constraints allow the infant to map auditory tokens onto perceived counterparts. On the other hand, *CATEGORIZE constraints forbid the classification of linguistic input, and *WARP constraints impede their modification. With respect to the initial ranking of these continuous auditory constraints, Boersma, Escudero and Hayes (2003) propose that all *CATEG constraints are ranked higher than the PERCEIVE constraints. This means that, initially, an infant cannot map the input onto any category. In addition, *CATEG constraints are ranked higher than the *WARP constraints that do not change the identity of the input in an auditorily noticeable way. Kewley-Port (1995) found that the just noticeable difference between F1 values is 40 Hz for adult listeners. Thus, *WARP constraints with a value of 40 Hz or below are ranked very low because they lead to a very small change between the input and the perceived category. To exemplify the workings of the three constraints families, Tableau (5) shows the initial perception grammar for a CE infant that is confronted with an F1 value of 670 Hz, which is a common F1 value for the CE /ɛ/.

(5) The null perception in the initial state in learning to perceive sound categories

[670 Hz]	*CATEG (/630/)	*CATEG (/670/)	PERCEIVE ([670])	*WARP (40)
/630 Hz/	*!			*
/670 Hz/		*!		
☞ /–/			*	

Here we can see that, in the initial state, the infant may not manage to perceive the input as any category, perhaps because she does not hear it as linguistic yet, in which case the input will result in a *null perception*. Therefore, some perceptual development needs to occur to allow the infant to be able to categorize the sounds of her language. Boersma, Escudero and Hayes employ the Gradual Learning Algorithm (GLA: Boersma and Hayes 2001) as the learning device responsible for such development. Thus, the GLA initially performs the classification of language sounds via their auditory distributions, a mechanism that can be called *auditory-driven perceptual learning*. In order to avoid the null perception of Tableau 3, the infant's GLA first acts as an *identity matching* device which will *force* the grammar to classify any auditory input as its perceived counterpart. That is, the GLA will tell the infant that she should have categorized [670 Hz] as /670/. As a result, the constraint *CATEG(/670/) will be demoted in order to increase the match between input and output. This identity matching mechanism is demonstrated in Tableau (6). Here we see that, because of the command given by her GLA, the infant automatically realizes that the null perception is incorrect, as depicted by the asterisks, and that she should have classified the auditory input as its perceived counterpart, as depicted by the check mark.

(6)   GLA identity matching procedure

[670 Hz]	*CATEG (/630/)	*CATEG (/670/)	PERCEIVE ([670])	*WARP (40)
/630 Hz/	*!			
√ /670 Hz/		*!→		*
☞ /–/			←*	

As we can see in the example, the identity matching procedure performed by the GLA will result in the lowering of the constraint with the value of the incoming auditory event, in this case 670 Hz, and in the rising of the PERCEIVE constraint for this same value. Consequently, the next time that the infant hears [670 Hz] it will be more likely that she perceives it as /670 Hz/. It is important to mention that although the infant will hear a large number of auditory inputs, not all *CATEG constraints will be demoted equally fast because the auditory values with which language sounds are produced commonly have particular frequency distributions. Consider, for instance, how F1 values are distributed in the production of CE /æ/ and /ɛ/. Figure 7 shows idealized F1 distributions of the CE vowels, assuming that they form Gaussian shapes with a standard deviation of 0.166 octaves.

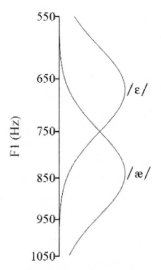

Figure 7.   F1 distributions of CE /æ/ and /ɛ/.

We can observe that the peaks of the two Gaussian curves lie at 670 and 840 Hz. These two values represent the most common tokens for the vowels /ɛ/ and /æ/ respectively. Boersma, Escudero and Hayes further propose that GLA auditory-driven learning changes the infant's perception grammar to appropriately cope with the distributional properties of her production environment. Tableau (7) illustrates how the infant perception grammar handles a rather uncommon F1 value, e.g. [710 Hz], in the vowel productions of CE speakers.

(7)   Infant perception after some identity matching learning

[710 Hz]	*CATEG (/750/)	*CATEG (/710/)	*CATEG (/670/)	*WARP (40)
☞ /670 Hz/			*	*
/710 Hz/		*		*
/750 Hz/	*!			

As we can see, the high frequency of 670 Hz in the CE environment has resulted in the low ranking of the constraint that limits its categorization as /670/. In contrast, because of the uncommon nature of auditory values such as 710 Hz and 750 Hz, the constraints that ban their perceived counterparts are high ranked. As a result, the infant's grammar will choose the most frequent candidate because of the low ranking of the corresponding *CATEG constraint. In the example of Tableau (7) we only see a simplified list of perceived candidates due to space limitations but it is of importance to bear in mind that any F1 value is a potential perceived candidate during auditory-driven learning.

Boersma, Escudero and Hayes (2003) explain how a reiteration of *frequency-driven categorization* leads to the mapping of several auditory inputs onto the most frequently perceived categories. That is, the infant's GLA adjusts the perception grammar in such a way that auditory values will be mapped onto a finite number of auditory categories, i.e. the most frequent ones. Crucially, this finite set of categories will automatically be turned into more abstract categories corresponding to the ones produced in the infant's environment. In the case of the CE infant, the two categories that result from the auditory-driven learning of the F1 distributions in Figure 7 can be called /mid-low/ and /low/.[6]

---

6. Although this paper only discusses the perception of two categories and not that of a system of vowel sounds, we use vowel height phonological features to refer to the categories present in the baby's lexicon. This is because the model proposes that sound categorization is unidimensional in early stages of acquisition and that the integration of dimensions, such as F1,

This GLA auditory-learning is compatible with the recent findings that suggest that infants are able to calculate the statistical distributions of the auditory values of sound productions and that this ability leads to the creation of phonetic categories (cf. Maye, Werker and Gerken 2002). Furthermore, it leads to the same warping of the infant perceptual space that has been shown to occur in the first year of life (Kuhl 1991).

With respect to further perceptual development, Boersma, Escudero and Hayes (2003) propose that once an abstract lexicon is in place the infant's GLA can re-rank the mapping constraints in the perception grammar when faced with mismatches between perceived and lexicalized representations. This second mechanism is known as lexicon-driven learning because the abstract lexical representations trigger re-rankings in the perception grammar, leading to optimal perception. For instance, imagine that a [785 Hz] production is intended as a /mid-low/ vowel but the child, by mistake, perceives it as a /low/ vowel, as shown in Tableau (8).

(8)   GLA lexicon-driven learning

[785 Hz] /b – mid vowel – k/	785 Hz not /mid-low/	785 Hz not /low/
√ /mid-low/	*!→	
☞ /low/		←*

At this point the baby has access to the semantic context of the words she hears, which in this case reveals that the speaker intended a word containing a /mid-low/ vowel, as shown in the input to the grammar. Therefore, the child will automatically notice that in this context the correct perception should have been /mid-low/, as depicted by the check mark. When confronted with this situation, the child's GLA re-ranks the constraints in the perception grammar so as to enable the perception of the next [785 Hz] token as /low/. Specifically, this is achieved by lowering the constraint against perceiving the acoustic value as /low/ and by simultaneously raising the one against perceiving the same value as /mid-low/, a procedure that was first proposed and described in Boersma (1998). This second type of perceptual learning results in the category

---

F2 and duration to form vowels such as /æ/ and /ɛ/ only occurs later in life, as will be mentioned in the next paragraph. In addition, the model proposes that adult sound categorization is characterized by the integration of multiple cues for the perception of sounds and therefore the modelling of adult L1 and L2 categorization employs vowel segments as the candidates of an adult perception grammar.

boundary shifts which have been shown to occur developmentally in infants and children (cf. Nittrouer and Miller 1997; Gerrits 2001; Jones 2003). The question for now is whether the same two types of learning mechanisms are present in adult L2 acquisition. The remainder of this article presents a phonological model for explaining the development of sound perception in second languages. This L2 model is based on the Linguistic Perception framework for sound perception and L1 acquisition discussed above.

3.   L2 Linguistic Perception of SIMILAR L2 sounds

The Second-Language Linguistic Perception (L2LP) model aims at describing, explaining, and predicting L2 sound perception at the initial, developmental, and end states. In this paper, the model will be applied to the acquisition of L2 sounds that are phonemically equivalent but phonetically different from L1 sounds, which are also called SIMILAR L2 sounds. For this L2 scenario, the model predicts that learners will equate two L2 phonemes with two L1 phonemes for purposes of lexical storage, as shown on the left of Figure 8. This lexical equation has an origin in perception because many tokens of the L2 sounds have auditory properties which are similar to the properties of the corresponding L1 sounds. However, this scenario also features a mismatch in the mapping from auditory events to phonological categories. This is because some tokens or phonetic realizations, commonly written between '[ ]', of the L2 categories are unlikely to be perceived as their L1 phonological counterparts, as depicted by the thick lines in Figure 8, right.

According to the L2LP model, if two L2 sounds are equated to a single sound in the L1, the learner faces the common NEW sounds scenario. But if two L2 sounds are equated to two L1 sounds, the learner faces a SIMILAR scenario. This differentiation between "new" and "similar" sounds is also found in many other models of L2 sound perception, such as Flege's *Speech Learning Model*

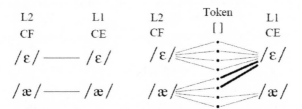

Figure 8.   Phonemic equation and perceptual mapping in the SIMILAR L2 perception scenario.

(Flege 1995, 2003), Best's *Perceptual Assimilation model* (Best 1995, Best and Tyler 2007), Major's *Ontogeny Phylogeny Model* (Major 2001, 2002), Kuhl's *Native Language Magnet* model (Kuhl 2000), and Brown's *Phonological Interference* model (Brown 1998, 2000). These proposals make diametrically opposite claims regarding L2 similar sounds, namely they either suggest that this scenario poses *no* L2 learning challenge (Brown, Best, and Kuhl), or that it poses *the greatest* L2 challenge (Major and Flege). The authors that follow the first approach share the idea that the presence of L2 sounds, features, or phonetic dimensions in the L1 guarantees the absence of an L2 perceptual learning problem, and therefore a SIMILAR scenario does not pose a challenge to either the L2 learner or the researcher. In contrast, the authors that follow the second approach claim that SIMILAR L2 sounds are the most difficult to acquire because the L2 learner will not be able to master them without an effect on their L1. For instance, Flege claims that SIMILAR L2 sounds will be equated to L1 sounds and therefore L2 learners will not be able to form new L2 categories for these sounds, which in turn results in non-native perception.

Thus, different approaches to L2 sound perception assume different and even opposite L2 tasks in a SIMILAR scenario. That is, one approach assumes that L2 learners will have *no* task when learning this type of sounds because of the assumption that having identical categories in L1 and L2 automatically turns the learner into a native-like perceiver. In contrast, the second approach claims that in this scenario the goal of L2 category formation is extremely difficult to achieve and learners may therefore never be able to attain full L2 proficiency when confronted with SIMILAR L2 sounds.

The L2LP model (cf. Escudero and Boersma 2004b and Escudero 2005) that is presented in this paper proposes an alternative approach to the development of SIMILAR L2 sounds. Unlike the first approach to the phenomenon, the L2LP proposes that SIMILAR sounds *do* pose a learning challenge, namely the adjustment of perceptual mappings. In addition, unlike the second approach, the L2LP claims that learners faced with this scenario needs to adjust their existing L1 categories instead of creating new L2 categories. Thus, the L2LP model, also unlike the second approach, claims that SIMILAR L2 sounds are easier to master than L2 sounds that do not exist in the learners' L1, i.e. NEW sounds. Table 2 shows the initial state, learning tasks and degree of difficulty that are hypothesized in the L2LP model.

As we can see, the L2LP assumes that both scenarios pose a learning challenge to the L2 learner. However, the degree of difficulty for these two scenarios is different depending on the learning tasks that need to be performed in order to attain optimal perception. Importantly, these different degrees of L2

Table 2.   Comparative initial states and learning tasks in the NEW and SIMILAR scenarios.

L2LP proposal	Prediction for NEW	Prediction for SIMILAR
Initial state	Too few categories	Same number of categories
Perceptual task	1. *Create* perceptual mappings 2. *Integrate* auditory cues	Adjust perceptual mappings and category boundaries
Representational task	1. *Create* phonetic categories 2. *Create* segments	None
Degree of difficulty	Very difficult	Not difficult

difficulty also refer to the number of learning mechanisms involved in the two scenarios. That is, the NEW scenario, in which the learning task is to create new perceptual mappings and categories, will involve both the learning mechanisms of category creation and of boundary shifting in L1 (cf. §2.2), while the SIMILAR scenario will *only* involve the boundary shifting mechanism. In the next sections, I show how the L2LP's principled separation between perception grammars and sound representations is used to more adequately explain the initial state, learning tasks, development and ultimate attainment in learning to perceive L2 SIMILAR sounds.

3.1   L2LP ingredient 1: comparing the L1 and the target L2

The L2LP model proposes that the first step into explaining L2 sound perception is to describe the optimal perception of each of the languages involved. In §2, it was mentioned that this hypothesized optimal perception was attested in the categorization of human listeners. Recall that the optimal perception hypothesis says that an optimal listener has a perception grammar that has been shaped by the acoustic properties of her production environment. Thus, if our aim is, for instance, to explain how CE listeners can learn to perceive CF /æ/ and /ɛ/, we must *first* describe the optimal perception of CE and of CF monolingual listeners.

Further, the L2LP model makes a principled distinction between perceptual mappings (performed by the perception grammar) and sound representations (constructed by the perception grammar). One of the model's main claims is that analysing mappings and categories separately results in an adequate description and explanation of the comparative knowledge underlying sound perception in listeners with different language backgrounds. For instance, the productions of the same abstract categories /æ/ and /ɛ/ exhibit different F1 distributions in CF and CE. The average F1 values for the CE vowels are 840 Hz and 681 Hz respectively, the acoustic distance between them is $\log2(840/681) = 0.3$ octaves, and therefore the boundary between their productions can be located at $\log2(840)-0.15 = 9.563$ octaves which is equivalent to 756 Hz. In contrast, the average F1 values for the CF vowels are 728 Hz and 557 Hz, the F1 distance between them is 0.39 octaves, and their boundary lies at 637 Hz. Therefore, optimal perceivers of each language will behave differently when categorizing the same set of F1 values, as shown in Figure 9. Note that the boundaries in the figure are only optimal if we assume that the input tokens only differ along the F1 dimension, i.e. if they have ambiguous duration values.

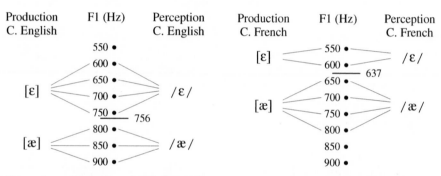

Figure 9.   CE (top) and CF (bottom) perceptual mappings and representations for /æ/ and /ɛ/.

We can observe that tokens between 637 and 757 Hz will be categorized as /ɛ/ by an optimal CE listener but as /æ/ by an optimal CF listener. Note that in both languages the tokens that have the boundary values boundaries, namely 756 Hz for CE vowel productions and 637 for CE, are the most ambiguous tokens for these two vowel categories. That is, assuming that the listeners' only choices are these two vowels, the tokens with boundary values will be categorized 50% of the time as /æ/ and 50% as /ɛ/ in each language. With respect to the cross-linguistic differences, tokens with values within the two languages' boundaries, i.e. between 637 Hz and 756 Hz, will be mainly categorized as /æ/ by CF listener but both as /ɛ/ and /æ/ by CE listeners. Thus, we can conclude that for vowel tokens with F1 values above 550 Hz, the CE and the CF optimal perception grammars may output the same two categories /æ/ and /ɛ/ but with different classification distributions, resulting from a difference in perceptual boundary locations.

An important prediction concerning the learning of L2 sounds is that there are two learning tasks, a perceptual and representational one. Crucially, when perceptual mappings are the only source of difference, the learner will just have a perceptual learning task. Thus, this L1 and target L2 comparison can be used to determine the initial state for the L2 learning process, at least if one assumes that L1 categories and L1 perception grammars are fully transferred to the initial state of L2 acquisition, as will be claimed in §3.2 below. In addition, the L1 and L2 comparison allows us to determine the L2 learning tasks, the characteristics of the mechanisms underlying L2 development, and the L1 perception that the learner needs to maintain, as will be described in §3.3–3.5.

3.2   L2LP ingredient 2: the initial state

A SIMILAR scenario will be first manifested as the equation of two L2 phonemes to the correspondent two L1 ones.[7] According to the L2LP model, this situation arises from the automatic and unconscious *reuse* or *copy* of the L1 categories and perception grammar. This L2 initial strategy finds a linguistic formalization in the Full Copying hypothesis, which is the speech perception interpretation of Schwartz and Sprouse's (1996) Full Transfer/Full Access hypothesis.[8] In the case of CE learners of CF, it is proposed that they will use their phonologically equivalent L1 categories /æ/ and /ɛ/ and their L1 optimal perception, i.e., their CE production distributions composed by the average productions and the optimal category boundary, to categorize CF vowels, as shown in Figure 10.

---

7.   It is important to acknowledge that this paper is restricted to one contrast of the L2 that is equated to another contrast in the L1. Clearly, this is a simplification of the acquisition of a vowel or consonant system in L2 acquisition. However, Escudero (2005: ch. 3) claims that every sound contrast in the target L2 could be seen as representing one of three main learning scenarios, namely NEW, SIMILAR and SUBSET. The first scenario refers to the learning of L2 sounds that do not exist in the learner's L1, a scenario, which was described in §3. The third scenario refers to L2 sounds which already exist in the L1 but have multiple L1 correspondents. That is, in this scenario, the L1 has more categories than the L2 and therefore the L2 categories constitute a *subset* of the L1 ones, a scenario which is fully described in Escudero (2005: ch. 6). In this paper, I concentrate on SIMILAR L2 sounds which are sounds that have the same number of counterparts in the L1 but have different production distributions.

8.   The same interpretation is found in Escudero and Boersma (2004b). Importantly, this interpretation provides the linguistic mechanism underlying Best's (1995) *two-category assimilation* and Flege's (1995) *equivalence classification* hypotheses.

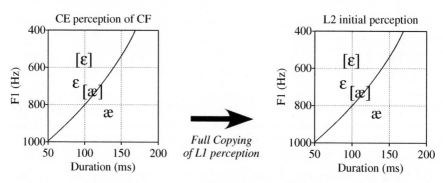

Figure 10.   Cross-language categorization of CF copied onto the L2 initial state. Between brackets: average CF productions. Curve: CE perceptual boundary.

Some support for Full Copying of L1 perception grammars and categories is shown in Escudero (2001) where Spanish learners of Scottish English had almost native-like perception of Scottish English /i/ and /ɪ/, while Spanish learners of Southern English used only duration differences to identify the same two vowels. These results can only mean that the Spanish learners copied their Spanish perception, which categorizes two Spanish vowels when confronted with Scottish English but a single Spanish vowel when confronted with Southern British English (cf. Escudero and Boersma 2004b).

Regarding empirical evidence in support of the use of L1 optimal perception to categorize foreign language stimuli, Escudero and Polka (2003) also tested the perception of CF tokens by monolingual CE listeners who were presented with the 60 CF tokens during the same perception experiment reported in §2.1. It was predicted that CE listeners would use their L1 optimal perception to classify the CF vowels, i.e., that they would integrate duration and F1 acoustic properties when identifying vowels. Figure 11 shows Escudero and

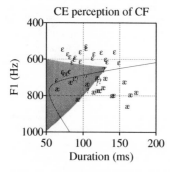

Figure 11.   Cross-language perception of CF /æ/ and /ɛ/ by CE monolingual listeners.

Boersma's (2004a) analysis of the findings. Note that the question marks in the figure represent the tokens that were not categorized as a single vowel by the majority of the listeners, viz. 6 out of 8.

In Figure 11, we observe how eight CE monolingual listeners classify CF /æ/ and /ɛ/ tokens as their own native CE /æ/ and /ɛ/ vowel categories. The solid line in the figure is the listener's perceptual category boundary line which connects the F1 and duration values that are likely to be perceived as both vowels. This line is computed from the responses that the listeners gave to the 60 CF tokens and therefore it represents their perception of non-native vowels or their *cross-language perception*. When comparing this cross-language category boundary line to the ones shown in Figure 9, it may seem that the CE cross-language perception of the CF vowels is closer to the CF native boundary than to the CE native perceptual boundary of the listeners. However, the influence of these listeners' L1 perception is shown in the categorization of the CF tokens in the grey region.

The grey region in Figure 11 represents the area were most native tokens, i.e. English tokens for CE listeners and French tokens for CF listeners, were perceived as /æ/ by CF listeners but as /ɛ/ by CE listeners, as shown in Figure 9 above. In this figure, we observe that, when having to categorize CF tokens, the CE listeners identified most of the CF tokens which fall in the grey region as /ɛ/. This cross-language categorization pattern does not follow the native CF perception but rather the listeners' use of L1 perception strategies. That is, unlike CF native listeners, the CE listeners rely on both vowel duration and F1 to identify vowel categories, a strategy which is shown by the diagonal shape of their cross-language category boundary.

As a result, CF tokens with relatively low F1 values, viz. at approximately 700 Hz, that are produced with a short vowel duration are most likely to be identified as /ɛ/ by these CE listeners, whereas they are categorized as /æ/ by the native CF listeners. In addition and as a result of the usage of their L1 perceptual boundary, the CE cross-language F1 boundary, which falls on the grey region, is 200 Hz lower than that of the native CF boundary.[9]

---

9. The monolingual CE listeners might have relied on other cues (apart from F1 and duration), such as F2 values, to categorize the CF tokens. If the listeners relied on F2 differences, a token with a low F1 value and a short duration may still yield an /æ/ native or cross-language categorization if its F2 value is too low to support /ɛ/ categorizations. In fact, it has been shown that when confronted with ambiguous tokens, English listeners may rely on cues that would only be secondary when categorizing unambiguous native tokens (cf. Hillenbrand, Clark and Houde 2000). However, for purposes of predicting the L2 initial state and development, the two cues considered in the present article, namely F1 and duration, seemed to be extremely informative precisely because L2 learners were shown to have developmentally adjusted their perception of those cues. Furthermore, this development clearly shows that L2 re-

3.3   L2LP Ingredient 3: predicting the L2 learning task

Given their initial state, beginning L2 learners will be able to differentiate between similar L2 sounds because these two L2 sounds 1) match two L1 categories and 2) have production distributions which overlap with the acoustic-auditory regions of two L1 categories. However, there will be a degree of mismatch between the L1 optimal perception grammar and the target language optimal perception grammar because of differences in the productions of the two categories involved. Figure 12 shows the region with the largest mismatch between the CE and CF vowel productions, which was shown for vowel perception in Figures 9 and 11 above.[10]

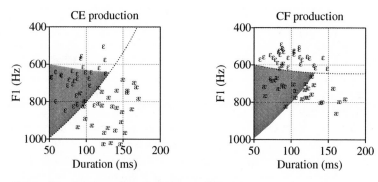

Figure 12.   Region of cross-language difference.

As we can see, about 50% of the CF /æ/ tokens were produced in the grey region while in CE only /ɛ/ tokens can be found in that same region. Thus, we can safely assume that CE listeners will perceive up to half of the CF tokens as the other L1 category with which they have equated the CF vowels, i.e. /ɛ/.[11] This means that CE beginning learners of CF are predicted to categorize many

---

categorization is possible and that it is performed through the adjustment of perceptual boundaries and perceptual cue weighting or trading, which is an instance of L1-like development.

10. When looking at the figures, one can also think of the top-right corner of the figure as a region of mismatch. However, only one token of the CF vowels and none of the CE vowels had values that fell on this acoustic area. Therefore, it cannot be said that there is a production mismatch in this area, and consequently it cannot be predicted that this area will constitute a problem in L2 perception because the learners may never hear tokens with such values.

11. However, as we have seen in the previous section, the CE listeners may be able to rely on other cues to correctly categorize the CF vowels as one of their two L1 categories. If we assume that they can only rely on F1 and/or duration the prediction of 50 % incorrect categorizations still holds.

tokens in that region as /ɛ/ and not as /æ/. In addition, the learners will some-times access words in their L2 lexicon that were not intended by the speaker of the target language because an inaccurate perception will trigger access of an incorrect lexical item. Therefore, their learning task will be to adjust their ini-tial L2 perception grammar, which is a copy of their L1 perception grammar, so as to shift their L1 boundary to the location of the L2 boundary, i.e. from the dotted line to the solid line shown in Figure 13.

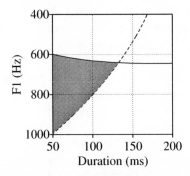

Figure 13. Region of cross-language perceptual mismatch (in grey) and L2 learning task for CE learners of CF. Dashed line: L2 initial state. Bold line: Target L2 boundary.

As can be seen, in order for a learner to obtaining native-like perception in CF, a *shift* in the category boundary needs to occur, i.e., from the dotted line to the solid line delimiting the grey region at the bottom and top respectively. This shift or adjustment, then, represents the L2 learning task because it defines the way in which the initial L2 perception grammar will need to change in order for the learner to acquire optimal L2 perception. In the case at hand, the initial L2 perception of CE learners of CF will need to change the perception of two dimensions, namely duration and F1, in order to turn their diagonal boundary, as represented by the dotted curve, into the CF optimal boundary, as represented by the solid line. That is, they must learn to ignore the durational differences between vowel tokens and to shift their F1 boundary between /æ/ and /ɛ/ to a higher location. Specifically, they need to classify the tokens in the grey region, i.e. tokens with durations shorter than 110 ms and with F1 values between 600 and 780 Hz, as their L2 /æ/ category instead of an L2 /ɛ/ category.

3.4   L2LP Ingredient 4: L2 development

The L2LP model provides a formal account of the learning mechanisms involved in the L2 learning task, an account that is based on the LP framework
discussed in §2.1 and in Escudero and Boersma (2004b). Crucially, it is proposed that L2 learners have access to the same GLA learning mechanisms
available for L1 learning, namely auditory-guided category formation and lex-
icon-guided boundary shifting (cf. §2.2).

In the learning of SIMILAR L2 sounds, it is predicted that L2 development
will only involve a change in the perception grammar because the copied L1
abstract phonological categories are retained and remain in use for L2 lexical
representation. Given that boundary shifts along different dimensions are also
the result of GLA lexicon-driven learning (cf. §2.1.2), the CE learners' task
can be performed by this L1-like learning mechanism. Recall that this type of
learning mechanism is activated when there is a mismatch between the perceived category and the speaker's intended word. For instance, if a beginning
CE learner perceives /bɛk/ when a CF speaker produces the French word *bac*
'ferry', GLA lexicon-driven learning will take place. That is, the semantic
context will tell the learner that she should have perceived a different vowel
category, namely the one contained in the word that was intended by the
speaker. Thus, the learners' GLA will demote the constraints against perceiving certain F1 and duration values as the L2 /æ/ category, as shown in Tableau
(9). Note that this constraint ranking is identical to the adult CE ranking shown
in Tableau (3) for duration but different for F1 constraints because of the new
value of 750 Hz as input to the grammar. That is, a value of 750 Hz is 0.69
standard deviations (s.d.) away from the mean F1 value for CE /ɛ/ but 0.87
s.d. away from the mean value for /æ/, and therefore this F1 value is less likely to be categorized as /æ/ than as /ɛ/ in the CE grammar:

(9)   Predicted lexicon-driven constraint re-ranking for Canadian English
       learners of Canadian French

[750 Hz, 85 ms] /bæk/	85 ms not /æ/	750 Hz not /æ/	750 Hz not /ɛ/	85 ms not /ɛ/
☞ /bɛk/			←*	←*
/bæk/	*!→	*→		

As proposed for L1 perceptual learning in Tableau (8) in §2.2 above, the error
in Tableau (9) will yield to the same lexical-driven perceptual learning performed by the Gradual Learning Algorithm, an adjustment which will gradual-

ly change the ranking of the constraints in the L2 perception grammar. In turn, this constraint re-ranking will lead to the two changes which could be observed in the L2 vowel categorization by CE learners of CF, namely 1) the CE learners learned to ignore the duration differences between the L2 vowels, and 2) they gradually shifted their initial F1 boundary location between the two L2 vowels. The deminishing importance of vowel duration is instantiated as a new ranking of duration-to-vowel cue constraints in the perception grammar. That is, duration constraints are now ranked in such a way that they play hardly any role in determining the winning L2 vowel category. As a consequence, the CE learner will exhibit a horizontal L2 boundary situated at a lower F1 value than her original L1 boundary. Figure 14 illustrates this gradual multidimensional boundary shift.

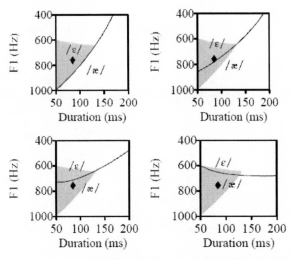

Figure 14.   Predicted category boundary shift for CE learners of CF /æ/ and /ɛ/.

In sum, it is predicted that in this scenario the learner will first equate two L2 categories to two L1 categories and therefore starts out with a near-optimal L2 perception. As a result of the mismatch between her copied L1 perception and the optimal target L2 perception, the learner will not be able to correctly categorize all L2 tokens. When faced with this situation, the learners' GLA, which in this situation acts as an error-driven constraint re-ranking mechanism triggered by mismatches between the output of perception and the lexicon, will change their perception grammars by small steps in order to decrease the probability of semantic mismatches. Finally, an optimal L2 perception will be attained when such mismatches no longer occur.

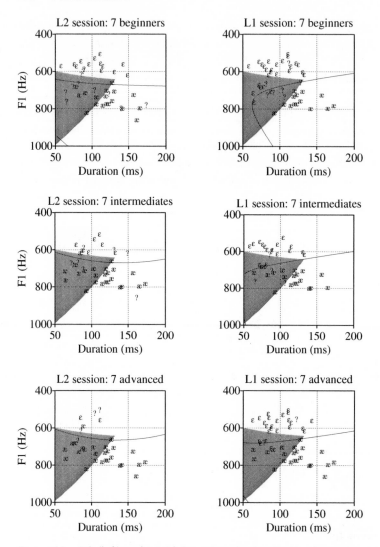

Figure 15. L2 (left) and L1 (right) categorization for the three groups of CE learners of CF.

As for empirical evidence that supports this prediction, Escudero (under review) examined the L1 and L2 perception of 21 CE learners of CF who were enrolled in a French language course at the McGill Language Centre. All learners were originally from non-French speaking regions of Canada that are outside the province of Quebec. They had monolingual Canadian English-speaking parents, and had come to Montreal at the age of 18 years. Their age at the time of testing was between 18 and 25. The learners were divided into three exposure groups, viz. beginning, intermediate, and advanced, on the basis of a language background questionnaire that determined their exposure to French in comparison with English. The target stimuli were the same 60 CF /æ/ and /ɛ/ tokens presented in the monolingual and cross-language experiments reported above, which were now presented as L2 stimuli. As for the response options, we asked the subjects to choose from five French keywords, viz. *qui* 'who', *dix* 'ten', *fait* 'do', *chez* 'at', and *ta* 'your'. The squares on the left of Figure 15 show the L2 perception for the three groups of learners while the squares on the right show the learners' L1 perception of the same CF tokens (see §3.5). Note that the question marks in the figure represent the tokens that were not categorized as a single vowel by the majority of the learners in each group, viz. 5 out of 7.

When looking at plot on the right of the figure, we can observe that none of the learner groups use duration differences when categorizing the L2 vowels, as shown by the horizontal shape of their category boundaries. This means that these learners needed just a little exposure to CF in order to acquire the optimal cue reliance, as can be inferred from the comparison of the first square on the left of Figure 15 with the CF boundary shown in Figure 6, above in §2.1. We can also observe a developmental adjustment in the location of the F1 boundary: the beginning learners incorrectly categorize F1 values in the grey region as CF /ɛ/, whereas the intermediate and advanced learners correctly categorize almost all tokens in the same region. Thus, taking the perception of the three groups together, it can be observed that learners categorize more and more L2 /æ/ vowels from the grey region as the optimal one, i.e. /æ/, as a function of their exposure level. This is visualized in Figure 16 below.[12] This means that CF /æ/ tokens produced with low F1 values and short durations that are categorized as /ɛ/ in monolingual CE perception are now being categorized as /æ/ in L2 CF. A ranked correlation test performed on the number of /æ/ responses for tokens that fall in the grey region and the learner's exposure level yielded a significant result (one-tailed Kendall's tau-b = 0.45, $N = 21$, $p = 0.004$, i.e. p from zero = 0.23%), which means that the observed development is statistically reliable.

---

12. As can be seen in the figure, one of the subjects in the intermediate group exhibits an unexpectedly low number of /æ/ responses. This seems to suggest that there are individual differences in the speed in which learners can achieve native-like performance in the learning of L2 similar sounds. A longitudinal study is needed to investigate the further development not only of this single outlier but also that of the other subjects who seem to, at this point in their acquisition process, conform to the model's predicted developmental path.

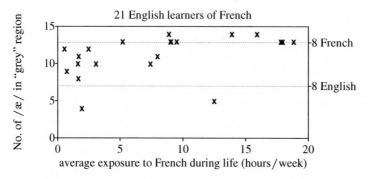

Figure 16. Categorization of the 15 CF /æ/ tokens that fall in the grey region during the learners' French session (L2 session). Horizontal dotted lines: Average monolingual CF and CE perception (8 listeners per language).

3.5   L2LP ingredient 5: the L2 end state

The interrelation between the L1 and the L2 perception systems can constrain the L2 end state as well as the L1 perception after L2 development has occurred. Cook (2002), following Francis (1999), proposes that there are three logical possibilities for how the representations of two language systems interact in the mind of a second language learner. Figure 17 shows an adapted version of Cook's graph for the possibilities (2002: 11). In a *separate* systems view, L1 and L2 sound categories are thought to belong to autonomous systems. The *mixed* view advocates that L1 and L2 sound systems are, in fact, a single representational system. This perspective has, in turn, two possibilities, namely *merged* and *integrated* systems: merged representations imply no language differentiation, whereas integrated representations refer assumes that the two languages are represented within the same system but are tagged differently. Finally, in the *connected* view, L1 and L2 representations are mostly distinct but they may share some elements or properties.

The L2LP model advances the separate perception grammars hypothesis which states that L2 learners and bilinguals have separate systems for perceiving their two languages, i.e., the left most option in the figure. In contrast, Flege's (1995) Speech Learning Model (SLM) suggests that the perception and representation of L1 and L2 sounds is handled within a common L1-L2 phonological space (p. 239) in which sounds from the two languages coexist, as in the integrated system view. These different views yield two different predictions for the L2 end state. That is, the L2LP predicts that an L2 learner can attain optimal L1 and L2 perception because they are handled by two different systems, whereas the SLM predicts that any L2 development will inevitably affect the L1 because L1 and L2 development occur within a common space that gets adjusted by L2 or L1 changes.

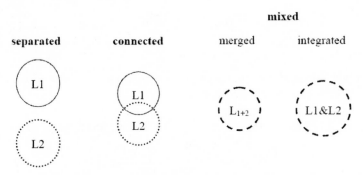

Figure 17.   Possible cognitive status of sound categories and perception processes in L2 learners (adapted from Cook 2002).

A key construct that can be used to evaluate these contradictory predictions may be Grosjean's (2001) hypothesis of the bilingual's *language modes* hypothesis which is defined as "the state of activation of the bilingual's languages and language processing mechanisms at a given point in time" (p. 2). According to this hypothesis the bilingual's languages can be activated selectively or in parallel depending on a number of linguistic and extra-linguistic variables, such as the language of the experimenter, the task, the stimuli, the instructions, etc., which Grosjean defines as a the state of continuum between a monolingual mode and a bilingual mode. The L2LP interpretation of this hypothesis presupposes that L2 learners and bilinguals exhibit different language modes as a result of the activation of separate perception grammars during online perception. Following this interpretation, an advanced L2 learner is predicted to have an optimal perception in the monolingual setting of each language.

Thus, in a SIMILAR scenario, learners are predicted to be able to adjust their L2 category boundaries without affecting their already optimal L1 boundaries, as shown in Figure 18. Importantly, these language setting effects are particularly relevant in the SIMILAR learning scenario because here we can test whether learners use the same number of categories while demonstrating different perceptual behaviour in the monolingual L1 and L2 conditions.

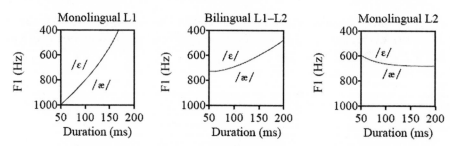

Figure 18.   Predicted three different types of perceptual behaviour in advanced Canadian English learners of Canadian French.

With respect to the available evidence in favour or against the hypothesis of separate grammars, Caramazza, Yeni-Komshian, Zurif and Carbone (1973), Elman, Diehl and Buchwald (1977), and Flege and Eefting (1987) found that bilinguals and L2 learners exhibit perceptual category boundaries that are at an intermediate location when compared to the monolingual L1 and L2 boundaries. This finding can have two possible interpretations. It can be said that the bilingual and L2 listeners possessed a single grammar or it can be said that they possessed two grammars that were both activated during the perception experiments. If the latter is the correct interpretation, it should be possible to gather L1-like and L2-like category boundaries from the same learners when they are conditioned to use only one of their languages. If this can be done, it would mean that the intermediate L1-L2 boundaries do not represent a property of sound perception in bilinguals and L2 learners, but they are the result of performance.

Thus, according to the L2LP model, the finding of intermediate perception boundaries results from the parallel activation of two grammars during online perception, and does not, therefore, confirm the existence of a single grammar. The L2LP model proposes that L1 and L2 are handled by two different grammars with the same constraints but different rankings. At any time, either of these two grammars can be activated for auditory input, depending on the linguistic and paralinguistic evidence for the activation of one language system and the inhibition of another. For ambiguous auditory events, i.e. tokens which belong to the distributions of both languages, the output of both grammars will be equally likely to become the chosen candidate. This is because in 50% of the cases the winner of one grammar will be chosen, and in 50% of the cases the winner of the other grammar will be chosen. Consequently, the category boundary between vowels which have similar distributions in the L1 and the L2 can exhibit intermediate properties between monolingual categorization, if the language of the incoming token is not clear or if the listener is in a fully bilingual mode. The result of the activation of two perception grammars, due either to ambiguous tokens or to an ambiguous language setting, is depicted in the middle plot of Figure 18.

Escudero (under review) presents data that support the hypothesis of separate perception grammars for bilinguals and L2 learners. In this study, the author conditioned CE learners of CF to use only one of their languages in two different testing sessions, namely a monolingual L1 session and monolingual L2 session. In each session, the learners listened to the same CF tokens of /æ/ and /ɛ/ embedded in the language condition of the session. For instance, in their French session, they were tested by a French experimenter, were addressed in French only, and were told that the stimuli they would hear were French. In addition, prior to the target perceptual experiment, the listeners were presented with a French passage and had to answer five general comprehension questions, all in French. This first task lasted for approximately 10 minutes and was used to enhance the use of French only. In the English session, the learners answered language background questions posed by a monolingual English-speaking experimenter, an activity that lasted 10 minutes and was performed prior to the English perception experiment.

Escudero's results show that the perception of the same CF tokens presented in the monolingual L1 condition turned out to be very different from the perception found in the monolingual L2 condition, as can be seen when comparing the squares on the right of Figure 15, above in §3.4, to the squares on the left. Figure 19 shows the learners' categorization of the CF /æ/ tokens that were produced in the grey region when listening to them as English, as opposed to the results of listening to them as French (Figure 16 above).

When comparing the results of Figures 16 and 19, it is easily observable that the learners perceive the same tokens differently depending on the language condition. Thus, the same ranked correlation performed for Figure 16 yields no effect of experience level when performed on the data shown in Figure 19. In addition, a paired-samples test conducted on the number of /æ/ responses in the results of the two language conditions confirms that the difference between listening to the same 15 CF tokens as French or as English is highly significant ($t = 4.51$, $N = 21$, $p < 0.0001$).

Thus, these findings suggest that L2 learners can achieve native-like L2 competence while maintaining their L1 perception in its original state. This means that L2 speakers have different ways of perceiving their two languages, L1 and L2, suggesting that they have two different perception grammars for them. Consequently, it can be said that the L2LP model's hypothesis that L2 speakers have two separate grammars is borne out and that the intermediate boundaries found in previous studies result from the activation of two separate grammars in a bilingual setting.

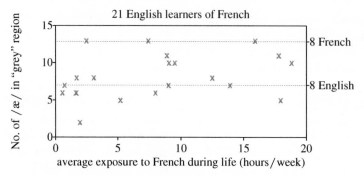

Figure 19. Categorization of the 15 CF /æ/ tokens that fall on the grey region category during the learners' English session (L1 session). Horizontal dotted lines: Average mononoligual CF and CE perception (8 listeners per language).

4.   Conclusions

In this paper, I argued that speech perception is a linguistic phenomenon that should be brought into the domain of phonological modelling. This claim is based on phonetic and psycholinguistic evidence that shows that adult speech perception is shaped by experience with a specific language, making it exclusively appropriate for that specific language. Further, I proposed a number of phonological, phonetic, and psycholinguistic criteria that a model should incorporate in order to arrive at a highly comprehensive and explanatory model for sound perception. Subsequently, I demonstrated that the LP model complies with these criteria. Importantly, the L1 acquisition extension of the LP model turned out to successfully lay out the mechanisms involved in learning to perceive the sounds of a language. With respect to the main objective of this paper, viz., explaining L2 sound perception, the L2LP model was shown to successfully describe, explain, and predict the learning of SIMILAR L2 sounds. This is summarized in Table 3.

Thus, I have shown that the L2LP model makes specific and explicit predictions for the perception of SIMILAR L2 sounds. First, the model predicts that listeners are optimal perceivers of their native language, a prediction that was borne out in the perception of /æ/ and /ɛ/ by monolingual CE and CF listeners. Second, it predicts that beginning L2 learners start with a copy of their L1 perception grammar and L1 perceived categories, a prediction that was confirmed by the perception of CE learners of CF because these learners made use of two L1 categories to perceive two L2 categories. Third, it was predicted that the learner would adjust her L1 perception to become an optimal L2 listener. It was found that the learners' perceptual boundaries of F1 and duration indeed gradually shifted in the direction of the boundaries for L2. Crucially, the model provides a formalization of the learning mechanism that leads to perceptual boundary shifting.

Table 3.   The five L2LP predictions for a SIMILAR L2 sound perception scenario and the evidence to support them.

L2LP ingredients	Predictions for SIMILAR	Finding
Optimal L1 & L2	CE and CF monolingual listeners will exhibit optimal L1 perception	Borne out
Initial state	Beginning CE learners will be equal to monolingual CE listeners	Partially borne out
Learning task	Boundary shift for CE learners	Borne out
Development	Lexicon-driven learning	Indirectly borne out
End state	CE learners will **attain** optimal L2 perception and will **maintain** their optimal L1 perception	Borne out

Finally, the L2LP hypothesizes that both L1 and L2 can be optimal because they are handled by two separate grammars. The data presented showed that CE learners of CF manifested a significant difference between their L1 and L2 perception of the same vowel tokens, thus confirming this prediction of the L2LP model. However, an even more rigorous procedure (especially with respect to the nature of the stimuli presented) is required to show whether the L1 perception of L2 learners remains monolingual-like and whether the difference between L1 and L2 perception increases with L2 exposure.

In sum, it can be concluded that the L2LP phonological proposal for L2 sound perception currently provides the most comprehensive description, explanation, and prediction of L2 sound perception. In this paper, it has been shown that the model can successfully handle the acquisition of L2 sounds that are phonemically equivalent but phonetically different from L1 sounds, which are also called SIMILAR L2 sounds. For the way the model handles other L2 sound learning scenarios such as NEW and SUBSET L2 sounds the interested reader is referred to Escudero and Boersma (2004b) and Escudero (2005).

References

Best, Catherine T.
1995   A direct realist view of cross-language speech perception. In: Wini-
              fred Strange (ed.), *Speech Perception and Linguistic Experience:*
              Theoretical and Methodological Issues in Cross-Language Speech
              Research, 171–203. Timonium: York Press.
Best, Catherine T., and Michael D. Tyler
2007   Nonnative and second-language speech perception: commonalities
              and complementarities. In: Ocke-Schwen Bohn and Murray J. Mu-
              nro (eds.), *Language Experience in Second-Language Speech Learn-*
              ing: In Honor of James Emil Flege, 13–34. Amsterdam: John Ben-
              jamins.
Boersma, Paul
1998   *Functional Phonology*. Ph.D. dissertation, University of Amsterdam.
              The Hague: Holland Academic Graphics.
Boersma, Paul, Paola Escudero, and Rachel Hayes
2003   Learning abstract phonological from auditory phonetic categories: an
              integrated model for the acquisition of language-specific sound cate-
              gories. In: Marie-Josep Solé, Daniel Recasens and Joaquín Romero
              (eds.), *Proceedings of the 15th International Congress of Phonetic*
              Sciences, 1013–1016. Barcelona: Causal Productions.
Boersma, Paul, and Bruce Hayes
2001   Empirical tests of the Gradual Learning Algorithm. *Linguistic In-*
              quiry 32: 45–86.
Broselow, Ellen
2004   Language contact phonology: richness of the stimulus, poverty of the
              base. *North-Eastern Linguistic Society* 34: 1–22.
Brown, Cynthia
1998   The role of the L1 grammar in the L2 acquisition of segmental struc-
              ture. *Second Language Research* 14: 136–193.
Brown, Cynthia
2000   The interrelation between speech perception and phonological acqui-
              sition from infant to adult. In: John Archibald (ed.), *Second Lan-*
              guage Acquisition and Linguistic Theory, 4–63. Oxford: Blackwell.
Bürki-Cohen, Judith, Joanne. L. Miller, and Peter D. Eimas
2001   Perceiving non-native speech. *Language and Speech* 44: 149–169.
Caramazza, Alfonso, Grace Yeni-Komshian, Edgar Zurif, and Ettore Carbone
1973   The acquisition of a new phonological contrast: the case of stop con-
              sonants in French-English bilinguals. *Journal of the Acoustical So-*
              ciety of America 5: 421–428.

Cook, Vivian J.
2002   Background to the L2 user. In: Vivian J. Cook (ed.), *Portraits of the L2 User*, 1–28. Clevedon: Multilingual Matters.
Dupoux, Emmanuel, Cristophe Pallier, Kazuhiko Kakehi, and Jacques Mehler
2001   New evidence for prelexical phonological processing in word recognition. *Language and Cognitive Processes* 5: 491–505.
Elman, Jeffrey, Randy Diehl, and Susan Buchwald
1977   Perceptual switching in bilinguals. *Journal of the Acoustical Society of America* 62: 971–974.
Escudero, Paola
2001   The role of the input in the development of L1 and L2 sound contrasts: language-specific cue weighting for vowels. In: Anna H.-J. Do, Laura Domínguez and Aimee Johansen (eds.), *Proceedings of the 25th Annual Boston University Conference on Language Development*, 50–261. Somerville, Mass.: Cascadilla Press.
Escudero, Paola
2005   *Linguistic Perception and Second Language Acquisition.* Ph.D. dissertation, Utrecht University.
Escudero, Paola
under review Evidence for gradual L2 re-categorization: boundary shifts in the L2 perception of Canadian French /æ/ and /ɛ/.
Escudero, Paola, Titia Benders, and Silvia C. Lipski
in press   Native, non-native and L2 perceptual cue weighting for Dutch vowels: the case of Dutch, German, and Spanish listeners. *Journal of Phonetics.*
Escudero, Paola, and Paul Boersma
2003   Modelling the perceptual development of phonological contrasts with Optimality Theory and the Gradual Learning Algorithm. In: Sundha Arunachalam, Elsi Kaiser and Alexander Williams (eds.), *Proceedings of the 25th Annual Penn Linguistics Colloquium. Penn Working Papers in Linguistics* 8: 71–85.
Escudero, Paola, and Paul Boersma
2004a   L2 re-categorization of an 'old' phonological contrast. Poster presented at the *9th Laboratory Phonology Conference*, University of Illinois at Urbana-Champaign.
Escudero, Paola, and Paul Boersma
2004b   Bridging the gap between L2 speech perception research and phonological theory. *Studies in Second Language Acquisition* 26: 551–585.
Escudero, Paola, and Linda Polka
2003   A cross-language study of vowel categorization and vowel acoustics. In: Marie-Josep Solé, Daniel Recasens and Joaquín Romero (eds.), *Proceedings of the 15th International Congress of Phonetic Sciences,* 861–864. Barcelona: Causal Productions.

Flege, James E.
1995   Second language speech learning: theory, findings, and problems. In: Winifred Strange (ed.), *Speech Perception and Linguistic Experience: Theoretical and Methodological Issues in Cross-Language Speech Research*, 233–277. Timonium: York Press.

Flege, James E.
2003   Assessing constraints on second-language segmental production and perception. In: Antje S. Meyer and Niels O. Schiller (eds.), *Phonetics and Phonology in Language Comprehension and Production*, 319–355. Berlin: Mouton de Gruyter.

Flege, James E., and Wieke Eefting
1987   Cross-language switching in stop consonant production and perception by Dutch speakers of English. *Speech Communication* 6: 185–202.

Francis, Wendy S.
1999   Cognitive integration of language and memory in bilinguals: semantic representation. *Psychological Bulletin* 195: 193–222.

Gerrits, Ellen
2001   *The Categorisation of Speech Sounds by Adults and Children*. Ph.D. dissertation, University Utrecht.

Gottfried, Terry L., and Patrice S. Beddor
1988   Perception of temporal and spectral information in French vowels. *Language and Speech* 31: 57–75.

Grosjean, François
2000   The bilingual's language modes. In: Janet Nicol (ed.), *One Mind, Two Languages: Bilingual Language Processing*, 1–22. Oxford: Blackwell.

Hillenbrand, James M., Michael J. Clark, and Robert A. Houde
2000   Some effects of duration on vowel recognition. *Journal of the Acoustical Society of America* 108: 3013–3022.

Hume, Elizabeth, and Keith Johnson
2001   A model of the interplay of speech perception and phonology. In: Elizabeth Hume and Keith Johnson (eds.), *The Role of Speech Perception in Phonology*, 3–26. New York: Academic Press.

Hyman, Larry M.
2001   The limits of phonetic determinism in phonology: *NC revisited. In: Elizabeth Hume and Keith Johnson (eds.), *The Role of Speech Perception in Phonology*, 141–186. New York: Academic Press.

Jacquemot, Charlotte, Christophe Pallier, Denis LeBihan, Stanislas Dehaene, and Emmanuel Dupoux
2003   Phonological grammar shapes the auditory cortex: a functional magnetic resonance imaging study. *Journal of Neuroscience* 23: 9541–9546.

Jones, Caroline
2003   *Development of Phonological Categories in Children's Perception
                of Final Voicing*. Ph.D. dissertation, University of Massachusetts at
                Amherst.
Jusczyk, Peter W., Anne Cutler, and Nancy J. Redanz
1993   Infants' preference for the predominant stress patterns of English
                words. *Child Development* 64: 675–687.
Kewley-Port, Diane
1995   Thresholds for formant-frequency discrimination of vowels in con-
                sonantal context. *Journal of the Acoustical Society of America* 97:
                3139–3146.
Kuhl, Patricia K.
1991   Human adults and human infants show a 'perceptual magnetic ef-
                fect' for the prototypes of speech categories, monkeys do not. *Per-
                ception & Psychophysics* 50: 93–107.
Kuhl, Patricia K.
2000   A new view of language acquisition. *Proceedings of the National
                Academy of Sciences USA* 97: 11850–11857.
Major, Roy C.
2001   *Foreign Accent.* Mahwah, NJ: Lawrence Erlbaum Associates.
Major, Roy C.
2002   The phonology of the L2 user. In: Vivian Cook (ed.), *Portraits of the
                L2 User*, 67–92. Clevedon: Multilingual Matters.
Maye, Jessica, Janet F. Werker, and Lou-Ann Gerken
2002   Infant sensitivity to distributional information can affect phonetic
                discrimination. *Cognition 82:* B101–B111.
McQueen, James M.
2005   Speech perception. In: Koen Lamberts and Rob Goldstone (eds.),
                The Handbook of Cognition, 255–275. London: Sage Publications.
Miller, Joanne L., and Emily R. Dexter
1988   Effects of speaking rate and lexical status on phonetic perception.
                *Journal of Experimental Psychology: Human Perception and Per-
                formance* 14: 369–378.
Miller, Joanne L., and François Grosjean
1997   Dialect effects in vowel perception: the role of temporal information
                in French. *Language and Speech* 40: 277–288.
Miyawaki, Kiichiro, Winifred Strange, Robert R. Verbrugge, Alvin M. Liberman,
James J. Jenkins, and Osamu Fujimura
1975   An effect of linguistic experience: the discrimination of [r] and [l] by
                native speakers of Japanese and English. *Perception & Psychophys-
                ics* 18: 331–340.

Nittrouer, Susan, and Marnie E. Miller
1997   Developmental weighting shifts for noise components of fricative-
            vowel syllables. *Journal of the Acoustical Society of America* 102:
            572–580.
Pater, Joe
2004   Bridging the gap between perception and production with minimally
            violable constraints. In: René Kager, Joe Pater and Wim Zonneveld
            (eds.), *Constraints in Phonological Acquisition*, 219–244. Cam-
            bridge: Cambridge University Press.
Pitt, Mark A., and James M. McQueen
1998   Is compensation for coarticulation mediated by the lexicon? *Journal
            of Memory and Language* 39: 347–370.
Polka, Linda, and Janet F. Werker
1994   Developmental changes in the perception of non-native vowel con-
            trasts. *Journal of Experimental Psychology: Human Perception and
            Performance* 20: 421–435.
Prince, Alan, and Paul Smolensky
1993   *Optimality Theory: Constraint Interaction in Generative Grammar*.
            New Brunswick: Rutgers University Center for Cognitive Science.
Schachter, Daniel L., and Barbara A. Church
1992   Auditory priming: implicit and explicit memory for words and voic-
            es. *Journal of Experimental Psychology: Learning, Memory, and
            Cognition* 18: 521–533.
Schwartz, Bonnie D., and Rex A. Sprouse
1996   L2 cognitive states and the Full Transfer/Full Access model. *Second
            Language Research* 12: 40–72.
Steriade, Donca
2001   Directional asymmetries in place assimilation: a perceptual account.
            In: Elizabeth Hume and Keith Johnson (eds.), *The Role of Speech
            Perception in Phonology*, 219–250. New York: Academic Press.
Strange, Winifred
1995   Cross-language study of speech perception: a historical review. In:
            Winifred Strange (ed.), *Speech Perception and Linguistic Expe-
            rience: Issues in Cross-Language Research*, 3–45. Timonium: York
            Press.
Tesar, Bruce, and Paul Smolensky
2000   *Learnability in Optimality Theory*. Cambridge, MA: MIT Press.
Werker, Janet F., and John S. Logan
1985   Cross-language evidence for three factors in speech perception. *Per-
            ception & Psychophysics* 37: 35–44.
Werker, Janet F., and Richard C. Tees
1984   Cross-language speech perception: evidence for perceptual reorgani-
            zation during the first year of life. *Infant Behaviour and Develop-
            ment* 7: 49–63.

Stress adaptation in loanword phonology: perception and learnability[*]

Ellen Broselow

1. The problem: learnability of interlanguage rankings

Under the widespread assumption that learning a phonological grammar means learning the language-specific rankings of phonological constraints, the framework of Optimality Theory forces us to ask not only what constraint rankings describe the data of a language, but also how those rankings could have been learned. The focus of this paper is on cases in which the second question is not so easily answered. Language contact situations confront speakers with types of structures that are not found in their native language, and in these situations we often find systematic adaptation patterns that are fairly consistent across speakers of the same native language. Analyses of loanword adaptation patterns have often posited fairly intricate webs of constraint rankings in the production grammar that cannot be motivated by the data of either the native or the foreign language. One possible explanation of such apparently unmotivated rankings is that they reflect the universal default. If this is the case, we should expect the same rankings to emerge in all situations where evidence to the contrary is lacking. But as Peperkamp (2005) has argued, there appears to be cross-linguistic variation in adaptation patterns that cannot be attributed to the data of either of the languages in contact. This leaves us with a puzzle: if we find interlanguage production grammar rankings that are a product neither of universal grammar nor of input data, what is their source? In this paper I argue that several adaptation patterns that appear to involve unlearnable rankings of production grammar constraints are actually an effect of the perception grammar.

I will consider two cases of loanword adaptation that have been analyzed in terms of crucial rankings of production grammar constraints, among them a constraint mandating preservation of foreign word stress. In each case, while

---

[*]   This paper has benefitted greatly from feedback from participants in my Fall 2003 seminar in language contact phonology, from colleagues at Stony Brook University, and from the NELS audience, and particularly from the careful comments of the editors and reviewers of this volume. Special thanks are due to Christina Bethin, Dan Finer, Yoonjung Kang, Miran Kim, and Zheng Xu.

the proposed rankings account for the adaptation patterns, it is unclear how these rankings could have been learned from the ambient data. I argue that in neither case are unlearnable rankings necessary; rather, the adaptation patterns can be seen as effects of interference from the native language grammar – specifically, that portion of the grammar that maps the acoustic signal onto phonological representations. I assume (following Boersma 1998) that the perception grammar defines which aspects of the acoustic signal are linguistically significant, causing listeners to misinterpret certain aspects of the contact structures. In this bipartite model, the inventory of structures presented by the contacting language is often richer than that presented by the native language input (the richness of the stimulus). But the listener's perception grammar maps this input onto a more restricted set of phonological representations, providing the adapter with an impoverished base, or set of underlying representations (Boersma 2000; Lassettre and Donegan 1998).

The paper begins with a survey of several types of ranking puzzles in language contact, followed by consideration of the sorts of rankings that we would expect to find in language contact phonology. I then consider examples of the adaptation of stress in borrowed words. The source stress is maintained in both Huave words borrowed from Spanish (Davidson and Noyer 1996) and in Fijian words borrowed from English (Kenstowicz [2003] 2007). However, the two borrowing languages differ in terms of the strategies used to resolve conflicts between the original stress position and the stress position dictated by the native language grammar: such conflicts are resolved in Huave by deletion of segments and in Fijian by lengthening of vowels. These different adaptation patterns have been described in the literature in terms of different rankings of a production grammar constraint MATCHSTRESS (or MAXSTRESS) directing that the position of the source stress should be maintained. But because this constraint is specific to loanwords, it is not clear how the early adapters could have learned its ranking. The contention of this paper is that the maintenance of source stress is not a function of the production grammar at all, but rather is determined by the native language perception/decoding principles that determine how foreign language stress is interpreted. In Huave, stress is demarcative, uniformly falling on the final syllable of the word, which causes Huave listeners to assume that stressed syllables are word-final in Spanish; thus, segmental material following the stressed syllable is lost in the mapping from acoustic signal to lexical representation. Similar loss of posttonic material is found in the adaptation of Spanish words by speakers of K'ichee', which also has uniformly word-final stress; in contrast, in Selayarese, where the position of stress is affected by morphological structure, listeners maintain foreign material following the stress foot. In Fijian, stress serves to enhance lexical contrasts of vowel length. I argue that Fijian listeners hearing a stressed syllable in a position that is normally not stressed interpret this as an indication of underlying vowel length.

2.   Ranking puzzles in language contact phonology

In the OT model of phonological acquisition, it has been proposed that the initial state involves a set of constraints in which markedness constraints are ranked above faithfulness constraints, ensuring that learners begin with the most restrictive grammar (Gnanadesikan [1994] 2004), or that while constraints may initially be unranked, the ranking process favors M >> F rankings (Hayes [1999] 2004; Prince and Tesar [1999] 2004). Aside from the bias toward markedness over faithfulness constraints, the learner establishes a ranking based on input from the ambient language. Where the input data are not sufficient to establish an exhaustive ranking of all constraints, the final state of the grammar could conceivably impose only a partial ranking (Ross 1996; Boersma 1998), or learners could choose an arbitrary ranking of otherwise unrankable constraints (Tesar and Smolensky 2000: 49); in the latter case, we need not assume that all learners would arrive at the same rankings. Given these assumptions, we can identify the following possible ranking patterns in the interlanguage grammar (the grammar that accounts for systematic behavior in loan adaptation and/or second language acquisition):

(1)   Possible ranking patterns in SLA or loan adaptation

  a. M >> F: putative default pattern
  b. F >> M: motivated by marked forms
  c. M >> M, F >> F: mysterious if not motivated by data

While M >> F rankings, as the default, need not be motivated by data, the other rankings are data-driven. But examination of language contact phonology reveals many examples of apparent production grammar rankings that are not obviously motivated by data other than language contact data:

1. Differential difficulty (M >> M): In this case, one foreign language structure is mastered more quickly than another, even though neither appears in the native language. One example of this pattern from second language acquisition involves final obstruent devoicing, which is attested for a number of speakers whose native language (such as Mandarin Chinese and Tswana) allows no obstruent codas of any type, and whose target language allows both voiced and voiceless obstruent codas (Wissing and Zonneveld 1996; Grijzenhout and van Rooij 2001; Eckman 1981; Flege and Davidian 1984; Flege, McCutcheon and Smith 1987; Yavas 1994; Broselow, Chen and Wang 1998; Broselow 2004; Broselow and Xu 2004). The M >> M pattern also underlies much of the evidence for lexical strata, analyzed by Ito and Mester (1995) as involving subgrammars specific to core and peripheral vocabularies.

2. Differential faithfulness (F >> F): In this case, certain aspects of contacting structures are preserved while others are lost. Thus, as discussed below, in borrowings from Spanish into Huave, the stress of the source word is preserved at the price of segmental unfaithfulness (Davidson and Noyer 1996), while in borrowings from Bahasa Indonesia into Selayarese, the source segmental structure is preserved while the source stress may be lost (Broselow 1999). Some F >> F rankings might be explained as the reflection of a universal perceptual similarity hierarchy (Steriade 2001), but some cases appear to violate proposed universal rankings. For example, as Kenstowicz ([2003] 2007) points out, English initial voiced stops in words borrowed into Fijian are realized as prenasalized stops, violating the putative universal ranking of production grammar constraints IDENT(nasal) >> IDENT(voice) proposed by Steriade (2001).

3. Differential repair strategies (F >> F or M >> F): In this case, the source language presents adapters with two or more structures that are equally impossible in the borrowing language, yet speakers use distinct repair strategies in adapting them. For example, in Wolof borrowings from French, obstruent-sonorant onsets are repaired by a copy vowel inserted between the two consonants (*kalas* from French *klas* 'class'), but [s]-stop onsets are repaired by insertion of a default vowel before the two consonants (*estati* from French *staty* 'statue,' Fleischhacker 2000). Since Wolof has no complex onsets of either type, the native language provides no basis for distinguishing them. Similar patterns are found in numerous languages (Broselow 1993; Fleischhacker 2000).

4. Ranking reversals (C1 >> C2, C2 >> C1): Many of the preceding cases involve rankings that are not motivated by the native language data, but are at least not inconsistent with it. In other cases, interlanguage patterns require an actual reversal of the rankings of the native language, even though the contacting language does not appear to present evidence for the new ranking. Thus in Malayalam, single voiceless consonants do not occur intervocalically. In Malayalee English, English intervocalic voiceless stops are realized as voiceless geminates (IDENT(voice) >> IDENT(mora)) although in Malayalam, length distinctions are preserved in preference to voicing distinctions (IDENT(mora) >> IDENT(voice), Mohanan and Mohanan 2003).

Various possible sources of such 'hidden' rankings (Davidson 2000) include the role of frequency in the data (Broselow 2004); the native speaker's articulatory program (Ussishkin and Wedel 2003); and the role of perception (Silverman 1992; Yip 1993; Kenstowicz 2001, [2003] 2007; Kang 2003; Peperkamp 2005). The central claim of this paper is that what at first glance appear to be 'hidden' rankings in the production grammar (that is, rankings that are not in any obvious way learnable from the data) either emerge from input frequency, or reflect rankings in the native language perception grammar that have been learned from native language data.

In the next three sections I consider cases of loan adaptation differing in the extent to which source language stress is preserved, and in the sorts of unfaithfulness that are tolerated to facilitate stress preservation. Two of these cases have been analyzed in the literature in terms of a production grammar constraint (MATCHSTRESS or MAXSTRESS), which applies only to borrowed words. The postulation of a stress preservation constraint, along with the assumption that constraints can be freely ranked across languages, predicts a wide variety of possible loan adaptation patterns. I will argue that whether or not the source stress is maintained in loanwords is a function not of the rankings of production grammar constraints, but rather of the role played by stress in the native language.

3. Adaptation of demarcative stress

3.1 Production grammar analysis of Huave adaptations

Huave, a language isolate spoken in southeastern Oaxaca State, Mexico, has borrowed a number of words from Spanish. Huave restricts stress to one of the two final syllables of the word, while Spanish words may have stress on any one of the three final syllables, creating conflicts between the Huave stress restrictions and the actual source stress. Davidson and Noyer (1996) analyze the adaptation patterns of the San Mateo del Mar dialect of Huave in terms of ranked constraints of the production grammar, some of which cannot obviously be motivated by either the Huave or the Spanish data.

In Huave native vocabulary, stress falls on a final syllable when that syllable is closed, and on the penultimate syllable when the final is light. Huave has no vowel length contrast, so syllable weight is dependent on the presence or absence of a coda consonant. Because all stems of major lexical categories and all suffixes end in a consonant, final stress is the overwhelmingly predominant pattern in Huave.[1]

(2)   Huave native vocabulary (Kreger and Stairs 1981)

    a. aráŋ   'he does'
    b. taraŋgás   'I did'
    c. taraŋgasán   'we did'
    d. ʃíke   'I'

Words have a single stress, with the exception of words containing a suffix or suffixes comprising more than two syllables, where a secondary stress falls on the root-final syllable and primary stress on the word-final syllable (Kreger and Stairs 1981: xvii).

To describe the Huave facts, Davidson and Noyer posit the following constraints, each apparently undominated in the native grammar:

(3)   Huave constraints

    a. TROCHAICFEET: feet are bimoraic trochees (CV́CV or CV́C).
    b. ALIGN-R: the right edge of a Prosodic Word is aligned with the right edge of a foot.
    c. FREE-V: a word should not end in a vowel.

Interestingly, these three constraints show different degrees of strength in borrowed words. The most nativized vocabulary items maintain the Huave pattern of final stressed and closed syllables, while still preserving the Spanish stress – if necessary, by deletion of segmental material in the final syllable of the source:

(4)   Loans into Huave from Spanish, stratum 1 (most nativized)

Spanish	*Huave*	
garabáto	garabát	'hook'
kardúmen	kardóm	'flock'
márso	márs	'March'
ígado	ík	'liver'

Davidson and Noyer attribute the maintenance of Spanish stress to a constraint MATCHSTRESS:

---

1. Kreger and Stairs (1981) mention a single morpheme which falls outside the stress domain, the enclitic *an* 'only'.

(5)   MATCHSTRESS: Stress falls on the same vowel in the source word as in the loanword (Davidson and Noyer 1996: 69).

In the core stratum, which contains the most nativized vocabulary, MATCH-STRESS, along with Huave stress constraints and FREE-V, is ranked above segmental faithfulness constraints. The following tableau illustrates the derivation of stratum 1 vocabulary from the Spanish forms. In the following tableaux, the inputs are the Spanish forms (written below in pipes), while the outputs are Huave surface forms:

(6)   Davidson and Noyer's production grammar, stratum 1

|garabáto| 'hook'	MATCHSTRESS	TROCHAICFEET, ALIGN-R	FREE-V	MAX
a.	gara(báto)			*!	
☞ b.	gara(bát)				*

|ígado| 'liver'	MATCHSTRESS	TROCHAICFEET, ALIGN-R	FREE-V	MAX
a.	(íka)do		*!	*	
b.	i(kádo)	*!		*	
c.	(íka)			*!	
☞ d.	(ík)				***

While the native vocabulary appears not to provide evidence for any ranking of FREE-V with respect to the stress constraints, the second stratum of more peripheral loanwords respects the stress constraints but not FREE-V:

(7)   Huave from Spanish, stratum 2

Spanish	*Huave*	
gwanábana	gwanába	'sweet-sop'
mandádo	mandáda	'command'

The facts of this less nativized stratum can be described by assuming a second subgrammar in which the constraint enforcing segmental faithfulness (MAX), while still dominated by the Huave stress constraints, is ranked above FREE-V:

(8)   Davidson and Noyer's production grammar, stratum 2

|gwanábana| 'sweet-sop'	MATCHSTRESS	TROCHAICFEET, ALIGN-R	MAX	FREE-V
a. gwa(nába)na		*!		*
b. gwana(bána)	*!			*
c. gwa(nában)		*!	*	
☞ d. gwa(nába)			**	*
e. gwa(náb)			**!*	

And finally, the third stratum of least nativized loanwords exhibits violations of both native stress constraints and FREE-V, while still preserving the Spanish stress:

(9)   Huave from Spanish, Stratum 3 (least nativized):

Spanish   *Huave*
mjérkoles   mjérkoles   'Wednesday'
médiko   médiko   'doctor'

(10)   Davidson and Noyer's production grammar, stratum 3

|médiko| 'doctor'	MATCHSTRESS	MAX	TROCHAICFEET, ALIGN-R	FREE-V
☞ a. (médi)ko			*	*
b. (médik)		*!	*	
c. (mé)dik		*!	*	
d. (médi)		*!*		*

The three strata therefore differ in their tolerance of MAX constraint violations (apocope): in stratum 1, apocope is tolerated to satisfy both the demand for right-aligned trochaic feet and final consonants (*garabát* from *garabáto, ík* from *ígado*); in stratum 2 apocope is tolerated to satisfy stress constraints but not the demand for final consonants (*gwanába* from *gwanábana*); in stratum 3, a loanword that has antepenultimate stress is fully segmentally faithful to the original (*médiko*). The three strata arise, Davidson and Noyer argue, from the differential ranking of the anti-deletion MAX constraints with respect to

MATCHSTRESS >> { TROCHAICFEET, ALIGN-R } >> FREE-V. Although both apocope (*garabát* from *garabáto*) and non-trochaic stress (*médiko*) are possible in loans, there are no cases in which both cooccur in a single form, because to derive a form such as **médik* from *médiko* would require the ranking FREE-V >> MAX >> { TROCHAICFEET, ALIGN-R }, a reversal of the markedness constraint rankings. The Huave data are therefore consistent with Ito and Mester's (1995) claim that while faithfulness constraints can be ranked differently in the subgrammars associated with different lexical strata, the relative rankings of markedness constraints are constant across strata. However, the ranking MATCHSTRESS >> { TROCHAICFEET, ALIGN-R } >> FREE-V is motivated by the loanword data rather than by any facts of the native language.

Additional complications ensue when we consider the treatment of Spanish complex onsets (forbidden in native Huave vocabulary), which are simplified by means of vowel insertion:

(11)   pláto   polát   'silver'
       brasáda   barasáda   'unit of measure' (*basáda, *sáda)

It is striking that while entire syllables may be deleted to preserve Spanish stress (*gwanába* from *gwanábana* 'sweet sop'), the strategy used to avoid complex onsets is insertion, rather than deletion. Davidson and Noyer elegantly describe these facts by ranking MATCHSTRESS and MAX(C,V) over *COMPLEXONSET, in turn ranked over DEP(V). This ranking makes vowel insertion the preferred repair strategy where there is a choice (as in the resolution of a complex onset violation). But the mandate that stress may neither leave its original syllable nor fall to the left of the penultimate syllable rules out vowel insertion as an option in posttonic position. Again, however, we must wonder how the original Huave adapters might have come up with such a ranking, in the absence of any evidence for either consonant deletion or vowel insertion in Huave. Thus, this analysis raises a number of thorny questions concerning the learnability of the constraint rankings:

1. *How would Huave speakers arrive at the ranking MATCHSTRESS >> MAX(C) >> *COMPLEXONSET >> DEP(V) (F >> F >> M >> F)?* This ranking is necessary to describe the pattern whereby segment deletion is used to maintain the Spanish stress, but vowel insertion is used to resolve complex onset violations. However, it is not clear how such a ranking might have been learned. Because Huave is a language in which all surface forms exhibit a regular stress pattern, the hypothesis of Richness of the Base requires us to assume that the stress constraints outrank any faithfulness constraints that would preserve lexi-

cally marked stress such as IDENTI-O(STRESS) (the typical M >> F ranking). Why, then, is MATCHSTRESS ranked so high? MATCHSTRESS could be argued to be an output-output constraint, a type which Hayes ([1999] 2004) has argued is ranked high by default. But this simply moves the question to another level: if we assume that all O-O constraints are ranked high in the absence of evidence to the contrary, why should an O-O constraint demanding faithfulness to stress outrank O-O constraints demanding faithfulness to segments? The pattern of faithfulness to stress over faithfulness to segments is not universal, as we shall see in the discussion of Selayarese below, and therefore must be explained as an effect of either the Huave grammar or the Spanish input.

2. *Why would Huave speakers rank stress constraints over FREE-V (M >> M)?* This ranking describes the fact that adapters give up the requirement that words end in consonants before they give up the requirements that the stress foot be aligned with the right edge of the word. But what would motivate such a ranking, when both the stress constraints and FREE-V are uniformly obeyed in Huave (for content words), and frequently violated in Spanish?[2]

3.2   Perception-oriented analysis of Huave adaptations

In this section I argue that what appear to be the effects of apparently unlearnable constraint rankings in Huave loan adaptation are actually a reflection of the native language perception grammar. Specifically, I argue that the unambiguously demarcative function of stress in Huave leads listeners with little or no knowledge of Spanish to assume that stressed syllables are word-final. The resulting forms, in which posttonic material is not analyzed as part of the word, are lexicalized, leading to what appears to be posttonic deletion in the earlier strata. The increasing faithfulness to Spanish segments seen in later strata is a function of increasing contact with Spanish, which forces listeners to revise the perception grammar, allowing a wider range of word shapes. This in turn forces a revision of the production grammar.

Before discussing the specifics of word adaptation, some information on the sociolinguistic context of the Huave adaptation patterns will be useful. As recently as 1961, 81% of Huave speakers in San Mateo del Mar were monolin-

---

2. I assume that Huave speakers distinguish content and function words, and that the presence of vowel-final function words in Huave would not contribute to demotion of Free-V. See Peperkamp (2004) for arguments that even infants distinguish content and function words, and that basic generalizations about stress are not disrupted by function words that interfere with general patterns.

gual in Huave (Diebold 1961: 104), and the community was "almost wholly preliterate" (Diebold 1961: 105). For those speakers with knowledge of Spanish, "Spanish was acquired relatively late in life, rarely in childhood", and only 6% could be considered fully bilingual [...] subordinate bilingualism in San Mateo involves very imperfect reproduction of Spanish, with a heavy load of interference from Huave" (Diebold 1961: 105). This situation has changed over the succeeding decades, so that at present, although "Huave is the language of everyday life [...] At least 90% of adults and 100% of children are now also completely fluent in Spanish; monolingual Huave speakers have become a negligible percentage of the population (this was not true 20 years ago)" (Kim and Park-Doob 2005). I will argue that the different strata of the Huave loanwords reflect the dramatic changes over time in adapters' familiarity with Spanish.

3.2.1 Faithfulness to stress vs. faithfulness to segments: Stratum 1

We begin by considering the most nativized words, which invariably end in stressed closed syllables (e.g., *ígado* is adapted as *ik* 'liver'). In the following discussion, I assume that the two mappings from the phonetic form – to a phonological surface representation, which encodes prosodic structure, and to a lexical representation, which serves as input to the production grammar – take place in parallel (see (22) in Boersma and Hamann this volume). I propose that the preservation of source stress over the preservation of source segments, which is encoded by Davidson and Noyer as a ranking of MATCHSTRESS over MAX, is in fact an effect of a high-ranked perception grammar constraint:

(12) Perception grammar constraint

ASSUMELEXWORDEDGE-V́C#: in mapping the acoustic signal to phonological representations, assume a word edge following each consonant preceded by a stressed vowel.

This constraint is one of a family of constraints aiding in the segmentation of the speech string into words (see for example the perception grammar constraints proposed by Boersma (2000) which posit word boundaries at the beginning and end of an utterance). For Huave, ASSUMEWORDEDGE-V́C# is undominated, serving as a filter on possible phonological representations. The high ranking of ASSUMEWORDEDGE-V́C# would cause listeners to assume that material following the stress foot is either part of the following word, or noise without linguistic significance. (An example of such nonsignificant articulations in English would be release of a phrase-final consonant, or a labial closure following a phrase-final vowel, coincident with simply shutting the mouth. The final consonant in colloquial English *nope* and *yep* most likely represents misanalysis of this closure as a segment.) In contrast to a constraint mandating that the right edge of a foot coincide with the right edge of a word, this constraint permits learners to segment strings into words on the basis of overt information present in the phonetic form.

I assume that at the initial stages of Huave-Spanish contact, ASSUMEWORD-EDGE-V́C# remained undominated in the Huave perception grammar, so that a Huave speaker first exposed to Spanish forms such as [*ígado*] 'liver' and [*garabáto*] 'hook' would posit a word boundary after each consonant following a stressed vowel (|*ig*|#*ado*, |*garabát*|#*o*). The forms identified as lexical items (|*ig*|, |*garabat*|) would then serve as input to the production grammar. Thus, the adapted forms *ík* and *garabát* would emerge not as a result of segment deletion in the production grammar, but as a result of a misanalysis of the lexical representation. It now becomes clear why final vowels are never deleted from Spanish forms with antepenultimate stress; for example, *médiko* 'doctor' never becomes **médik*. In Davidson and Noyer's account this is the reflection of the production grammar ranking TROCHAICFEET >> MAX >> FREE-V. In the perception-oriented account, apocope is a function of misparsing, not of truncation in the production grammar. The Huave perception grammar provides no reason to parse *médiko* as *médik#o*, because *médik* would not be a legal Huave word shape. If any misparsing occurred, the resulting form would be **méd* (on analogy with *ík* 'liver' from *ígado*).

We must now consider whether the strategy of assuming that a stressed syllable marks the end of a lexical unit is a realistic one. A good deal of evidence suggests that even very young children make use of stress information in segmenting words, and that their segmentation patterns reflect the normal position of stress in a language (see for example Jusczyk 1999; Thiessen and Saffran 2003; Werker and Curtin 2005). The same principles have been shown to guide adults' segmentations, using a variety of experimental paradigms. For example, Cutler and Butterfield (1992) found that in both natural 'slips of the ear' and in experimental investigation of English listeners' segmentation of highly attenuated speech, "listeners tend to insert boundaries before strong syllables and delete them before weak syllables [...] the rhythmic properties of the input guide listeners' hypotheses about the placement of lexical boundaries in imperfectly perceived speech" (Cutler and Butterfield 1992: 232).[3] Since initial con-

---

3. The rankings of the segmentation constraints in the perception grammar of English and Huave listeners will of course differ, with ASSUMEWORDEDGE-V́C ranked low in the English

tact with a foreign language, particularly in the absence of orthographic information, is a situation likely to lead to 'imperfectly perceived speech', it seems reasonable that Huave listeners should have segmented Spanish strings according to Huave patterns.

However, in some cases this erroneous segmentation might entail positing that the remnant is also a word, which would appear to violate the Possible Word Constraint of Norris, McQueen, Cutler and Butterfield (1995), who found that listeners had difficulty recognizing (for example) 'egg' in strings like *fegg*, where the remnant [f] is not a possible word. This principle militates against Huave listeners segmenting *garabáto* as *garabát#o*, since [o] would not fulfill the Huave requirement that all words contain a bimoraic foot. Later work, however, indicates that the Possible Word Constraint as originally stated is too strong; Cutler, Demuth and McQueen (2002) found that when the remnant was a syllable, rather than a single segment, word detection was not hampered; Sesotho listeners efficiently detected *rora* in *jirora*, even though the minimal word size in Sesotho is bisyllabic, and therefore *ji*, the remnant left when *rora* is identified as a word, is not a possible Sesotho word. It is therefore plausible that the Huave speakers could have identified a string like *garabát* as a word, even where the string *garabáto* could not be segmented into two possible words (though in non-final position, the final [o] could plausibly be assigned to the following word).

A second possible objection to the account of the Huave data comes from work by Peperkamp and Dupoux (2002), who argue that adult speakers of languages in which stress is invariably utterance-final exhibit 'deafness' to stress in other languages, manifested in their difficulty in distinguishing CVCV words differing only in the position of stress (as contrasted with their ability to perceive segmental contrasts in such words). These results appear to be inconsistent with our claim that Huave speakers use stress to determine word structure. But in Peperkamp and Dupoux's experimental paradigm, listeners were presented with already segmented 'words'. Their subjects' task was therefore very different from that of speakers in a language contact situation attempting to segment foreign language strings into words.[4]

---

perception grammar, but in both languages, constraints relating stress and word edges will play a role.

4. Altmann (2006) presents experimental results that are problematic for Peperkamp and Dupoux's claim that invariant utterance-edge stress leads to the greatest degree of stress deafness. Briefly, Altmann found that Arabic speakers, whose language assigns stress to one of the final three syllables of a word, depending on syllable weight, showed greater difficulty in cross-linguistic perception of stress than speakers of French or Turkish, where stress is always assigned at the utterance edge.

I assume, therefore, that the least nativized loanwords represent words that entered the lexicon at a stage in which the Spanish forms were filtered through the native Huave perception grammar. At this stage, Huave ASSUMEWORD-EDGE-V́C# was ranked more highly than, for example, the constraint that accounts for the results of Cutler and Butterfield (1992) showing the tendency of English speakers to posit a word boundary before a stressed syllable. At this stage Spanish forms are interpreted as consistent with Huave restrictions, and so provide no pressure to restructure the production grammar:

(13)   Stratum 1 (*ígado* → *ik*) perception grammar (= Huave native grammar)

ASSUMEWORDEDGE-V́C# >> ASSUMEWORDEDGE-#STRESSEDSYLL

A form such as *ígado* would emerge from the perception grammar in truncated form. (Below I concentrate only on the relationship between stress and truncation, ignoring various segmental issues such as the Spanish [d/ð] alternation. I also take no stand on whether the change from [g] to [k] in the loanword is a function of misperception or misproduction.)

(14)   Input to perception grammar: 'liver'

[ígado]		ASSUMEWORDEDGE-V́C#	other word edge constraints
a.	|ígado|#	*!	*
☞ b.	|ig|# (or |ik|#)		*

The output of the perception grammar would then be submitted to the production grammar. Derivation of the Huave surface form is trivial, since the lexicalized form satisfies all Huave constraints:

(15)   Input to production grammar

|ig|		ALIGN-R, TROCHAICFEET	FREE-V	MAX
☞ a.	ík			
b.	í		*!	*

Because at this early stage all lexical representations were assumed to conform to Huave restrictions, there was no motivation to alter the ranking of constraints in the production grammar.

3.2.2 Posttonic deletion vs. pretonic insertion

The asymmetry in pretonic and posttonic repair tactics, illustrated by vowel insertion in forms like *polát* (Spanish *pláto* 'silver') and *barasáda* (Spanish *brasáda* 'unit of measure') but deletion in forms like *ik* 'liver' (Spanish *ígado*) is now unsurprising. Material was lost in positions where the perception grammar defined it as not part of the relevant word, or as not linguistically significant (e.g., as an effect of consonantal release), but preserved where the grammar defined it as potentially contrastive. On this account, preservation of perceived segments is the norm, and deletion is not a grammatical process; rather, the apparent deletion of posttonic material results from incorrect identification of right word edges.

It would not be surprising if missegmentation also occasionally led to confusion concerning the beginnings of words as well. In Huave, a word can only be preceded by a phrase boundary, by $\acute{V}$C, or by $\acute{V}$CV (the latter following a function word). Spanish, however, allows a wider range of options, and the Huave speaker might be expected to occasionally misparse the left edges of words in running Spanish speech. Indeed, borrowings from Spanish evidence both the addition of material at the left edge, in *arintf* from Spanish *ránt͡ʃo* 'ranch', and the loss of pretonic material, in forms like *nimál* 'animal' from Spanish *animál* and *maríl* 'yellow' from Spanish *amaríʎo* (Diebold 1961: 107).[5] This pretonic truncation, if analyzed as part of the production grammar, would require the ranking ONSET >> MAX(V). But such a ranking would contradict the ranking required for the native vocabulary, which must permit vowel-initial words (which are relatively common). The adaptation pattern would therefore represent a reversal of the normal situation found in a stratified lexicon, in which the core vocabulary obeys a ranking of M >> F while the more peripheral vocabulary obeys the ranking F >> M, and the loss of the initial vowel could not be a function of nativization, but rather would represent an emergence of the unmarked effect. Such an effect does not, however, hold generally for Huave loanwords – see, for example, *asét* 'oil'.[6] Given the sporadic nature of initial deletion, the best analysis appears to be as an effect of misparsing rather than as an effect of the production grammar.

---

5. For the sake of clarity, I have adopted Davidson and Noyer's (1997) transcription system in rendering Diebold's forms. Diebold transcribes these forms as *àrìtf*, *nìmál* and *màrìil*, respectively.
6. In Diebold's transcription, *àsét* (Diebold 1961: 107).

3.2.3   Requirement for right-aligned stress foot vs. requirement for final consonant

In the account sketched above, the most nativized (stratum 1) loanwords represent an early stage in which Huave speakers segmented Spanish strings in terms of Huave word structure, and their erroneously segmented forms were then lexicalized. However, increasing contact with speakers of Spanish would inevitably have confronted Huave speakers with lexical, syntactic, and meta-linguistic evidence for words of shapes that were incompatible with Huave restrictions, resulting in the restructuring of both the perception and (conse-quently) the production grammars. As we saw above, the first restriction to go is the requirement that all words end in a consonant (resulting in forms like *gwanába* 'sweet-sop' from *gwanábana*), while the last restriction to be aban-doned is the requirement that all words end in a bimoraic trochaic foot (*médiko* 'doctor'). The relative strength of these requirements is described in Davidson and Noyer's (1997) account in terms of the ranking of the stress constraints over FREE-V. I will argue that their relative strengths are actually a function of the input to the adapters – that is, the extent to which each is violated in the Spanish data.

While Spanish words may violate both the Huave stress constraints and FREE-V, they do so with differing degrees of frequency. Eddington (2000) finds, among the 4,829 most frequent Spanish words, that 2,850 (59%) are vowel-final while 1,979 (41%) are consonant-final. Therefore, the majority of Spanish words end in vowels, violating FREE-V. In contrast, a majority of Spanish words obey the requirement that words end in a right-aligned bimoraic trochaic foot. This requirement is satisfied by slightly more than 68% of the words in Eddington's corpus: words ending in V́CV total 2,494 (51.6%) and words ending in V́C total 798 (16.5%). In contrast, fewer than a third of the words in Eddington's corpus violate the stress constraints; these are of three types, words with antepenultimate stress (274, or 5.6%), consonant-final words with penultimate stress (1085, or 22.4%), and vowel-final words with final stress (178, or 3.6%). Therefore, the input to Huave speakers will contain more forms consistent with the Huave stress constraints than forms consistent with the requirement that words be consonant-final:

(16)   Percentage of Spanish words consistent with Huave constraints

a. stress constraints: 68%
b. FREE-V: 41%

As Huave speakers begin to recognize words ending in vowels, they will begin to create a perception grammar distinct from that motivated solely by the native language data. Such a grammar will admit the possibility of words ending in V́CV. They will hear a relatively smaller number of words that do not end in a bimoraic foot, and misanalysis of such forms should persist longer. In particular, words like *médiko*, which constitute only 5.6% of the input, will take longer to become established as possible lexical representations. It seems likely that such words are characteristic of the pronunciation of bilinguals who have developed two clearly distinct grammars, one of which (the Huave grammar) imposes predictable stress on all words, and the second of which (the Spanish grammar) maintains lexically marked stress.

3.3   Other languages with demarcative stress: K'ichee' and Selayarese

Davidson and Noyer's (1997) account of stress preservation as a function of the ranking of MATCHSTRESS leads us to expect that various rankings of this constraint could be found in different language contact situations. In contrast, the alternative analysis developed above ascribes stress preservation to specific properties of the borrowing language: the perception grammar of Huave speakers leads them to missegment foreign language utterances. In order for such missegmentation to arise, certain conditions are required, both phonological and sociolinguistic. First, the borrowing language must have clearly demarcative stress, oriented toward the word edge, while the source language must allow stress in positions farther from the word edge than are possible in the borrowing language. Second, borrowing must occur under conditions that do not present borrowers with unambiguously segmented speech: generally, through an aural route rather than through orthography, through connected speech rather than citation forms, and in a situation in which listeners have limited knowledge of the source language and little explicit instruction or correction from speakers of the source language. We would expect that given the same conditions, other languages should exhibit similar deletion of segmental material peripheral to the stress. We now consider two additional cases of loan adaptation into languages with demarcative stress, one in which source stress is routinely preserved, and one in which it is not.

3.3.1   K'ichee'

K'ichee', a member of the Quichean branch of eastern Mayan, is similar to Huave in allowing only words ending in stressed closed syllables. Like Huave, K'ichee' has also borrowed heavily from Spanish. Isaacs and Wolter (2003) present the following data from the Nahualá dialect spoken in western Guatemala:

(17)	*Spanish*	*K'ichee'*	
	atáke	atá:k	'attack'
	baráto	barát	'barracks'
	kadéna	kadé:n	'chain'
	gánas	gá:n	'desire'
	mansána	mansá'n	'apple'
	antónia	tó'n	'Antonia'
	durásno	turá's	'peach'

As in Huave, the position of Spanish stress is maintained in words borrowed into K'ichee', and the stressed syllable is rendered final by deletion of posttonic segmental material.[7] The sensitivity of K'ichee' speakers to the stress pattern of their language is apparently established early; according to Demuth (1996), the first words of children acquiring K'ichee' as their first language are monosyllabic, with truncation of pretonic syllables (e.g., [lóm] for [jolóm] 'head'). This pattern contrasts with the early productions of learners of Dutch, English, and Sesotho, who tend to produce disyllabic trochees, the preferred word structure of their ambient languages. Note that the difference between the simplification patterns of children acquiring K'ichee' and adult K'ichee' speakers adapting Spanish loans rules out the possibility that the adult adaptation pattern represents an initial-state default ranking.

The similarities in loan adaptation by speakers of Huave and K'ichee' are striking. These similarities are, furthermore, expected, given the account sketched above in which uniformly demarcative stress leads to missegmentation of words that do not conform to the native language pattern in which stress position and word boundary position correspond. However, an alternative account of the correspondence between the Huave and K'ichee' adaptations is possible: that MATCHSTRESS is universally highly ranked, by default. We now turn to a third language which shows that this cannot be the case.

---

7. The Spanish stressed vowel is realized as either a long vowel or a glottalized vowel (represented as *v'* by Isaacs and Wolter).

3.3.2   Selayarese

In many ways, the stress system of Selayarese is quite similar to that of Huave; both prefer a trochaic foot at the right edge of the word, ranking TROCHAIC-FEET and ALIGN-R(WORD,FOOT) high. However, Selayarese differs from Huave in that Selayarese codas do not contribute to syllable weight, so all feet are bisyllabic, yielding penultimate stress:

(18)   Selayarese native stress (Basri 1999; Broselow 1999)

      sampúlo   'ten'
      bálaŋ   'creek'
      kalihára   'ant'

Selayarese has borrowed a large number of words from Bahasa Indonesia (BI). While many BI words also have penultimate stress, the BI prohibition on stressed schwa leads in some cases to final stress. As the forms below illustrate, Selayarese borrowers ignore the source stress of BI words, assigning them stress according to Selayarese restrictions. (Because Selayarese lacks schwa, BI schwa is realized as a full vowel in Selayarese, though the quality of this vowel is not entirely predictable. For discussion of the segmental changes motivated by Selayarese segmental and syllable structure restrictions, see Basri 1997, Broselow 1999).

(19)   *Bahasa Indonesia*   *Selayarese*
       gəmúk   gómmoʔ   'fat'
       sədəkáh   sidákka   'alms'
       səbáb   sábaʔ   'cause'
       bənáŋ   bánnaŋ   'thread'

The Huave strategy of deleting posttonic material would obviously not be viable for Selayarese speakers, since their goal is penultimate stress. However, Selayarese speakers could in principle use vowel insertion to bring loan words with final stress into conformity with the native stress restrictions – as they in fact do with borrowed subminimal forms, such as *bom* 'bomb,' which is realized as *bóʔoŋ*. It is not obvious why BI *bənáŋ*, for example, should not also be realized with vowel insertion (*banáʔaŋ), which would both preserve the source stress and place it in the normal Selayarese penultimate position. But insertion of segments is used only in monosyllabic words; in longer words, Selayarese speakers simply shift the original stress to the normal Selayarese position (*bánnaŋ*).[8] We could describe this pattern by the ranking { TROCHAICFEET, ALIGN-R } >> DEP >> MATCHSTRESS (since if MATCHSTRESS is part of the grammar of Huave, it must be part of the grammar of all languages). The ranking TROCHAICFEET >> DEP is consistent with the facts of Selayarese, which indeed has no words smaller than two syllables. But the low ranking of MATCHSTRESS would need to be explained.

We see the same disregard for source stress in another class of words. Many Selayarese roots end in [r], [l], or [s], none of which is a possible coda (Mithun and Basri 1986; Broselow 1999). When one of these consonants occurs in root-final position, it is followed by a copy of the preceding vowel. Words with a final epenthetic vowel take stress on the antepenultimate syllable:

(20)   lámbere   'long'
        sússulu   'burn'
        maŋkásara   'Makassar'
        sáhala   'profit'

Note that the epenthetic vowel fails to appear before a vowel-initial (nonclitic) suffix (cf. *lámbere/lambéraŋ* 'longer'), in contrast to underlying vowels, which always appear (*tirére/tireré-aŋ* 'thirsty/thirstier').

This association of antepenultimate stress with a final epenthetic vowel in native vocabulary has been analyzed by ranking HEAD-DEP, which directs that an epenthetic vowel may not be part of the main stress foot (Alderete 1999), above ALIGN-R. This ranking favors the formation of a bisyllabic foot containing only underlying vowels over the formation of a perfectly right-aligned foot:

(21)   HEAD-DEP: Stress foot includes only underlying vowels (Alderete 1999)

	|lamber|		HEAD-DEP	ALIGN-R
	a.	lam(bére)	*!	
☞ b.		(lámbe)re		*

This pattern is also respected in loanwords, which take antepenultimate stress with a final epenthetic vowel, regardless of the stress of the source:

---

8. The one exception is *korá?aŋ* 'Koran' (Hasan Basri, personal communication). Clearly, there are sociolinguistic factors that could mandate greater faithfulness in this case.

(22)   *Bahasa Indonesia*   *Selayarese*
   sénter   séntere   'flashlight'
   kəlás   kálasa   'class'
   bərás   bérasa   'rice'
   bələbás   balábasa   'ruler'

The Selayarese speakers could easily have preserved the source stress by adapting BI *kəlás* (for example) as *kalása rather than *kálasa*. There would be nothing objectionable in the surface form **kalása;* as the minimal pair *sáhala* 'profit' (from root |sahal|) and *sahála* 'sea cucumber' (from |sahala|) shows, the presence of [r, l, s] surrounded by identical vowels is a necessary but not a sufficient condition for antepenultimate stress.

Again, we could describe this pattern by a production grammar ranking { HEAD-DEP, TROCHAICFEET } >> { ALIGN-R, DEP } >> MATCHSTRESS. But we would need to explain how Selayarese speakers would have converged on this ranking – particularly since, as we know from the Huave case, low ranking of MATCHSTRESS is not universal. Let us therefore consider the ways in which the Selayarese situation differs from the Huave situation.

First of all, Selayarese speakers are very likely to have a good command of Bahasa Indonesia, the lingua franca of Indonesia, and the language of formal education. Second, while stress serves unambiguously in Huave to mark word edges, the role of stress in Selayarese is not nearly so straightforward. Clearly, the epenthetic forms muddy the relationship between stress and word edges. An additional complicating factor is the presence of clitics, which fall outside the stress domain, though they still participate in certain aspects of word-level phonology (Basri, Broselow and Finer 2000). Clitic attachment may result in stress as far back as the preantepenult:

(23)   géle -ma - kaŋ 'we are no longer...'

A sequence of three syllables, only the first of which is stressed, could correspond to any of the following morphological structures in Selayarese (though the interpretation in (24c) is possible only if the onset of the third syllable is one of [r, l, s] and if the vowels of the two poststress syllables are identical):

(24)   Possible grammatical structures for σσσ (where {,} indicate PWd edges)
   a. σσ)} # {(σ..   (separate grammatical words)
   b. (σσ)}- σ #   (grammatical word plus clitic)
   c. (σσ)σ}#   (root plus epenthetic vowel)

Thus, Selayarese listeners, unlike Huave listeners, cannot use stress to reliably demarcate words, and cannot disregard segmental material following the stress foot (indeed, such material may encode lexical contrast in Selayarese, as in *bótoro* 'gamble' vs. *bótolo* 'bottle'). Rather than simply using stress to recover native language word structure, Selayarese listeners must attend to both stress and segmental structure.

The Selayarese adapters' cavalier treatment of foreign stress may seem surprising given that stress in principle can function to signal lexical contrast in Selayarese: stress is the only cue distinguishing epenthetic from nonepenthetic roots (as in the minimal pair *sáhala* (from |sahal|) 'profit' vs. *sahála* (from |sahala|) 'sea cucumber').[9] But in fact, the functional load of this contrast is extremely low; this minimal pair may be the only one, and the vast majority of words of the shape ...V r,l,s V# (where the last two vowels are identical) are epenthetic forms, with antepenultimate stress.

3.4   Interim summary

We have seen that in two languages with clearly demarcative, word-edge stress (Huave and K'ichee'), posttonic material tends to be truncated in loan adaptation. We trace this not to a ranking of production grammar constraints, but rather to the tendency of such words to be misparsed in the perception grammar. We now turn to another case of loanword adaptation that has been analyzed similarly to the Huave case, involving a high-ranking production grammar constraint mandating source stress. In Fijian, stress does serve as a signal of lexical contrast. However, stress falls predictably on long vowels, and I will argue that vowel length, not source stress, is what Fijian listeners attend to.

4.   Adaptation of lexically contrastive stress

4.1   Stress and length: Production grammar analysis

In the adaptation of loanwords in Fijian, analyzed by Schütz (1978, 1983, 1999) and Kenstowicz ([2003] 2007), source stress is preserved not by unfaithfulness to segments but by unfaithfulness to vowel length. Here again I will argue that the preservation of stress is not an effect of MATCHSTRESS, but ra-

---

9.   We should expect listeners whose language uses stress in this way to be sensitive to foreign stress (as argued by Peperkamp and Dupoux 2002; Peperkamp 2004).

ther a reflection of speakers' misinterpretation of the source words, guided by their perception grammar.

In Fijian, as in Huave, main stress falls on a final heavy syllable, otherwise on the penult (Schütz 1978, 1983, 1999, 2004; Kenstowicz [2003] 2007; Hayes 1995). (Note, however, that Schütz (1999: 146) argues that it is the rightmost foot of a phrase, rather than of each word, that is most prominent.) We can therefore assume that Fijian, like Huave, has high-ranked TROCHAICFEET and ALIGN-R. Fijian differs from Huave in that where syllable contrasts in Huave reside in the presence or absence of a syllable coda, Fijian has only open syllables, but does employ a contrast between long and short vowels. Secondary stress in Fijian falls on all long vowels, giving rise to contrasts such as that between (25b) and (25c). Strings of light syllables are organized into bisyllabic trochaic feet, as in (25d):

(25) Fijian Native Vocabulary (Schütz 1999; Kenstowicz [2003] 2007; Hayes 1995)[10]

a. ma(káwa)   'old'

b. (màða)(wá:)   'worthless'

c. (mà:)(ðáwa)   'week'

d. (kàmba)(tá-ka)   'climb with it' (Hayes 1995: 144)

The requirement of a bimoraic trochee at the right edge of a word forces shortening of a vowel in penultimate position in native vocabulary:

(26) a. (síβi)   'exceed' (from |si:βi|)

b. (sì:)(βí-ta)   'exceed, trans.' (Hayes 1995: 145, from Dixon 1988)

Note that lengthening the final vowel would be an alternative means of satisfying the right edge bimoraic foot requirement (*(sì:)(βí:)). Although this would produce an acceptable word structure (cf. *(ndrè:)(ndré:)* 'difficult', Scott 1948: 739), this option is not chosen; vowels are never lengthened in native vocabulary.

We do see lengthening, however, in loans from English. When English stress falls on the penultimate syllable, the English stressed vowel can serve as

---

10. Much previous work employs Fijian orthography, in which *c* represents a voiced interdental fricative, *j* a palatal affricate (derived, at least historically, from |ti|), and *v* a voiced bilabial fricative, while *b,d,q* represent voiced prenasalized labial, dental, and velar stops, respectively. I have translated the orthography into phonetic transcription. The reader is referred to Schütz (1978) for discussion of the impact of loanwords on the segmental inventory of Fijian.

the head of a bisyllabic foot, as in (27a). But when stress falls on the final syllable, the stressed vowel must be lengthened to retain stress, as in (27b):

(27)   English stress preservation

    a.   pa(ʧáma)   'pajama'
         ta(βáko)   'tobacco'

    b.   mba(zá:)   'bazaar'
         ŋgi(tá:)   'guitar'

  (vs. (ʧéli)   'jelly')

When the English stress falls on the antepenultimate syllable, we see one of two patterns. Either the stressed vowel is lengthened, forming a foot on its own, as in (28a), or the final vowel is lengthened, making the antepenult the head of a bisyllabic foot, as in (28b):

(28)   English antepenultimate stress

    a. (kò:)(lóni)   'colony'
       (tà:)(féta)   'taffeta'

    b. (kàli)(kó:)   'calico'
       (pòli)(ó:)   'polio'

Thus, the English main stress vowel always receives some stress, although the main stress of the Fijian adaptation may fall on an originally unstressed vowel (as in *kò:lóni* 'colony'). We should note that (as pointed out by Schütz 1978: 25) that not all tense English vowels are realized in Fijian as long (for example, 'eagle' is *ikéli*, not **i:kéli* and 'deaconess' is *ndikonési*, not **ndi:konési*). Thus, Fijian borrowers do not appear to identify the English tense/lax contrast as equivalent to their long/short contrast. In this they differ from Japanese borrowers, as illustrated by Japanese *ʧi:pu* 'cheap' vs. *ʧikiN* 'chicken';[11] this difference is no doubt related to the intimate relationship between vowel length and stress which holds in Fijian but not in Japanese.

Kenstowicz ([2003] 2007) analyzes the Fijian adaptation patterns by a ranking reminiscent of that posited for Huave: TROCHAICFEET, ALIGN-R, and MAXSTRESS (= Davidson and Noyer's MATCHSTRESS) dominate faithfulness constraints (in this case, DEPMORA: "do not add a mora"). The contrast between the patterns illustrated in (28a) and (28b) is accounted for by a constraint that minimizes the perceptual difference between source and output:

---

11. This contrast is generally realized in English by some combination of spectral and durational cues, depending on the dialect (Escudero 2001; Escudero and Boersma 2004).

(29)   PP-2: a short unstressed V may not be realized as a long stressed V.

Kenstowicz assumes that the 'colony' pattern represents the default. However, the 'calico' pattern can be derived with the same grammar, if we assume that Fijians analyze the final V of 'calico' as underlyingly long, so that PP-2 allows it to be stressed:

(30)   Kenstowicz's production grammar, 'colony'

|koloni|	TROCHAICFEET, ALIGN-R	MAX STRESS	DEP MORA	PP-2
☞ a. (kò:)(lóni)			*		
b. (kòlo)(ní:)				*	*! (i → í:)
c. ko(lóni)		*!			

(31)   Kenstowicz's production grammar, 'calico'

|kaliko:|	TROCHAICFEET, ALIGN-R	MAX STRESS	DEP MORA	PP-2
a. (kà:)(líko)			*!		
☞ b. (kàli)(kó:)					
c. ka(líko)		*!			

Kenstowicz's analysis provides an elegant account of this complex array of data. However, it leaves unanswered some of the same sorts of questions we have been pondering:

1.   Given that lengthening is never attested in native vocabulary, what evidence would have caused Fijians to rank MAXSTRESS above DEP-MORA, and DEPMORA over PP-2 (as required to prevent the lengthening of unstressed vowels, choosing (e.g.) *ta(βáko)* 'tobacco' over **(tà:)(βáko))*?
2.   Why do we find two different patterns for adaptation of proparoxytones like *(kò:)(lóni)* 'colony' and *(kàli)(kó:)* 'calico'?
3.   Why do we find an asymmetry between Fijians' interpretations of English pretonic tense vowels/diphthongs and final tense vowels/diphthongs? Kenstowicz ([2003] 2007) notes that an English tense vowel before the English main stress is always realized as long (*ò:méka* 'ome-

ga', *tò:píto* 'torpedo'), while an English tense vowel in final position may be realized as either long or short (*kàlikó:* vs. *tò:píto, kò:lóni*).

4.2   Stress and length: Perception-oriented analysis

In Kenstowicz's analysis, Fijians correctly perceive English stress, and their production grammar constraints are ranked so as to preserve the English main stress, by vowel lengthening if necessary. In contrast, Schütz (1978, 1983, 2004) proposes that "English words are interpreted in Fijian in terms of an important phonological unit: the *accent group*" (Schütz 1983: 566). Both Kenstowicz and Schütz assume that lengthening is an effect of the imperative to maintain similarity between the stress patterns of the English and Fijian forms; Schütz (1983: 570) argues that "For cases in which merely changing the placement of accent (and hence grouping) would not improve the prosodic fit, syllables can be lengthened to attract the accent." My proposal is somewhat different: that Fijians actually misinterpret English stress as length in certain contexts – that is, in mapping the acoustic signal of English words onto the phoneme categories of their native language, Fijians use prominence patterns to decode phonemic length contrasts.

A Fijian vowel may be stressed either by virtue of occupying a prominence-conferring position (head of a bisyllabic foot), or by being long. Therefore, in Fijian, any vowel that is stressed and is not in a prominence-conferring position must be long. Because the grouping of syllables into feet is predictable (in shorter words – but see §4.3 for discussion of longer words), I assume that lexical representations for words of up to three syllables generally encode length contrasts rather than footing contrasts, which are assigned by the production grammar on the basis of the underlying arrangement of long and short vowels in a word.

On this account, Fijians hear a final stressed vowel (as in *mbazá:* 'bazaar') as long because in Fijian, the only way a final vowel can achieve greater prominence than the vowel preceding it is by virtue of being long. In contrast, a penultimate stressed vowel (as in *taβáko* 'tobacco') need not be analyzed as long, because it occurs in a prominence-conferring position. The variation seen in stressed antepenultimate vowels (as in *kàlikó:* 'calico' vs. *to:píto* 'torpedo' or *kò:lóni* 'colony') also makes sense: as Schütz (1983) points out, the Fijian grammar provides two possible routes to prominence in this position: as head of a bisyllabic foot (as in *(kàli)(kó:)*) or as a long vowel (as in *(kò:)(lóni)*). I will argue below that the variation is not entirely random, but instead depends on subphonemic cues: inherent length differences in English vowels, which Fijian listeners interpret as signalling contrastive length differences.

The asymmetric behavior of pretonic and posttonic vowels also falls out from this account. While we see variation in the lengthening of final posttonic vowels (*kàlikó:* 'calico' vs. *to:píto* 'torpedo'), tense vowels immediately preceding the English main stressed syllable are consistently lengthened, as in *ò:méka*, while lax prestressed vowels, as in *patʃáma*, are not. Lax vowels, of course, are unstressed in English, while tense vowels in prestress position receive some degree of stress. Apparently, Fijian listeners interpret the different prominence patterns of words like 'omega' and 'pajama' in accord with the principles of Fijian grammar, which does not allow adjacent stressed monomoraic syllables (Schütz 1978, 1983, 2004). The secondary prominence on the initial syllable of 'omega' translates to the Fijian pattern illustrated by *(mà:)(ðáwa)* 'week'; the last two (strong-weak) syllables form a bisyllabic trochaic foot, and the antepenultimate syllable receives stress by virtue of its long vowel. In contrast, the closest analogue to the prominence pattern of 'pajama', with a single stress in penultimate position, is found in words like *ma(káwa)* 'old'.

We can formalize these observations in a set of perception grammar constraints which allow Fijian speakers to decode the acoustic cues of English to determine the prominence profile of a word and from that to recover the length contrasts which, in Fijian, determine foot structure. (For the moment, I will equate prominence with stress, though this will be refined shortly). These constraints are presumably precisely the same ones that Fijian speakers use to determine the lexical representations of unfamiliar native words, as they spell out the contexts in which prominence signals vowel length:

(32)   Fijian perceptual mapping constraints

    a. FINALVLONG: If the final V is more prominent than the preceding V, then assume it is long.

    b. CLASH→LONG: If two prominent vowels are adjacent, assume the first V is long (that is, a stress clash signals length).

    c. *LONGV: Assume all vowels are short.

Consider first contrasts in bisyllabic words like *ŋgitá:* 'guitar' vs. *fíβa/βíβa* 'fever'. The input to the perception grammar is the source pronunciation, from which the listener must extract the phonological structure. I assume that Fijian listeners hear the main stress in the English surface form, indicated as a stress mark on the English phonetic form in square brackets, as a prominence peak, though not necessarily the only such peak in a word. The listener's job is then to translate the acoustics of the English form, including its prominence pattern, into a representation that encodes the significant contrasts of the borrower's language. In Fijian, this involves determining where stress is a function of position and where stress is a function of length. Again, I assume that mapping to the phonological and the lexical forms takes place in parallel; here I concentrate on the recovery of the length contrasts on which footing is parasitic.

(33)   Inputs to perception grammar: 'guitar', 'fever'

[gitá]		FINALVLONG	CLASH→LONG	*LONGV
a.	|ŋgiːtaː|			**!
b.	|ŋgita|	*!		
c.	|ŋgiːta|	*!		*
☞ d.	|ŋgitaː|			*

[fívə]		FINALVLONG	CLASH→LONG	*LONGV
a.	|fiːβaː|			*!*
☞ b.	|fiβa|			
c.	|fiːβa|			*!
d.	|fiβaː|			*!

These same constraints will derive the contrast between proparoxytones with unstressed vs. stressed initial vowels; the perceived length of secondarily stressed vowels before the main stressed vowel is on this account a function of CLASH→LONG.

(34)   Inputs to perception grammar: English 'pajama', 'omega'

[pədʒámə]		FINALVLG	CLASH→LONG	*LONGV
☞ a.	|patʃama|			
b.	|paːtʃama|			*!
c.	|patʃamaː|			*!
d.	|paːtʃamaː|			*!*

[òmégə]	FINALVLG	CLASH→LONG	*LONGV
a. |omeka|		*! (ò, é)	
☞ b. |oːmeka|			*
c. |omekaː|		*! (ò, é)	*
d. |oːmekaː|			**!

The constraints above also predict the final lengthening in 'calico' if we assume that listeners perceive the final full vowel of 'calico' as more prominent than the reduced penultimate vowel:

(35)   Input to perception grammar: English 'calico'

[kǽlɨko]	FINALVLG	CLASH→LONG	*LONGV
a. |kaliko|	*! (o > ɨ)		
b. |kaːliko|	*! (o > ɨ)		*
☞ c. |kalikoː|			*
d. |kaːlikoː|			**!

However, as noted above, not all words with stress patterns similar to 'calico' are adapted with final lengthening; alongside *kàlikó:* 'calico' we find *kò:lóni* 'colony'. We can account for this variability in the interpretation of poststress vowels if we assume that the information Fijian speakers use in determining the relative prominence of vowels includes finer phonetic details, such as inherent length differences. Schütz's (1978) corpus of Fijian loanwords contains fifteen words that are trisyllabic in English, have initial stress in English, and are realized as trisyllabic in Fijian (that is, do not undergo vowel insertion). Of these fourteen, five follow the 'colony' pattern of initial lengthening (36a), seven follow the 'calico' pattern of final lengthening (36b), and three have no lengthening, thereby losing the original English stress (36c); the latter group perhaps represents borrowings through orthography:

(36)   English trisyllabic proparoxytones

    a. Fijian (σ:)(σσ)

colony	(kò:)(lóni)
company	(kà:)(mbáni)
taffeta	(tà:)(féta)
Lucifer	(lù:)(séfa)
governor	(kò:)(βána)

    b. Fijian (σσ)(σ:)

calico	(kàli)(kó:)
polio	(pòli)(ó:)
radio	(rèti)(ó:)
editor	(èndi)(tá:)
battery	(mbàti)(rí:)
motorcar	(mòto)(ká:)
pinafore	(βìni)(βó:)

    c. Fijian σ(σσ)

cylinder	si(línda)
officer	o(βísa)
vinegar	βi(nínga), βi(níka)[12]

Although the prosody of the adapted form is not entirely predictable, neither is the choice of strategy entirely random. First, final [o] is always long in the adapted form. There are good phonetic reasons why [o] might be more often interpreted as underlyingly long than final [i] (or [ɪ]) or schwa. As is well established, English vowels exhibit inherent length differences independent of the increased length conferred by stress or intonation. Average durations for American English (using Crystal and House's notation) are presented below:

(37)   American English vowel durations (Crystal and House 1988)

ɔɪ > au > ai > o > ɔ > ʉ > a > ei > æ > ɜ > u > i > ...
298 202 160 155 146 138 134 133 131 116 114 107...msec

Thus, while 'calico' and 'colony' are similar in their prosodic structures, they differ in the inherent durations of their final vowels, with [o] on average nearly 50 ms longer than [i] (even assuming a source pronunciation with a tense final [i]).

---

12. Schütz (1983: 571) points out that "vowel lengthening is common for English words ending in -r" as in *motoka:* 'motorcar', but that some forms "have become standardized without compensatory lengthening, and as a result, the prosodic fit seems rather loose."

Evidence exists that inherent vowel length differences of this type, though not linguistically significant in English, may influence speakers of other languages. Peng and Ann (2001) have found, in Singapore English, Nigerian English, and the English of Spanish speakers, pronunciations like *illusTRAtor, frusTRAted, exerCISE, CHInese, autoBIography*. Based on a survey of such unfaithful stressings, they conclude that "If a multisyllabic word develops a primary stress placement distinct from L1, primary stress in L2 falls on the syllable whose vowel lasts the longest" (Peng and Ann 2001: 14). Furthermore, Kiparsky (2004: 22) argues that in Finnish, "the sonority hierarchy determines fixed secondary stress in loanwords", with vowels of greater sonority attracting stress. The stress-sonority relationship obtains in various native language grammars as well; for example, in Gujarati (de Lacy 2002, 2006), the preference for penultimate stress (*apwána* 'to give') is overridden in favor of stressing a syllable containing [a] rather than some less sonorous vowel (*pátini* 'wife', *hoʃijár* 'clever'). Although "loanwords often retain the source language's stress in defiance of the stress rules" (de Lacy 2006: 242), Kiparsky (2004) points out that some borrowed words, such as *sinemá* 'cinema', do change their stress pattern to accord with the sonority-stress relationship.

The lengthening of final [o] in words like 'calico' and the lack of lengthening of the prosodically similar final [i] in words like 'colony' can now be seen as an interpretation of relative prominence based in part on inherent duration of the English vowels, as compared to the expected duration of the corresponding Fijian vowel categories with which they are identified. The Fijian listeners' task in interpreting the lexically significant features of an unfamiliar trisyllabic word is to determine which syllable, if any, contains a long vowel. The final vowel of 'calico' is significantly longer than the penultimate vowel, but the final vowel of 'colony' is shorter – too close to its reduced neighbor to be identified as long. The initial vowel of 'colony', on the other hand, is inherently longer than the other two vowels of the word, and this length difference is further enhanced by the main stress on this vowel, making it a good candidate for analysis as an underlyingly long vowel. We can encode this pattern by means of one additional constraint in our perception grammar:

(38) ANTEPENULTVLONG: If the antepenultimate V is more prominent than the final or penultimate vowel, then assume the antepenultimate V is long.

The tableau below illustrates the mapping of the source words to underlying representations. bringing ANTEPENULTVLONG into play. In 'calico' (realized as *(kàli)(kó:)*) the initial vowel receives the durational enhancement of main stress, but the final vowel has the benefit of inherently greater length, making them comparable. In 'colony' (realized as *(kò:)(lóni))*, on the other hand, the initial vowel has the advantage over the remaining vowels in the word both in terms of stress-based prominence and inherent duration. The initial vowel of 'vinegar' (realized as *βi(niŋga))*, in contrast, is too short relative to the other vowels to be perceived as underlyingly long:

(39)   Inputs to Fijian perception grammar: English proparoxytones 'calico', 'colony', 'vinegar'

[kǽlɪko]	FINALVLG	CLASH→LONG	ANTEPVLG	*LONGV
a. |kaliko|	*! (o > ə)		√ (æ ≈ o)	
b. |ka:liko|	*! (o > ə)			*
☞ c. |kaliko:|			√ (æ ≈ o)	*
d. |ka:liko:|				**!

[kɔ́ləni]	FINALVLG	CLASH→LONG	ANTEPVLG	*LONGV
a. |koloni|			*! (ɔ > ə,i)	
☞ b. |ko:loni|				*
c. |koloni:|			*! (ɔ > ə,i)	*
d. |ko:loni:|				**!

[vínəgə]	FINALVLG	CLASH→LONG	ANTEPVLG	*LONGV
☞ a. |βiniŋga|				
b. |βi:niŋga|				*!
c. |βiniŋga:|				*!
d. |βi:niŋga:|				*!*

While in principle any vowel of a trisyllabic form could be long in the underlying representation, the Fijian production grammar limits the positions in which length contrasts are manifested. Recall that long vowels are shortened in penultimate position when they precede a short vowel, as illustrated in (26) *síβi* 'exceed' (the underlying long vowel surfaces in *sì:βi-ta* 'exceed, trans.'). Furthermore, Schütz (1999) notes a tendency for pre-penultimate vowels to

shorten where their shortening makes possible incorporation of the long syllable into a bimoraic foot. This shortening is illustrated in the form *ßakata:kila:*
'reveal it' in which "the first vowel [...] retains its length only in a formal pronunciation" (Schütz 1999: 140, note 4); "in faster speech" this form is pronounced as *(ßaka)(taki)(la:)* (Schütz 1999: 145). Thus even though the perception grammar constraints above make possible the analysis of a loanword on
first encounter as V:-V-V:, such a structure would most likely be altered to V-
V-V: in less formal speech, with this structure serving as the input to subsequent listeners.

The underlying representations that emerge from the perception grammar,
submitted to the production grammar, will result in the footings below:

(40)   Inputs to Fijian production grammar: 'calico', 'colony', 'vinegar'

|kaliko:|		ALIGN-R	TROCHAICFEET, BIMORAIC	MAXMORA	PARSESYLL
☞ a.	(kàli)(kó:)				
b.	(kà)(líko:)		*!		
c.	ka(líko:)		*!		*

|ko:loni|		ALIGN-R	TROCHAICFEET, BIMORAIC	MAXMORA	PARSESYLL
a.	(kò:lo)(ní)		*!*		
☞ b.	(kò:)(lóni)				
c.	ko:(lóni)				*!

|ßininga|		ALIGN-R	TROCHAICFEET, BIMORAIC	MAXMORA	PARSESYLL
a.	(ßìni)(ŋgá)		*!		
b.	(ßì)(níŋga)		*!		
☞ c.	ßi(níŋga)				*

In summary, the account above implements the generalization that upon en-
countering new words, the Fijian listener must determine the position of lexically contrastive length, by listening for prominence in positions where prominence is not automatic. The interpretation of greater-than-expected relative

length as signaling prominence is reasonable in terms of the Fijian prosodic system; Scott (1948) describes stressed short vowels as "half long" (Scott 1948: 743). Once the English forms have been mapped to Fijian underlying representations encoding contrastive length distinctions, the production grammar of Fijian will assign stress precisely as it does with native vocabulary. In this account, there is no need to assume loan-specific constraints or rankings, since the task is the same for all new vocabulary, whether native or foreign: to map the acoustic signal onto an underlying representation which encodes lexically contrastive information, and to assign stress on the basis of that information.

4.3   Comparison of production-oriented and perception-oriented accounts

We are now in a position to compare analyses of Fijian loanword adaptation. In Kenstowicz's analysis, the Fijian listener correctly perceives the position of main stress in the English word. The production grammar limits the degree of perceptual deviance between underlying and phonetic forms – specifically, by triggering lengthening of the English main stressed vowel if necessary to preserve stress on that vowel. The constraints of the production grammar refer only to phonological categories such as long vs. short, stressed vs. unstressed, and participate in crucial ranking relationships that are motivated solely by the loanword data. The second analysis, in contrast, assumes that lengthening of vowels in loanwords is an effect of a perception grammar that allows listeners to recover from the acoustic signal those aspects of the native language that are contrastive (such as vowel length). The representation provided by the perception grammar then serves as input to the production grammar, which assigns stress according to Fijian principles. The constraints of the perception grammar may refer to fine-grained, non-categorical aspects of phonetic detail, such as relative vowel duration, predicting the possibility of variation in words with similar English stress patterns but different relative inherent vowel durations, as seen in *kò:lóni* 'colony' vs. *kàlikó:* 'calico' vs. *βiníŋga* 'vinegar'.

At this point one might reasonably object that if a production grammar can account for the Fijian patterns, there is no motivation for adding another component to the model. But in fact, much of the analysis in the preceding section would be necessary to Kenstowicz's analysis as well. Given a proparoxytone with no underlying long vowels, Kenstowicz's grammar would always derive the *kò:lóni* 'colony' pattern. In order to derive the *kàlikó:* 'calico' pattern, it is crucial that Fijian listeners analyze the final vowel of 'calico' as long. Thus, along with the production constraint MAXSTRESS, the production analysis must contain an implicit perceptual component that identifies certain source vowels as underlyingly long.

However, Kenstowicz provides two additional arguments for the account of Fijian stress based on a production grammar which preserves the English stress position. The first concerns words longer than three syllables. Kenstowicz discusses words like *(tàle)βi(sóni)* 'television' which, in contrast to native forms like *li(nàmu)(nráu)* 'arm-2dual possessor' (Hayes 1995: 144), allow two adjacent unstressed syllables. The tolerance of stress lapse is, Kenstowicz argues, in conflict with the native language grammar, which would favor the footing **ta(lèβi)(sóni)*; therefore, the actual footing of 'television' must be explained as a function of the stress conserving constraint. This argument depends on the assumption that the native language grammar provides a default footing pattern for strings of light syllables, an assumption challenged by Schütz (1983), who argues that "Longer forms, especially those with an uneven number of syllables, offer the potential for alternate groupings, dependent upon accent placement" (Schütz 1983: 569). Indeed, there seems to be consensus among writers on Fijian that stress patterns in native vocabulary containing strings of more than four light syllables are not predictable. For example, Hayes (1995), citing forms such as *(mbàti)ka(síβi)* 'kind of fish', characterizes Fijian as "a language with predictable primary stress but phonemic secondary stress" (Hayes 1995: 144), and Kenstowicz ([2003] 2007: 9) concedes that "To the extent that these items are no longer decomposed in the minds of Fijian speakers, there is a precedent for the lapses observed in loans." In other words, Fijian speakers cannot predict the footing pattern of new words consisting of more than three light syllables, and must therefore listen for cues to (lexically contrastive) footing in new words. It therefore seems reasonable that Fijian listeners hearing English 'television' would interpret the prosodic pattern of this word as indicating that the first two syllables form a bisyllabic foot. This is precisely the position of Schütz (1983), who argues that in longer borrowings, "We assume that one grouping sounds closer to the English model than the other" (Schütz 1983: 569).

A second argument for Kenstowicz's stress preservation analysis concerns the treatment of forms with epenthetic vowels. While trisyllabic forms with initial stress may undergo lengthening of either the initial or the final syllable (*kò:lóni* vs. *kàlikó:*), initially-stressed words that become trisyllabic through medial epenthesis invariably lengthen the final syllable:[13]

---

13. The sole exception to this generalization is *si(liβa)* 'silver'. Schütz's (1978) corpus contains no parallel words with final stress in the source pronunciation.

(41)   Bisyllables with medial epenthesis
   (wìsi)(kí:)   'whiskey'
   (ndòke)(tá:)   'doctor'
   (sìsi)(tá:)   'sister'
   (ràka)(βí:)   'rugby'

Kenstowicz's ([2003] 2007) analysis of the data in (41) makes use of a high-ranked constraint *v́, which bans stress on epenthetic vowels. The most direct way to preserve stress on the initial vowel in a word like 'whiskey' would be to lengthen it. But lengthening the initial vowel would force the epenthetic vowel into the head of a bisyllabic foot, resulting in the nonoccurring realization *(wì:)(siki), which violates *v́. Therefore, Fijians choose the alternate route of lengthening the final vowel, which allows the initial syllable to be head of a bisyllabic foot: (wìsi)(kí:). Kenstowicz appeals to these facts as an argument against a perceptual account of lengthening, pointing out that "not all long vowels in Fijian adaptations can be attributed to a putative equation of stress = length at the level of the perceptual scan (Silverman 1992). We therefore conclude that the main stress of English is translated as a stress in Fijian rather than as a length that in turn attracts a stress" (Kenstowicz [2003] 2007: 10).

   Indeed, it seems highly unlikely that the final vowels of all forms with medial epenthesis would be consistently perceived as longer than the preceding (stressed) vowel, as required to explain the lengthening of final vowels in loanwords in the perception-based analysis outlined above. However, this final lengthening is precisely what would be expected if words like 'whiskey' are perceived by the Fijian listener as trisyllabic forms. This is the proposal advanced by Schütz (1978), who argues that "each English consonant that is not followed by a vowel is interpreted as a Fijian CV syllable" (Schütz 1978: 18). Schütz presents two arguments for this view. First, the unaccented syllable of a bisyllabic foot is typically reduced, even in native vocabulary, so that the phonetic distance between C and CV is fairly small: "certain syllables are so reduced that their phonetic manifestation is merely a lengthened consonant" (Schütz 1978: 14). Second, the choice of epenthetic vowel is dependent on the preceding consonant, with a preference for [u] after labials and [i] after coronals. This suggests "that the release of a certain consonant in this class is perceived as a particular vowel" (Schütz 1978: 22). In a production-oriented approach, the choice of epenthetic vowel is an effect of the mandate to minimize the perceptual distance between the (accurately perceived) English form and the output of the Fijian production grammar. The perception-oriented approach advocated here would view this instead as an effect of the interpretation of the

English phonetics in terms of Fijian lexical categories. Because, for example, an unstressed syllable [si] may be realized (noncontrastively) as a lengthened [s] in Fijian, the Fijian listener maps the [s] of 'whiskey' to the sequence [si] in underlying representation. On this view, the final vowel of 'whiskey' is clearly longer than what is perceived as the preceding (highly reduced) vowel, and should be analyzed as long. Words like 'whiskey' are thus similar to words like *(kàli)(kó:)* 'calico'.

This proposal is consistent with the adaptation patterns of words like 'beacon' or 'belt', with an initial stressed syllable followed by either an unstressed vowel plus an epenthetic vowel, or by two epenthetic vowels. Such forms, by hypothesis, will be perceived as trisyllabic. We would expect the initial vowel to be perceived as clearly longer than the two following vowels (and therefore, by ANTEPENULTVLONG, as long), just as in words like *(kò:)(lóni)* 'colony'. Indeed, words of this type always lengthen the initial vowel:

(42) Epenthetic forms with antepenultimate lengthening

    a. (mbì:)(kéni)   'beacon'
       (mbò:)(nísi)   'bonus'
    b. (mbè:)(léti)   'belt'
       (fi:)(límu)   'film'

As Schütz (1990: 121) points out, these words are subject to the same tendency toward shortening that affects prepenultimate vowels in native vocabulary; Schütz cites shortened forms *mbeleti* 'belt', *mbikeni* 'beacon' and *mbonisi* 'bonus'.

In contrast to epenthetic forms with initial English stress, forms with a stressed vowel followed by a single epenthetic vowel do not lengthen the stressed vowel:

(43) Epenthetic forms without lengthening

    mba(lúni)   'balloon'
    ŋga(rátʃi)   'garage'

Again, these facts are consistent with the theory outlined above, since there is no perception grammar constraint that would force a penultimate vowel followed by a less prominent vowel to be analyzed as long.

At this point we should ask why Fijian speakers behave differently from Huave speakers, since in both languages the right edges of words are invariably aligned with the main stress foot. In other words, stress in Fijian serves to signal phonemic vowel length contrasts, but also to mark the edges of words.

Why, then, do Fijians not attend to stress in the same way that Huave speakers do, assuming a word boundary at the right edge of the stress foot? One possible answer is that the languages are actually quite different in terms of the relationship between stress and word edge: while Huave appears to have one clearly perceptible stress per word, Fijian has a rich system of secondary stress which makes the strategy of projecting word edges after stressed syllables a risky one.

5.   Conclusion

One great virtue of the Optimality Theoretic approach is that it forces us to ask not only whether a grammar is consistent with a set of data, but also how that grammar could have been learned. In the cases discussed above, asking this question has led us to consider alternative analyses of the data which shed light on the division of labor between the production and perception modules of the grammar. We have now seen that loan adaptation in two languages, both of which have been described by means of a crucially ranked production grammar constraint demanding stress preservation in loanwords, is amenable to an alternative analysis in which the mapping from the acoustic signal to underlying phonological representations is mediated by the native language perception grammar. This mapping accounts for the facts of loanword stress using only rankings (of both perception and production grammar constraints) that are motivated by the native language data. In Huave, the preservation of source stress was argued to reflect the demarcative function of Huave stress, while source stress preservation in Fijian was argued to be a byproduct of the identification of stress with length.

Our larger conclusion is that what at first appeared to be unlearnable rankings in the production grammar are actually a reflection either of input frequency or of the workings of a perception grammar. This approach has several desirable consequences. First, we can eliminate loan-specific constraints like MATCHSTRESS from the grammar. This in turn allows us to make much stronger predictions about the range of possible adaptation patterns. For example, a model that includes a MATCHSTRESS constraint in the repertoire of production grammar constraints predicts that all combinations of native stress system and stress conservation in loanword adaptation should be logically possible, due to free ranking of MATCHSTRESS. In contrast, a model such as the one proposed above ties the treatment of stress in loanwords to the function of stress in the native language. We would not expect, for example, to find a language that is like Huave in all respects except that it ranks MATCHSTRESS low.

Much work obviously remains to be done in developing a complete model of native language perception/decoding processes, but language contact phonology provides a rich source of insights into this aspect of language.

References

Alderete, John
1999   Head dependence on stress-epenthesis interaction. In: Ben Hermans and Marc van Oostendorp (eds.), *The Derivational Residue in Phonological Optimality Theory*, 29–50. Amsterdam: John Benjamins.
Altmann, Heidi
2006   *The Perception and Production of Second Language Stress: A Cross-Linguistic Experimental Study*. Ph.D. dissertation, University of Delaware.
Basri, Hasan
1997   Phonological nativization of loanwords in Selayarese. Manuscript, Stony Brook University.
Basri, Hasan
1999   *Phonological and Syntactic Reflections of Morphological Structure in Selayarese*. Ph.D. dissertation, Stony Brook University.
Basri, Hasan, Ellen Broselow, and Daniel Finer
2000   Clitics and crisp edges in Makassarese. In: Catherine Kitto and Caroline Smallwood (eds.), *Proceedings of the Sixth International Meeting of the Austronesian Formal Linguistics Association*, 25–36. Department of Linguistics, University of Toronto.
Boersma, Paul
1998   *Functional Phonology: Formalizing the Interactions Between Articulatory and Perceptual Drives*. Ph.D. dissertation, University of Amsterdam. The Hague: Holland Academic Graphics.
Boersma, Paul
2000   The OCP in the perception grammar. *Rutgers Optimality Archives* 435.
Boersma, Paul, and Silke Hamann
this volume   Introduction: models of phonology in perception.
Broselow, Ellen
1993   Transfer and universals in second language epenthesis. In: Susan Gass and Larry Selinker, (eds.), *Language Transfer in Language Learning*, 71–86. Amsterdam/Philadelphia: John Benjamins.

Broselow, Ellen
1999   Stress, epenthesis, and segment transformation in Selayarese loans.
                In: Steve S. Chang, Lily Liaw and Josef Ruppenhofer (eds.), *Pro-
                ceedings of the Twenty-fifth Annual Meeting of the Berkeley Linguis-
                tics Society*, 311–325. Berkeley: Berkeley Linguistics Society.
Broselow, Ellen
2004   Unmarked structures and emergent rankings in second language
                phonology. *International Journal of Bilingualism* 8: 51–65.
Broselow, Ellen, Su-I Chen, and Chilin Wang
1998   The emergence of the unmarked in second language acquisition.
                Studies in Second Language Acquisition 20: 261–280.
Broselow, Ellen, and Zhang Xu
2004   Differential difficulty in the acquisition of second language phonol-
                ogy. *International Journal of English Studies* 4: 135–163.
Crystal, Thomas H., and Arthur S. House
1988   The duration of American-English vowels: an overview. *Journal of
                Phonetics* 16: 263–84.
Cutler, Anne, and Sally Butterfield
1992   Rhythmic cues to speech segmentation: evidence from juncture mis-
                perception. *Journal of Memory and Language* 31: 218–236.
Cutler, Anne, Katherine Demuth, and James McQueen
2002   Universality versus language-specificity in listening to running
                speech. *Psychological Science* 13: 258–262.
Davidson, Lisa
2000   Hidden rankings in the final state of the English grammar. In: Gra-
                ham Horwood and Se-Kyung Kim (eds.), *Ruling Papers II*, 21–48.
                New Brunswick: Rutgers University.
Davidson, Lisa, and Rolf Noyer
1996   Loan phonology in Huave: nativization and the ranking of faithful-
                ness constraints. In: Brian Agbayani and Sze-Wing Tang (eds.), *Pro-
                ceedings of the West Coast Conference on Formal Linguistics* 15,
                65–80. Palo Alto: CSLI.
de Lacy, Paul
2002   *The Formal Expression of Markedness.* Ph.D. dissertation, Universi-
                ty of Massachusetts at Amherst.
de Lacy, Paul
2006   *Markedness: Reduction and Preservation in Phonology.* New York:
                Cambridge University Press.
Demuth, Katherine
1996   The prosodic structure of early words. In: James Morgan and Kathe-
                rine Demuth (eds.), *Signal to Syntax: Bootstrapping from Speech to
                Grammar in Early Acquisition,* 171–184. Mahwah, N. J.: Lawrence
                Erlbaum Associates.

Diebold, A. Richard
    1961   Incipient bilingualism. *Language* 37: 97–112.
Dixon, Robert M. W.
    1988   *A Grammar of Boumaa Fijian.* Chicago: University of Chicago Press.
Eckman, Fred
    1981   On the naturalness of interlanguage phonological rules. *Language Learning* 31: 195–216.
Eddington, David
    2000   Spanish stress assignment within the analogical modeling of language. *Language* 76: 92–109.
Escudero, Paola
    2001   The role of the input in the development of L1 and L2 sound contrasts: language-specific cue weighting for vowels. In: Anna Do, Laura Domínguez and Aimee Johansen (eds.), *Proceedings of the 25th Annual Boston University Conference on Language Development*, 250–261. Somerville, Mass.: Cascadilla Press.
Escudero, Paola, and Paul Boersma
    2004   Bridging the gap between L2 speech perception research and phonological theory. *Studies in Second Language Acquisition* 26: 551–585.
Flege, James, and Richard Davidian
    1984   Transfer and developmental processes in adult foreign language speech production. *Applied Psycholinguistics* 5: 323–347.
Flege, James, Martin McCutcheon, and Steven Smith
    1987   The development of skill in producing word final English stops. *Journal of the Acoustical Society of America* 82: 433–447.
Fleischhacker, Heidi
    2000   Cluster-dependent epenthesis asymmetries. In: Adam Albright and Taehong Cho (eds.), *UCLA Working Papers in Linguistics* 7: 71–116.
Gnanadesikan, Amalia
    2004   Markedness and faithfulness constraints in child phonology. In: René Kager, Joe Pater and Wim Zonneveld (eds.), *Constraints in Phonological Acquisition*, 73–108. Cambridge: Cambridge University Press. First published on *Rutgers Optimality Archive* 67 [1995].
Grijzenhout, Janet, and Bertus van Rooij
    2001   Voicing phenomena in Zulu-English: an OT account of the emergence of the unmarked in second language acquisition. *SFB 282 Working Papers* 119.
Hayes, Bruce
    1995   *Metrical Stress Theory: Principles and Case Studies.* Chicago: University of Chicago Press.

Hayes, Bruce
2004   Phonological acquisition in Optimality Theory: the early stages. In: René Kager, Joe Pater and Wim Zonneveld (eds.), *Constraints in Phonological Acquisition*, 158–203. Cambridge: Cambridge University Press. First published on *Rutgers Optimality Archive* 327 [1999].

Isaacs, James, and Lynsey Wolter
2003   Vowel length, weight and stress in K'ichee'. Talk presented at the *Trilateral Phonology Weekend (TREND) 2003,* University of California at Santa Cruz.

Ito, Junko, and Armin Mester
1995   The core-periphery structure of the lexicon and constraints on re-ranking. In: Jill Beckman, Laura Walsh Dickey and Suzanne Urbanczyk (eds.), *University of Massachusetts Occasional Papers in Linguistics 18: Papers in Optimality Theory*, 181–209. Amherst, Mass.: Graduate Linguistics Student Association.

Jusczyk, Peter
1999   How infants begin to extract words from speech. *Trends in Cognitive Science* 3: 323–328.

Kang, Yoonjung
2003   Perceptual similarity in loanword adaptation: English post-vocalic word-final stops to Korean. *Phonology* 20: 219–274.

Kenstowicz, Michael
2001   The role of perception in loanword phonology. *Linguistique Africaine* 20.

Kenstowicz, Michael
2007   Salience and similarity in loanword adaptation: a case study from Fijian. *Language Sciences* 29: 316–340. First published on *Rutgers Optimality Archive* 609 [2003].

Kim, Yuni, and Mischa Park-Doob
2005   Fieldwork strategies for endangered dialects of Huave. Poster presented at the Workshop *Challenges and Issues in Endangered Language Fieldwork* at the LSA Annual Meeting, Oakland.

Kiparsky, Paul
2004   Universals constrain change: change results in typological generalizations. Manuscript, Stanford University.

Kreger, Glenn, and Emily Stairs
1981   *Diccionario Huave de San Mateo Del Mar.* Tlalpan, Mexico: Instituto Lingüístico de Verano.

Lassettre, Paul, and Patricia Donegan
1998   Perception in Optimality Theory: the frugality of the base. In: Benjamin Bergen, Madelaine Plauché and Ashlee Bailey (eds.), *Proceedings of the 24th Annual Meeting of the Berkeley Linguistics Society*, 346–355. Berkeley: Berkeley Linguistics Society.

Mithun, Marianne, and Hasan Basri
1986   The phonology of Selayarese. *Oceanic Linguistics* 25: 210–252.
Mohanan, K. P., and Tara Mohanan
2003   Towards a theory of constraints in OT: emergence of the not-so-unmarked in Malayalee English. *Rutgers Optimality Archive* 601.
Norris, Dennis, James McQueen, Anne Cutler, and Sally Butterfield
1997   The possible-word constraint in the segmentation of continuous speech. *Cognitive Psychology* 34: 191–243.
Peng, Long, and Jean Ann
2001   Stress and duration in three varieties of English. *World Englishes* 20: 1–27.
Peperkamp, Sharon
2004   Lexical exception in stress systems: arguments from early language acquisition and adult speech perception. *Language* 80: 98–126.
Peperkamp, Sharon
2005   A psycholinguistic theory of loanword adaptations. In: Marc Ettlinger, Nicolas Fleischer and Mischa Park-Doob (eds.), *Proceedings of the 30th Annual Meeting of the Berkeley Linguistics Society*, 341–352. Berkeley: Berkeley Linguistic Society.
Peperkamp, Sharon, and Emmanuel Dupoux
2002   A typological study of stress 'deafness'. In: Carlos Gussenhoven and Natasha Warner (eds.), *Laboratory Phonology 7*, 203–240. Berlin: Mouton de Gruyter.
Prince, Alan, and Bruce Tesar
2004   Learning phonotactic distributions. In: René Kager, Joe Pater and Wim Zonneveld (eds.), *Constraints in Phonological Acquisition*, 245–291. Cambridge: Cambridge University Press. First published on *Rutgers Optimality Archive* 353 [1999].
Ross, Kie
1996   *Floating Phonotactics: Variability in Infixation and Reduplication of Tagalog Words.* M.A. thesis, University of California at Los Angeles.
Scott, Norman C.
1948   A study in the phonetics of Fijian. *Bulletin of the School of Oriental and African Studies* 12: 737–752.
Schütz, Albert
1978   English loanwords in Fijian. In: Albert Schütz (ed.), Fijian language studies: borrowing and pidginization. *Bulletin of the Fiji Museum* 4, 1–50.
Schütz, Albert
1983   The accenting of English loanwords in Fijian. In: Frederick Agard, Gerald Kelley, Adam Makkai and Valerie Makkai (eds.), *Essays in Honor of Charles F. Hockett*, 565–572. Leiden: Brill.

Schütz, Albert
1990   Prosody and its effect on phonological processes in Fijian: a syn-
                chronic study. In: Jeremy Davidson (ed.), *Pacific Island Languages:
                Essays in Honour of G. B. Milner*, 119–127. Honolulu and London:
                University of Hawaii Press and School of Oriental and African Stu-
                dies.
Schütz, Albert
1999   Fijian accent. *Oceanic Linguistics* 38: 139–151.
Schütz, Albert
2004   English loan words in Fijian. In: Jan Tent and Paul Geraghty (eds.),
                Borrowing: A Pacific Perspective, 253–294. Canberra: Pacific Lin-
                guistics.
Silverman, Daniel
1992   Multiple scansions in loanword phonology: evidence from Canto-
                nese. *Phonology* 9: 289–328.
Steriade, Donca
2001   The phonology of perceptibility effects: the P-map and its conse-
                quences for constraint organization. Manuscript, University of Cali-
                fornia at Los Angeles.
Tesar, Bruce, and Paul Smolensky
1998   Learnability in Optimality Theory. *Linguistic Inquiry* 29: 229–268.
Thiessen, Erik, and Jenny Saffran
2003   When cues collide: use of stress and statistical cues to word bounda-
                ries by 7- to 9-month-old infants. *Developmental Psychology* 39:
                706–716.
Ussishkin, Adam, and Andrew Wedel
2003   Gestural motor programs and the nature of phonotactic restrictions:
                evidence from loanword phonology. In: Mimu Tsujimura and Gina
                Garding (eds.), *Proceedings of West Coast Conference on Formal
                Linguistics* 22: 505–518. Somerville, Mass.: Cascadilla Press.
Werker, Janet, and Suzanne Curtin
2005   PRIMIR: a developmental framework of infant speech processing.
                Language Learning and Development 1: 197–234.
Wissing, Daan, and Wim Zonneveld
1996   Final devoicing as a robust phenomenon in second language acquisi-
                tion: Tswana, English and Afrikaans. *South African Journal of Lin-
                guistics*, Supplement 34: 3–24.
Yavas, Mehmet
1994   Final stop devoicing in interlanguage. In: Mehmet Yavas (ed.), *First
                and Second Language Phonology*, 267–282. San Diego, CA: Singu-
                lar.
Yip, Moira
1993   Cantonese loan word phonology and Optimality Theory. *Journal of
                East Asian Linguistics* 2: 261–291.

Perception of intonational contours on given and new referents: a completion study and an eye-movement experiment[*]

Caroline Féry, Elsi Kaiser, Robin Hörnig,
Thomas Weskott and Reinhold Kliegl

1. Introduction

Two factors have facilitated the study of the interplay between speech perception and phonology: first, we now have the benefit of various technological advances that allow for the collection and analysis of data on perception that were unavailable 20 years ago, and second, theoretical progress. In the framework of Optimality Theory (Prince and Smolensky 2004; McCarthy and Prince 1993), research has led to the formulation of perceptually grounded constraints that interact with constraints motivated by other modules of the linguistic system. See for instance Smolensky (1996), Steriade (1995, 1999) and Flemming (1995), who have modeled in Optimality Theory the influence of perception on the usual production grammar. A further progress is proposed by Boersma (1998 et seq.), who models perception itself in Optimality Theory.

In this paper, by presenting a completion experiment and an eye-tracking study and by implementing the results in an Optimality-Theoretic model, we rely on both the technological and the theoretical advances. Traditionally, phonological theory draws heavily on production, a fact which is explained by the ease with which articulatory facts, like the position of the tongue, can be analyzed as opposed to the difficulties encountered in the study of perception. It has been observed repeatedly, however, that the way we perceive contrasts in sound structure has an influence on phonological systems and sound changes, and vice-versa, and that we articulate sounds or sound sequences depending on how we perceive them (see for instance Ohala 1981; Lindblom 1990; Steriade 1999). To cite well-known examples, palatalization arises as a consequence of

---

[*] This paper is part of the projects A1 and C1 of the SFB 632 'Information structure', funded by the DFG. We thank the organizers, Paul Boersma and Silke Hamann, and the participants of the workshop 'Speech perception in or outside phonology' of the 27th DGfS conference, where we presented this paper. Many thanks to Sabine Kern, Petra Grüttner and Anja Kuschmann for technical help.

coarticulation between a coronal and a high vowel, and final devoicing as a consequence of a reduction of final obstruents to plain voiceless ones. If neutralization arises as a result of palatalization or final devoicing, contrasts are lost. But clearly, the maintenance of a contrast may be in some cases more important than the reduction of articulatory effort, even when perception is not maximally guaranteed, such as in non-prominent syllables (see Hume 1994 and Ćavar 2004, for instance). On a more abstract level, perception and production may not be separable into distinct cognitive modules, since these two components have necessarily evolved in parallel.

The articulation of sounds and the intonation of melodies are achieved by manipulating the physical acoustic waves, and their perception is translated into impressions by the auditory system. Phonological systems, on the other hand, are symbolic in nature, and abstract away from concrete phonetic events. Once we have learned a language, we do not need to physically produce or perceive speech sounds in order to access its phonology. The problem that phonologists face is providing the best model of the relationship between phonetics and phonology. To this purpose, the classification of sounds in categories has proved very useful for the study of phonemic systems and allophonic alternations, as well as for the study of tonal patterns (see Pierrehumbert 1980, and below). The theoretical question which we try to answer in this paper is how tonal structures relate to the expectation of listeners, and to provide a model of our results.

Section 2 gives an overview of the main theoretical issues relating to intonation and its perception. Studies of the perception of tonal structures have observed categorical classes in the alignment of peaks (horizontal dimension) as well as the height of peaks (vertical dimension; Pierrehumbert and Steele 1987; Kohler 1990; Ladd and Morton 1997). Other studies find that misplaced accents induce more difficulty than exaggerated or insufficient ones (Gussenhoven 1983; Birch and Clifton 1995; Hruska, Alter, Steinhauer and Steube 2001), with this difference being attributed to the difficulty of processing incorrect prosodic information as compared to merely inappropriate prosodic information. Only few processing studies have focused on the perception of qualitatively different accents, like rising and falling ones, and the kind of anticipatory expectation they elicit (but see Féry and Stoel 2006 for such a study in German).

In §3 and §4, we report two experiments which we conducted in order to examine these issues in German. Experiment 1 is a completion experiment with a forced-choice task between two possible object completions: one that refers to a character that has already been mentioned in the preceding discourse ('discourse-given') and one that refers to a referent that is being mentioned for the first time ('discourse-new'). In Experiment 2, the eye movements of listeners were tracked as they heard spoken descriptions of scenes, so as to test whether specific on-line referential processes are involved in the processing of accents. Upon hearing an early falling accent sequence, German listeners should expect the upcoming noun to be discourse-given, whereas an early rising sequence should trigger anticipation of a discourse-new referent. This experiment adapted the material and experimental design of Kaiser and Trueswell (2004), an eye-movement experiment on word order in Finnish which showed that comprehenders extract pragmatic implications of word order incrementally as a sentence unfolds in real time, and even anticipate upcoming referents based on information encoded in word order.

The results of the sentence completion study and the eye-tracking experiment confirmed our predictions. Sentences with falling accents triggered more completions with the discourse-given character and showed anticipatory eye movements to the discourse-given referent at the onset of the second noun, even before participants had enough acoustic information to recognize this word. In contrast, sentences with rising accents triggered more answers with a discourse-new character – as compared to a (hypothetical) baseline – and showed anticipatory eye movements to a discourse-new referent.

Section 5 introduces a model of tone perception. An important finding of our experiments is that listeners have expectations regarding the discourse-status of the verbal arguments well ahead of their realizations. If listeners know that the German sentence they are processing is a declarative sentence, they can deduce the information status as discourse-new or discourse-given just by the way the tonal structure of the sentence is unfolding. As is shown in §5, such a result speaks strongly in favor of phonological processing of spoken material, and a model of perception has to take these observations into account.

2. Background

2.1 Tonal structure of German

German is an intonation language, which means that it uses pitch accents to express grammatical relationships and information structure (see von Stechow and Uhmann 1986 for instance). In intonation languages, the tonal structure of utterances is relatively flexible. Most researchers who study intonation agree that two kinds of intonational markings are necessary: (i) boundary tones, which delimit prosodic phrases and (ii) pitch accents, associated with lexically stressed syllables which are focused or topicalized. Syllables lacking a lexical stress can carry a pitch accent if necessary for the information structure. We use the term 'focus' in the sense of 'prominent' or 'new' (Rooth 1985; von Stechow and Uhmann 1986 among others), and 'topic' in the sense of 'about-ness' (see e.g. Reinhart 1981; Jacobs 2001; *inter alia*). If a constituent is a topic in German, it gets a special rising tone, and the sentence is felt to be 'about' this constituent. In our material, both focus and topic are signaled by pitch accents. If accenting is normal or unmarked (on the object in an SVO sentence), wide focus is assumed. The notion of wide focus is used in contrast with narrow focus, a situation in which only part of the sentence is prominent. In our sentences (see below), both wide and narrow focus are used. A pitch accent on the verb induces narrow focus on this constituent. An early rising accent signals a topic. We refer the reader to Rooth (1985, 1992) for a semantic definition of focus. Here, it suffices to say that focus denotes the part of the sentence which the speaker wants to signal as new, or as particularly promi-nent. Many researchers also agree that tones are morphemic, and that they arise both in the lexicon (for tone languages) and in the postlexical grammar (for all languages), when words are put together to deliver meanings. Pitch accents may appear on any syllable in a sentence, if necessary for a felicitous conversa-tion. The term 'nuclear accent' refers to an accent that is the last one in the sentence and which is perceived as the strongest one, whereas prenuclear ac-cents are those realized early in the sentence, before the nuclear one. Nuclear accents and prenuclear accents are realized by a small inventory of pitch ac-cents, the distribution of which is relatively well-studied. In German, nuclear accents are always bitonal (falling or rising), but prenuclear ones may be less complex and consist of just a high tone, or just a low tone. The nuclear accent is the last pitch accent in the Intonation Phrase (IP), an entity which corres-ponds roughly to a sentence. In a neutral realization of (1), for instance as an answer to the question 'What happens next?', the object *Krankenschwester* 'nurse' carries the nuclear accent and the subject *Arzt* 'doctor' has a prenuclear accent. The location of the neutral nuclear accent is conditioned by grammati-cal principles. In the kind of sentences which we focus on in this paper (transi-tive matrix clauses with SVO order), the default location of the nuclear accent is on the last argument of the verb, namely on the direct object (see von Ste-chow and Uhmann 1986; Cinque 1993; Féry and Samek-Lodovici 2006, among others). (In example (1), as in the other examples in this paper, small caps highlight the words which carry pitch accents. The square bracket and the subscripted F highlight the focus structure of the sentence, namely the promi-nent or new information.)

L*H   H* L   L$_I$
(1)   [Der ARZT befragt gleich die KRANKENSCHWESTER]$_F$
       'The doctor asks/questions soon the nurse'

In a declarative sentence, the nuclear accent has a falling contour, and the pre-nuclear accent is rising. This is indicated in (1) by means of the so-called auto-segmental-metrical notation system, which has been originally developed by Pierrehumbert (1980) for English, following a proposal by Bruce (1977) for Swedish, but which has in the meantime been adapted for a number of languages, among others for German (see Féry 1993; Grabe 1998; and Grice, Baumann and Benzmüller 2005; among others). L*H is a rising accent, the starred tone L* is associated with the accented syllable, and the following tone is a 'trailing' tone, which shows that the entire excursion is rising. Rising into-nation (L*H) has been interpreted as expressing topicality, openness and non-finality. In contrast, a falling accent such as H*L expresses focus and finality. The pitch contour of this sentence, one of our stimuli, is reproduced in Figure 1.

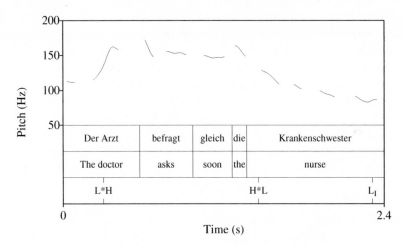

Figure 1.   Contour with late fall.

In most cases, nuclearity means finality, since the last accent is generally per-ceived as the most prominent of the sentence, even though its acoustic corre-lates may be less prominent than those of the prenuclear accents. This is due to the regular downstep of the melodic peaks which is part of the tonal characte-ristics of German, as well as of other languages. The H of the final H*L is lower than the H of the initial L*H. At the end of the phrase, the tone L$_I$ indi-cates that the global contour of the sentence is falling. This is a boundary tone which is associated with the last syllable of its domain rather than with a prominent syllable. A final L_I contrasts with a final H_I, which is typical for a question intonation or a so-called continuation intonation. In a sentence like (1), the falling pattern is induced by the last pitch accent, located on the first and second syllables of *Krankenschwester*, and the remainder of the sentence, in this case the two last syllables of this word, are low and flat. Between the two accents, the voice may remain relatively high, since there is no further tonal specification between the last high tone of *Arzt* and the first high tone of *Krankenschwester*. However, there may in general be a dip between the two high tones of a sentence like (1), especially when more syllables intervene between the two H tones. This dip is found in other languages, as well (see Pierrehumbert 1980 for English).

2.2   Given and new in intonation

The distribution of pitch accents depends on the information structure of a particular sentence. Elements that are part of the background by virtue of having already been introduced into the discourse are deaccented, especially if they occur after the nuclear accent, i.e., in a 'postnuclear' position. This is illustrated by the question-answer pair in (2). In (2B), *Krankenschwester* is introduced by the preceding question (2A), and for this reason, it is no longer able to carry the nuclear accent of the sentence. It is now the noun phrase that answers the question, *der Arzt*, that carries the nuclear accent, and the rest of the sentence has a low and deaccented intonation. Notice that, in naturally-occurring dialogue of this type, the answer is often elliptical, i.e., the deaccented part of the sentence is elided. In fact, the repetition of the given material, though grammatical, is not completely natural.

(2)   A: Wer befragt gleich die Krankenschwester?
             who questions soon the nurse
             'Who asks soon the nurse?'

             H*L   L_I
      B: [Der ARZT]_F befragt gleich die Krankenschwester
             the   doctor   questions soon the nurse
             'The doctor asks/questions soon the nurse.'

In contrast, in the question-answer pair in (3), *befragt* answers the preceding question and thus receives the nuclear accent. In this case, even though *der*

Arzt is backgrounded, it still carries a rhythmical prenuclear accent. This prenuclear accent can be less prominent than in an all-new, entirely-focused utterance as in (1) above, but does not need to be (see §2.3). As mentioned above, a
marked rising tone in this position is readily interpreted as topical. This sentence is also part of our stimulus set and is illustrated in Figure 2.

(3)   A: Was macht der Arzt gleich mit der Krankenschwester?
             what does the doctor soon with the nurse
             'What does the doctor do with the nurse?'

               L*H   H*L   L₁
        B: Der Arzt [BEFRAGT]F gleich die Krankenschwester
             the doctor questions   soon the nurse
             'The doctor asks/questions soon the nurse.'

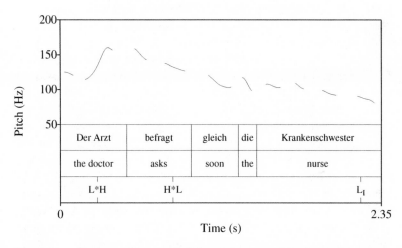

Figure 2.   Contour with an early fall and deaccented final material.

In German, a rising tone (L*H) must be followed by a falling tone (H*L) in a
declarative sentence, since the last accent of a declarative is always falling. A
falling tone is the last tone of an IP and there is no following accent in this
case.

2.3   Perception of tones

Earlier research on the perception of tones has investigated the relationship between accent location and information structure, or between accent quantity and information structure, and the findings indicate that listeners are reasonably sensitive to the relation between accents and tones. Gussenhoven (1983) and Birch and Clifton (1995) examine the role of prenuclear accents on the verb in a VP consisting of a verb plus an argument or an adjunct in English, and find that a prenuclear accent on a verb is tolerated in a sentence where only the nuclear accent is required. In Gussenhoven's study, this result is much stronger when the VP consists of a verb plus argument (as in the VP *share a flat*, where an accent structure with a single accent on *flat* is preferred) than when it consists of a verb plus adjunct (as in *skiing in Scotland*, where a structure with two accents, one on *skiing* and one on *Scotland* is readily accepted). In an experiment in which listeners had to decide how well pairs of question-answer sequences make sense, Birch and Clifton also find that listeners accept both absence and presence of prenuclear accent on the verb in focused VP (with the nuclear accent on the postverbal element). The distinction between prenuclear, nuclear and postnuclear accents has been investigated in Dutch (Nooteboom and Kruyt 1987; Krahmer and Swerts 2001), and German (Hruska, Alter, Steinhauer and Friederici 2001). The findings show that prenuclear accents on given material are readily accepted whereas unlicensed (post)nuclear accents are not. For example, the sentence in (1) with the nuclear accent on the object is perceived as deviant in the context of question (2A) which is asking about the subject of the sentence.

Studies bearing on the perception of tones as indicators of givenness and newness have been conducted for English by Jannedy (2002) and by Welby (2003), and for German by Féry and Stoel (2005). These authors find a sensitivity not only to presence and absence or quantity of accents, but also to the quality of accents. Simply put, topics require topical accents and foci require focal accents. In these studies, a whole sentence was presented to listeners at once and judgments were elicited on the basis of the complete sentence plus a context preceding the sentence. These studies corroborate the finding that prenuclear accents on given material are much more readily accepted than unlicensed postnuclear accents. Unlicensed nuclear accents located later than the licensed ones are felt to sound inappropriate. The difference of acceptability between prenuclear and postnuclear accents is explained by the observation that a supplementary prenuclear accent can get an interpretation in which the prenuclear accent is information structurally prominent, for instance by virtue of being a topic. We will see below that the readiness to accept a prenuclear accent, but to reject an inadequate nuclear accent has influenced our results, as well.

Some studies have also explicitly addressed the question of whether the perception of intonation is categorical or gradient. This issue has proved to be particularly hard to tackle since tonal patterns are realized by real voices, with their own fundamental frequency, quality, intensity, range and so on, all of them being aspects which are gradient in nature. Nevertheless, some interesting clear categories have emerged. First, using a series of equal-sized temporal shifts of F0 peaks across the constant accented syllable /lo/ in the utterance *Sie hat ja gelogen* 'she's been lying', Kohler (1990) finds three intonation categories: 'early', 'medial' and late peaks, being associated with parallel changes along the semantic dimension from 'established' (early peak) to 'new' (middle) and 'surprising' (late).[1] As a second example, Pierrehumbert and Steele (1987) asked American English speakers to imitate 15 different synthesized realizations of the phrase *only a millionaire* which differed from each other in the timing of the intonational peak: the tokens were synthesized to form a continuum such that the peak of one token was 20 ms later than the peak of the preceding token. Pierrehumbert and Steele hypothesized that if speakers were able to reproduce these fine differences, then peak alignment must be gradient. But speakers were not. Their realizations clustered around two values which are shown with the help of tone sequences in (4) and (5).

$L_I H^*L \quad H^*L \quad H_I$
(4)   ONly a MILlionaire

$L_I H^*L \quad L^*HL \quad H_I$
(5)   ONly a MILlionaire

A third, slightly more controversial example comes from Ladd and Morton (1997) who find categoriality in the interpretation of height of pitch accents in British English. There is an abrupt change in the interpretation of pitch accents, which skips from normal to emphatic when the height of the pitch accent is gradually increased.

The present study differs from the earlier studies in that it investigates the perception of tonal structures incrementally, before the sentence has ended. It assumes categoriality in the type of accents used: a falling accent is a final focus accent, and a rising accent is a non-final topical or pre-nuclear accent. Like production, speech perception is a process that occurs over time. As a

---

1.   Unfortunately, Kohler does not elaborate the concepts 'established', 'new' and 'surprising.'

sentence unfolds, listeners – on the basis of different kinds of information – develop expectations of what the speaker will produce. We assume that different kinds of phonological components exert an influence on the listener's expectations. Our study is not the first one to investigate the kind of hypotheses that listeners make on the basis of what they have heard at a particular point in time. The influence of the initial sequence of segments is a domain which has been extensively studied in the psycholinguistic literature. In the domain of syntax, word order also plays an important role, especially in languages with flexible word order like German and Finnish. But up to now, only very few studies have investigated the anticipatory effect that the not-yet-completed tonal structure has on listeners for the perception of entire sentences.

The next two sections present two studies that we conducted in order to investigate whether listeners have specific expectations about the information structure of sentences; in particular, whether listeners expect that an upcoming constituent will be discourse-new (mentioned for the first time) or discourse-given (already mentioned in the discourse) on the basis of the intonational information they have heard. However, since listeners usually have no explicit knowledge of the tonal contours of utterances, it is not possible to investigate their expectations and intuitions concerning the fundamental frequency directly. Our investigation had thus to be indirect and relied on the following well-established facts about German (see Büring 1997; Grabe 1998; Grice, Baumann and Benzmüller 2005; Féry 1993 for more detailed discussion of these points):

- a declarative sentence has a global falling contour,
- a bitonal falling accent is the last one in a declarative Intonation Phrase,
- a bitonal rising tone is not last in a declarative sentence,
- a focus is realized with the last falling tone of the utterance, and
- a prenuclear accent (topical or not) is realized with a rising tone.

By studying the kind of expectations that participants develop with respect to the discourse status (discourse-given versus discourse-new) of not yet pronounced referents, we were able to gather indirect evidence that listeners are indeed sensitive to the implications that certain tonal realizations bring with them.

3.   Completion experiment (Experiment 1)

3.1   Material and procedure

The same set of sixteen experimental items was used in both the completion experiment discussed in this section and in the Visual World experiment discussed in section 4 (see Tanenhaus, Spivey-Knowlton, Eberhard and Sedivy 1995 for details concerning the Visual World paradigm). The decision to use both types of procedure was motivated by a desire to compare results from an off-line experiment with those of an on-line experiment, in order to investigate the processing role of intonational information. It is important to note that although the off-line sentence completion experiment lets us investigate whether comprehenders use intonation to predict the discourse status of upcoming referents, an off-line study cannot tell us at what stage in the course of language processing this information is used. Both visual and auditory materials were adapted from Kaiser and Trueswell (2004) to meet the need of our design, and translated into German. The visual stimuli consisted of full-screen color pictures depicting three characters and other objects that made up coherent scenes. The three characters were of approximately the same size and positioned such that one was on the left side of the picture, one was in the middle, and one was on the right. A sample picture with a patient, a doctor, and a nurse is shown in Figure 3.

Figure 3.   A sample visual experimental stimulus.

As for the auditory stimuli, brief verbal passages were prepared that told a simple story involving the characters shown in the picture. The sample picture in Figure 3 was accompanied by the following passage:

(6)   a. An der Empfangstheke des Krankenhauses lehnen ein Arzt und eine Krankenschwester.
       'On the hospital reception desk are leaning a doctor and a nurse,'

      b. Die Uhr zeigt fast zwei.
       'It is almost two o'clock.'

      c. Der Arzt befragt gleich die Krankenschwester / die Patientin.'
       'The doctor asks soon the nurse / the patient.'

      d. Die Krankenschwester schaut nervös.
       'The nurse looks nervous.'

Prior to the target sentence (6c), two of the characters were mentioned in the first sentence of the passage (the doctor and the nurse in (6a)) and hence were discourse-given. The third character (the patient) was not mentioned in the first two sentences and hence was still discourse-new. The target sentence was preceded by a distractor sentence which referred to an element in the picture different from the three characters (the clock in (6b)). The complete set of speech materials was recorded in one session with a male speaker of German. No acoustic manipulations were performed.

The subject of the target sentence always refered to an already-mentioned entity, whereas the object refered to either an already-mentioned referent (e.g. the nurse) or a discourse-new referent (e.g. the patient). The adverb *gleich* 'soon' was inserted between the verb and the postverbal object in all experimental items in order to separate the two words from each other. The pitch on *gleich* was low or high, depending on the accent on the postverbal noun (compare Figures 1 and 2). As shown in (7), four versions of each target sentence were recorded by crossing the discourse status of the referent of the object noun phrase (discourse-new vs. discourse-given) with the new and given referents (doctor, nurse). The pitch on *gleich* is also explicitly noted, since it is this word which serves as reference point in both our experiments. In the subsequent discussion, we will often use the terms 'high/low tone on *gleich*' simply as a convenient shorthand label for the two different intonational patterns we are investigating (late fall and early fall, respectively).

(7)   a. *Late fall*, the object is new (congruent)

      L*H   H   H*L L$_I$

      [Der ARZT befragt gleich die PATIENTIN]$_F$

      the doctor questions soon the patient

      b. *Early fall*, the object is given (congruent)

      L*H   H*L   L   L$_I$

      Der Arzt [BEFRAGT]$_F$ gleich die Krankenschwester

      c. *Late fall*, the object is given (incongruent)

      L*H   H   H*L   L$_I$

      [Der ARZT befragt gleich die KRANKENSCHWESTER]$_F$

      the doctor questions soon the nurse

      d. *Early fall*, the object is new (incongruent)

      L*H   H*L   L   L$_I$

      Der Arzt [BEFRAGT]$_F$ gleich die Patientin

For the completion experiment, two variants of target sentence fragments were used. In the first one, called *late fall*, the object is realized with a falling nuclear accent (and the subject has a rising prenuclear accent). This is the variant illustrated in (1) and Figure 1, as well as in (7a and c). In the second variant, called *early fall*, there is a falling nuclear accent on the verb (and the subject has a rising prenuclear accent). This is the variant illustrated in (3) and Figure 2, as well as in (7b and d). Fragments were obtained by truncating the target sentences so that the second noun phrase is removed, e.g., *Der Arzt befragt gleich* ... 'The doctor asks soon ...'. Two presentation lists were constructed by randomly combining the 16 target stories with 20 filler stories (also adopted from Kaiser and Trueswell 2004). Each pair of consecutive target items was separated by at least one filler item. Fillers were designed to vary in the number of characters in the picture and in whether the characters were mentioned in the story. Within a presentation list, eight of the target trials appeared with the high tone pattern and eight appeared with the low tone pattern. Reverse order lists were also generated to control for trial order.

Thirty-two native speakers of German were tested individually on a PC. Each trial began with the presentation of the picture stimulus. After a 1000 ms delay, participants heard the corresponding passage ending with the target sentence fragment via earphones. Participants were asked to complete the passage by ticking one of two options which were presented to them on a sheet of paper (e.g. the nurse or the patient).

3.2   Hypotheses

As noted in section 2.2, we hypothesized that in the late fall variant (with a high tone on *gleich*), the rising accent on the subject would be interpreted as the topical non-final accent which must be followed by another accent. We therefore expected participants to complete the sentence fragments more often with the discourse-new referent (e.g. the patient) in this condition. On the other hand, in the variant with the early fall (and a low tone on *gleich*), the falling contour on the verb should be interpreted as the last accent of the sentence. In this case, we expected participants to complete the sentence fragments more often with the discourse-given referent (e.g. the nurse).

Hypotheses:

H1: High tone on *gleich* (late fall) prompts completion with discourse-new referent.
H2: Low tone on *gleich* (early fall) prompts completion with discourse-given referent.

3.3   Results

The results of the completion task are summed up in Figure 4. When hearing a low tone on *gleich*, the participants completed the target sentence fragments more often with the discourse-given referent than with the discourse-new referent (76% vs. 24%). When confronted with a high tone on *gleich*, completions with the discourse-new referent increased remarkably and were even somewhat more frequent than completions with the discourse-given referent (56% vs.

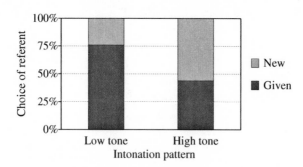

Figure 4.   Results of the sentence completion task.

44%). Tests revealed that the difference between the answers to the two intonation patterns was statistically significant ($p < 0.05$) (see Weskott *et al.* submitted for detail).

3.4 Discussion

Our results show that the choice of the referent in the sentence completion was dependent on the intonational variant. This shows that participants were sensitive to prosody. Discourse-status depended on intonation as predicted: With a low tone on *gleich*, completions with discourse-given referents were chosen more frequently than with discourse-new referents. With a high tone on *gleich*, completions with discourse-given referents were reliably reduced. It is tempting to infer that only the low tone pattern influenced completions whereas the high tone pattern had no influence, since completions with referents of either discourse status were nearly equally frequent in this last condition. We have, however, independent evidence from a comparable study on word order (not discussed in this paper, but see Weskott *et al.* submitted) that participants in general exhibit a preference for completions with discourse-given referents in this task (see also Kaiser and Trueswell 2004 for related discussion regarding a preference for already-mentioned referents). In light of these data, we take the results of the high tone condition as an indication that the rising accent counteracts the discourse-given bias and pushes participants to choose discourse-new referents more often than they otherwise would have.

When considering these results, one needs to keep in mind another factor that may have contributed towards the apparent discourse-old bias that we observed in the results. First, it is important to note that even the discourse-given character can, under certain circumstances, receive an accent – namely, when it is interpreted contrastively. In the semantic interpretation of focus, a contrastive accent is interpreted as generating a set of alternatives (in the sense of Rooth 1985, 1992). Thus, a rising accent on the subject can occur when the object is discourse-new information or when it is discourse-given and contrastive. As a result, a rising accent on the subject may also trigger completions with the already-mentioned referent as the object. However, the sentences used in this experiment did not provide any explicit cues that would push participants towards a contrastive interpretation of the object, and thus we regard the risk of contrast and discourse-oldness being confounded as very low.

Furthermore, since the discourse-new referent is displayed in the picture from the beginning, we cannot exclude the possibility that participants will interpret this character as 'visually given'. In other words, we might also expect some responses in which participants opted for the discourse-new (but visually given) referent even if the accent on the verb is falling. It is not unheard of for languages to distinguish between different kinds of givenness, see. e.g. Baumann (2006) and Birner and Ward (1998).

In sum, the results of the first experiment show that different intonational patterns create different expectations regarding the discourse status of upcoming referents. However, on the basis of the sentence completion experiment, we cannot tell at what stage of processing the intonational information is used. Are listeners extracting information from the intonational patterns at the same time as they parse the sense? Or is intonational information used at a later stage of processing, after the sentence fragment has already been comprehended? On the basis of the results of the off-line sentence completion task, we can conclude that listeners are sensitive to information that intonation carries regarding the discourse status of not-yet-mentioned entities, but we do not know whether intonational information is being processed at the same time as the propositional meaning of the sentence, or at a later stage of processing. In order to investigate this question, we used eye-tracking in a visual world paradigm (Experiment 2).

4.   Visual World experiment (Experiment 2)

4.1   Material and procedure

The auditory stimulus material in this experiment consisted of the same passages used in Experiment 1, but now the sentences were not truncated, i.e., we used entire target sentences instead of target sentence fragments; sample items are given in (7). Four presentation lists were constructed by randomly combining the 16 target stories with 32 filler stories. Each pair of consecutive target items was separated by at least one filler item. Within a presentation list, eight of the experimental trials appeared with the low tone pattern and eight trials appeared with the high tone pattern. For both of these prosodic patterns, the target sentence of half of the trials mentioned the discourse-given referent and the target sentence of the other half of the trials mentioned the discourse-new referent. Each target item was then rotated through these four conditions, generating four different presentation lists. The fillers had the same overall setting as in the preceding experiment, except that the final sentence of eight filler stories described the picture incorrectly. The total sample of 48 trials were individually randomized for each participant.

A new group of 40 native speakers of German (none of whom participated in the completion experiment), were tested individually. Each trial began with the presentation of the picture stimulus. After a 1000 ms delay, participants heard the corresponding passage via earphones. Participants were instructed to press a key whenever they noticed an erroneous description. While participants listened to the passages, their eye movements were recorded by a SMI-iViewX eye-tracking system. The basic idea of the Visual World paradigm is to track which of the referents in the picture participants attend to by determining which referent is fixated at any point in time. We implemented the Visual World paradigm in order to check whether intonational cues can trigger anticipatory eye movements towards the referent with the appropriate discourse status. Incorrect descriptions were included to ensure that participants would pay attention to both the visual and the auditory stimulus. The advantage of this method over the one used in Experiment 1 is that speakers do not perform a given task consciously, and that the method is less invasive. Eye fixations on referents indicate the likelihood of the referent as the intended object in the target sentence. It has being shown independently that people tend to look at what is being talked about. We can thus infer from the proportion of fixations how likely a potential referent was considered to be mentioned in each case (Allopenna, Magnuson and Tanenhaus 1998; and Tanenhaus, Magnuson, Dahan and Chambers 2000).

4.2   Hypotheses

According to our hypotheses, summed up below, an early fall melody (accompanied with a low tone on *gleich*) is interpreted as standing for an unaccented object, and participants will show a preference for fixating the discourse-given referent (e.g., the nurse) more often than the discourse-new referent. On the other hand, a late fall melody (accompanied by a high tone on *gleich*) is interpreted as signaling an upcoming accented (and hence discourse-new) object, and thus we predict that participants will tend to fixate the discourse-new referent (e.g., the patient) more often than the discourse-given one. This hypothesis claims that accent patterns trigger anticipatory eye movements towards the discourse-given referent (when a falling accent has already been heard) or towards the discourse-new referent (when only a rising accent has occurred, and a falling accent is expected to follow) before the segmental information of the actual second noun phrase becomes available. In order to test this, we identified the offset (end point) of the adverb *gleich* 'soon' as the critical event at time $t_0 = 0$. The critical noun, of course, starts right at the offset of *gleich*.

Thus, we predict a main effect of prosody (whether the voice is low or high) shortly after the critical event.

Hypotheses

H1: Low tone on *gleich* (early fall) prompts anticipatory fixations of discourse-given referent.
H2: High tone on *gleich* (late fall) prompts anticipatory fixations of discourse-new referent.

It follows from the hypotheses that two of the four experimental conditions are congruent, whereas two are incongruent. If the early fall pattern triggers anticipatory fixations of the discourse-given referent and the upcoming noun phrase turns out to refer to the discourse-given referent, the anticipatory fixations are correct. Likewise, if the late fall pattern triggers anticipatory fixations of the discourse-new referent and the upcoming noun phrase mentions the discourse-new referent, the anticipatory fixations prove to be correct. However, when the object noun phrase does not refer to the anticipated referent (i.e. when the object is discourse-given after a late fall pattern, or discourse-new after early fall pattern), we assume that attention has to be reallocated from the anticipated referent to the actually mentioned referent. We predict that this reallocation of attention is reflected in a delayed increase of preferred fixations of the mentioned referent.

4.3   Results

We report the results within the time window beginning 1000 ms before and ending 1000 ms after the critical event (offset of *gleich*). This time window covers nearly the whole target sentence. Fixations were determined by using a velocity-based saccade detection algorithm (Engbert and Kliegl 2003). Fixation probabilities for the discourse-given referent and the discourse-new referent were averaged within ten segments à 200 ms. In Figure 5, we plot difference scores, which were calculated by subtracting the probability of fixating on the discourse-new referent from the probability of fixating on the discourse-given referent. Accordingly, positive scores indicate preferred fixations of the discourse-given referent, whereas negative scores indicate preferred fixations of the discourse-new referent.

FixProb(Given) - FixProb(New)

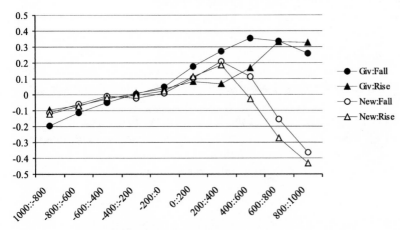

Figure 5. Fixation probability for the discourse-given referent minus fixation probability for the discourse-new referent in Experiment 2 for target sentences mentioning the discourse-given (Given) and the discourse-new (New) referent, paired with an early fall accompanied with a low tone pattern on *gleich* (Early Fall) or with a late fall accompanied with a high tone pattern on *gleich* (Late Fall).

Analyses of variance revealed an increasing tendency to fixate the discourse-given referent until about 300 ms after the critical event, indicating a general bias towards the discourse-given referent. In the time slices from 200 ms until 600 ms after the critical event, fixations of the discourse-given referent were reliably more frequent with a low tone on *gleich* (Fall) as compared to a high tone on *gleich* (Rise). In other words, participants' fixations on discourse-old vs. discourse-new referents are significantly influenced by the intonational pattern of the sentence. It is well-known that it takes about 200 ms to program and launch an eye movement (Matin, Shao and Boff 1993), and thus the eye movements occurring 200 ms after the offset of *gleich* were actually programmed during the offset of *gleich*, i.e. before the onset of the subsequent noun (the object). Note also that the mean onset of the postverbal noun phrase was within that time window (113 ms after the onset of *gleich*). The finding that there is a significant difference in the 'given referent-new referent' difference scores already in the 200–400 ms time slice indicates that participants are indeed launching anticipatory eye movements. In other words, they are making use of the intonation information very quickly and efficiently to make predictions about the next referent.

Finally, in the time slice from 400 ms until 600 ms after the critical event, the lexical content of the noun has an effect. Thus, in the incongruous conditions (a late fall/high tone on *gleich* followed by a given object, and an early fall/low tone on *gleich* followed by a discourse-new object), the anticipatory looks turn out to be incorrect, and thus we see a re-allocation effect, as participants make use of the lexical content of the noun to fixate the mentioned referent. In contrast, in the congruous conditions (a late fall/high tone on *gleich* followed by a new object, and an early fall/low tone on *gleich* followed by a given object), the lexical content of the noun confirms the expectations participants built up based on the intonational pattern. Not surprisingly, this effect persists until the end of the time window. Note that by the end of the trials, participants' fixations mirror their overall target choices.

4.4   Discussion

Experiment 2 confirms the finding of Experiment 1, that participants are sensitive to intonation. Crucially, Experiment 2 also tells us about the time-course of this sensitivity. In addition to an early general preference to attend to the discourse-given referent, we saw in Figure 6 that prosody affected fixations of referents very shortly after the critical event. The data suggest that the participants were launching anticipatory looks to one of the two referents even before they had enough phonological information to recognize the word – in other words, it seems that participants are very efficiently and quickly making use of the information carried by the intonational contour of the sentence. Moreover, the reallocation effect discussed above shows that whenever the anticipation prompted by the accent pattern turned out to be misleading, it took participants some time to shift their attention to the actually mentioned referent, as indicated by a slower increase of preferred fixations of the mentioned referent. As a whole, Experiment 2 shows that participants make use of intonational information very quickly during on-line processing, and that the discourse-level information carried by intonation, like that encoded in word order (see Weskott *et al.* submitted and Kaiser and Trueswell 2004 on Finnish) can be used to predict upcoming referents.

5.   Modeling tonal perception and production[2]

On the basis of this observation and of existing models of phonological perception in Optimality Theory, we develop in this section a model of the perception of intonation, to our knowledge the first of this kind. Our results are important for a theory of perception of tonal contours since they provide evidence for a preplanning of upcoming tonal events. Hearers develop expectations about the yet-to-come tonal patterns while a sentence enfolds.

The material presented in the preceding sections leads us to assume three levels in perception, one of which being the phonological level, and the other two are those which Boersma (this volume) and Boersma and Hamann (this volume) call phonetic and underlying respectively, as shown in (8). The lowest level is the acoustic signal, in our case a melody or tune. The intermediate level is the surface form (the phonological level in our terminology), which corresponds to pitch accents, boundary tones etc. (see section 2) and the highest level is the semantico-conceptual one (the underlying form), which corresponds to the meaning of phonological tones. We thus follow McQueen and Cutler (1997) among others, who assume that perception involves two separate processes: perception *per se* (equivalent to the prelexical level of psycholinguistics) and recognition (corresponding roughly to the lexical level). The perceptual operation transforms the raw fundamental frequency into phonological objects, which can be understood as tonal morphemes (Liberman 1975; Pierrehumbert 1980; Ladd 1996), and the recognition operation interprets these morphemes as abstract concepts with their own meanings (topic in our example (8)).

According to the conventions of this book, the single arrows in Figure 6 indicate that the interpretation of a rising melody as a pitch accent is language-dependent. In a language without pitch accent, this kind of pitch excursion may signal something else, like a lexical tone or the boundary of a phonological domain. It must be noted that the same kind of pitch excursion can also be interpreted as a boundary tone in German if it is located on an unstressed syllable at the end of an IP, for instance. In other words, the task of the hearer while perceiving a certain tonal pattern is to regognize it as a specific type of phonological object which is then identified as the bearer of a specific meaning, like topic, focus, new referent, etc. The two processes can happen in parallel since it must be the case that the process of identification (recognition) influences the process of perceiving (translation of F0 contours into tonal morphemes).

---

2.   Many thanks to Paul Boersma and Silke Hamann who discussed the formal aspects of tonal perception with us.

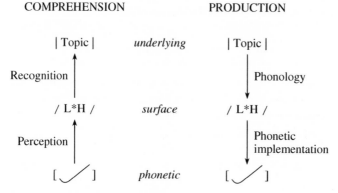

Figure 6.   Model of tone processing

We do not dwell on the phonetic level here, and refer the readers to Boersma (this volume) who discusses several possible interpretations for it. Instead, we concentrate on the phonological level. There are two major arguments emerging from our study which speak in favor of the phonological level. First, as shown in §3, pitch excursions are uninterpretable as such. It is the phonological system of a specific language which allows the listeners to interpret falling and rising tones as pitch accents, boundary tones or lexical tones. Listeners translate a rising pitch excursion into something abstract like a topic because they understand it as a certain kind of pitch accent, and pitch accents have themselves meanings (see for instance Pierrehumbert and Hirschberg 1990; Steedman 2000; and Gunlogson 2001 for the meaning of tones). Second, the results of Experiments 1 and 2 suggest an intermediate level that allows listeners to plan ahead which tones are still to come, and to infer the discourse-status of the not yet introduced referents. As we demonstrated in this paper, when listeners start to process an utterance which they know to be declarative, they anticipate a final falling tone. As long as this falling tone has not been perceived, listeners keep expecting it, and process the tonal contours associated on referents, verbs and so on, according to this expectation. More specifically, every rising tone is interpreted as a non-final one.

We assume a model of grammar in which the language forms which underlie production and perception are the same, similarly to the parity model (Liberman and Whalen 2000) or to the Optimality-Theoretic model, among others which make this assumption. Since each of these two aspects of language needs the other one to function, and since they evolved simultaneously, this is a reasonable assumption to make. In this view, models of auditory perception are identical to models of production. A caveat is necessary however: modeling perception and production must be carefully distinguished from the 'actions' or processing involved in language. It is evident that language perception involves different functions from those needed in production. The articulatory gestures are only truly present in production, and even if theories like the motor theory are right in postulating an articulatory component in perception, it is clear that perception involves an auditory and a visual component which are subordinate in production.

In order to make our model more specific, we propose an Optimality-Theoretic view on intonation, adapted from Gussenhoven (2004), who shows how prespecified tones are aligned and associated with texts. In the following we consider both how perception as well as production can be expressed in Optimality Theory. As Smolensky (1996) first showed, Optimality Theory provides a framework in which the constraints entering the evaluation of candidates work in two directions, making this model of grammar ideal for evaluating both production and perception with the same tools.

We assume that sequences of tones associate and are aligned with segmental material or with edges of prosodic constituents in ways determined by specific constraint rankings. Our experimental material contained three kinds of tones: a bitonal falling pitch accent H*L, used to express a 'focus', which was the final tone in our sentences, a bitonal rising pitch accent L*H standing for 'topic' or simply prenuclearity, and a final boundary tone L_I, which is responsible for declarativity. Of course, a complete grammar of the intonation of German includes more than this small inventory of tones, but for the sake of this paper, it is sufficient. The starred tones H* and L* associate with metrical heads of the Intonation Phrase, H and L concatenate to the right of the starred tone and L_I aligns with the right edge of the Intonation Phrase. For the sake of simplicity, we assume that H*L and L*H are associate as a single entity with the segmental material.

Some of the relevant constraints are listed in (9). The first constraints are ASSOCIATE constraints which require that segmental material independently specified for focus or topic associate with certain tones. The metrically most prominent syllable of such information structural categories has to associate with the starred tone. The last constraint in (9) is an ALIGN constraint which lets the right edge of an Intonation Phrase coincide with the boundary tone L_I.

(9)   a. ASSOCIATE (Focus, H*L): Associate the prominent syllable of a focus with H*L.

       b. ASSOCIATE (Topic, L*H): Associate the prominent syllable of a topic with L*H.

       c. ALIGN (IP, L_I, R): Align L_I with the rightmost syllable of the IP.

Optimality-Theoretic tableaux (10) and (11) illustrate this simple grammar for our sentences. In both tableaux, candidate (a) is the winner, since it fulfills all constraints. The other candidates violate one constraint each. The constraints are not ranked, as they do not interfere which each other here. The input consists of the morpho-syntactic material with its information structure. The right boundary of the Intonation Phrase is also indicated in the input, since L_I is aligned with this boundary. In (10), the whole VP is focused, whereas in (11), only the verb is focused. The stress pattern of the words entering the input is calculated independently, and can be considered as part of the input. The lexical stress of the input words is underlined in the input. The small caps in the candidates indicate which syllable is supposed to be accented. This accent is then realized by a bitonal tone such as H*L, which appears on a focus. In (10), the argument of the verb carries the accent, rather than the verb itself (see Féry and Samek-Lodovici 2006 for constraints to this effect). And in (11), the verb itself carries the bitonal tone. In (10) and (11), there is no topic, and the second constraint is vacuously fulfilled.

(10)   [befragt die PATIENTIN]$_F$

...[be<u>fra</u>gt die Pa<u>tie</u>ntin]$_F$]$_I$	ASSOC (Foc, H*L)	ASSOC (Top, L*H)	AL (IP, L$_I$,R)
☞ a. H*L L$_I$ [befragt die PaTIENTin]$_F$]$_I$			
b. H* L L$_I$ [befragt die PaTIENTin]$_F$]$_I$	*!		
c. L$_I$ H*L [befragt die PaTIENTin]$_F$]$_I$			*!

(11)   [befragt]$_F$ die Patientin

...[be<u>fra</u>gt]$_F$ die Pa<u>tie</u>ntin]$_I$	ASSOC (Foc, H*L)	ASSOC (Top, L*H)	AL (IP, L$_I$,R)
☞ a. H*L L$_I$ [beFRAGT]$_F$ die Patientin]$_I$			
b. H*L L$_I$ [beFRAGT]$_F$ die Patientin]$_I$	*!		
c. H* L L$_I$ [beFRAGT]$_F$ die Patientin]$_I$	*!		
d. L$_I$ H*L [beFRAGT]$_F$ die Patientin]$_I$			*!

The operations of association and alignment are further restricted by general constraints on the intonation structure which regulate the usual association of tones with tone bearing units (TBUs, in German, syllables). The four most important ones according to Gussenhoven (2004) are: (i) the fact that TBUs are usually associated with no more than one tone (NOCROWDING, NOCONTOUR), (ii) tones prefer to be associated with only one TBU (NOSPREADING), (iii) tones and TBUs do not delete and are not freely epenthesized (MAX, DEP), and (iv) they do not change their value, even if a markedness constraint like OCP militates in this direction (IDENT): in German, for instance, a hat pattern, implying two adjacent high tones is well tolerated.

Interpretative constraints attribute meanings to tones: a bitonal H*L for instance is interpreted as a focus, and a L tone at the end of an Intonation Phrase is interpreted as the boundary tone of a declarative sentence. In the same way, a bitonal rising tone gets an interpretation as a non-final or as a topical accent. In hearing such a tone on the stressed syllable of a constituent, hearers know that more material is to come. The interpretative constraints (12) are the mirror images of the constraints in (9).

(12) a. INTERPRET (H*L, Focus): Interpret H*L as a focus.

  b. INTERPRET (L*H, Topic): Interpret L*H as a topic.

  c. INTERPRET (L_I, R): Interpret L_I as the boundary tone of a declarative IP.

Tableau (13) illustrates how a bitonal tone on *Patientin*, the object of a VP, allows us to formulate hypotheses about the focus structure of this VP. This tone structure is compatible with a narrow focus on *Patientin*, but also on the whole VP. It is, however, not compatible with a narrow focus on the verb. In (14), a bitonal accent on *befragt* is compatible only with narrow focus on this verb (at least when the whole VP is new in the discourse).

(13) H*L stands for a wide focus domain

$H*L\ L_I$, be<u>fragt</u> die Pat<u>ie</u>ntin	INTERP (H*L, Foc)	INTERP (L*H, Top)	INTERP (L_I, IP, R)
$H*L\ L_I$ ☞ a. [befragt die PaTIENtin]$_F$			
$H*L\ L_I$ ☞ b. befragt die [PaTIENtin]$_F$			
$H*L\ L_I$ c. [beFRAGT]$_F$ die Patientin	*!		

(14)   H*L stands for a narrow focus domain

H*L L₁, be<u>fragt</u> die Pa<u>tien</u>tin	INTERP (H*L, Foc)	INTERP (L*H, Top)	INTERP (L₁, IP, R)
H*L L₁ ☞ a. [beFRAGT]_F die Patientin			
H*L L₁ b. beFRAGT [die Patientin]_F	*!		

In the same way, hearers interpret a rising tone as a topic. Tableau (15) is the Optimality-Theoretic tableau to this effect. Candidate (15b) is eliminated because a rising tone is interpreted as a focus.

(15)   L*H stands for a topic

L*H, der <u>Arzt</u>	INTERP (H*L, Foc)	INTERP (L*H, Top)	INTERP (L₁, IP, R)
L*H ☞ a. [der ARZT]_T			
L*H b. [der ARZT]_F		*!	

Evidently, the model we have offered in this section needs to be elaborated. But, even if the analysis is rather short for reasons of space, we think that we have demonstrated the existence and importance of a phonological level between the phonetic and the underlying level in the perception of intonation. In an Optimality-Theoretic approach like the one developed here, the phonological tones are interpreted as pragmatic discourse concepts, and pragmatic discourse concepts are realized as phonological tones. The speaker produces tones in order to highlight some constituents and the hearer interprets the tones correctly. This allows speakers and hearers to communicate and comprehend not only lexical and semantic contents, but also the discourse structure like focus, topic, new and given information.

6.   Conclusion

In phonology, there has been a bias towards the study of production rather than perception. The reason for this difference is to be found in the poor access to the mechanisms underlying perception as compared to the possibilities offered by vocal tract modeling or experimental work on speech production. In this paper, we have presented two experiments bearing on the issue of perception. Our domain of investigation has been tonal contours in German and the expectations that listeners have, on the basis of the global intonation contour of a sentence, concerning the information structure of not-yet-perceived constituents. The first experiment was a forced-choice completion task using truncated sentences, where subjects had to choose between two possible object completions: one of them referring to a discourse-given and the other one referring to a discourse-new character. The results show an overall tendency in favor of the given constituent, which is confirmed by similar experiments we performed bearing on word order, not presented in this paper. However, this preference is modulated by accent type: participants were more likely to choose the given referent when they heard a sentence with an early falling accent than when they heard a tonal pattern giving them reasons to assume that the last accent was still to come, in which case participants were more likely to opt for the discourse-new referent. The second experiment was an eye-tracking experiment, using the complete versions of the sentences that were truncated in the first experiment. Thus, the participants heard the same sentences, but this time in their entirety. We tracked the eye movements of the listeners while they listened to a tonal pattern varying between early accent on the verb and late accent on the object, and assumed that the amount of fixation of the referents reflect the probabilities that the referents are considered as possible objects. Again, we saw a clear effect of the prosody on the preference for the upcoming, not yet heard object. As a whole, the two experiments indicate that not only do listeners use intonation to predict the discourse-status of upcoming referents, they do so very quickly and efficiently during on-line processing.

Altogether, our findings illustrate that in an intonation language like German, specific tonal contours, reflecting specific accent patterns and pragmatic meanings, can result in expectations regarding the discourse status of a yet-to-be-heard constituent. Furthermore, our experimental results show that a certain amount of anticipation helps the listeners to interpret tonal contours. The time frame inside of which such contours are processed is much longer than the one needed for the perception (and processing) of single segments or single words. Pitch excursions need language-specific phonologies in order to be interpretable. A model of perception must take this fact into account, and integrate a phonological level able to model the grammar of intonation.

References

Allopenna, Paul D., James S. Magnuson, and Michael K. Tanenhaus
   1998   Tracking the time course of spoken word recognition: evidence for
                continuous mapping models. *Journal of Memory and Language* 38:
                419–439.
Baumann, Stefan
   2006   *The Intonation of Givenness. Evidence from German.* Tübingen:
                Niemeyer.
Birch, Stacy, and Charles Clifton, Jr.
   1995   Focus, accent, and argument structure: effects on language compre-
                hension. *Language and Speech* 38: 365–391.
Birner, Betty J., and Gregory Ward
   1998   *Information Status and Noncanonical Word Order in English.* Ams-
                terdam/Philadelphia: John Benjamins.
Boersma, Paul
   1998   *Functional Phonology: Formalizing the Interactions Between Arti-
                culatory and Perceptual Drives.* Ph.D. dissertation, University of
                Amsterdam. The Hague: Holland Academic Graphics.
Boersma, Paul
   this volume Cue constraints and their interactions in phonological perception and
                production.
Boersma, Paul, and Silke Hamann
   this volume Introduction: models of phonology in perception.
Bruce, Gösta
   1977   Swedish word accent in sentence perspective. *Travaux de l'Institut
                de Linguistique de Lund* 12.
Büring, Daniel
   1997   *The 49th Bridge Accent.* Berlin: Mouton de Gruyter.
Ćavar, Malgorzata
   2004   *Perception and Production of Polish Palatals.* Ph.D. dissertation,
                University of Potsdam.
Cinque, Guglielmo
   1993   A null theory of phrase and compound stress. *Linguistic Inquiry* 24:
                239–297.
Engbert, Ralf, and Reinhold Kliegl
   2003   Microsaccades uncover the orientation of covert attention. *Vision
                Research* 43: 1035–1043.
Féry, Caroline
   1993   *German Intonational Patterns.* Niemeyer, Tübingen.

Féry, Caroline, and Ruben Stoel
2006   Gradient perception of intonation. In: Gisbert Fanselow, Caroline Féry, Matthias Schlesewsky and Ralf Vogel (eds.), *Gradience in Grammar: Generative Perspectives*, 145–166. Oxford: Oxford University Press.

Féry, Caroline, and Vieri Samek-Lodovici
2006   Focus projection and prosodic prominence in nested foci. *Language* 82: 131–150.

Flemming, Edward
1995   *Auditory Representations in Phonology*. Ph.D. dissertation, Stanford University.

Grabe, Esther
1998   *Comparative Intonational Phonology: English and German*. Ph.D. dissertation, Universiteit of Nijmegen.

Grice, Martine, Stefan Baumann, and Ralf Benzmüller
2005   German intonation in autosegmental-metrical phonology. In: Sun-Ah Jun (ed.), *Prosodic Typology: The Phonology of Intonation and Phrasing*, 55–83. Oxford: Oxford University Press.

Gunlogson, Christine
2001   *True to Form: Rising and Falling Declaratives as Questions in English*. Ph.D. dissertation, University of California at Santa Cruz.

Gussenhoven, Carlos
1983   Testing the reality of focus domains. *Language and Speech* 26: 61–80.

Gussenhoven, Carlos
2004   *The Phonology of Tone and Intonation*. Cambridge: Cambridge University Press.

Hruska, Claudia, Kai Alter, Karsten Steinhauer, and Anita Steube
2001   Misleading dialogues: human's brain reaction to prosodic information. In: Ch. Cavé, I. Guaïtella and S. Santi (eds.), *Oralité et gesturalité: Interactions et comportements multimodaux dans la communication*. 425–430. Paris: L'Harmattan.

Hume, Elizabeth
1994   *Front Vowels, Coronal Consonants and their Interaction in Nonlinear Phonology*. New York: Garland.

Jacobs, Joachim
2001   The dimensions of topic-comment. *Linguistics* 39: 641–681.

Jannedy, Stefanie
2002   *Hat Patterns and Double Peaks: The Phonetics and Psycholinguistics of Broad Versus Late Narrow Versus Double Focus Intonations*. Ph.D. dissertation, Ohio State University.

Kaiser, Elsi, and John C. Trueswell
2004   The role of discourse context in the processing of a flexible word-order language. *Cognition* 94: 113–147.

Kohler, Klaus J.
1990   Macro and micro F0 in the synthesis of intonation. In: Kingston, John, and Mary Beckman (eds.), *Papers in Laboratory Phonology I: Between the Grammar and the Physics of Speech*, 115–138. Cambridge: Cambridge University Press.

Krahmer, Emiel, and Marc Swerts
2001   On the alleged existence of contrastive accents. *Speech Communication* 34: 391–405.

Ladd, D. Robert
1996   *Intonational Phonology*. Cambridge: Cambridge University Press.

Ladd, D. Robert, and Rachel Morton
1997   The perception of intonational emphasis: continuous or categorical? *Journal of Phonetics* 25: 313–342.

Liberman, Mark Y.
1975   *The Intonational System of English*. Ph.D. dissertation, MIT.

Liberman, Alvin M., and Douglas H. Whalen
2000   On the relation of speech to language. *Trends in Cognitive Sciences* 4: 187–196.

Lindblom, Björn
1990   Explaining phonetic variation: a sketch of the H&H theory. In: William J. Hardcastle and Alain Marchal (eds.), *Speech Production and Speech Modeling*, 403–40. Dordrecht: Kluwer Academic Publishers.

Matin, Ethel, K.C. Shao, and Kenneth R. Boff
1993   Saccadic overhead: information processing time with and without saccades. *Perception & Psychophysics* 53: 372–380.

McCarthy, John J., and Alan S. Prince
1993   Generalized alignment. In: Geert Booij and Jaap van Marle (eds.), *Yearbook of Morphology 1993*, 79–153. Dordrecht: Kluwer.

McQueen, James, and Anne Cutler
1997   Cognitive processes in speech perception. In: William J. Hardcastle and John Laver (eds.), *The Handbook of Phonetic Sciences*, 566–586, Oxford: Blackwell.

Nooteboom, Sieb G., and Johanna G. Kruyt
1987   Accents, focus distribution, and the perceived distribution of given and new information: an experiment. *Journal of the Acoustical Society of America* 82: 1512–1524.

Ohala, John J.
1981   The listener as a source of sound change. In: Carrie Masek, Roberta A. Hendrick, Mary Frances Miller (eds.), *Proceedings of the Chicago Linguistics Society*, 178–203. Chicago.

Pierrehumbert, Janet
1980   *The Phonology and Phonetics of English Intonation*. Ph.D. dissertation, MIT.

Pierrehumbert, Janet, and Julia Hirschberg
    1990   The meaning of intonational contours in the interpretation of dis-
                course. In: Philip R. Cohen, Jerry Morgan and Martha E. Pollock
                (eds.), *Intentions in Communications*, 271–311. Cambridge: MIT
                Press.

Pierrehumbert, Janet, and Susan Steele
    1987   How many rise-fall-rise contours? In: *Proceedings of the XI Meeting
                of the International Congress of Phonetic Sciences*, Volume 3, 145–
                147. Tallinn: Estonian Academy of Sciences.

Prince, Alan, and Paul Smolensky
    2004   *Optimality Theory: Constraint Interaction in Generative Grammar.*
                Cambridge: MIT Press.

Reinhart, Tanya
    1981   Pragmatics and linguistics: an analysis of sentence topics. *Philosopi-
                ca* 27: 53–94.

Rooth, Mats
    1985   *A Theory of Focus Interpretation.* Ph.D. dissertation, University of
                Massachusetts, Amherst.
    1992   A theory of focus interpretation. *Natural Language Semantics* 1, 75–
                116.

Smolensky, Paul
    1996   On the comprehension/production dilemma in child language. *Lin-
                guistic Inquiry* 27: 720–731.

Stechow, Arnim von, and Susanne Uhmann
    1986   Some remarks on focus projection. In: Werner Abraham and Sjaak
                de Meij (eds.), *Topic, Focus and Configurationality*, 295–320. Ams-
                terdam: John Benjamins.

Steedman, Mark
    2000   Information structure and the syntax-phonology interface. *Linguistic
                Inquiry* 31: 649–689.

Steriade, Donca
    1995   Positional neutralization. Unfinished manuscript, University of Cali-
                fornia, Los Angeles.

Steriade, Donca
    1999   Phonetics in phonology: the case of laryngeal neutralization. In:
                Matthew Gordon (ed.), *UCLA Working Papers in Linguistics* 2: 25–
                46.

Tanenhaus, Michael K., Michael J. Spivey-Knowlton, Kathleen M. Eberhard, and Julie
C. Sedivy
    1995   Integration of visual and linguistic information in spoken language
                comprehension. *Science* 268: 1632–1634.

Tanenhaus, Michael K., James S. Magnuson, Delphine Dahan and Craig Chambers
    2000   Eye movements and lexical access in spoken-language comprehension: evaluating a linking hypothesis between fixations and linguistic processing. *Journal of Psycholinguistic Research* 29: 557–580.
Welby, Pauline
    2003   Effects of pitch accent position, type and status on focus projection. *Language and Speech* 46: 53–58.
Weskott, Thomas, Robin Hörnig, Elsi Kaiser, Caroline Féry, Sabine Kern, and Reinhold Kliegl
    submitted   Information structure and the discourse status of postverbal reference.

Lexical access, effective contrast, and patterns in the lexicon

Adam Ussishkin and Andrew Wedel

1. Introduction

Patterns in the physical, extra-grammatical world and patterns in grammar often show suggestive relationships. For example, gradient biases in articulation and perception are frequently mirrored in categorical patterns in phonological grammars. This relationship has led linguists from many different theoretical backgrounds to suggest that there exist some mechanism(s) by which a gradient tendency derived from the environment can be transformed into an element of the grammar (e.g., Baudouin de Courtenay [1895] 1972; Donegan and Stampe 1979; Prince and Smolensky [1993] 2004; Archangeli and Pulleyblank 1994; Blevins 2004; Hayes and Steriade 2004; Wedel 2004). If we accept that there exist some general mechanism(s) for grammar-external biases to influence grammar and/or lexical structure, the most general hypothesis is that biases anywhere along the pathway from production through perception may come to be reflected in grammar or the lexicon. A diagram of processes and representations in this pathway that may be of interest to the phonologist is shown in Figure 1 below.

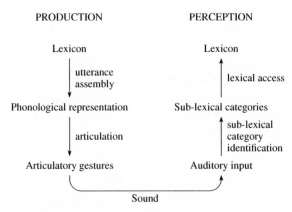

Figure 1. Heuristic schematic of steps in the pathway from production through perception

Many papers in this volume provide examples of phonological patterns based in biases in the mapping from percepts to sub-lexical categories in perception ("Sub-lexical category identification" in Figure 1). In this paper, we argue that some surface patterns in language can arise through asymmetries in the ease of lexical access ("Lexical access" in Figure 1). Successful lexical access requires that the sounds from which words are built be contrastive; that is, absent external determination from context, differently signifying utterances must sound recognizably different. Although many have argued or assumed that sound-contrast itself is a primitive notion of grammatical systems (e.g., Jakobson 1978; Flemming 1995; Padgett 2003), sound-contrast makes its direct functional contact with language use in the process of lexical access, rather than at some more abstract level. However, lexical access is not an all-or-nothing process, as we will review below, and some percepts can be more rapidly and successfully mapped to a lexical category than others. It has been argued elsewhere that these asymmetries can influence the system of sound contrasts within a language (Wedel 2004: ch. 2; Blevins 2004: ch. 8). Here, we present evidence that lexical access asymmetries can leave their traces in lexical and grammatical patterns as well. In the process, we review evidence that sound-contrast is only one of several influences on the ease of lexical access, and introduce a new term, *effective contrast*, that describes the combined interaction of these influences on lexical access in the context of the larger system. We argue that the concept of effective contrast, rather than sound-contrast alone, provides better insights into the data.

Specifically, we will present an argument that two distinct surface patterns in language – (i) the stem-suffix faithfulness distinction (Jakobson [1965] 1990: 414; Willerman 1994; McCarthy and Prince 1995; Bybee 2004), and (ii) the tendency for small stems to resist alternation (Wedel 2002) – may share a source in biases found within the process of lexical access, that is, the mapping from sub-lexical categories to lexical entries ("Lexical access" in Fig. 1). Below, we summarize research on this lexical access step suggesting that at least three competing factors influence its efficiency: lexical neighborhood density, relative lexical token frequency, and morpho-phonological alternation. We then propose that lexicons and grammars may evolve to balance these influences in such a way that acts to support lexical access efficiency, using patterns in morpheme structure from a variety of languages as evidence.

The remainder of this paper is structured as follows. First, we provide a discussion of neighborhood density and its relationship to lexical access. We then introduce token frequency as a factor that can mitigate inhibitory effects of high neighborhood density. We discuss how these two factors combine to yield a functional notion of *effective contrast* that goes beyond traditional ideas relating to sound-contrast. We then turn to two types of phenomena that on the surface might seem unrelated to each other. First, we introduce distinctions in contrast that play out in stems vs. affixes, showing how the usual cross-linguistic pattern can be explained once factors like neighborhood density and token frequency are taken into account. We then examine the unusual pattern observed in Modern Hebrew, which turns not to be so unusual once our notion of contrast is broadened to include effective contrast. Second, we discuss contrast distinctions that appear to be dependent on morpheme size. In the same section, we examine phonological alternations in Catalan that seem to pattern exceptionally in stems whose segment number falls below a particular threshold. By expanding our notion of contrast to include effects of neighborhood density the exceptional behavior observed in small stems receives a principled explanation.

2. The neighborhood density effect and sound contrast

In the last twenty years, research on the process of matching a sound-percept to an entry in the mental lexicon has shown that the efficiency with which a word is recognized is affected by the number of other similar words in the lexicon. For example, in the lexical decision task, the speed and accuracy with which it can be determined if a phonologically licit sequence of sounds corresponds to an actual word is inversely related to the number of similar words in the lexicon (Luce 1986; see also Goldinger, Luce and Pisoni 1989; Cluff and Luce 1990; Luce and Pisoni 1998).

For the purposes of these studies, similarity is usually operationally defined as a Hamming distance of one segment (Luce 1986), in which a lexical entry will be counted as similar to another if it can be changed into the other by adding, subtracting or changing one segment. For example, entries that are similar to the lexical entry *cat* under this definition include *cast*, *at*, *sat*, *kit*, and *can*. (This is clearly a very coarse measure of similarity; that it is sufficient for experimental purposes is perhaps a testament to the robustness of this phenomenon.) The set of words that are identified by this measure are termed that word's lexical *neighbors*. In the lexical decision task for example, experiments show that English-speaking subjects are able to decide that a sound string with few neighbors like *orange* is a real word more rapidly and accurately than a string with many neighbors like *cat*. This is termed the neighborhood density effect, illustrated graphically below in Figure 2.

low-density neighborhood   high-density neighborhood

Figure 2.   Lexical access in a low-density neighborhood (the left oval) is faster and more accurate than in a high-density neighborhood (the right oval); figure adapted and extended based on Dirks, Takayanagi, Moshfegh, Noffsinger and Fausti (2001).

In Figure 2, ovals represent lexical neighborhoods and bars represent lexical entries. The distance between bars represents the degree of phonemic similarity. The lexical entry represented by the solid bar on the left is accessed more efficiently because it has relatively few neighbors. On the right, the lexical entry represented by the solid bar has many more near neighbors, and is found to be accessed less efficiently. The Neighborhood Activation Model (Luce 1986; Luce and Pisoni 1998 and references therein) accounts for the neighborhood density effect by proposing that a sound sequence activates all lexical entries in the lexicon relative to their degree of similarity to the stimulus. Selection of a lexical entry as the best match to the sound sequence is made on the basis of differential levels of activation, with the lexical entry with greatest relative activation most likely to be selected.

By positing a competition between activated lexical entries for recognition, the Neighborhood Activation Model predicts that entries in high-density phonological neighborhoods will be recognized less efficiently than entries occurring in low-density neighborhoods, because when an input activates words in a high-density neighborhood, there will be many competitors with similar activation levels. Rephrased in terms of phonotactics, the Neighborhood Activation Model predicts that entries that share many segments in sequence with other entries will be responded to less quickly and accurately than those that have rarer segments and segment sequences. Over the last two decades, many studies using a variety of methodologies have confirmed these predictions (e.g., Luce 1986; Goldinger, Luce and Pisoni 1989; Cluff and Luce 1990; Metsala 1997; Newman, Sawusch and Luce 1997; Wright 1997; Luce and Pisoni 1998; Vitevitch and Luce 1998; Vitevitch, Luce, Pisoni and Auer 1999; Boyczuk and Baum 1999; Dirks, Takayanagi, Moshfegh, Noffsinger and Fausti 2001; Scarborough 2002).

Although the Neighborhood Activation Model is couched in terms of 'neighbors' and 'density', it can be rephrased in terms of contrast, a term more familiar to the linguist. A lexical item in a high-density neighborhood, such as *cat*, is a lexical item that does not contrast highly with other words in the English lexicon, that is, very nearly all of the features that make up the lexical entry *cat* are required to distinguish it from all its neighbors. A word like *cat* then can be thought of as having a relatively low phonemic contrast within the English lexicon. A lexical item in a low-density neighborhood on the other hand, such as *orange*, is highly contrastive: it is distinguished from its nearest neighbors by a large number of features. The useful insight to be gained from this line of research is that for the purposes of lexical access, the contrast of a lexical item may be largely dependent on the number and similarity of its actual lexical neighbors, rather than possible words or any other more abstract factor.

3.   Frequency and effective contrast

Alongside neighborhood density, lexical frequency also has a strong effect on the efficiency of lexical access: all else being equal, the higher a lexical item's relative token frequency, the more rapid and accurate its access (e.g., Gordon 1983; Dirks *et al.* 2001). The factors of neighborhood density and relative frequency interact, as a sufficiently high relative token frequency can mitigate the deleterious effects of a dense neighborhood on lexical access (Luce 1986). This is illustrated below in Figure 3.

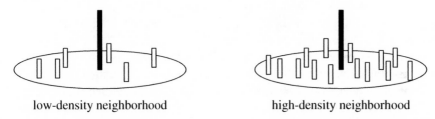

low-density neighborhood   high-density neighborhood

Figure 3.   High relative frequency mitigates the otherwise inhibitory effect of high neighborhood density: Access efficiency can be similar for the low-density neighborhood (leftmost oval) and the high-density neighborhood (rightmost oval) when the target item has a higher token frequency relative to its neighbors.

In Figure 3, as before in Figure 2, ovals represent lexical neighborhoods, bars represent lexical entries, and the distance between bars represents degree of phonemic similarity. New to Figure 3 is the factor of token frequency, illustrated using bar height, where the higher a bar, the higher its token frequency. On the left, the lexical entry represented by the solid bar is accessed relatively efficiently because it is very frequent relative to its lexical neighbors, which are, in addition, few and far between. On the right, the lexical entry represented by the solid bars has many more neighbors, but is still accessed efficiently because it is much more frequent than any of those neighbors.

The diagrams in Figure 3 illustrate the finding that a high relative token frequency renders access efficiency less sensitive to neighborhood density; in other words, a high frequency lexical item in a dense neighborhood may be accessed nearly as efficiently as one in a low density neighborhood. Thus, efficiency of access is affected by (at least) two factors. On the one hand, the lower a lexical entry's phonemic contrast with other entries (i.e., the denser its neighborhood), the lower its efficiency of access. On the other hand, the more often a lexical entry is accessed (i.e., the higher its token frequency), the more efficient that access is.

Over the last century, a variety of linguistic theories have grappled with accounting for the maintenance of phonemic contrast in synchronic grammars and/or over diachronic change (e.g., Martinet 1955; Lindblom 1986; Flemming 1995; Padgett 2003). Lexical access efficiency provides a useful frame for thinking about contrast, because in functional terms, lexical items that are accessed efficiently are definitionally those that contrast well. Because the degree to which a lexical item contrasts with its neighbors is not solely a function of its phonemic contrast, we suggest that a reconception of contrast in terms of the composite influences on access, may be useful for guiding hypotheses about patterns of contrast. To distinguish this idea from the notion of contrast defined in terms of strictly sound-based difference (whether phonemic, featural or cue-based), we use the term *effective contrast*, first introduced in Ussishkin and Wedel (2002). Because effective contrast is sensitive to both sound contrast and relative token frequency, two lexical items can have the same effective contrast but be in neighborhoods of different densities. For example, a relatively frequent lexical entry in a dense neighborhood may have the same effective contrast as an infrequent one in a sparse neighborhood. Terms such as effective contrast which refer to a composite property are often useful; for example, the *watt* is a familiar term for the composite notion of power. Wattage is defined as the product of voltage and amperage with the result that a given number of watts can be achieved through a higher voltage and lower amperage, or vice versa. Returning to effective contrast, the combined influence of neighborhood density and relative frequency on lexical access is often expressed in the literature by the descriptors 'hard' versus 'easy', where a word may be 'easy' because it is high frequency despite being in a dense neighborhood, or because it is in a sparse neighborhood, despite being low frequency (e.g., Luce 1986; Wright 1997; Scarborough 2002).

4. The stem-affix faithfulness distinction

We turn now to our first set of data, which focuses on the distinctions in contrast played out in stems vs. affixes. This distinction has been long noted by many researchers, going back at least as far as Jakobson ([1965] 1990; see also Willerman 1994; Bybee 2004). The distinction itself can be very simply stated: cross-linguistically, it has been observed that within individual languages, affixes tend to be shorter than stems, and to make use of a less marked subset of the overall inventory of segments and structures. Theoretical linguists have proposed that this distinction be encoded via a universal preference to preserve contrast in stems (allowing for a wider array of contrasting segments and structures) while disallowing as much contrast in affixes. In Optimality Theory, this preference has been elevated to the status of a universal metaconstraint, known as the Stem-Affix Faithfulness Metaconstraint (McCarthy and Prince 1995), which bifurcates faithfulness into two types: FAITH-STEM and FAITH-AFFIX. If FAITH-STEM is always ranked above FAITH-AFFIX, with a markedness constraint sandwiched in between the two, the prediction is that affixes will never allow an instance of the marked structure to surface, contrary to stems, whose higher-ranking faithfulness allows that structure to serve as a way to contrast. This proposed universal would then describe, for instance, why in Arabic relatively marked segments (such as pharyngeal consonants) occur in stems but never in affixes. A skeletal ranking illustrating the metaconstraint is given in (1):

(1)   Stem-affix faithfulness metaconstraint (McCarthy and Prince 1995)

       FAITH-STEM » MARKEDNESS » FAITH-AFFIX

Rather than appealing to a descriptive device such as the McCarthy and Prince metaconstraint, the account proposed here provides a psycholinguistically grounded explanation for the distinct behavior of stems vs. affixes.[1] First, like all function morphemes, an individual affix is likely to have a much higher token frequency than any given stem (Segalowitz and Lane 2000 and therein). Second, affixes as a group have a much lower *type* frequency than stems – from language to language, the tendency is to find a much larger number of stems than affixes. Clearly, then, this distributional difference between stems and affixes motivates a possible separation of one from the other in terms of how the grammar might treat them. Whether this separation is embodied in the lexicon or not, the relatively high frequency of affixes relative to stems should

---

1. For conceptually parallel accounts of the influence of experience and token frequency on the mapping from percepts to sublexical categories, see Boersma (1998) and Hume (2004).

allow them to evolve lower phonemic contrast without sacrificing effective contrast. And both of the two affix-stem distinctions noted above, (i) limitation on the set of component phonemes, and (ii) shorter length, reduce the number of ways that affixes can differ from one another. This reduction in the size of the contrast space occupied by affixes results in a higher average neighborhood density, which is equivalent to a lower phonemic contrast under the gradient notion of contrast proposed here.

Earlier, we proposed that in the balance between reduction of markedness and maintenance of contrast, effective contrast is the functional factor that mediates between them. This understanding of the conflict between maintenance of contrast and minimization of markedness predicts that reduction in markedness will have the least impact for morphemes with the highest effective contrast, whether due to a sparse neighborhood or high relative token frequency. Consistent with this notion, Zipf noted long ago that there is a strong, inverse correlation between the frequency of a morpheme and its length (Zipf [1935] 1968: 173). We undertook a casual test of this finding for a large set of English derivational affixes by plotting the lexical frequency of the affixes against their phoneme number. A power curve fit to the data showed a significant inverse correlation ($p < .01$)[2].

In recent work, Bybee (2004) suggests that the tendency for affixes to be composed of less marked elements is unsurprising due to their greater frequency in production, because lenition proceeds more rapidly in high-frequency items (see Bybee 2001). However, if this were the only factor governing lenition, we would be unable to explain the many examples of contrast-enhancing effects (e.g., Kirchner 1997; Smith 2002) and effects of morpheme realization, in which affixal material retains some minimal phonological exponence even when the phonology would otherwise prefer full deletion (e.g., Yip 1998; Kurisu 2001). Furthermore, there is evidence that speakers use more contrastive phonetic detail when producing words in high-density lexical neighborhoods (e.g., Goldinger and Summers 1989; Wright 1996; Scarborough 2002), suggesting that frequency is not the only factor influencing the degree of lenition in individual production events. We suggest that while lenition may proceed through small changes over individual productions, the rate with which lenited production exemplars can drive changes in the underlying form of a lexical entry may be

---

2. Derivational affixes were taken from http://indodic.com/affixListEnglish.html. Frequency was counted from the set of words of 5 per million frequency or greater in the Newdic database after hand-correcting the list to remove spurious matches. Newdic contains a phonemic wordlist of English with frequencies, and can be found at http://www.lexicon.arizona.edu/~hammond/newdic.html.

influenced by the effective contrast of the entry (Wedel 2006; Blevins and Wedel to appear).

5. Allomorphy and effective contrast

Tsapkini, Kehayia and Jarema (1999) show that phonological difference between a derived form and a base slows the lexical access of derived forms in auditory presentation. If allomorphy generally imposes a processing cost on some members of a paradigm, allomorphy, low sound-contrast and low frequency all share an inhibitory effect on lexical access. Given our hypothesis that lexical and grammatical systems evolve to maintain adequate effective contrast, rather than solely sound-based contrast, it follows that we may find that allomorphy is less frequent in paradigms where effective contrast is already low, through low sound contrast and/or low frequency.

In addition to the cross-linguistic tendency for affixes to contain material that is less marked than stems, a second relevant tendency instantiating the stem-affix asymmetry concerns alternation. Alternation is more prevalent in affixes than in stems. As an example, consider the English regular plural suffix, which undergoes voicing assimilation to match its voicing with the final segment of the stem it attaches to. A priori, this voicing assimilation might be expected on cross-linguistic grounds to have regressively affected the stem-final segment, but instead, spreads voicing progressively to the suffix. Harmony processes provide yet a more dramatic case; since such processes are overwhelmingly stem-controlled (e.g., Baković 2003). That is, harmony tends to affect affixal segments, resulting in alternation in the phonological realization of affixes but not stems.

This asymmetry in alternation can also be described via the McCarthy and Prince metaconstraint. Since alternation in Optimality Theory is driven by ranking markedness above faithfulness, high-ranking FAITH-STEM protects stems from undergoing alternation, but since FAITH-AFFIX is ranked below the markedness constraint the effects of the markedness constraint emerge in affixes. In other words, the metaconstraint provides coverage for two sets of facts: a cross-linguistic tendency for stems to contain more highly marked structures and segments than affixes, as well as a similarly broad tendency for affixes to undergo alternation rather than stems.

6.   Avoidance of alternation in affixes: the Neighborhood Activation Model predicts the Hebrew pattern

In Modern Hebrew (hereafter referred to simply as "Hebrew"), verbal derivational affixes (and some inflectional affixes) occur as patterns of two vowels (sometimes with a concomitant prefix), resulting in the system of verbal classes known as *binyanim*. This type of nonconcatenative templatic morphology has been analyzed as a word-based phenomenon (Bat-El 1994, 2003; Ussishkin 1999, 2000, 2005), rather than on the traditional but language-specific basis of the consonantal root. These researchers argue, on the basis of morphological and phonological evidence, that Hebrew presents robust evidence in favor of a word-based model for Semitic. This evidence comes from several domains, including the preservation of consonant clusters in denominal verbs, vowel transfer effects in denominal verbs, and templatic effects within the verbal system as a whole. Recent psycholinguistic evidence from studies by Berent, Marcus and Vaknin (2007) demonstrate a need for whole-word storage in Hebrew, thus strengthening the view that the word-based model, which finds much psycholinguistic support in other languages, is also a valid approach to Semitic.

Under the word-based approach, Hebrew requires a ranking in which FAITH-AFFIX outranks all other faithfulness constraints, including FAITH-STEM. Such a situation contradicts the metaconstraint proposed by McCarthy and Prince (1995), but is necessary in order to achieve what is known as melodic overwriting, the mechanism by which nonconcatenative templatic morphology is carried out. Hebrew verbs are prosodically restricted to two syllables, and are formed by concatenating a bisyllabic base form with a bivocalic affix. Given the maximal word size of two syllables, as established by Ussishkin (2000, 2005), the resulting complex form can only accommodate the affixal material by deleting base material. The following section details the relevant data.

As an example of melodic overwriting in nonconcatenative templatic morphology, consider the following paradigm, which presents verbs derived from the base verbal form *gadal* 'he grew'.

(2)   The verbal paradigm for *gadal*, 'to grow'

Base form	*+affix*	*Derived form*	*Gloss*
[gadal]			'he grew'
	/i e/	[gidel]	'he raised'
	/u a/	[gudal]	'he was raised'
	/hi i/	[higdil]	'he enlarged'
	/hu a/	[hugdal]	'he was enlarged'

For each derived form, it is clear that the output has failed to parse part of the original base form: namely, the vowels of the base. This is schematically represented for the derivation of the form *gidel* from the base form *gadal* in the following diagram:

(3)   Melodic overwriting: affix vowels overwrite base vowels

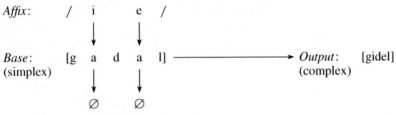

Given the bisyllabic maximum, the only way for the affix /i e/ to be realized is by violating FAITH-STEM, because material in the stem must be deleted to accommodate the affix. In other words, if the metaconstraint were universally obeyed a language like Hebrew would be predicted as impossible. The upshot is that we need to weaken the status of the metaconstraint from a universal to a tendency, thus reducing its explanatory power. The next question, then, concerns both the metaconstraint's viability and the real source for the tendency it describes in most cases. In such cases the metaconstraint seems to adequately describe the observation that affixes tend to be less marked than stems, as well as the observation that if a stem and an affix compete for phonological exponence the stem tends to win. How can we maintain these observations – valid in most languages – while at the same time capturing a seemingly abnormal pattern like melodic overwriting in Hebrew?

The Neighborhood Activation Model predicts that affixes will tolerate markedness reduction better than stems because affixes are more frequent. This higher relative frequency endows affixes with a high effective contrast, so that any effect of phonemic markedness reduction is mitigated. Likewise, the relatively lower number of affixes means that affixes will be unlikely to have many near neighbors, again resulting in a high tolerance for markedness reduction given the resulting high effective contrast. However, any special conditions resulting in lower effective contrast for affixes, such as an unusually high number of high frequency neighbors, should make affix faithfulness a higher priority.

In Hebrew, affixes for different verbal classes are composed of two vowels, sometimes with a concomitant prefix. Given the five-vowel inventory of Hebrew (*i, e, a, o, u*) a total of only 25 possible affixes exist. Compare this with, e.g., English, where the contrast space available to affixes is much larger. In

Hebrew, seventeen of the 25 possibilities are actually attested, so there exist few opportunities to further reduce phonemic contrast without neutralization to homophony. Therefore, because of special restrictions on what may serve as verbal affixal material, verbal affixes are all near neighbors of one another, as the following table shows:

Table 1.   Extant bivocalic melodies in Modern Hebrew (from Ussishkin 2005): the first vowel of the affix is represented by the vowels in the leftmost column; the second vowel of the affix is represented by the vowels in the topmost row, and each attested combination is provided in the intersecting cells.

V1 \ V2	i	e	a	o	u
i	past tense of hifʕil forms	past tense of piʕel forms	past tense of some piʕel forms; past tense of nifʕal forms; deverbal noun of paʕal	infinitive of some paʕal forms	deverbal noun of piʕel forms
e	past tense of some hifʕil forms	some sego-late nouns	some sego-late nouns		
a	present tense of some hifʕil forms; infinitive and future stem of some hifʕil forms	present tense stem of piʕel forms; infinitive stem of piʕel forms	past tense of paʕal forms	some nominal and adjectival forms	participle of paʕal forms
o	present tense of some hifʕil forms	present tense of paʕal forms; past tense of some piʕel forms	nominal pattern		
u			past tense of puʕal and hufʕal forms; present tense stem of puʕal and hufʕal forms		

With the potential contrast space almost filled (shading in the table indicates gaps), we can understand that neutralization of any phonemic contrast is likely to result in neutralization of a morphological contrast, thus explaining the need to maintain a high level of phonemic contrast in order to maintain the necessary effective contrast. In other words, high token affix frequency in Hebrew is not sufficient to guarantee a high enough effective contrast. This is illustrated below in Figure 4.

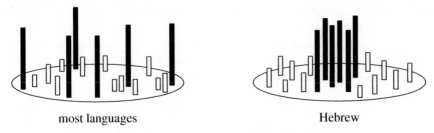

most languages   Hebrew

Figure 4.   Affix neighborhood density in most languages vs. Hebrew

In Figure 4, the ovals represent regions of the lexicon and the bars represent lexical entries. Bar height represents token frequency. The solid bars are representative of affix entries. For the case depicted on the left, which is meant to represent the commonly found situation in most languages, affixes are distributed relatively evenly throughout lexical space, due to the facts that affixes are relatively few and that affixal material is drawn from a relatively large set of elements, at least in contrast to Hebrew where affixes tend to be vocalic. For Hebrew, represented on the right, affixes are taken from a very limited set of elements that are very similar to each other — vowels. Therefore, Hebrew verb class affixes are grouped very closely together in lexical space.

Above we saw that the high frequency of affixes relative to their neighbors makes their access efficient even when phonemic contrast is low. In Hebrew, however, we see that verbal affixes are *not* more frequent than their near neighbors, because since those neighbors are affixes they have the same type of phonological content, so in effect relative frequency is cancelled out as a factor in effective contrast. Unlike in other languages, the high frequency of a verbal affix in Hebrew cannot compensate for a low phonemic contrast, with the result that phonemic contrast must be maintained to preserve adequate effective contrast; essentially, in the Hebrew case, effective contrast is equivalent to phonemic contrast. Hebrew demonstrates that FAITH-AFFIX must outrank FAITH-STEM in cases where following the metaconstraint would obliterate the contrast between affixes entirely. This important functional motivation for the reversal of the metaconstraint has precedence in work of Boersma (1998: 189), who states, for Mixtec tone deletion based on an analysis in Zoll (1996), "it is more important to keep *some* information about the affix than to keep *all* the information about the base."

7.   Avoidance of allomorphy in small stems

Morpheme length is a very robust predictor of neighborhood density, as illustrated for English below in Figure 5.[3] This obtains because while the number of *possible* words increases exponentially with phoneme number, the rate of increase in the number of *actual* words with phoneme number is much slower. Phrased differently, relatively more of the *possible* small words are also *actual* words (see Frauenfelder, Baayen and Hellwig 1993 for additional discussion).

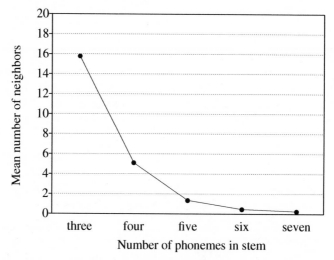

Figure 5.   The mean number of neighbors decreases with stem length in English.

This strong relationship between morpheme length and neighborhood density provides us an indirect way to test the prediction that phonological alternation should be avoided in high density neighborhoods, because it allows us to rephrase the prediction in terms of morpheme length.

---

3.   Neighborhood densities for stems of a given length were obtained from the Newdic English database (see footnote 2 above).

7.1   Final stop devoicing in Catalan

Catalan exhibits the cross-linguistically common pattern of devoicing under-lyingly voiced obstruents word-finally, as illustrated in (4) below.

(4)   Word-final devoicing in Catalan.

	Stem	*Masculine*	*Feminine*	*Gloss*
a.	/bɛrd/	[bɛrt]	[bɛrða]	'green'
b.	/sɛrt/	[sɛrt]	[sɛrta]	'certain'

If Catalan were under pressure to avoid alternation in dense neighborhoods, it could in principle accomplish this in two ways: (i) final devoicing could be waived for lexical items in dense neighborhoods, or (ii) lexical items in dense neighborhoods could preferentially end with underlyingly unvoiced stops, which do not alternate. Because Catalan does not ever violate final-stop de-voicing, strategy (i) can be discounted. To examine whether strategy (ii) is employed, all monomorphemic nouns and adjectives ending in p/b, t/d, and k/g in the Diccionari Catalá Invers amb Informació Morfológica (Mascaró and Rafel 1990) were collected and categorized by number of segments.[4] The data is presented in graphic form in Figure 6 below.

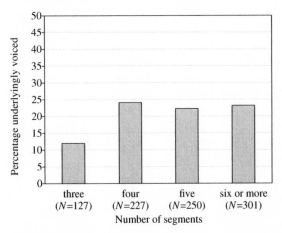

Figure 6.   Stem-final stop voicing by number of segments in Catalan (*N* is the sam-ple size).

---

4.   By Catalan orthographic convention, alternating stems are consistently written with a voiced stop, and non-alternating stems with an unvoiced stop. Multimorphemic forms were identified and discarded with the help of a native informant.

The data shown in Figure 6 suggests that 3-segment noun and adjective stems are less likely to end in an underlyingly voiced stop than longer stems. Chi-square analysis confirms this, indicating that the 3-segment class is distinct from the classes with more segments taken together at a confidence of greater than 0.01. None of the classes with greater than three segments are significantly distinct from each other. Note that the cross-linguistic preference for unvoiced stops is in evidence here as well, as even in sparser neighborhoods, i.e., for those forms with greater than three segments, stops are underlyingly voiced on average in only about 22% of the stems.

7.2   Distribution of final stops in English

The hypothesis that alternation is marked in high-density lexical neighborhoods provides an account for the relative paucity of underlyingly voiced stops in small stems in Catalan. Under this same hypothesis however, if there is no alternation, then there should be no relation between stem size and the proportion of voiced to unvoiced final stops. English can serve as a test for this hypothesis: as English does not exhibit final-stop devoicing, there is no alternation in the voicing of stem-final stops under suffixation. Therefore, the proportion of voiced to unvoiced stem-final stops should be constant regardless of stem size.

To test the hypothesis, monomorphemic words in the Newdic database of English[5] between three and six segments ending in [b/p], [d/t] and [g/k] were collected and categorized by segment number. To avoid peripheral vocabulary, only words with a frequency of 5 per million or greater were included. Figure 7 below shows the pooled percentage of stems ending in voiced stops by segment number.

In contrast to Catalan, English displays no relative preference for unvoiced stops in smaller stems, consistent with the hypothesis that the pattern in Catalan derives from the alternation in voicing of final stops in noun and adjective stems under suffixation. Examination of the graph shows however that English, like Catalan, displays the expected overall preference for unvoiced stem-final stops.

---

5.   This is a phonemic list of English words annotated with frequencies from Francis and Kucera (1982), available at http://www.speech.cs.cmu.edu/cgi-bin/cmudict.

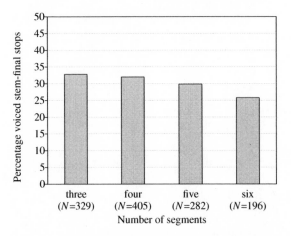

Figure 7. Stem-final stop voicing by segment number in English.

7.3 Word-internal alternations in Catalan

The two alternations shown in the previous sections are located at the right word edge. Are alternations in other domains also under-represented in small stems? Vowel reduction-driven alternations in Catalan provide a good test case for this question. In Catalan, a subset of the vowels that appear in stressed syllables are neutralized in unstressed syllables, as illustrated below in (5).

(5)   Vowel reduction in Catalan
       Stressed position   *Unstressed position*

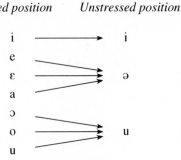

The relevant feature of this pattern for our purposes here is that the non-high vowels [a, ɛ, e, o, ɔ] alternate with [ə] and [u] in unstressed syllables, but the high vowels [i, u] remain constant.

Primary stress in Catalan is default-penultimate, but there are many suffixes, particularly in the verbal paradigm, that are underlyingly stressed, resulting in stress shift upon suffixation as illustrated below.

(6)   Stress-shift under suffixation in Catalan verbs.

	Verb stem	+ 1sg. pres. ind. /-o/	+ 1pl. pres. ind. /-ém/	Gloss
a.	/din/	[dínu]	[diném]	'eat lunch'
b.	/sum/	[súmu]	[sumém]	'add'
c.	/don/	[dónu]	[duném]	'give'
d.	/pas/	[pásu]	[pəsém]	'pass'

The first person singular present indicative suffix /-o/ is not underlyingly stressed, so suffixation to a verb stem such as /din/ 'eat lunch' results in surface stress on the verb stem under default penultimate stress. The first person plural present indicative /-ém/, on the other hand, is underlyingly stressed, such that the same verb stems surface without stress under suffixation as shown in the third column in (6). In these forms, we can see that the difference in the positions of stress between the first person singular present indicative and the first person plural present indicative suffixed forms does not change the vowel quality of the stem vowel if it is high. Compare (6a–b) with (6c–d), in which, upon stress shift, the stem vowel alternates between [o] and [u] in (6c) and [a] and [ə] in (6d). The existence of both underlyingly unstressed and underlyingly stressed suffixes in the verbal paradigm results therefore in an alternation between surface vowels in verb stems containing underlyingly non-high vowels. Monosyllabic verb stems with underlyingly high vowels in contrast show no alternation in vowel quality across the verbal paradigm.[6]

The hypothesis advanced here, namely that alternation is avoided in dense lexical neighborhoods, predicts then that in Catalan, verb stems in dense neighborhoods should preferentially contain high vowels over non-high vowels, because the latter alternate under suffixation.

To test this prediction, all monomorphemic mono- and disyllabic verb stems containing between two and six segments were collected from a small Catalan/English dictionary (Sabater and Freixinet 1990), and divided into ini-

---

6. Because stresslessness and secondary stress alternate by syllable in Catalan, in disyllabic verb stems one of the two syllables will always license a full vowel. The first syllable of disyllabic verb stems was arbitrarily chosen in this analysis for comparison.

tial-syllable high vowel and non-high vowel classes. The proportion of verbs with an initial-syllable non-high vowel is shown plotted against segment number in Figure 8 below.

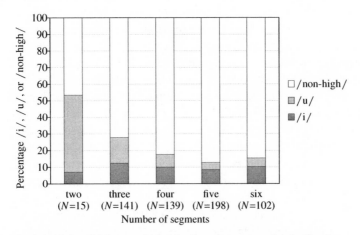

Figure 8. Verb-initial syllable vowel identity by segment number in Catalan

The graph in Figure 8 makes clear that as segment number decreases below four, the proportion of verb stems with initial non-high vowels decreases relative to those with initial high vowels. Chi-square analysis shows that the two and three segment classes are distinct from each other ($p < .05$), each from the larger classes taken together ($p < .01$), and that the 4–6 segment classes are not significantly distinct from one another.[7] As segment number is a reliable proxy for neighborhood density, these results are consistent with the hypothesis that the probability of alternation is inversely correlated with neighborhood density, at least at the relatively high densities experienced by short stems. The decrease in correlation with segment number as segment number increases could have at least two sources. First, neighborhood density falls exponentially with increase in size (cf. Figure 5 above), with the result that the relative decrease in neighborhood density grows progressively smaller as segment size goes up. We therefore might expect any association of word length with the probability of alternation to fall off exponentially with increasing length as well. Beyond that however, it is possible that for longer words effective contrast is high enough that any decrease in lexical access efficiency associated with allomorphy is simply no longer significant.

---

7. These significances were calculated using the Bonferroni correction for multiple comparisons within a data set.

Note that because the vast majority of the verb stems under five segments are monosyllabic, the results presented here are unlikely to be due to distinctions in syllable number given that the 2-segment class is distinct from the 4-segment class ($p < .01$). Furthermore, the majority of the 5-, and all of the 6-segment stems in the sample are disyllabic, but do not form statistically distinct classes relative to the majority monosyllabic 4-segment verb stems.

Could the paucity of alternating short stems be due solely to homophony avoidance, rather than a more general reduction in lexical access efficiency in high density neighborhoods? A contextual neutralization of contrast is more likely to result in accidental homophony in a dense neighborhood than a sparse one, so avoidance of neutralizing segments also avoids the contextual creation of homophones. However, the Catalan verb stem data are not consistent with the hypothesis that homophony avoidance is the primary source of avoidance of non-high vowels in short verb stems. In the Catalan vowel system in (5), /i/ and /u/ differ in that an unstressed [i] can only correspond to a stressed [i] in a related form, while an unstressed [u] can correspond to stressed [u], [o], or [ɔ] in a related form. If avoidance of accidental homophony under stress-shift has been a significant driving force in the evolution of Catalan verbs, then we should find a preference for [i] in short verbs, and avoidance of all alternating vowels including [u].[8] This is not the case however. As shown in Figure 8, [u] is in fact much more common than [i] in short verbs, which is at odds with the hypothesis that homophony avoidance is responsible for this pattern.

The converging pattern of non-alternation in small stems found within the diverse class comprising final devoicing and vowel reduction in Catalan suggest that the phenomenon may derive from a general property of allomorphy, rather than something specific to a particular kind of alternation. In conjunction with the hypothesis that allomorphy imposes some cost on lexical access, the finding that allomorphy is relatively rare in the densest parts of the lexicon supports the proposal that effective contrast is under optimizing pressure in the lexicon.

8.   Conclusion

This paper represents an initial foray into a new domain, asking whether there is support for the hypothesis that biases in lexical access may drive the development of lexical and grammatical patterns. Evidence from a wide range of psycholinguistic experiments shows that all kinds of words are not accessed

---

8.   We are grateful to an anonymous reviewer for bringing this point to our attention.

equally well, but rather, (i) neighborhood density, (ii) frequency, and (iii) allo-morphy, all influence the efficiency of access. In functional terms, contrast comes down to the ability to efficiently map a sound onto a lexical entry, so it is a sensible question to ask whether it may be this *effective* contrast that has a more significant influence on language patterns, rather than a more abstract system of sound-contrast per se. In support of this proposal, we have summa-rized data suggesting that a wide variety of observed patterns may result from pressure to maintain adequate effective-, as opposed to sound-contrast within the lexicon:

– Stems often exhibit more marked structures than affixes.
– Stems are less likely to alternate than affixes.
– Small stems are less likely to alternate than larger stems.

Additional work to support or refute this hypothesis is necessary (see Blevins and Wedel to appear). For example, in languages where small stems are prefe-rentially composed of non-alternating phonemes, it could be fruitful to trace the diachronic development of such stems. In addition, there remains a need to confirm the correlation of avoidance of allomorphy in small stems with neigh-borhood density. On the psycholinguistic front, further experimental work needs to be done to investigate the processing cost of alternation. For instance, some Hebrew affixes alternate to satisfy phonotactic requirements, though these requirements are no longer necessarily transparent. Does this affect the processing of these affixes compared to affixes that don't alternate? Pursuing work in these directions will help in determining if this research program – looking outside what linguists strictly define as the grammatical domain – is viable as an explanatory track for the linguistic tendencies examined here.

References

Archangeli, Diana, and Douglas Pulleyblank
   1994   *Grounded Phonology.* Cambridge: MIT Press.
Baković, Eric
   2003   Vowel harmony and stem identity. *Rutgers Optimality Archive* 540.
Bat-El, Outi
   1994   Stem modification and cluster transfer in Modern Hebrew. *Natural Language and Linguistic Theory* 12: 571–596.

Bat-El, Outi
2003   Semitic verb structure with a universal perspective. In: Joseph Shim-
            ron (ed.), *Language Processing and Language Acquisition in a Root-
            Based Morphology*, 29–59. Amsterdam: John Benjamins.
Baudouin de Courtenay, Jan
1972   An attempt at a theory of phonetic alternations. In: Edward Sankie-
            wicz (ed.), *A Baudouin de Courtenay Anthology*, 144–212. Bloo-
            mington: Indiana University Press. Abridged translation of: *Versuch
            einer Theorie phonetischer Alternationen: Ein Kapitel aus der Psy-
            chophonetik*, Trübner, Strassburg/Cracow [1895].
Berent, Iris, Gary Marcus, and Vered Vaknin
2007   Roots, stems, and the universality of lexical representations: evi-
            dence from Hebrew. *Cognition* 104: 254–286.
Blevins, Juliette
2004   *Evolutionary Phonology: The Emergence of Sound Patterns*. Cam-
            bridge: Cambridge University Press.
Blevins, Juliette, and Andrew Wedel
to appear   Inhibited sound change: an evolutionary approach to lexical compe-
            tition. *Diachronica*.
Boersma, Paul
1998   *Functional Phonology*. Ph.D. dissertation, University of Amsterdam.
            The Hague: Holland Academic Graphics.
Boyczuk, Jeffrey, and Shari Baum
1999   The influence of neighborhood density on phonetic categorization in
            aphasia. *Brain and Language* 67: 46–70.
Bybee, Joan
2001   *Phonology and Language Use*. Cambridge: Cambridge University
            Press.
Bybee, Joan
2004   Restrictions on phonemes in affixes: a cross-linguistic test of a popu-
            lar hypothesis. Manuscript, University of New Mexico.
Cluff, Michael, and Paul Luce
1990   Similarity neighborhoods of spoken two-syllable words: retroactive
            effects on multiple activation. *Journal of Experimental Psychology:
            Human Perception and Performance* 16: 551–563.
Dirks, Donald, Sumiko Takayanagi, Anahita Moshfegh, P. Douglas Noffsinger, and
Stephen Fausti
2001   Examination of the Neighborhood Activation Theory in normal and
            hearing-impaired listeners. *Ear and Hearing* 22: 1–13.
Donegan, Patricia, and David Stampe
1979   The study of Natural Phonology. In: Daniel A. Dinnsen (ed.), *Cur-
            rent Approaches to Phonological Theory*, 126–173. Bloomington:
            Indiana University Press.

Flemming, Edward
1995   *Auditory Representations in Phonology.* Ph.D. Dissertation. UCLA.
Francis, W. Nelson, and Henry Kucera
1982   *Frequency Analysis of English Usage: Lexicon and Grammar.* Boston: Houghton Mifflin.
Frauenfelder, Uli, R. Harald Baayen, and F. M. Hellwig
1993   Neighborhood density and frequency across languages and modalities. *Journal of Memory and Language* 32: 781–804.
Goldinger, Stephen, Paul Luce, and David Pisoni
1989   Priming lexical neighbors of spoken words: effects of competition and inhibition. *Journal of Memory and Language* 28: 501–518.
Goldinger, Stephen, and W. Van Summers
1989   Lexical neighborhoods in speech production: a first report. *Research on Speech Perception Progress Report* 15: 331–342. Bloomington.
Gordon, Barry
1983   Lexical access and lexical decision: mechanisms of frequency sensitivity. *Journal of Verbal Learning and Verbal Behavior* 18: 24–44.
Hayes, Bruce, and Donca Steriade
2004   The phonetic bases of phonological markedness. In: Bruce Hayes, Robert Kirchner and Donca Steriade (eds.), *Phonetically Based Phonology*, 1–34. Cambridge: Cambridge University Press.
Hume, Elizabeth
2004   Deconstructing markedness: a predictability-based approach. In: *Proceedings of the Berkeley Linguistics Society* 30.
Jakobson, Roman
1990   Quest for the essence of language. In: Linda R. Waugh and Monique Monville-Burston (eds.), *On Language: Roman Jakobson*, 407–421. Cambridge: Harvard University Press. First published in *Diogenes* 13: 21–37 [1965].
Jakobson, Roman
1978   *Six Lectures on Sound and Meaning.* Cambridge: MIT Press.
Kirchner, Robert
1997   Contrastiveness and faithfulness. *Phonology* 14: 83–111.
Kurisu, Kazutaka
2001   *The Phonology of Morpheme Realization.* Ph.D. dissertation, University of California at Santa Cruz.
Lindblom, Björn
1986   Phonetic universals in vowel systems. In: John J. Ohala and Jeri J. Jaeger (eds.), *Experimental Phonology*, 13–44. Orlando: Academic Press.
Luce, Paul
1986   Neighborhoods of words in the mental lexicon. *Research on Speech Perception Progress Report No. 6.* Bloomington: Indiana University, Psychology Department, Speech Research Laboratory.

Luce, Paul, and David Pisoni
    1998   Recognizing spoken words: the Neighborhood Activation Model. *Ear and Hearing* 19: 1–38.
Martinet, André
    1955   *Economie des changements phonétiques.* Berne: Francke.
Mascaró, Joan, and Joaquim Rafel
    1990   *Diccionari Catalá Invers amb Informació Morfológica.* Barcelona: Liberigraf.
McCarthy, John, and Alan Prince
    1995   Faithfulness and reduplicative identity. In: Jill Beckman, Laura Walsh Dickey and Suzanne Urbanczyk (eds.), *University of Massachusetts Occasional Papers* 18: *Papers in Optimality Theory*, 249–384.
Metsala, Jamie
    1997   An examination of word frequency and neighborhood density in the development of spoken-word recognition. *Memory and Cognition* 25: 47–56.
Newman, Rochelle, James Sawusch, and Paul Luce
    1997   Lexical neighborhood effects in phonetic processing. *Journal of Experimental Psychology* 23: 873–889.
Padgett, Jaye
    2003   The emergence of contrastive palatalization in Russian. In: D. Eric Holt (ed.), *Optimality Theory and Language Change*, 307–335. Dordrecht: Kluwer Academic Press.
Prince, Alan, and Paul Smolensky
    2004   *Optimality Theory: Constraint Interaction in Generative Grammar.* London: Blackwell. First appeared as Technical Report of the University of Colorado Computer Science Department [1993].
Sabater, M.S., and J.A. Freixinet
    1990   *Hippocrene Concise Dictionary, Catalan-English/English-Catalan.* Hippocrene Books: New York.
Scarborough, Rebecca A.
    2002   Effects of lexical confusability on the production of coarticulation. *UCLA Working Papers in Linguistics* 101.
Segalowitz, Sidney, and Korri Lane
    2000   Lexical access of function versus content words. *Brain and Language* 75: 376–389.
Smith, Jennifer
    2002   *Phonological Augmentation in Prominent Positions.* Ph.D. dissertation, University of Massachusetts, Amherst.
Tsapkini, Kyrana, Eva Kehayia, and Gonia Jarema
    1999   Does phonological change play a role in the recognition of derived forms across modalities? *Brain and Language* 68: 318–323.

Ussishkin, Adam
1999   The inadequacy of the consonantal root: Modern Hebrew denominal
              verbs and output-output correspondence. *Phonology* 16: 401–442.
Ussishkin, Adam
2000   *The Emergence of Fixed Prosody.* Ph.D. dissertation, University of
              California at Santa Cruz.
Ussishkin, Adam
2005   A fixed prosodic theory of nonconcatenative templatic morphology.
              Natural Language and Linguistic Theory 23: 169–218.
Ussishkin, Adam, and Andrew Wedel
2002   Neighborhood density and the root-affix distinction. In: Maki Hiro-
              tani (ed.), *Proceedings of the North-Eastern Linguistic Society* 32:
              539–549. University of Massachusetts, Amherst: GLSA.
Vitevitch, Mike, and Paul Luce
1998   When words compete: levels of processing in perception of spoken
              words. *Psychological Science* 9: 325–329.
Vitevitch, Mike, Paul Luce, David Pisoni, and Edward Auer
1999   Phonotactics, neighborhood activation and lexical access for spoken
              words. *Brain and Language* 68: 306–311.
Wedel, Andrew
2002   Phonological alternation, lexical neighborhood density, and marked-
              ness in processing. Poster presented at *Laboratory Phonology 8*,
              Yale University.
Wedel, Andrew
2004   *Self-Organization and Categorical Behavior in Phonology.* Ph.D.
              dissertation, University of California at Santa Cruz.
Wedel, Andrew
2006   Exemplar models, evolution and language change. *The Linguistic
              Review* 23: 247–274.
Willerman, Raquel
1994   *The Phonetics of Pronouns: Articulatory Bases of Markedness.* Ph.D.
              dissertation, University of Texas at Austin.
Wright, Richard
1997   Lexical competition and reduction in speech: a preliminary report.
              Research On Spoken Language Processing: Progress Report No. 21
              (1996–1997), Indiana University.
Yip, Moira
1998   Identity avoidance in phonology and morphology. In: Steven La-
              Pointe, Diane Brentari and Patrick Farrell (eds.), *Morphology and its
              Relation to Phonology and Syntax*, 216–246. Stanford: CSLI Publi-
              cations.

Zipf, George K.

1968   *The Psycho-Biology of Language: An Introduction to Dynamic Phi-
lology.* Cambridge, Mass.: MIT Press. First edition: Houghton-
Mifflin, Boston [1935].

Zoll, Cheryl

1996   *Parsing Below the Segment in a Constraint Based Framework.* Ph.D.
dissertation, University of California at Berkeley.

Phonology and perception: a cognitive scientist's perspective

James L. McClelland

As a researcher who has long been interested in the perception, use, and acquisition of language, the title of this volume, *Phonology in Perception*, already piques my interest. Closer examination reveals an exciting development: a diverse group of researchers grounded deeply in the discipline of linguistics are grappling with details of the actual human processing of language, something that would have been almost unthinkable just a few years ago. Every chapter speaks to issues of processing and learning about spoken language and refers to data from experimental psycholinguistics. These developments lend hope to the idea that the distinction between linguistic and psychological approaches to language will gradually fade away, replaced by an interdisciplinary investigation of language, encompassing the structure, use and acquisition of language and even language change. The remarks I make below are offered in the spirit of hastening this integration.

The authors of the various chapters raise a number of issues and questions, either explicitly or implicitly, that lie at the heart of debates within psychological as well as linguistic circles.

- Is language special or does it reflect the operation of domain general principles?
- What is built in, and what is learned, about language?
- Can phonology be treated separately from the sensory and motor processes that are required for overt communication?
- What are the different levels of representation of language, in what form is information represented within each, and how are they interrelated?
- How formal can/should our system of representing language information be? What is the actual status of any such formalization?
- In what form should regularities of language be captured? What is the status of such constructs as rules, constraints, and preferences?
- How can we best capture gradient aspects of language, and do such gradient aspects belong within linguistic theory?

In what follows I will comment briefly on each of these issues. Before I start I would like to make two more general observations.

First, the book exudes a refreshing openness to a very broad range of alternative approaches. As in any field, each author has a particular viewpoint and a particular argument to make in support of that viewpoint; yet for the most part the authors seem open to and interested in the ideas and insights that emerge from the approaches of others. This seems a far cry from an earlier day when clashes of perspectives appeared to be framed in starker, sometimes almost doctrinal terms – and it also seems a very healthy development. Each perspective has its strengths, and it is by seeing these strengths in juxtaposition to each other that we have the greatest chance of being able to find ways to combine the best of each into an ultimately more satisfying synthesis.

Second, the book reflects broad currents within the field, visible both in other work on phonology as well as many other aspects of language use, processing, and learning. Sticking close to phonology, one case in point is Joan Bybee's book on *Phonology and Language Use* (Bybee 2001). Though not focused on the role of perception per se, Bybee argues there for an approach in which phonology is shaped by the use of language, and reflects processes and principles of a general cognitive nature. Other relevant work clearly bridging the fields of linguistics and psycholinguistics includes, for example, the work of Janet Pierrehumbert and others who take an exemplar approach to phonological and lexical representation (Pierrehumbert 2001).

Now on to the issues! Rather than summarize or evaluate arguments made by other authors in this book, I will simply present findings and viewpoints coming from my own background as a cognitive scientist interested in many aspects of cognition, including language.

– Is language special or does it reflect the operation of domain general principles?

This question raged for years within the psychologistic community, with strong proponents for the view that language was special, both at the level of language as a whole (cf. Fodor 1983) and speech as a specific aspect of language (Liberman 1996).

My own view on this question is that language reflects the operation of domain general mechanisms subject to the particular constraints imposed by the task of linguistic communication – a position that appears to be quite close to the Natural Phonology position described in the chapter by Balas (this volume). This view has been supported over the years by the joint success of two closely related models, one of context effects in visual letter perception and one of context effects in speech perception. The first of these, the interactive activation model of letter perception (McClelland and Rumelhart 1981), addressed a phenomenon known as the word superiority effect – the finding that we see letters better when they fit together with their neighbors to spell a word than when they occur in isolation or in a jumbled array of unrelated letters. The model embodied a few simple principles – that when we perceive we rely on graded representations (activations, similar to probability estimates), that activation depends on the propagation of activation via weighted connections (whose values correspond approximately to subjective estimates of conditional probabilities), and that activation spreads, both from the stimulus 'up' and from higher-level representations 'down'. The ideas in this model draw their initial inspiration from properties of neurons, which of course provide the substrate for all aspects of human cognition, and they are closely related to ideas that suffused a number of neural network models proposed as solutions to 'constraint satisfaction problems' that arise in a wide range of domains, including visual scene recognition as well as printed and spoken language perception. Indeed, Jeff Elman immediately recognized the relevance of these ideas for understanding a wide range of findings in the perception of speech sounds, leading us to formulate the TRACE Model of speech perception relying on the same principles (McClelland and Elman 1986).

It is important to note that the TRACE model is not the same as the interactive activation (IA) model. In the IA model, we treat the printed word as arriving at the senses all at once, while in TRACE the speech stream unfolds sequentially over time. This required an elaboration of the architecture of the IA model in a direction that makes the TRACE model somewhat specialized for the processing of speech. A host of issues arise in the case of speech perception that do not arise in the perception of printed words – the ephemeral nature of speech, the absence of word boundaries in the speech stream, and effects of co-articulation are three differences between speech and print. The differences in architecture may reflect the structuring role played by the differences in the task demands of speech perception and visual letter perception, rather than innately pre-specified differences in the neural machinery of speech perception. The work of Sur demonstrating that auditory cortex takes on properties of visual cortex if it receives visual instead of auditory input supports a strong role for experience.

It may be worth noting that the models mentioned here can now be seen as early instantiations of probabilistic models that are enjoying wide popularity today, extending to all aspects of human and machine intelligence including natural language processing. Yet, whenever such models are used, there is always some question of domain-specificity, since a model for any particular domain will always include a set of units, and an arrangement of these units, that is to some extent domain-specific. We will consider this issue jointly with the second question I raised at the outset.

– What is built in, and what is learned, about spoken language?

The question of what is specific of language, and to what extent whatever is specific must be innately specified, has of course been central in all aspects of linguistic and psycholinguistic inquiry, including in phonology. The issue also comes up in the context of the models mentioned above. In the interactive activation model, there is a structured arrangement of units corresponding to hypotheses about a presented visual stimulus at three levels: a feature level, a letter level, and a word level. In the TRACE model, there are also the same three levels, but, of course, different speech-specific features and a phonemic level in place of the letter level.

Given that written language is not ubiquitous and has only been in use for less than 4000 years, and given the differences in the world's orthographies, it never seemed sensible to assume that the particular feature or letter units needed for perception of written words in any particular language could have been innately pre-specified. Rather, it seems likely that such units came into use as a result of a socio-cultural process working in interaction with available technology for written communication, and that adaptation of the perceptual and motor systems of a child learning how to read and write is largely a matter of learning.

We face what has often been viewed as a very different situation with spoken language, in that, first, spoken language has been with us for much longer than written language, and, second, there are evident commonalities across languages at both the featural and phonological levels. These points, taken together with the fact that the featural and phonological characteristics we see across human languages are not widely exploited in the communication systems used by other species, seem like strong points in favor of the view that somehow the basic building blocks of speech are 'special' to human spoken language and arise as a result of evolution rather than learning.

I consider it important to try to understand how language might have special characteristics that are not built in, or at least not built-in as such. To be sure, there are special characteristics of the human vocal tract that make it better suited to spoken language production than the vocal tracts of other organisms, and these characteristics are clearly given to us by evolution rather than produced in response to experience. Even here, however, the ability of parrots to mimic speech places limits on just how special or unique we should see the elements of human speech production to be.

Within relatively broad constraints established by what we can produce and the effects of alterations in production on perception, a range of perspectives remain viable regarding the extent to which we need to see the units of speech production and perception as innately given. One that I myself find particularly congenial is the idea that the phonological systems found in the world's languages might reflect an optimization over several constraints. (1) Messages should be as easy as possible to produce (2) their characteristics should be perceptually salient and (3) different messages should be mutually distinct from one another. These ideas were introduced by Lindblom and colleagues (e.g. Lindblom, MacNeilage and Studdert-Kennedy 1984) and are being actively pursued by other phonologists (Flemming [1995] 2002; Boersma and Hamann 2008). The suggestion is that these simple principles, together with the physical characteristics of the articulators and the consequences for the sounds that they can produce, could explain the emergence of phonological systems consisting of a largely combinatorial system of phonemes built around contrasts such as manner and place of articulation. Given just a little in the way of an innately predetermined ability to produce the relevant repertoire of gestures, the rest can be left to the same forces that shape the world's orthographies: a socio-cultural process working in interaction with available technology for spoken communication, with the adaptation of perceptual and motor systems within the individual child learning to understand and speak being very largely a matter of learning.

– Can phonology be treated separately from the sensory and motor processes that are required for overt communication?

This issue lies at the heart of the present volume and, perhaps, could be a defining issue for the future investigation of phonology: the general theme of the book is essentially that we will ultimately reap important rewards if we allow the sensory and motor processes involved in the perception and production of speech to affect our thinking about the structure of phonology. To me, as an outsider to the field, the idea that this issue was one that required any discussion comes as quite a shock. True, speech perception researchers once made quite a big deal out of the idea that there was a special 'speech mode' of perception quite distinct from perception of non-speech (cf. Liberman 1996), but even these researchers treated speech as organized around the recovery of the underlying articulatory gestures that, they believed, were what the perceptual processing of speech aimed to uncover. Thus, the notion that the discipline of phonology might, within certain branches of Optimality Theory at least, be construed as the study of a completely abstract system of essentially arbitrary constraints seems to me strange and foreign. Luckily, this is not the position taken by the authors of the articles in this book, and so from that point of view, perhaps little more need be said about it. On the other hand, to the extent that the issue is alive at all as a differentiating feature of contemporary perspectives on phonology, perhaps some of the evidence from the field of speech perception that points forcefully toward a role of specifically auditory factors in speech perception is worth a brief mention.

There is now a very large literature that shows how characteristics thought at one time to be special to the perception of speech also arise in non-speech contexts. As one case in point, the categorical perception of the distinction between /b/ and /p/ was once thought to be a special characteristic of the speech mode. But as early as the 1970's, researchers noted that a similar tendency toward categorical perception occurs with the distinction between plucked and bowed violin sounds (Cutting, Rosner and Foard 1976). Other work showed that such distinctions tended to be perceived categorically by non-human animals (Kuhl and Miller 1975). The particular contrasts used in particular languages appear to be influenced by properties of the acoustic signal, but do vary from language to language (Kuhl 1991). It is now widely noted that the tendency for speech perception to be categorical is more marked for consonants than vowels, and it turns out that there is a parallel tendency among non-speech sounds, such that the tendency toward categorical perception is far greater among sounds marked by rapid transitions or abrupt changes, and weaker in perception of sounds distinguished by their steady state characteristics (Mirman, Holt and McClelland 2004). The data are consistent with the view that an intra-linguistic contrast (between consonants and vowels) has a non-linguistic basis, grounded in a distinction in processing between transient and steady-state signals.

A further and perhaps even more telling set of findings relates to the cross-influence of non-speech stimuli on the perception of speech. A key phenomenon taken at first as a sign of the special speech mode of processing was the finding of compensation for coarticulation. A following /l/ pulls a preceding stop forward and a following /r/ tends to push it back. Perceivers compensate for this, tending to perceive an ambiguous sound falling about half way between /d/ and /g/ as a /g/ when followed by an /l/ but as a /d/ when followed by an /r/. Strikingly, however, the same effect can be obtained by following the ambiguous sound by a tone stimulus (Wade and Holt 2005) that is not perceived as speech but that contains frequencies matching those of the third formant onset frequency of /l/ (relatively high) or /r/ (relatively lower). The phenomenon is explained by the authors by assuming that perceptual systems use neighboring frequencies as reference points. Frequencies below a context reference will be heard as relatively lower (more /d/ like) and frequencies above a context reference will be heard as relatively higher (more /g/ like) (Lotto and Kluender 1998). Thus the perception of the category of a spoken language sound appears to be highly dependent on general purpose auditory processing mechanisms.

– What are the different levels of representation of spoken word forms, in what form is information represented within each, and how are they interrelated?

These are among the central questions of this book, and certainly they are the focus of the introductory chapter by Boersma and Hamann (this volume). They are also very complex questions, and the answers are clearly not independent.

Several models reviewed in the introductory chapter propose an underlying form, a surface form, and two phonetic forms, an auditory phonetic form and an articulatory phonetic form. There, the motivation for considering these different forms arises in the context of capturing phonological phenomena, particularly those that may depend on aspects of perception. Here I will discuss these issues from the point of view of the processing mechanisms involved in perception and production.

It seems uncontroversial enough to think that most utterances arise because speakers have something in mind to say; so there must be some intended communicative content; and when they speak, they produce a sequence of muscular contractions driving the articulators. Although it is possible to imagine otherwise, most theories do posit that the intended communicative content is first translated into some sort of underlying representation capturing aspects of the intended articulation (e.g. the sequence of abstract phonological segments contained in the message, generally embellished with stress and structure markings), which is then further transformed to produce the overt muscle contractions and resulting trajectories of the articulators. So, we have at least three representations: the intended message, the underlying representation of articulatory content, and the actual sequence of muscle contractions and movement patterns in the articulators.

Proceeding toward the receiving side, it seems uncontroversial to state that the process of articulation gives rise to an auditory waveform. Perceptible visual cues are also produced and are known to play a role in speech perception; it seems likely that such cues will ultimately play a role in explaining some phenomena in phonology, but I will not consider them further here. The auditory waveform gives rise to internal processes within the listener, which appear to involve formation of both a perceptual representation – what the listener thinks s/he heard – and a conceptual representation, roughly, the message the perceiver construes the speaker to have intended to communicate. On the perceiving side, then, there would appear to be three forms: the auditory waveform, the percept, and the message-as-received.

So far of course I have said very little, attempting to be as neutral as possible. To say more than this is to begin to specify one particular theory; a theory specifying, for example, the actual form and structure of intended communicative content; the form and structure of a percept or of the underlying representation of articulatory content; and the aspects of articulation and resulting auditory waveform that are relevant to speech perception. It is apparent that these matters are far from settled.

For example, there are many models of human language processing that posit the existence of lexical entries or lexical units that are supposed to mediate between intended communicative content and the percept on the input side and the underlying representation of the intended articulation on the output side. The TRACE model of speech perception is an example of a model that contains such units on the perceptual side, and Levelt and his collaborators (Levelt, Roelofs and Meyer 1999) have proposed that speech production involves an essential stage of lexical unit (lemma) selection as an intermediary between meaning and speech.

While these early models contained processing units corresponding to conventional lexical and phonological units (words and phonemes), more recent models employ learned distributed representations. One such model is shown in Figure 1 (it is similar to models implemented in Dilkina, McClelland and Plaut 2008 and Rogers *et al.* 2004). The model illustrates the approach my colleagues and I take to characterizing the mechanisms involved in understanding and speaking, as well as in perceiving objects and events in the world and then taking action. Pools of units correspond to different types of perceptual representations – percepts of printed or spoken words, or of actual objects – as well as plans for actions of different types, including producing the correct spoken word for a presented object (saying ball in the example). The model includes an integrative layer that receives projections from and sends projections to the different perceptual and output layers respectively. The figure also includes a direct pathway from the pool corresponding to the speech percept to the pool corresponding to the articulatory plan (Hickok and Poeppel 2003) as well as pathways from a visual word-form representation to both the speech percept and articulatory plan representations (Mechelli *et al.* 2005). Additional unlabeled pools of units are included to represent other possible inputs (haptic, olfactory) and other possible types of output (possibly including emotional responses, for example).

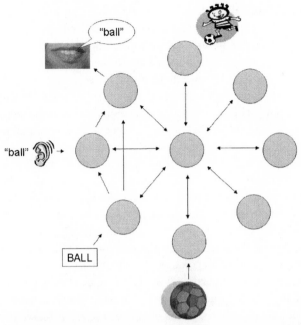

Figure 1.   A schematic rendition of the distributed connectionist model of semantic and lexical knowledge, extending a similar figure in Dilkina, McClelland and Plaut (2008). Each circle stands for a pool of neuron-like processing units over which patterns of activation represent some aspect of experience with objects or words. The number and functions of all of the pools of units involved are not known, but the cognitive neuroscience literature assigns specific brain areas that correspond to some of the pools of units in the model. As one example, there is a 'visual word form area' corresponding to the pool that represents the pattern corresponding to the visual form of a word (lower right pool of units in the figure). Other pools are associated with auditory word forms and articulatory word forms. Still other pools are associated with representations of the visual forms of objects, the actions we take on objects, etc. A single integrative layer is shown in the middle of the figure, with bidirectional arrows to each of the other pools. According to the theory (Rogers *et al.* 2004; Dilkina, McClelland and Plaut 2008), bidirectional connections from each of the surrounding pools to the integrative pool in the middle allow input arising in any of the pools to give rise to the corresponding output on any of the other pools. Thus on hearing the word 'ball' activation would propagate from the auditory representation layer to the integrative layer, and from there to all the other layers, allowing the network then to pronounce the word and visualize its spelling, and also to imagine the object and the action one might take upon it, among other things.

Existing implemented models of this type (e.g., Dilkina, McClelland and Plaut 2008) learn to map from patterns on the visual and spoken input layers to appropriate output layers, and do so without employing individual processing units corresponding either to individual words or to individual concepts. Instead, the models rely on learned distributed representations that mediate between the different input and outputs, and that are acquired through a neural network training algorithm. Each item develops its own learned distributed representation over the integrative layer that mediates between all of the different types of information about both words and objects (the same representation mediates representations of the spelling, sound, and articulation of the word 'ball' and the associated conceptual knowledge of what balls look like, how they move, how we interact with them, etc.). At first all items rely on highly overlapping patterns of activation, but as learning proceeds these become differentiated, increasing distinctiveness but not completely eliminating overlap. While these learned distributed representations function like concepts or lexical entries in some ways, they are graded, distributed representations whose patterns of overlap reflect similarity relations. As such they show tendencies to generalize and to degrade gracefully under damage in ways that are not intrinsic to models containing discrete units or entries for individual lexical items.

Models of this type have been highly successful in accounting for the effects of a neurological disorder thought to affect the brain analog of the integrative layer – the anterior temporal cortex. Among the findings is the fact that patients with this disorder lose specific information about concepts as well as specific information about words, while still preserving more general knowledge about words and objects. Patients still know what typical objects look like, and make errors that "typicalize" exceptional properties of objects (drawing, for example, a human-like ear in place of an elephant's ear when drawing a picture of an elephant). Patients also still know typical spelling-sound correspondences, and typicalize exceptional aspects of word's spellings, and our models do the same (McClelland, Rogers, Patterson, Dilkina and Lambon Ralph 2008). No discrete lexical or conceptual units are employed in capturing both correct normal performance as well as the effects of brain damage.

For simplicity, implemented versions of our models use one dedicated unit to stand for each phoneme in the phonological input pool, a unit for each letter in the word form pool, and a unit for each phoneme in the speech percept pool, and another unit for each phoneme in the speech output pool. In this respect they are like many other models and psychological theories that contain explicit phoneme units. In our case, however, we view this, not as a representation of reality but as a simplification. Just as words and concepts need not be represented by individual dedicated units, so also even phonemes and graphemes might not really be represented by such units either. Because hearers appear to be sensitive to auditory detail and speakers produce the same 'phoneme' in different ways that are often lexical-item-specific (e.g., the silence and following burst release associated with the /t/ in 'softly' are briefer that those associated with the /t/ in 'swiftly'; Hay 2001) it has been suggested that spoken language representation might contain far more articulatory or auditory detail than is naturally captured by thinking that a word's phonological form is represented as a string of discrete units. Indeed, models that map from raw acoustic input via an intermediate layer of learned distributed representations onto some sort of meaning-like representation have been developed (Kaidel, Zevin, Kluender and Seidenberg 2003), and we plan to incorporate such learned distributed reprsentations in future implementations of the model shown in Figure 1.

With these efforts as context, the idea that human mental processing of language may involve neither lexical nor phonological units in any kind of explicit form becomes more and more of a possibility. Within this context, we can ask, just what is the status of the different levels of representation postulated in linguistic theories of phonology?

The proposal that arises from a distributed connectionist perspective is to view the units and levels found in linguistic theory as useful approximations that serve to succinctly characterize clusters of material that is similar in some respect rather than strictly identical. For example, we use the symbol [p] to represent a wide range of slightly different articulatory gestures that share several properties and have similar acoustic consequences. To distinguish useful subsets of these we use additional markings, for example, to distinguish aspirated and unaspirated variants. We recognize a regularity within this class of sounds, which is that aspiration tends to be reduced or absent when /p/'s follow /s/'s but to be present to a greater degree and more often when /p/'s occur in word-initial position. These are useful descriptive statements even if in fact aspiration is a matter of degree, and even if there is overlap in the frequency distributions for different degrees of aspiration in the different types of contexts.

In light of the above, I often find debates in linguistics about the relative merits of different formalisms for capturing regularities to be unnecessary. In fact it is my belief that no such formalism will ever really do full justice, and that there are many with considerable utility.

- How formal can/should our system of representing language information be? What is the actual status of any such formalization?
- In what form should regularities of language be captured? What is the status of such constructs as rules, constraints, and preferences?
- How can we best capture gradient aspects of language, and do graded strength parameters have a role in linguistic theory?

The three issues above seem intimately intertwined, and I've already begun to indicate the general nature of my own preferred answer. Although these questions do not come up overtly in most of the papers in this volume, the chapter by Balas (this volume) does raise them explicitly in her contrast between Natural Phonology and OT. We have, on the one hand, within OT, a seeming commitment to a program quite similar in some ways to Chomsky's program in syntax, seeking a very abstract and formal characterization of the principles of phonological structure. As characterized by Balas, 'classic' OT is treated as a purely formal system, devoid of sensory-motor content, stipulating a set of universal constraints that govern phonological forms and different only between languages in how the constraints are ranked. OT then invites us, we are told, to see learning as a matter of establishing constraint rankings, a task that should be simpler, than, say, learning exactly how the constraints should be structured or formulated. On the other hand, Natural Phonology is cast as a framework within which very general pressures – e.g. to keep messages short and simple but also distinct – operate in conjunction with characteristics of the articulatory apparatus of speech, the ways in which articulation shapes sound, and the ways in which sound is processed by mechanisms of auditory processing to shape the characteristics of phonological forms.

    To me, it is clear that both approaches have their virtues, especially when viewed as ways of helping to channel researcher's thinking toward insights into the nature and structure of natural languages. As an outsider to the field of phonology, particularly to the full and by now very complex literature on OT, it is difficult to have a definitive take on the prospects for the OT program in the form stated above. However, from my own research in one circumscribed sub-area in phonology -- the rimes found in English word forms – it seems to me that the search for a simple list of universal constraints can take us part, but not all the way, toward a characterization of the details of phonological structure. I therefore see OT as being a useful formalism, but one that should be viewed as providing only an approximate characterization of the real underlying nature of phonological structure.

    As an illustration of these points, let us consider the data in Figure 2. The figure displays a partial ordering of each of several different rime types occurring in monomorphemic, monosyllabic word forms in the CELEX English corpus (Baayen, Piepenbrock and van Rijn 1993). The figure encompasses all of the rime types in the corpus containing a short (V) or long (VV) vowel, and a single stop consonant plus no more than one pre-stop consonant – a nasal, an l, or an alveolar fricative. The numbers written next to each rime in the figure indicate the average per-vowel[1] occurrence rates in the corpus of monosyllabic, monomorphemic English word lemmas of each type. Thus, for example, for the form Vt there are 113 such lemmas summing over the 5 short vowels included in the corpus, producing an average per vowel occurrence rate of 22.6 for this rime type.

　　Within these rime types, several very general principles seem to hold. Four very simple, and arguably[2] universal constraints – keep it short, simple, coronal, and unvoiced – do a good job of capturing ordinal relationships among the occurrence rates of the different types of rimes listed in the figure. There is a preference for short relative to long vowels. There is a preference for simpler forms – those without the added consonant – compared to their more complex counterparts. There is a preference for coronal relative to non-coronal stop consonants, and a preference for unvoiced relative to voiced stops. The constraints are represented in the figure by placing forms that violate a given constraint below those that adhere to it, and connecting members of the same minimal pair – a pair of forms that are the same except that one violates exactly one more constraint than the other – with an upward arrow. Where the arrow is solid, the data are consistent with the constraint, in that either (i) the form at the top of the arrow has a greater occurrence rate than the form at the bottom of the arrow or (ii) neither form occurs at all (see the figure caption for more details). Of the 140 minimal pairs encompassed by the figure, there are 135 where the occurrence rates are consistent with the constraints, and only 5 case that are inconsistent, indicating strong overall consistency with the four simple constraints.

---

1. The CELEX English corpus uses Southern British English pronunciations. The counts exclude forms containing relative rare vowels of each of the short and long types. Five short and 10 long vowels are included. See McClelland and Vander Wyk (2006) for more details.

2. I say 'arguably' here to make it clear that any claim of universality will require more detailed specification of the constraints. In particular, the context in which these universals apply must be specified. A preference for relatively simpler forms seems likely to operate generally. A preference for unvoiced relative to voiced and coronal as opposed to non-coronal articulation in codas of monomorphic monosyllabic word forms appears widespread, as does a preference for short over long vowels in forms that contain stop consonants in the coda. Some or all of these preferences may be at work in other contexts, but may be overridden in other contexts by counter-veiling factors.

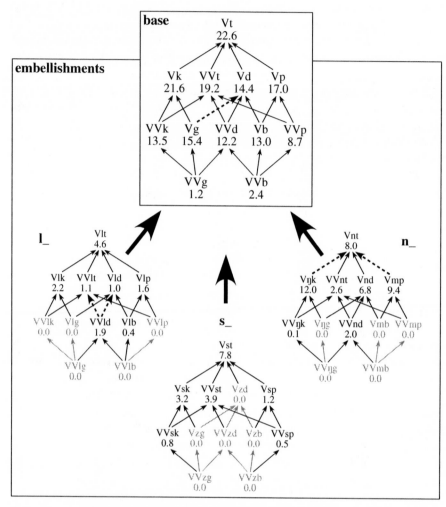

Figure 2.   Partial ordering graph showing graded influences of several constraints. The base subgraph in the small box at the top shows the rime types containing a single coda stop consonant which may be either voiced or unvoiced, coronal or non-coronal, and is preceded by a short (V) or long (VV) vowel. Numbers shown are the average per-vowel occurrence rates in the corpus, as described in the text. Arrows indicate dominance relationships according to the four constraints described in the text. Solid arrows are used in cases where the occurrence rates are consistent with the constraints, and dotted arrows indicate cases where the occurrence rates violate the constraints. The other three sub-graphs within the larger box

Clearly, these data at least provide evidence for each of these four constraints, and leaving them simply as abstract principles might be viewed as a good, first-order summary of this data. Here we characterize these constraints in the simplest possible form:

*VV (disprefer long vowels)
*X (disprefer added segments of any type)
*Voi (disprefer voicing of coda obstruents)
*NC (disprefer non-coronals)

One the one hand, we could see these constraints as compatible with an OT approach, in that they are very abstractly formulated and possibly universal. On the other hand, it is also possible to view some of these constraints as so general that they are not really specific to language. One possibility is that, at least in part, all of these constraints reflect a pressure to keep word forms shorter in duration. Of course, forms containing fewer segments and short vowels rather than long vowels do take less time to articulate. Somewhat less obvious is the finding that violations of Voicing and Coronality are also associated with longer spoken word form durations (Vander Wyk and McClelland in preparation). Thus, it may be that all these constraints reflect a very general preference for shorter word-forms, a constraint that does not seem on the face of it to require an appeal to a construct such as Universal Grammar.

On the other hand, these constraints, without further details, do not provide a full account of the data. If we wish to explain in more detail exactly which forms do occur and which forms do not, or if we wish to address the occurrence rates quantitatively, we will need to specify additional information. Here we seem to pass beyond what is ordinarily offered in the abstract framework of Optimality Theory. Even just to address whether a particular rime type does or does not occur, we already run into difficulty, if we try to rely on the standard constraint ranking logic of OT. If *Voi outranks Faithfulness, then no voiced coda obstruents should occur, but if Faithfulness outranks *Voi, then coda

---

indicate corresponding data for cases where the rime contains a pre-stop /l/, pre-stop /s/, or pre-stop nasal segment. The solid arrows from each of these three sub-graphs to the sub-graph in the box indicates that in every case, the presence of the pre-stop segment reduces the occurrence rate of each form in the subordinate sub-graph, compared the corresponding base form in the base subgraph. As one example, the occurrence rate of Vst, a form in the pre-stop /s/ subgraph, is less than the occurrence rate of Vt, a form in the base subgraph. Adapted with permission from McClelland and Vander Wyk (2006).

obstruents should occur without penalty. Clearly, none of the abstract constraints under consideration individually outranks faithfulness, since forms violating each of these constraints do occur in the language. However, when a rime type violates several of the constraints, it may well not occur in the language. Some form of constraint cumulation appears to be in order, violating a principle employed in standard versions of OT. Simply specifying that up to two violations are allowed but that a third is not[3] might capture some of the data, but some forms that violate three constraints do occur (VVnd as in *find* violates *VV, *X, and *Voi) and some that violate three constraints do not (Vmb violates *X, *Voi, and *NC, and there are no words containing this rime type – the *b* in *bomb*, for example, is not pronounced).

One way to go beyond the limits of standard OT is to stay with the idea of very abstract constraints, but to return to the approach taken in Harmony Theory, the predecessor of OT, which relied on weighted parameters and a quantitative rule for combining the weights. Appeals to graded constraints are, of course, quite common in phonological research (e.g., Harris 1994), including work undertaken within the OT framework (Boersma 1998; Burzio 2000), and quite a lot of formal work is now being undertaking using some form of graded constraint representation (e.g., Hayes and Wilson 2008). In addition to the notion that constraints have continuous-valued weights, it will be useful to allow continuous variation in the degree to which a particular constraint is violated by a particular word form. Allowing the total extent of constraint violation to be given by the product of a continuous-valued weight specifying the importance of the constraint times a continuous-valued score specifying the degree of the violation should simplify, for example, the analysis of many of the phenomena reviewed in the chapter on cue constraints by Boersma (this volume).

In McClelland and Vander Wyk (2006), we proposed an extremely simple version of this idea, in which the underlying constraint violation score (CVS) associated with a form is a simple linear function of the set of constraints that it violates:

$$CVS_i = \Sigma_j\, C_{ij}\, w_j$$

Here the subscript i indexes different rime types, and the subscript j indexes constraints. w_j refers to the strength or weight of constraint j, and C_{ij} takes the value 1 if the rime type violates constraint j, and is 0 otherwise. Smaller CVS values are associated with 'better' forms.

---

3. Even this appears to violate the standard version of OT, in which counting of violations is not allowed (Prince and Smolensky 2004).

To relate this formula to the actual occurrence rates of forms in English, we found that the following function provided a better fit to the data in the table than other formulations:

$$S_i = B - \text{CVS}_j \; ; \quad R_i = [S_i]+$$

The expression simply states that the strength (S_i), or tendency to occur, of a particular rime type is equal to a (positive) baseline occurrence rate B, less the constraint violation score. The notation $R_i = [S_i]+$ indicates that the predicted occurrence rate of the form, R_i, is simply equal to S_i if the value of S_i is greater than 0; otherwise, R_i is equal to 0. Note that B itself already reflects constraints operating on the simplest form included (Vt). The remaining constraints cumulated in the *CVS* for a given item include one for Long relative to Short vowels, and one for voiced relative to unvoiced obstruents in the coda. There are additional constraints corresponding to penalties for non-coronal articulation and for adding additional segments over and above the vowel and one stop consonant. In fitting the data, we found that some types of added segments appeared to exert a greater cost than others, and different ways of being non-coronal also appeared to vary in cost. Thus, we found it useful to include a separate constraint violation weight for each type of pre-stop coda consonant (pre-stop /s/, prestop /l/, prestop nasal) and a separate constraint violation weight for each for the two types of non-coronal stops (velars and labials). The version of this model that we used to fit the data in along with some additional data not shown had ten[4] numeric parameters (the baseline B plus nine constraint weights), and accounted for 85% of the variance in the observed occurrence rates. It also correctly predicted that 38 of the 40 rime types that do occur would occur, and only incorrectly predicted that 4 rime types would occur that do not occur. All of the mispredictions were relatively small in magnitude (i.e., the 4 forms predicted to occur that do not occur were predicted to occur with low rates). This level of success in our model supports the view that it may be worthwhile to consider integrating graded constraints in a more thoroughgoing way into phonological theory, and to treat what has become the standard version of OT as a simplification that may be useful for some purposes.

While inclusion of graded constraint weights and graded degrees of constraint violation should help, even this may not be enough to account for all the subtleties in the real data. Even in the data summarized in Fig. 2, there are a few deviations in the partial ordering predictions that would still be unexplained. As one example: the type VVld occurs less frequently than Vld, even

---

4. In fact our fits used a data set including forms containing post-stop /t/ and post-stop /s/, requiring 1 more weight for each of these two types of added segments, for a total of 10.

though the former has a long vowel. Furthermore, there appear to be some constraint interactions: we find that non-coronal place of articulation interacts strongly both with consonant voicing and with the presence of a nasal segment (see Figure 3). How are these additional features of the data to be explained?

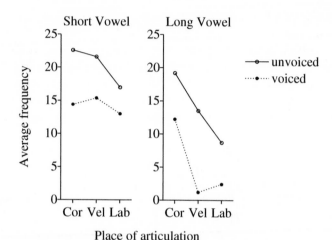

Figure 3.   Average per vowel occurrence rates for the six forms in the base subgraph of Fig. 2. Each data point represents a rime type, consisting of a single vowel, which may be short or long and a single stop consonant, which may be unvoiced or voiced, and which may have a coronal (cor) velar (vel) or labial (lab) articulation. It is evident that the constraint against non-coronals is greater when the vowel is long, and may be amplified further when the consonant is voiced. Adapted with permission from McClelland and Vander Wyk (2006).

A number of possible explanations can be envisioned. As suggested by Natural Phonology, some of these may well involve details of interactions between the actual gestures required to produce adjacent segments and/or effects of attempts to combine such gestures on perceptibility. For example, the gesture required to produce an /l/ may interact with the gestures required to produce neighboring vowel segments in ways that make some long vowels more compatible with a following /l/ than some short vowels, or may shift the perceived quality of the preceding vowel. Another possible type of explanation may revolve around the idea that the distribution of word forms in the language is a solution to an optimization problem, in which the distribution of rime types in the language is thought of as a compromise solution, influenced both by simplicity as well as perceptual distinctiveness of the resulting word forms.

The point of reviewing these ideas here has been to suggest that the succinct statement of abstract constraints, as in some versions of Optimality Theory, should be viewed, not as a matter of fundamental theoretical principle, but as a matter of simplicity that allows a good approximate description of the facts of phonological structure in a very compact and straightforward form. A full understanding will require appeals to the actual magnitudes of particular specific instances of constraints, as well as appeals to particular details of articulation. On this view, OT may be a useful notational framework that facilitates understanding in some cases, but it should not be viewed as the one true way to characterize phonological structure. I would, in fact, suggest that the search for the 'true' abstract framework for capturing phonological (or any other aspect of linguistic) structure may no longer be the best path toward a fuller understanding. We should continue the effort to provide useful ways of summarizing facts about language structure, but view these as essentially descriptive activities, without seeing alternative approaches as in fundamental opposition to each other.

References

Baayen, R. Harald, Richard Piepenbrock, and Hedderik van Rijn
   1993   *The CELEX Lexical Database (CD-ROM)*. Philadelphia, PA: Linguistic Data Consortium, University of Pennsylvania.
Balas, Anna
   this volume   Why can Poles hear "Sprite", but not "Coca-Cola"? A Natural Phonological account.
Boersma, Paul
   1998   *Functional Phonology: Formalizing the Interactions Between Articulatory and Perceptual Drives*. Ph.D. dissertation, University of Amsterdam. The Hague: Holland Academic Graphics.
Boersma, Paul
   this volume   Phonological perception as an interplay between structural and cue constraints.
Boersma, Paul, and Silke Hamann
   2008   The evolution of auditory dispersion in bidirectional constraint grammars. *Phonology* 25: 217–270.
Boersma, Paul, and Silke Hamann
   this volume   Introduction: models of phonology in perception.

Burzio, Luigi
2000   Missing players: phonology and the past-tense debate. In: Kleanthes K. Grohmann and Caro Struijke (eds.), *University of Maryland Working Papers in Linguistics* 10: 73–112.
Bybee, Joan L.
2001   *Phonology and Language Use*. Cambridge: Cambridge University Press.
Cutting, James E., Burton S. Rosner and Christopher F. Foard
1976   Perceptual categories for musiclike sounds: implications for theories of speech perception. *The Quarterly Journal of Experimental Psychology* 28: 361–378.
Dilkina, Katia, James L. McClelland and David C. Plaut
2008   A single-system account of semantic and lexical deficits in five semantic dementia patients. *Cognitive Neuropsychology* 25: 136–164.
Flemming, Edward
1995   *Auditory Representations in Phonology*. Ph.D. dissertation, University of California, Los Angeles. Published London and New York: Routledge [2002].
Fodor, Jerry A.
1983   *Modularity of Mind*. Cambridge, Mass.: MIT Press.
Harris, John
1994   *English Sound Structure*. Oxford: Blackwell.
Hay, Jennifer
2001   Lexical frequency in morphology: is everything relative? *Linguistics* 39: 1041–1070.
Hayes, Bruce, and Colin Wilson
2008   A maximum entropy model of phonotactics and phonotactic learning. *Linguistic Inquiry* 39: 379–440.
Hickok, Gregory, and David Poeppel
2004   Dorsal and ventral streams: a framework for understanding aspects of the functional anatomy of language. *Cognition* 92: 67–99.
Keidel, James L., Jason D. Zevin, Keith R. Kluender, and Mark S. Seidenberg
2003   Modeling the role of native language knowledge in perceiving nonnative speech contrasts. In: Marie-Josep Solé, Daniel Recasens and Joaquín Romero (eds.), *Proceedings of the 15th International Congress of Phonetic Sciences*, 2221–2224. Barcelona.
Kuhl, Patricia K.
1991   Human adults and human infants show a "perceptual magnet effect" for the prototypes of speech categories, monkeys do not. *Perception and Psychophysics* 50: 93–107.
Kuhl, Patricia K., and James D. Miller
1975   Speech perception by the chinchilla: voiced-voiceless distinction in alveolar plosive consonants. *Science* 190: 69–72.

Levelt, Willem J. M., Ardi Roelofs, and Antje S. Meyer
1999   A theory of lexical access in speech production. *Behavioral and Brain Sciences* 22: 1–38.

Liberman, Alvin M.
1996   *Speech: A Special Code.* Cambridge, MA: MIT Press.

Lindblom, Björn, Peter F. MacNeilage, and Michael Studdert-Kennedy
1984   Self-organizing processes and the explanation of phonological universals. In: Brian Butterworth, Bernard Comrie and Östen Dahl (eds.), *Explanations for Language Universals*, 181–203. Berlin: Mouton.

Lotto, Andrew J., and Keith R. Kluender
1998   General contrast effects in speech perception: effect of preceding liquid on stop consonant identification. *Perception & Psychophysics* 60: 602–619.

McClelland, James L., and Jeffrey L. Elman
1986   The TRACE Model of speech perception. *Cognitive Psychology* 18: 1–86.

McClelland, James L., Timothy T. Rogers, Karalyn Patterson, Katia N. Dilkina, and Matthew R. Lambon Ralph
in press   Semantic cognition: its nature, its development, and its neural basis. In: Michael Gazzaniga (ed.), *The Cognitive Neurosciences IV*. Boston, MA: MIT Press.

McClelland, James L., and David E. Rumelhart
1981   An interactive activation model of context effects in letter perception. Part 2: an account of basic findings. *Psychological Review* 88: 375–407.

McClelland, James L., and Brent C. Vander Wyk
2006   Graded constraints in English word forms. Manuscript, Department of Psychology, Carnegie Mellon University.

Mechelli, Andrea, Jennifer T. Crinion, Steven Long, Karl J. Friston, Matthew R. Lambon Ralph, Karalyn Patterson, James L. McClelland, and Cathy J. Price
2005   Dissociating reading processes on the basis of neuronal interactions. *Journal of Cognitive Neuroscience* 17: 1753–1765.

Mirman, Daniel, Lori L. Holt, and James L. McClelland
2004   Categorization and discrimination of non-speech sounds: differences between steady-state and rapidly-changing acoustic cues. *Journal of the Acoustical Society of America* 116: 1198–1207.

Pierrehumbert, Janet
2001   Exemplar dynamics: word frequency, lenition and contrast. In: Joan L. Bybee and Paul Hopper (eds.), *Frequency and the Emergence of Linguistic Structure*, 137–157. Amsterdam: John Benjamins.

Prince, Alan, and Paul Smolensky
2004   *Optimality Theory: Constraint Interaction in Generative Grammar.* Oxford: Blackwell.

Rogers, Timothy T., Matthew R. Lambon Ralph, Peter Garrard, Sasha Bozeat, James L. McClelland, John R. Hodges, and Karalyn Patterson
  2004   The structure and deterioration of semantic memory: a neuropsycho-logical and computational investigation. *Psychological Review* 111: 205–235.

Vander Wyk, Brent C., and James L. McClelland
  in preparation Constraints affecting occurrence rates of English word forms also af-fect spoken word duration.

Wade, Travis, and Lori L. Holt
  2005   Effects of later-occurring non-linguistic sounds on speech categori-zation. *Journal of the Acoustical Society of America* 118: 1701–1710.

Index